PARENTING AND THE CHILD'S WORLD: INFLUENCES ON ACADEMIC, INTELLECTUAL, AND SOCIAL-EMOTIONAL DEVELOPMENT

MONOGRAPHS IN PARENTING SERIES

Marc H. Bornstein, Series Editor

Borkowski, Ramey, and Bristol-Powers   Parenting and the Child's World:
Influences on Academic, Intellectual, and Social-Emotional Development

Bornstein   Parenting: Essential Readings

Cowan, Cowan, Ablow, Johnson, and Measelle   The Family Context of
Parenting in Children's Adaptation to School

Bornstein and Bradley   Socioeconomic Status, Parenting, and Child Development

PARENTING AND THE CHILD'S WORLD: INFLUENCES ON ACADEMIC, INTELLECTUAL, AND SOCIAL-EMOTIONAL DEVELOPMENT

John G. Borkowski
University of Notre Dame

Sharon Landesman Ramey
University of Alabama at Birmingham

Marie Bristol-Power
*National Institute of Child Health
and Human Development*

This publication is the result of a conference supported by the Robert Wood Johnson Foundation and the National Institute of Child Health and Human Development.

2002

LAWRENCE ERLBAUM ASSOCIATES, PUBLISHERS
Mahwah, New Jersey   London

Editor: Bill Webber
Editorial Assistant: Erica Kica
Cover Design: Kathryn Houghtaling Lacey
Textbook Production Manager: Paul Smolenski
Full-Service Compositor: TechBooks, Inc.
Text and Cover Printer: Hamilton Printing Company

This book was typeset in 10/12 pt. Times Roman, Bold, and Italic.
The heads were typeset in Americana and Americana Bold.

Lawrence Erlbaum Associates, Inc., Publishers
10 Industrial Avenue
Mahwah, New Jersey 07430

Library of Congress Cataloging-in-Publication Data

Parenting and the child's world : influences on academic, intellectual, and social-
emotional development / [edited by] John G. Borkowski, Sharon Landesman
Ramey, and Marie Bristol-Power.
    p.   cm. — (Monographs in parenting)
    Follow-up papers for a conference held on Bethesda, Maryland in August
1999, sponsored by the Robert Wood Johnson Foundation and the National
Institute of Child Health and Human Development.
    Includes bibliographical references and index.
    ISBN 0-8058-3832-5 (alk.paper)
    1. Parenting. 2. Child rearing. 3. Parent and child. I. Borkowski, John
G., 1938– II. Ramey, Sharon L. III. Bristol-Power, Marie. IV. Series.
HQ755.8 .P379126 2002
649'.1—dc21   2001040281

Printed in the United States of America
10 9 8 7 6 5 4 3 2 1

Contents

Series Foreword
Monographs in Parenting

Parenting is fundamental to the success of the human race. Everyone who has ever lived has had parents, and most adults in the world become parents. If opinions about parenting abound, surprisingly little solid scientific information or considered reflection exists about parenting. *Monographs in Parenting* intends to redress this imbalance: The chief aim of this series of volumes is to provide a forum for extended and integrated treatments of fundamental and challenging contemporary topics in parenting. Each volume treats a different perspective on parenting and is self-contained, yet the series as a whole endeavors to enhance and interrelate studies in parenting by bringing shared perspectives to bear on a variety of concerns prominent in parenting theory, research, and application. As a consequence of its structure and scope, *Monographs in Parenting* will appeal—individually or as a group—to scientists, professionals, and parents alike. Reflecting the nature and intent of this series, contributing authors are drawn from a broad spectrum of the humanities and sciences—anthropology to zoology—with representational emphasis placed on active contributing authorities to the contemporary literature in parenting.

Parenting is a job whose primary object of attention and action is the child—children do not and cannot grow up as solitary individuals—but parenting is also a status in the life course with consequences for parents themselves. In this forum, parenting is defined by all of children's principal caregivers and their many modes of caregiving. *Monographs in Parenting* will encompass central themes in parenting:

Who Parents?

Biological and adoptive mothers, fathers, single-parents, divorced, or remarried parents can be children's principal caregivers, but when siblings, grandparents, and non-familial caregivers mind children their "parenting" will be of interest as well.

Whom Do Parents Parent?

Parents "parent" infants, toddlers, children in middle-childhood, and adolescents, but special populations of children include multiple births, preterm, ill, developmentally delayed or talented, and aggressive or withdrawn children.

The Scope of Parenting

Parenting includes genetic endowment and direct effects on children of experiences that parents provide, including parents' beliefs and behaviors; parenting's indirect influences take place through parents' relationships with each other and their connections to community networks; the positive and negative effects of parenting are both topics of concern.

Factors that Affect Parenting

Evolution and history; biology and ethology; family configuration; formal and informal support systems, community ties, and work; social, educational, legal, medical, and governmental institutions; economic class, designed and natural ecology, and culture—as well as children themselves—each helps to define parenting.

The Nature, Structure, and Meaning of Parenting

Parenting has pleasures, privileges, and profits as well as frustrations, fears, and failures that will be explored.

MONOGRAPHS IN PARENTING

The first volumes planned in the series include:

John G. Borkowski, Sharon Landesman Ramey, and Marie Bristol-Power's *Parenting and the Child's World: Influences on Academic, Intellectual, and Social-Emotional Development,* a collection that identifies multiple parenting influences on specific domains of child and adolescent development.

Marc H. Bornstein's *Parenting: Essential Readings,* a volume that collects classic and modern landmark papers in parenting studies.

Philip A. Cowan, Carolyn Pape Cowan, Jennifer Ablow, Vanessa Kahen Johnson, and Jeffrey R. Measelle's *The Family Context of Parenting in Children's Adaptation to School,* a treatise on the roles of parents and associated family factors in children's academic and social adjustment to elementary school.

Marc H. Bornstein and Robert H. Bradley's, *Socioeconomic Status, Parenting, and Child Development,* a set of essays that delves deeply into interrelations between social class and parenting and their consequences.

Contemporary parenting studies are diversified, pluralistic, and specialized. This fragmented state needs counterforce in an arena that allows the extended in-depth exploration of cardinal topics in parenting. *Monographs in Parenting* vigorously pursues that goal.

Marc H. Bornstein
Series Editor

Preface

In August 1999, the Robert Wood Johnson Foundation and the National Institute of Child Health and Human Development (NICHD) cosponsored a conference in Bethesda, Maryland, on parenting and child development. This book contains follow-up papers for most of the presentations made at that conference, plus several additional contributions.

The conference was stimulated by the publication of a book by Judith Rich Harris, *The Nurture Assumption: Why Children Turn Out the Way They Do.* Harris offers a startling answer to the questions, "How much credit do parents deserve when their children turn out well? How much blame when they turn out badly?" Based on her review of the scientific literature on parenting effects, she believes that "the assumption that what influences children's development, apart from their genes, is the way their parents bring them up . . . is wrong." This starkly stated conclusion captured widespread media attention, with inadequate balance or attention to the fact that Harris concentrates almost exclusively on outcomes in the domain of personality—a construct assumed to have a large biological and genetic component, based on twin, sibling, and adoption studies.

The tremendous public interest in this topic and the potential policy implications for a new understanding of the nature and extent of parenting influences, in conjunction with other important influences on child development, warranted the conference and the resultant book. The Bethesda conference was not intended to debate the correctness of Harris' position per se. Rather, we began by recognizing that there are multiple sources of influence on children's development, including parenting behavior, family resources, genetic and other biological factors, as well as social influences from peers, teachers, and the community at large.

During the past decade, there has been vigorous new research about the specific influences of parenting on children's development. The effects of parenting on three domains of development are especially important: (1) children's academic achievement and intelligence, (2) social-emotional development, and (3) risk-taking behaviors during the adolescent years. These research agendas have been diverse in terms of populations studied, methodologies used, designs employed (naturalistic versus interventions to change outcomes), and conceptual or theoretical models used to guide data collection and analyses.

The book is divided into four main sections. Part 1 is about the conceptual and methodological foundations of parenting research. Two chapters—by Judith Harris (chapter 1) and David Rowe (chapter 2)—present arguments for challenging the "nurture assumption" and provide supporting evidence for the importance of genetic and peer influences. Next, counterarguments are presented by Eleanor Maccoby (chapter 3) and Sharon Ramey (chapter 4); they develop conceptual frameworks for analyzing specific parenting influences on specific domains of child and adolescent development.

Part 2 analyzes the role of parenting on academic achievement and personal competence. Philip and Carolyn Cowan (chapter 5) describe a set of family intervention studies that enhance school success and reduce behavior problems. Next, data from the NICHD Early Child Care Network on parenting influences on children in child care are presented by Margaret Owen (chapter 6). Craig Ramey and colleagues (chapter 7) discuss how center-based treatments can improve parenting effectiveness. In chapter 8, Fred Morrison and Ramie Cooney summarize the multiple pathways that lead from parenting practices to academic achievement. Relatedly, John Borkowski and colleagues (chapter 9) describe how "inadequate" adolescent parenting can produce significant delays in children's intelligence, competence, and school success.

Emotional and social development as affected by parenting practices is the focus of Part 3. Alan Sroufe (chapter 10) describes how infant attachment becomes reflected in successful adolescent and adult development. The role of maternal depression in children's behavioral and psychobiological development is the focus of Lara Embry's and Geraldine Dawson's contribution (chapter 11). Next, Ken Dodge (chapter 12) describes how effective and ineffective parenting practices moderate and/or mediate children's aggressive behaviors. In the same view, Tom Dishion and Bernadette Bullock (chapter 13) describe how intervention programs can alter adolescent problem behaviors. Mark Cummings and colleagues (chapter 14) show how maternal conflict can impact children's emotional and social development. The section ends with Steve Suomi's analyses (chapter 15) of how parents and peers influence socialization processes in primates and the implications of these data for understanding human development.

Part 4 presents various environmental and cultural influences on parenting children with and without disabilities. Sharon McGroder and colleagues (chapter 16) report data on the role of parents in shaping the developmental impact of recently enacted welfare-to-work programs. The final two chapters in this section—by Dennis Hogan and Michael Msall (chapter 17) and Laraine Glidden (chapter 18)—focus on the special role of parents in rearing children with physical and/or mental disabilities.

Part 5 concludes our coverage of contemporary research on parenting and its impact on multiple domains of child and adolescent development. Margaret

Feerick and colleagues at the NICHD (chapter 19) review trends in NIH funding for parenting research and suggest new research directions. In the final chapter, John Borkowski and colleagues (chapter 20) use basic research findings to construct a "mental model" of parenting practices and then translate this model into an instructional format (RPM3) that can be used by parents in responding retroactively and proactively to the daily challenges they face in rearing children from infancy through adolescence.

In this text, we search for when, where, and how parenting matters and the major antecedents and moderators of effective parenting. The contributions, in the main, focus on the major conceptual issues and empirical approaches that underlie our understanding of the importance of parenting for child development in academic, socio-emotional, and risk-taking domains. Additional goals are to show how culture and parenting are interwoven, to chart future research directions, and to help parents and professionals understand the implications of major research findings. The publication of this book will be followed by a parenting brochure that will launch a national campaign to support and improve parenting practices in the United States.

PARENTING AND THE CHILD'S WORLD: INFLUENCES ON ACADEMIC, INTELLECTUAL, AND SOCIAL-EMOTIONAL DEVELOPMENT

I

Parenting Research: Conceptual and Methodological Foundations

1

Beyond the Nurture Assumption: Testing Hypotheses About the Child's Environment

Judith Rich Harris

Parenting isn't what it used to be. When I was a child, back in the 1930s and '40s, parental use of the words "I love you" was pretty much reserved for death-bed declarations. Today those words are given out daily, like vitamins. In the homes in which my childhood friends and I grew up, spankings were routine. For really bad transgressions, the punishment was administered with a belt or a ruler. Today I have a 5-year-old granddaughter who has never been hit—never received any sort of physical punishment at all. The trend, over the course of this century, has been clear: away from strict, authoritarian styles of childrearing (Alwin, 1988; Wolfenstein, 1953) and away from a reliance on physical punishment as a routine way of ensuring obedience (Graziano, Hamblen, & Plante, 1996; Socolar, Winsor, Hunter, Catellier, & Kotch, 1999). Worries that the children might damage the furniture have given way to worries about damaging their self-esteem.

Have these dramatic changes in behaviors and attitudes toward children had their expected effects? Are today's children happier, more self-confident, or less aggressive than the children of the 1930s and '40s? Alas, there is no evidence of a

Address correspondence to: 54 Crawford Road, Middletown, NJ 07748 or 72073-1211 @compuserve.com.

change for the better. Rates of childhood depression and suicide, for example, have gone up, not down (Myers, 1992). And adult personality has not shown secular changes to parallel the changes in childrearing styles. Here's what personality researchers Robert McCrae and Paul Costa (1988) concluded about the effects of the "fundamental changes in childrearing practices in the first half of this century":

> The use of corporal punishment declined, children were given more voice in the family, and fathers became less distant. Yet large-scale cross-sectional studies comparing adults born within the time span from the 1900s to the 1950s show little difference in basic personality dimensions. . . . Adults show the same distribution of personality traits regardless of the era in which they were raised. (p. 418)

THE NATURE (AND NURTURE) OF THE EVIDENCE

When developmental psychologists first started asking why children differ from one another, the answer was not "nature and nurture": The answer was simply "nurture." Why are some children fearful? Because their fathers scared them by making loud noises. Why are some children autistic? Because their mothers didn't love them enough. Why are some children aggressive? Because their parents reinforced them for behaving that way.

When it became impossible to ignore the contribution of the child's genes, nature was simply added on as an afterthought. It was acknowledged that children differ from each other at birth, but the acknowledgment came slowly and reluctantly. Today most developmentalists continue to favor environmental explanations, particularly those that involve the influence of parents. Faced with ambiguous evidence—evidence that could be used to support either nature or nurture—they demand to see nature's credentials but let nurture pass with a smile and a nod. This bias is part of a pattern of thought I call the "nurture assumption": the strongly held belief that parents are the most important part of the child's environment (Harris, 1998a).

Evidence is ambiguous when it is compatible with more than one explanation. Take, for example, the finding that babies who have warm, secure relationships with their mothers also tend to get along better with other people, such as peers (Sroufe, Egeland, & Carlson, 1999). This correlation can be explained in either of two ways. Perhaps babies learn something from their relationships with their mothers that helps them to get along better with other people. Or perhaps some babies are born with qualities (a cheerful disposition, a winning smile) that stand them in good stead in all their relationships. The first explanation is the one that is favored by researchers who study infant attachment.

A similarly ambiguous correlation comes from research on emotional expressiveness. Parents who express their emotions freely are found to have children who also tend to express their emotions freely (Eisenberg, Cumberland, & Spinrad, 1998a). Again, two explanations are possible. Perhaps parents teach their children, by example or training, to express emotions or to keep them bottled up. Or perhaps children inherit from their parents a tendency to be emotionally expressive or inexpressive. The first explanation is the favored one.

More precisely, the favored explanation nowadays is that both nature and nurture play a role. This compromise solution has been embraced so enthusiastically that its logical flaw has been overlooked. A correlation that could be due to a genetic effect, an environmental effect, or a combination of the two effects does not constitute proof that both effects are present. Before we can conclude that the correlation is due to a combination of the two effects, we need proof that it is not due solely to one or the other. To obtain such proof, we need methods that will allow us to unconfound the two effects by varying them independently.

EVIDENCE FROM BEHAVIORAL GENETICS

The methods of behavioral genetics were devised by researchers who believed that most correlations between parents and children result from a combination of genetic and environmental effects and who sought a way to tease them apart. This could be done, the researchers reasoned, in one of two ways: by eliminating the genetic portion of the correlation by studying adopted children, or by controlling for it statistically on the basis of estimates made by studying identical and fraternal twins.

Interestingly enough, both of these methods led to the same unexpected conclusion: that the home environment—the environment provided by the parents—had little or no effect on the personality, intelligence, or mental health of the children reared in that home (see Harris, 1995, 1998a). Once researchers were able to subtract the effects of the genes, nearly all the effects previously attributed to the home environment vanished. Children somewhat resemble their biological parents and siblings in personality, but the genes they have in common can account for almost all of the resemblances. These results indicate that being reared by conscientious parents does not, on average, make children more (or less) conscientious, that being reared by sociable parents does not, on average, make children more (or less) sociable, and that being reared by open-minded parents does not, on average, make children more (or less) open-minded (Bouchard, 1994).

This doesn't mean, of course, that all the variation in psychological characteristics is due to differences in genes; in fact, genes probably account for no more than half of the variance. But behavioral geneticists have so far been unable to discover the source of the other half—the environmental half. There are personality differences between siblings who grew up in the same home that cannot be attributed either to differences in genes or to any measured differences in environment

(Bouchard, 1994; Reiss, 2000; Turkheimer & Waldron, 2000). We know they are not genetic, because these unexplained differences show up in identical twins as well as in other kinds of sibling pairs (fraternal twins, biological siblings, and adoptive siblings). The correlation in personality traits, as measured by standardized tests, is only about .50 for identical twins reared together; it is close to zero for adoptive siblings (Plomin & Daniels, 1987).

Some developmentalists (e.g., Collins, Maccoby, Steinberg, Hetherington, & Bornstein, 2000) believe that the personality differences between children reared in the same home can be attributed to interactions between genes and environment. The idea is that children with different genetic endowments react differently to the same environmental influences, and that therefore we shouldn't expect children reared in the same home to turn out alike. However, this idea cannot explain the differences in personality found between identical twins raised in the same home. If there is no genetic difference, an interaction between genes and environment cannot produce a difference—it has to be a difference in environment. To account for the behavioral genetic results, we need an explanation that can apply to all kinds of sibling pairs, including identical twins, because the same results—that is, results leading to the same conclusions—are consistently found for all kinds of sibling pairs.

Shortcomings of Behavioral Genetic Methods

Behavioral genetic studies, like studies in developmental psychology, are designed to look for the sources of the individual differences among their participants. Researchers in both fields are asking the same question: Why does one baby turn out this way and another turn out that way? Researchers in both fields are limited by the range of participants they study and the range of environments they study. Developmentalists who study children reared in white, middle-class American families cannot assume that their results will hold true for children reared in Yemen or Zimbabwe. Neither can behavioral geneticists. Furthermore, both research methods are completely insensitive to any factors that are common to all of the participants. If every parent whose child took part in a given study had a magic formula for making children smarter or less aggressive or more conscientious, its effects would be invisible to the researchers, whether they used traditional developmental methods or behavioral genetic methods. For both kinds of researchers, the goal is to account for the variance measured within their pool of participants. Any factors that do not contribute to the variance will not be picked up by either method.

From my point of view, the most important drawback of behavioral genetic methods is that they cannot distinguish between the environment that siblings share within the home and the environment they share outside the home. For example, children who are adopted into middle-class homes tend to have higher

IQs than those who are adopted into working-class homes (see Maccoby, this volume). Is that because of what these children learned from their adoptive parents, or because of what they experienced outside the home? Behavioral genetic studies do not provide an answer. Children whose families differ in socioeconomic level lead different lives both at home and outside the home. They live in different neighborhoods, go to different schools. There are cultural differences in the norms of the children's peer groups. These outside-the-home influences affect children's attitudes toward reading, schoolwork, and other intellectual activities, and in the long run can increase or decrease a child's intelligence (Harris, 1998a). These effects do not show up in adoption studies in which all the adoptive parents belong to the same social class, and in the United States almost all adoptive parents are middle- or upper-middle-class. What behavioral genetic studies of adopted children do show, however, is that within the measured range of socioeconomic classes, differences among the parents—differences in their attitudes and behaviors regarding school achievement, reading, leisure-time activities, and so on—have no lasting effects on the intelligence of their adopted children (Plomin, Chipuer, & Neiderhiser, 1994).

DEFENDING THE NULL HYPOTHESIS

The behavioral genetic findings came as a shock to everyone, including the researchers themselves. They hadn't intended their studies to be a *test* of the hypothesis of parental influence—they had expected to *confirm* it. Many behavioral geneticists looked for explanations that would allow them to continue to believe that parents have important effects on their children. Others began to express their doubts (Rowe, 1994) or their bafflement (Bouchard, 1994).

Developmentalists also reacted in various ways. Most simply ignored the unsettling findings. Others tried to explain them away (e.g., Hoffman, 1991) or attacked behavioral genetic methods (e.g., Baumrind, 1993). Admittedly, behavioral genetic methods are not perfect, but they are an important step ahead of traditional methods of studying child development, because they provide a way to skim off genetic effects in order to get closer to a true estimate of environmental effects. Moreover, the findings produced by behavioral genetic methods have proven to be remarkably robust and replicable—more so than those reported in most other areas of psychology, including developmental. But weak findings may be accepted if they are in accord with prior assumptions, and robust findings discounted if they conflict with prevailing beliefs. If behavioral genetic studies had produced the results that everyone expected them to—results showing that the environment provided by parents does have important effects on the children— would anyone be questioning the validity of their methods?

The reaction to the behavioral genetic findings bears witness to the power of the nurture assumption. In other fields of science, researchers begin with the null hypothesis—the hypothesis, for example, that a certain drug is no better than a placebo in treating a certain disease. But the hypothesis that one style of parenting is no better than any other in its long-term effects (and that differences in outcome are due to factors other than parenting) has never been taken seriously in developmental psychology. Here, for example, is what Eisenberg, Cumberland, and Spinrad (1998b) said in reply to my commentary (Harris, 1998b) on their article in *Psychological Inquiry*: "The conclusion that parenting has no effects does not follow from the fact that we do not know the degree to which the obtained effects are due to genetic versus environmental effects" (p. 327).

In other words, Eisenberg and her colleagues are saying that I cannot use ambiguous evidence to prove that parenting has no effects. They are right, of course: I cannot prove that parenting has no effects. You can't prove the null hypothesis—all you can do is to accept it or reject it at some level of confidence. But in scientific research, the null hypothesis is supposed to be the starting point—the square from which you move only if you have evidence that enables you to reject it. To say, "We are going to go on believing in parental influence until someone disproves it" reveals an a priori bias. It's like the medical researchers saying, "We are going to go on believing that this drug is effective until someone proves otherwise."

The correlations that make up so much of the data of developmental psychology are ambiguous because they could result from genetic effects, they could result from the effects of the parents' behavior on the child, they could result from the effects of the child on the parents' behavior, or they could result from all of these effects (and others) mixed together, in unknown proportions. Evidence of this sort cannot be used to reject the null hypothesis of zero parental influence because it is not inconsistent with the null hypothesis.

Other Evidence

Although I cannot prove the null hypothesis, I have found a fair amount of evidence that supports my conclusion that parents have little or no influence on how their children turn out. Consider, for instance, the only child. Children without siblings bear the full brunt of their parents' positive and negative attention, and miss out on some aspects of family life that most of us take for granted, and yet researchers have failed to find any consistent differences in personality or adjustment between children who do or do not have siblings (Falbo & Polit, 1986; Falbo & Poston, 1993; Veenhoven & Verkuyten, 1989).

Then there are the recent studies on the effects of day care (NICHD Early Child Care Research Network, 1998; Scarr, 1997). No important differences in behavior or adjustment have been found between children who started full-time daycare in early infancy and children who spent their first three years at home. If parenting matters, shouldn't it matter whether a child gets a lot or a little of it? And isn't a mother who is with her child all day likely to dispense a different style of parenting than one who sees her child only for an hour in the morning and an hour in the evening?

A third example comes from studies of the language development of the children of immigrants—one of the findings that psycholinguist Steven Pinker "knew to be true but had filed away in that mental folder we all keep for undeniable truths that do not fit into our belief systems" (1998, p. xi). He is referring to the fact that the children of immigrants, if they grow up in a neighborhood where everyone speaks English without a foreign accent, will end up speaking English without a foreign accent. Even if they continue to speak their parents' language at home, English will become their primary language. These children do not end up with a compromise between the language they learned from their parents and the one they learned outside the home. They end up, pure and simple, with the language they learned outside the home—with the language of their peers, to be precise, even if it is not the language of most of the adults in their community (Bickerton, 1983).

When the child of aggressive parents behaves aggressively, or the child of agreeable parents is agreeable, the observed similarities could be due to genetic influences, environmental influences, or some combination of the two. But when the child of English-speaking parents speaks English, or the child of a Southerner speaks with a southern accent, we know they didn't inherit their language or accent from their parents. It is this freedom from genetic influence that makes language or accent such a good test of the assumption that parents are the most important influence on a child's development. In the absence of genetic effects, it is much easier to see how the environment affects behavior.

CONTEXT-SPECIFIC LEARNING

According to my theory of development, which I call *group socialization theory* (Harris, 1995, 1998a), children learn separately how to behave at home and how to behave outside the home. When they are together, parents do influence their children's behavior, and children do influence their parents' behavior. These mutual influences play an important role in the family's home life, but they do not necessarily play a role in the way family members behave outside the home. If children discover that what they learned at home is not useful outside of the home—and this is true for many aspects of social behavior, because behaviors that are appropriate at home commonly turn out to be inappropriate in the classroom or the playground—they will cast off what they learned at home and acquire new behaviors.

Children are not constrained to carry into a new context what they learned in an old one; "transfer of training" is the exception, not the rule (Detterman, 1993). It is true that there are correlations—usually small—between a child's behavior in two different contexts, but the evidence suggests that these correlations have a genetic source rather than an environmental one (Harris, 2000). The things children learn can be left behind if they don't prove useful in the new context, but what they are born with goes with them wherever they go. Children who are timid in one social context are not necessarily timid in another, but there are some children who are timid in every context (Rubin, Hastings, Stewart, Henderson, & Chen, 1997). Research has shown that it is the genetic component of timidity that transfers from one context to another and the environmental component that is context-specific (Cherny, Fulker, Corley, Plomin, & DeFries, 1994; see Saudino, 1997).

The idea that learned behavior is specific to the context in which it was learned can explain some of the puzzles in the literature. For example, birth order effects on personality are generally found when people are tested in contexts that evoke the family of origin, but are generally not found when they are tested in a neutral setting (Harris, 1998a; 2000).

Context-specific learning can also explain some of the discrepancies in research on the effects of punishment. In 1997, two studies on this topic—one by Straus, Sugarman, and Giles-Sims, the other by Gunnoe and Mariner—appeared in the same issue of a medical journal. Both used a longitudinal design to answer the question: Does the child who receives many spankings become more aggressive?

The answer that was reported in newspapers around the country was *yes*. Straus and his colleagues (1997) reported that children who received frequent spankings from their mothers tended to become more aggressive over time. The researchers' widely quoted conclusion was that if parents would only stop hitting their kids, it could "reduce the level of violence in American society" (p. 761).

The other study went unmentioned by the newspapers. Gunnoe and Mariner (1997) used a similar design but got different results. These researchers found no tendency for the children who got frequent spankings to become more aggressive. If anything, the trend was in the opposite direction.

The reason the two studies produced different results, I believe, was that different methods were used to measure aggressiveness. The first group of researchers measured the child's aggressiveness *at home*; the second measured aggressiveness *outside the home*. The first group of researchers assumed that a child who becomes more aggressive at home will also be more aggressive outside the home; the second showed that this did not happen.

SOCIALIZATION AND PERSONALITY

How do children learn to behave outside the home? According to group socialization theory, they do it by identifying with a group of people they see as being similar to themselves—for most children today this means others of the same age and sex—and taking on the norms of that group.

Over the course of middle childhood, boys who started out timid become less timid, but girls who started out timid are less likely to change (Kerr, Lambert,

Stattin, & Klackenberg-Larsson, 1994). The change in timid boys has been attributed by Jerome Kagan (1994; Kagan, Arcus, & Snidman, 1993) to the influence of their parents, but he has provided surprisingly little evidence for this assertion—as far as I have been able to determine, one unpublished doctoral dissertation (Arcus, 1991) involving 24 babies followed only to the age of 21 months.

My explanation for why timid boys get less timid—that it is a consequence of assimilation to the norms of the boys' peer group—is consistent with Eleanor Maccoby's views on gender development. Maccoby (1990, 1998; Maccoby & Jacklin, 1987) has concluded that the behavioral differences between boys and girls do not appear to be due to different treatment by the parents or to identification with the same-sex parent. She attributes the differences (those that do not have a biological basis) to the fact that the girls' and boys' peer groups of middle childhood have different cultures—or, as I would put it, different behavioral norms. In the girls' peer group, it is okay to behave in a shy or inhibited manner; in the boys' peer group it is not.

Because appropriate behavior in every society depends on whether you are a male or a female, an adult or a child, the child's first job is to figure out what sort of person he is or she is. This is a cognitive process: The child figures out what social categories are available in her society, then she figures out which one she belongs in. In childhood, the social category is usually the same as the peer group, but it doesn't have to be. A child can identify with a group even if it rejects her. This is not about friendship or the influence of friends, but the effects of what social psychologist John Turner (1987) called *self-categorization*.

When children split up into different groups (which is more likely to occur in larger schools and classes than in smaller ones), differences between the groups widen. Children sort themselves into groups partly on the basis of shared interests and propensities, in which genetic predispositions no doubt play a role (Scarr & McCartney, 1983), but once they have done that, environmental influences work to exaggerate the traits that brought them together in the first place. The jocks become jockier, the nerds become nerdier. The kids who were rejected from other groups because they were weird or aggressive form a group of their own and become weirder and more aggressive. When young people with antisocial tendencies come together in a group—either of their own accord or as the result of well-meaning action by a social service or law enforcement agency—group socialization theory predicts that they will become even more antisocial. Dishion (this volume; Dishion, McCord, & Poulin, 1999) has recently reported that this is indeed what happens.

Over time, the members of groups tend to become more alike in those behaviors and attitudes that are the defining characteristics of their group. But in other ways—especially in those aspects of behavior we call "personality"—the members of groups tend to become *less* alike. Personality differences among the members widen as a consequence of differentiation within the group. Groups differentiate among their members by assigning higher or lower status to them and by typecasting them in different roles, and these differences in role or status can leave permanent marks on the personality. I attribute the variation in personality not explained by genes mainly to differentiation within the group. This is the most speculative part of group socialization theory, the part for which I currently have the least evidence. Although much data exists, most of it is useless, because the research design provided no control for genetic influences. The cause-or-effect question (is the child maladjusted because he was rejected, or was he rejected because he was already behaving in an odd or unpleasant way?) is as much a problem in research on peer effects as in research on parenting. In *The Nurture Assumption* (Harris, 1998a) I suggested one way to get around this problem without using behavioral genetic methods: Study the personality development of boys who are small for their age. Such boys tend to have low status in their peer groups. The existing evidence is skimpy but supports my prediction that small or slow-maturing boys have a greater than average risk of maladjustment, both in childhood (Richman, Gordon, Tegtmeyer, Crouthamel, & Post, 1986) and adulthood (Jones, 1957).

THE EXPERIMENTAL METHOD

Most studies in child development use a correlational design that provides no control for genetic influences or for the effects of the child's behavior on the parents. As Cowan, Powell, and Cowan (1998) have pointed out:

> In studies of parent-to-child effects, causality is virtually impossible to determine. Because almost all studies of parents and children are correlational in design, it is not possible to establish whether parents' behaviors are affecting the child, the child's behaviors are affecting the parents, the child's behavior is a product of the parent-child relationship, or the child's behavior is attributable to familial and extrafamilial factors that are separate from parenting. (p. 7)

The use of longitudinal methods does not solve the cause-or-effect problem, according to Cowan et al. (1998):

> The inference problems in determining the direction of effects cannot be completely resolved with longitudinal designs. The fact that a parent's behavior at Time 1 is highly correlated with a child's behavior at Time 2 does not establish parental influence, because the parent's Time 1 behavior may have been influenced by the child's behavior prior to the Time 1 assessment or by other factors in the parent's experience. (pp. 7–8)

An additional problem is that the parent's behavior, as well as the child's, is influenced in part by genetic predispositions (see Rowe, this volume). If the child is the biological offspring of the parent, there are likely to be correlations in behavior due to the fact that child and parent share 50% of their genes.

Some researchers attempt to control for the child's genetic predispositions by using a measure of temperament made in the first year of life. If this early measure does not prove to be a good predictor of a child's later personality or behavior, the poorness of the prediction is taken as evidence that the child has changed as a result of environmental influences. There are three things wrong with this reasoning. First, these early measures of temperament might lack validity, as well as reliability—the test might not be measuring the right thing. Second, the concept of temperament is far too narrow to include all the psychological variables (many of which have a genetic component) that may contribute to the personality or behavior of an older child. Finally, genes contribute not just to the way individuals start out, but also to the way they change over time. There are genes that kick in early and genes that kick in late, and an adequate research design has to control for all of them.

Cowan and Cowan (this volume; Cowan et al., 1998), have concluded that the best way to test parental influence is to use the experimental method, rather than the correlational method. The kind of experiment they advocate is called an *intervention study*. With this design, families are randomly assigned to experimental and control conditions; only the experimental group receives the intervention. The random assignment makes it unnecessary to control for genetic effects, because the two groups are presumed to be approximately equal in their genetic assets and liabilities. An intervention study is the most straightforward way to test my assertion that parents have no important long-term effects on their children's personalities or on the way their children behave outside the family context.

Let me first make my predictions clear. I do not question the fact that it is possible to change the way children or adolescents behave in a given context. If an intervention succeeded in teaching parents better ways of interacting with their children, I would expect the result to be an improvement in family relationships and in the way the children behave in the presence of their parents. My prediction in this case is no different from the prevailing one.

I also agree that it is possible to improve children's behavior at school. But now there is a difference in predictions because, according to my theory, improving a child's behavior at school would require an intervention in the school or in a social context similar to the school (where peers are present and parents are not). My theory predicts that an intervention that affects only the home environment will not change the child's behavior in school—except under one condition. If the children whose families took part in the intervention attended the same school and belonged to the same peer group, changes in behavior that occurred at home could be brought along to the school and retained. According to group socialization theory, behaviors and attitudes common to a culture are passed down from the parents' group to the children's group (Harris, 1995). By changing the behaviors or attitudes of the majority of the parents of children in a given peer group, it should be possible to change the behaviors or attitudes of the peer group. Unfortunately, it is difficult to test this hypothesis against the existing literature, because most reports of intervention studies do not mention whether the children in the intervention group associated with each other in school or in the neighborhood.

I will, therefore, put this exception aside for now and make the strong prediction that home-based interventions will not modify the child's behavior in school, though they might modify it at home. A proper test of this prediction requires that there be no attempt to change the child's environment outside the home—the intervention must be focused entirely on the home—and that the child's behavior outside the home be assessed by objective observers who are blind to the experimental or control group assignment of the participating families.

Do Home-Based Interventions Change the Child's Behavior Outside the Home?

There is a surprising dearth of intervention studies that meet these criteria. In many of the studies in which parents were taught better ways of dealing with their children, the children's behavior was assessed only at home. Other studies lacked a control group, or modified the children's environment in the school as well as the home by enlisting teachers as well as parents in the intervention, or combined two or more of these drawbacks. For example, in the widely cited study by Webster-Stratton (1984), the children's behavior was assessed only at home immediately after the intervention. It was assessed at school at the 1-year follow-up, but for this assessment there was no control group. In another study by the same researcher (Webster-Stratton, 1998), the children's behavior was assessed both at school (a Head Start classroom) and at home, but the intervention took place in both places—both the teachers and the parents were taught strategies for managing children's misbehavior. The same teachers judged the children's school behavior in the postintervention assessment.

A few studies do meet my criteria. In this chapter I will look closely at two of the best: Dishion and Andrews (1995) and Forgatch and DeGarmo (1999).

The design of the Dishion and Andrews study is exemplary. A total of 158 high-risk families were randomly divided into three intervention groups, of which only one, called "parent focus," received solely a parent-training intervention. (The other two intervention groups were "teen focus"—teenagers met in groups of seven or eight with a counselor; and "parent and teen focus"—a combination of the parent-training and teen group-counseling interventions). There were also two control groups (in the first, participants received newsletters and videotapes; in the second there was no intervention at all). People in the intervention groups received 12 weekly 90-minute training or counseling sessions. Results consisted of observers' reports of parent–adolescent conflict, parents' reports of adolescents' behavior at home, and teachers' reports of their behavior at school, made immediately after the intervention and one year later. The teachers did not know (unless their students told them) the experimental or control group assignments of the participating families.

According to the reports of the parents and observers, the parent-focused intervention reduced the amount of family conflict. For my purposes, the important question is: Did the adolescents' behavior at school also improve? The abstract of the article says that it did: "The parent intervention conditions showed immediate beneficial effects on behavior problems at school" (Dishion & Andrews, 1995, p. 538). The data, however, are less convincing. There was a small, "statistically marginal effect" ($p < .10$) immediately after the intervention: The adolescents in the parent-focus condition showed "reductions in school behavior problems" compared to the control conditions (p. 543). A post hoc analysis comparing both groups that included a parent-focused intervention with both control groups brought the significance level up slightly, but it still failed to hit the magic number: $p < .06$. One year later, these marginal effects had disappeared.

Figure 1.1 shows my graph of Dishion and Andrews' (1995) results. These are the means of teachers' ratings of adolescents' externalizing behavior; higher scores mean more troublesome behavior. Notice in this graph that the preintervention

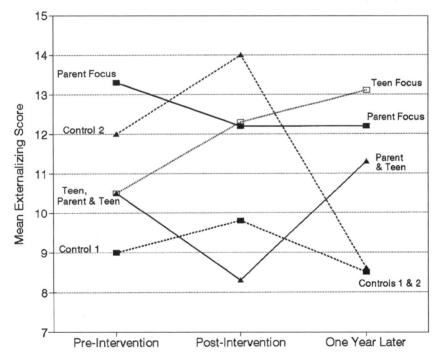

FIG. 1.1. Teachers' ratings of adolescents' behavior at school, using the Child Behavior Checklist Externalizing scale (data from Dishion and Andrews, 1995, p. 544). Higher scores mean more troublesome behavior. Solid lines identify the two groups that included a parent-focused intervention; dashed lines identify the two control groups.

differences between the groups were larger than most of the postintervention changes. The only result—no doubt a fluke—that shows up clearly in these data is that, one year after the intervention, the adolescents in the two control groups were behaving better in school than the adolescents in any of the three intervention groups.

The study by Forgatch and DeGarmo (1999) also used a well-designed procedure. The participating families were recently separated single mothers and their sons in Grades 1 to 3. The intervention consisted of group parent-training sessions for the mothers ($n = 153$) over a period of 14 to 16 weeks, with midweek phone calls from the trainers to encourage use of the recommended parenting behaviors. The control group ($n = 85$) got no intervention at all. Results consisted of observations of mother–child interactions by researchers and assessments by the mothers, teachers, and the children themselves. The teachers, who were unaware that the families were participating in a study, were asked to rate the children's externalizing behavior, prosocial behavior, and adaptive functioning.

My interest is again in the teachers' ratings. According to Forgatch and DeGarmo, these ratings yielded results that were "contrary to [their] expectations" (1999, p. 718) but not to mine: There were no significant differences between the intervention and control groups in any of the behaviors judged by the teachers. The researchers responded to this setback by carrying out a post hoc path analysis. The path analysis showed that the intervention was significantly associated with an increase in effective parenting, and that an increase in effective parenting was significantly associated with an improvement in school adjustment. What the path analysis revealed was a correlation: The mothers who improved as a result of the intervention had children who behaved better in school.

At first glance this seems like a perfectly reasonable way to look at these data. Naturally, we wouldn't expect the intervention to have beneficial effects on children's behavior in school unless the mother's parenting improved! But there is a serious, though subtle, problem with the post hoc analysis. What it does, in effect, is turn an experimental design into a correlational design.

As Cowan and Cowan (this volume) point out, the power of intervention designs derives from the random assignment of participating families to the intervention or control conditions. The random assignment is what makes it unnecessary to control for genetic effects: We can assume that there are no systematic genetic differences between the experimental and control groups. But this reasoning works only for group-versus-group comparisons. Looking for correlations within the experimental group destroys the randomness of the design, because it is logically equivalent to dividing up the parents in the experimental group into two subgroups—those who profited from the intervention and those who did not—and reporting the results only for the children of the better subgroup. Though the experimental group *as a whole* and the control group *as a whole* can be regarded as genetically equivalent, we cannot skim off the top performers in the experimental group and assume that this select subgroup is genetically equivalent to the control group. It is not surprising that mothers who respond well to the social and intellectual demands of an intervention would have biological offspring who respond well to the social and intellectual demands of school. Thus, the observed correlation could have been due to heritable differences in personality or intelligence between those members of the intervention group who did and not profit from the intervention. All we can legitimately conclude from the results of Forgatch and DeGarmo's (1999) study is that if we take two genetically equivalent groups of people and provide the parents in one group with an intervention designed to improve their parenting, on the average the children in this group will behave no better in school than the children in the group that did not receive the intervention (see also Cowan and Cowan, this volume).

I have no doubt that parent-training interventions can improve a family's home life; there are beneficial effects on parenting and, consequently, beneficial effects on the way the children behave at home. But my survey of the intervention literature led me to conclude that home-based interventions cannot improve the children's behavior at school, and others have come to the same conclusion. Wierson and Forehand (1994), in an article summarizing the results of two decades of parent-training interventions (many of them carried out by Forehand himself), reported that such training improves the parents' behavior toward the child both in the clinic and at home, and improves the child's responsiveness to the parents in both places. "However," Wierson and Forehand admitted, "research has been unable to show that the child's behavior is modified at school" (p. 148).

There is no need, however, to be discouraged about the potential usefulness of interventions. It is possible to modify children's behavior in any context, but to do so requires an intervention in that context. Awareness of this principle appears to be spreading; many researchers (e.g., Capaldi, Chamberlain, Fetrow, & Wilson, 1997; Henggeler & Borduin, 1990) are switching to "multimethod" or "multisystemic" interventions, designed to reach children both at home and in one or more outside-the-home settings. Group socialization theory predicts that such interventions will be more effective if they are aimed at a group of children—children who are members of the same peer group—and that their effects will be more lasting if the children remain in contact with each other after the intervention ends. But the group approach also has its hazards: As Dishion and his colleagues have learned (1999; this volume), bringing high-risk or antisocial young people together in a group can make their behavior worse rather than better.

Can parents do anything? Of course they can. Although individual mothers and fathers have little power to modify their children's behavior outside the home, parents can exert a great deal of power if they get together. For example, if one parent prevented her child from watching violent TV shows, my prediction is that it would not make a difference, because her child would pick up his attitude toward violence from peers who do watch these shows. But if all the parents in a given school or neighborhood prevented their children from watching violent TV shows, that could make a big difference. According to group socialization theory, neighborhoods, schools, the media, and the parents *as a group* have effects on individual children through their effects on the norms of their peer groups.

GOALS FOR FUTURE RESEARCH

Testing theories of development is a difficult job and a vitally important one. Developmentalists should bring to this job the same rigorous methods that have been used so successfully in medical research. That means using "blinded" procedures whenever possible. It means not using designs in which the same informants contribute the data on both sides of the correlations. It means not using correlations to draw conclusions about causes and effects, unless there are data of other kinds to back up the conclusions. It means using existing methods, or devising new methods, to separate genetic and environmental effects, because we cannot achieve an accurate understanding of how the environment affects the child without first understanding what the child brings to that environment.

Scientific advances will be made only if researchers start from a level playing field on which all hypotheses are given equal treatment, and if no assumptions— not even the nurture assumption—are regarded as sacred.

ACKNOWLEDGMENTS

I thank Joan Friebely for her assistance in gathering reference materials and Charles S. Harris for his helpful comments.

REFERENCES

Alwin, D. F. (1988). From obedience to autonomy: Changes in traits desired in children, 1924–1978. *Public Opinion Quarterly, 52,* 33–52.

Arcus, D. M. (1991). *Experiential modification of temperamental bias in inhibited and uninhibited children.* Unpublished doctoral dissertation, Harvard University.

Baumrind, D. (1993). The average expectable environment is not good enough: A response to Scarr. *Child Development, 64,* 1299–1317.

Bickerton, D. (1983, July). Creole languages. *Scientific American, 249,* 116–122.

Bouchard, T. J., Jr. (1994, June 17). Genes, environment, and personality. *Science, 264,* 1700–1701.

Capaldi, D. M., Chamberlain, P., Fetrow, R. A., & Wilson, J. E. (1997). Conducting ecologically valid prevention research: Recruiting and retaining a "whole village" in multimethod, multiagent studies. *American Journal of Community Psychology, 25,* 471–492.

Cherny, S. S., Fulker, D. W., Corley, R., Plomin, R., & DeFries, J. C. (1994). Continuity and change in infant shyness from 14 to 20 months. *Behavior Genetics, 24,* 365–380.

Collins, W. A., Maccoby, E. E., Steinberg, L., Hetherington, E. M., & Bornstein, M. H. (2000). Contemporary research on parenting: The case for nature *and* nurture. *American Psychologist, 55,* 218–232.

Cowan, P. A., Powell, D., & Cowan, C. P. (1998). Parenting interventions: A family systems perspective. In W. Damon (Series Ed.) & I. E. Sigel & K. A. Renninger (Vol. Eds.), *Handbook of child psychology: Vol. 4. Child psychology in practice* (5th ed., pp. 3–72). New York: John Wiley and Sons.

Detterman, D. K. (1993). The case for the prosecution: Transfer as an epiphenomenon. In D. K. Detterman & R. J. Sternberg (Eds.), *Transfer on trial: Intelligence, cognition, and instruction* (pp. 1–24). Norwood, NJ: Ablex.

Dishion, T. J., & Andrews, D. W. (1995). Preventing escalation in problem behaviors with high-risk young adolescents: Immediate and 1-year outcomes. *Journal of Consulting and Clinical Psychology, 63,* 538–548.

Dishion, T. J., McCord, J., & Poulin, F. (1999). When interventions harm: Peer groups and problem behavior. *American Psychologist, 54,* 755–764.

Eisenberg, N., Cumberland, A., & Spinrad, T. L. (1998a). Parental socialization of emotion. *Psychological Inquiry, 9,* 241–273.

Eisenberg, N., Cumberland, A., & Spinrad, T. L. (1998b). The socialization of emotion: Reply to commentaries. *Psychological Inquiry, 9,* 241–273.

Falbo, T., & Polit, D. F. (1986). Quantitative research of the only child literature: Research evidence and theory development. *Psychological Bulletin, 100,* 176–189.

Falbo, T., & Poston, D. L., Jr. (1993). The academic, personality, and physical outcomes of only children in China. *Child Development, 64,* 18–35.

Forgatch, M. S., & DeGarmo, D. S. (1999). Parenting through change: An effective prevention program for single mothers. *Journal of Consulting and Clinical Psychology, 67,* 711–724.

Graziano, A. M., Hamblen, J. L., & Plante, W. A. (1996). Subabusive violence in child rearing in middle-class American Families. *Pediatrics, 98,* 845–848.

Gunnoe, M. L., & Mariner, C. L. (1997). Toward a developmental-contextual model of the effects of parental spanking on children's aggression. *Archives of Pediatrics and Adolescent Medicine, 151,* 768–775.

Harris, J. R. (1995). Where is the child's environment? A group socialization theory of development. *Psychological Review, 102,* 458–489.

Harris, J. R. (1998a). *The nurture assumption.* New York: Free Press.

Harris, J. R. (1998b). The trouble with assumptions [commentary on Eisenberg, Cumberland, & Spinrad]. *Psychological Inquiry, 9,* 294–297.

Harris, J. R. (2000). Context-specific learning, personality, and birth order. *Current Directions in Psychological Science, 5,* 174–177.

Henggeler, S. W., & Borduin, C. M. (1990). *Family therapy and beyond: A multisystemic approach to treating the behavior problems of children and adolescents.* Pacific Grove, CA: Brooks/Cole.

Hoffman, L. W. (1991). The influence of the family environment on personality: Accounting for sibling differences. *Psychological Bulletin, 110,* 187–203.

Jones, M. C. (1957). The later careers of boys who were early or late maturing. *Child Development, 28,* 113–128.

Kagan, J., with Snidman, N., Arcus, D., & Reznick, J. S. (1994). *Galen's prophecy.* New York: Basic Books.

Kagan, J., Arcus, D., & Snidman, N. (1993). The idea of temperament: Where do we go from here? In R. Plomin & G. E. McClearn (Eds.), *Nature, nurture, and psychology* (pp. 197–210). Washington, DC: American Psychological Association.

Kerr, M., Lambert, W. W., Stattin, H., & Klackenberg-Larsson, I. (1994). Stability of inhibition in a Swedish longitudinal sample. *Child Development, 65,* 138–146.

Maccoby, E. E. (1990). Gender and relationships: A developmental account. *American Psychologist, 45,* 513–520.

Maccoby, E. E. (1998). *The two sexes: Growing up apart, coming together.* Cambridge, MA: Harvard University Press.

Maccoby, E. E., & Jacklin, C. N. (1987). Gender segregation in childhood. *Advances in Child Development and Behavior, 20,* 239–287.

McCrae, R. R., & Costa, P. T., Jr. (1988). Recalled parent–child relations and adult personality. *Journal of Personality, 56,* 417–434.

Myers, D. G. (1992). *The pursuit of happiness: Who is happy—and why?* New York: Avon.

NICHD Early Child Care Research Network. (1998). Early child care and self-control, compliance, and problem behavior at twenty-four and thirty-six months. *Child Development, 69,* 1145–1170.

Pinker, S. (1998). Foreword. In J. R. Harris, *The nurture assumption* (pp. xi–xiii). New York: Free Press.

Plomin, R., Chipuer, H. M., & Neiderhiser, J. M. (1994). Behavioral genetic evidence for the importance of nonshared environment. In E. M. Hetherington, D. Reiss, & R. Plomin (Eds.), *Separate social worlds of siblings: The impact of nonshared environment on development* (pp. 1–31). Hillsdale, NJ: Lawrence Erlbaum Associates.

Plomin, R., & Daniels, D. (1987). Why are children in the same family so different from one another? *Behavioral and Brain Sciences, 10,* 1–60.

Reiss, D., with Neiderhiser, J. M., Hetherington, E. M., & Plomin, R. (2000). The relationship code: Deciphering genetic and social influences on adolescent development. Cambridge, MA: Harvard University Press.

Richman, R. A., Gordon, M., Tegtmeyer, P., Crouthamel, C., & Post, E. M. (1986). Academic and emotional difficulties associated with short stature. In B. Stabler & L. E. Underwood (Eds.), *Slow grows the child: Psychosocial aspects of growth delay* (pp. 13–26). Hillsdale, NJ: Lawrence Erlbaum Associates.

Rowe, D. C. (1994). *The limits of family influence.* New York: Guilford Press.

Rubin, K. H., Hastings, P. D., Stewart, S. L., Henderson, H. A., & Chen, X. (1997). The consistency and concomitants of inhibition: Some of the children, all of the time. *Child Development, 68,* 467–483.

Saudino, K. J. (1997). Moving beyond the heritability question: New directions in behavioral genetic studies of personality. *Current Directions in Psychological Science, 6,* 86–90.

Scarr, S. (1997). Why child care has little impact on most children's development. *Current Directions in Psychological Science, 6,* 143–148.

Scarr, S., & McCartney, K. (1983). How people make their own environments. A theory of genotype Æ environment effects. *Child Development, 54,* 424–435.

Socolar, R. R. S, Winsor, J., Hunter, W. M., Catellier, D., & Kotch, J. B. (1999). Maternal disciplinary practices in an at-risk population. *Archives of Pediatrics and Adolescent Medicine, 153,* 927–934.

Sroufe, L. A., Egeland, B., & Carlson, E. A. (1999). One social world: The integrated development of parent-child and peer relationships. In W. A. Collins & B. Laursen (Eds.), *Relationships as developmental contexts* (pp. 241–261). Mahwah, NJ: Lawrence Erlbaum Associates.

Straus, M. A., Sugarman, D. B., & Giles-Sims, J. (1997). Spanking by parents and subsequent antisocial behavior of children. *Archives of Pediatrics and Adolescent Medicine, 151,* 761–767.

Turkheimer, E., & Waldron, M. (2000). Nonshared environment: A theoretical, methodological, and quantitative review. *Psychological Bulletin, 126,* 78–108.

Turner, J. C., with Hogg, M. A., Oakes, P. J., Reicher, S. D., & Wetherell, M. S. (1987). *Rediscovering the social group: A self-categorization theory.* Oxford, UK: Basil Blackwell.

Veenhoven, R., & Verkuyten, M. (1989). The well-being of only children. *Adolescence, 24,* 155–166.

Webster-Stratton, C. (1984). Randomized trial of two parent-training programs for families with conduct-disordered children. *Journal of Consulting and Clinical Psychology, 52,* 666–678.

Webster-Stratton, C. (1998). Preventing conduct problems in Head Start children: Strengthening parenting competencies. *Journal of Consulting and Clinical Psychology, 66,* 715–730.

Wierson, M., & Forehand, R. (1994). Parent behavioral training for child noncompliance: Rationale, concepts, and effectiveness. *Current Directions in Psychological Science, 3,* 146–150.

Wolfenstein, M. (1953). Trends in infant care. *American Journal of Orthopsychiatry, 23,* 120–130.

2

What Twin and Adoption Studies Reveal About Parenting

David C. Rowe

University of Arizona

One of the most persistent questions in the field of development is: How do parents influence the development of their child's intelligence and personality? To answer this question, one approach is for researchers to look for correlations between the way the parents behave toward the child and the way the child turns out—*child outcomes*. Very often, these correlations are then used to infer environmental effects on the child: the environment provided by the parent is assumed to be the cause of the child outcomes. For example, if the parents have a good vocabulary and often engage the child in conversation, and this child does better in school, it is assumed that the parents' verbal behavior stimulated intellectual growth in the child. If the parents' method of discipline is harsh or inconsistent and the child is found to be disruptive or aggressive, then this is because the parents failed to teach (by instruction or example) self-control or the proper social norms. In other words, parental treatment is usually considered to be an "environmental influence" that has the capacity to shape the children's development.

Address correspondence to: School of Family and Consumer Sciences, Box 210033, University of Arizona, Tucson, AZ 85721, Phone: 520-621-7127; Fax: 520-621-3401; e-mail: dcr091@ag. arizona.edu

Harris (1998) called this assumption about the power of parental treatments to mold children "the nurture assumption" because it is so pervasive in American culture. Following from it, correlations between parental behavior and children's developmental outcomes are taken as evidence of an environmental influence, especially when other variables (e.g., birth order, parental education, income, family size) are statistically controlled.

Flaws in this inference were recognized long ago by behavioral scientists (Bell, 1968; Burks, 1938) and have been brought to the attention of the general public in several books (Cohen, 1999; Harris, 1998; Rowe, 1994; Wright, 1998). Bell articulated the evidence that the association between a parent's and child's behavior also contains information about the child's influence on the parent, as well as vice versa. This means that parental behavior itself has been adapted to the child's individual development.

Behavioral genetic theory gave another reason for doubting the causality of parent–child associations. As far back as the 1930s, pioneers in behavioral genetics such as Burks (1938) recognized that genetic influences could play a role in creating correlations between parenting and child outcomes. She further realized that the possibility of genetic influences posed difficulties for any research design based solely on biological families. Such designs combine genetic and environmental effects and so can overestimate environmental influence if part, or all, of the association between parental behavior and child outcome arises from shared heredity. To control for such genetic influences on intellectual development, Burks conducted an adoption study. It revealed familial social class to be considerably less influential on children's intellectual development than findings from studies of biological families would have led one to believe. The belief in strong parental influence, founded on studies of biological families, was in error.

Burks' insight unfortunately was lost in the changes in social philosophy and ethical thinking that followed the Second World War (Degler, 1991). Because of the terrible crimes committed by the Nazi regime, and partly justified by its ideology of racial superiority, it became socially unacceptable—especially in educated circles—to use biology to explain various aspects of human behavior, such as individual differences in intelligence.

Now, building on the advances in molecular biology as well as those in psychology, we can go back to a more balanced view (Plomin, Owen, & McGuffin, 1994). We are in an era when behavioral effects of single genes can be examined in experimental animals. In knockout animals, a gene is rendered nonfunctional by molecular genetic methods, and the animals are bred to be homozygous for it. In transgenic animals, a gene from another species is added to an animal. Knockouts and transgenic animals permit the examination of the effect of single genes on behavior. For example, a knockout induced hyperactivity in mice (Giros et al., 1996). In another dramatic finding, the introduction of a gene from the monogamous prairie vole into transgenic mice changed the mice from highly polygynous to nearly pair-bonding in response to a dose of vasopressin (Young et al., 1999).

In human studies, advances in genetic linkage and association studies have also identified single genes with behavioral effects, for example, a polymorphism in the aldehyde dehydrogenase gene is one reason for lower alcoholism rates in Koreans and Japanese men than in European men (Wall & Ehlers, 1995). In another instance, a gene involved in the metabolism of the neurotransmitter dopamine is associated with attention deficit hyperactivity disorder in childhood (Waldman et al., 1998). Despite the remarkable scope of these new discoveries, we know that genes do not determine behavior in any sort of rigid way. But it has become abundantly clear that genes can influence behavior. We can no longer afford to ignore the role of the genes.

What does it mean to say that a correlation between parenting behavior and child outcome could be due—partly or entirely—to genetic influences? In order for this to happen, a necessary condition is that there has to be some genetic influence on parents' behavior. One way this can come about is that variations in parenting behavior are due, at least in part, to genetic variations among parents.

Genes of a parent could influence parenting behavior directly. The new methods of molecular genetics have not yet identified in people any specific "parenting genes." Researchers who investigated genes in the mouse, however, succeeded inadvertently. Brown, Ye, Bronson, Dikkes, and Greenberg (1996) were studying a gene called fosB. Like a symphony conductor who directs the action of many instruments, the fosB protein activates and controls the expression of many other genes. The fosB protein, in particular, is found in regions of the brain required for nurturing behavior, and so among its cascade of effects could be some on nurturing behavior. To explore the function of fosB in the nervous system, Brown et al. created an inbred line of mice in which the fosB gene was rendered nonfunctional. In these knockout mice, they found a very high rate of infant mortality. Naturally, a first thought was that the gene's absence had an adverse affect on the physical development of the pups. But that proved not to be the case. The pups', deaths turned out to be due to a deficiency in the mothers, not in the pups' development: The mothers who lacked a fosB gene failed to retrieve their pups when the pups ventured away from the nest. This absence of a single gene led to a failure in nurturing, which put the pups at risk because they failed to return to the nest for the mother's protective warmth and nutritive milk. Interestingly enough, these mice were normal in other respects, so that the behavioral deficit of the female mice was specific to their nurturing behaviors.

In humans, we do not have evidence of direct genetic effects on parenting behavior, but there is ample evidence of indirect effects. Indirect effects occur because genes influence many parental characteristics. We know that differences in personality traits and intellectual abilities are partly due to genetic variations among individuals who can be parents themselves. If these characteristics in turn influence parenting styles, they are then also genetically influenced. Reflect on the characteristics of shy versus outgoing and agreeable versus hostile. A shy and hostile parent is probably not an emotionally warm parent. An outgoing and agreeable parent is probably a warm parent.

My colleagues and I found associations between parenting behaviors and the "big five" dimensions of personality (Losoya, Callor, Rowe, & Goldsmith, 1997). The big five dimensions were identified because they are repeatedly found in factor analyses of data from individuals answering self-report questions about their behaviors and in data from raters of friends and acquaintances. The big five dimensions are: extraversion, agreeableness, conscientiousness, emotional stability, and intellectual orientation. These trait names label just one pole of a trait dimension. For example, the opposite end of extraversion is shyness and introversion. Parents of children who were eight years old or younger completed several self-report parenting scales. Items were combined to form a parenting dimension that we called positive support; it refers to showing more affection and attention to children. The same parents completed a measure of the big five. Each of these personality dimensions correlated positively with self-report of parental support, with the correlation coefficients ranging from .34 for extraversion to .47 for intellectual orientation. We found that the conventionally thought of positive pole of each trait was associated with more positive support. Extroverts were more supportive than introverts. Emotionally stable parents managed more attention to their children than neurotic parents. A good amount of variation in parenting style is statistically associated with these personality characteristics. Genes that influence parents' personalities thus also appear to influence their behaviors toward their children.

We also know that genes influence intelligence. Social scientists use one scale, called the HOME, to measure the quality of family environments. The home environments of high IQ parents earn higher scores on the HOME than those of lower IQ parents. High IQ parents are more likely to show all the kinds of behaviors that are conventionally accepted as good in American society—for instance, giving a child more intellectual stimulation and the "just right" kind of parenting that blends affection with an appropriate amount of control.

Our study of personality dimensions and parenting had a further purpose (Losoya et al., 1997). We also wanted to discover whether genetic influences led to different styles of parenting. Thus, we sampled not only individuals who were parents, but also those who were siblings. Our sampling strategy, which relied on advertisements placed in major newspapers like the *New York Times*, was designed to locate three kinds of sibling pairs that vary widely in their genetic relatedness: identical twins (completely related genetically), fraternal twins (related 50%), and adoptive siblings (related 0%).

This research design was intended to test whether genes or family environment had the greater influence on parenting behaviors. Consider an environmental theory first. One way that parenting behaviors might be acquired is through observation of one's own parents. All siblings in this study were reared together by the same parents (the grandparents of their young children), so if parenting style is learned by observing one's parents, we would then expect the siblings to use similar parenting styles with their own children. But that is not what we found.

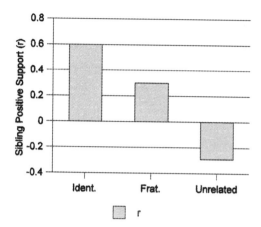

FIG. 2.1. Sibling correlations for positive support in identical, fraternal, and adoptive (unrelated) siblings.

Figure 2.1 shows the findings for the positive support dimension of parental behavior. The height of the bars represent the degree to which the siblings parent their children (who are cousins) in similar ways. The height represents the correlation coefficient between siblings; a correlation of 0 would mean that siblings do not parent at all alike. A correlation of 1.0 would mean exactly identical parenting styles. A negative correlation means a dissimilarity in the parenting styles of the siblings. The associations followed genetic relatedness for positive support (attention and affection). Identical twins were most alike in their parenting, fraternal twins were in the middle, and the adoptive siblings were slightly dissimilar. This rank order held for two other dimensions of parenting: criticism and strictness (called *negative affect*) and imposition of rules (called *control*). If adoptive children learn anything at all about parenting from observing their own parents, they take away very different lessons.

CHILD EFFECTS: GENES OF CHILDREN INFLUENCE PARENTS

Genetic differences among children may elicit or provoke different parenting styles. To take a really extreme example, Kip Kinkel murdered his parents and young children at his elementary school in Oregon. His mother and father were constantly concerned about him; his father even sought psychological advice for his son from a fellow airline passenger who was a clinical psychologist. Mr. Kinkel did not need to take these same steps for Kip's sister, a school cheerleader and popular student. Kip's obsession with guns and violence was provoking different behaviors from his parents. To take a less extreme example, parents need to spend less time monitoring the behavior of an inactive child than a highly active child. The highly active child might run into a street, break toys, or otherwise move out of bounds, and parents must exert greater monitoring and control over such children.

The examples are called *child effects* in the literature on child development (Bell, 1968; Bell & Chapman, 1986). Developmental scientists try to solve the problem of child effects by using longitudinal designs. The basic idea is to determine whether a change in a children's behavior from two ages is predictable from a change from parental treatment. To the extent that the child's genes undergo no changes between the two ages, this longitudinal method is a feasible strategy. When genetic influences are constant they cannot account for change. However, the constancy of genetic influences is not always true. Women and men develop secondary sexual characteristics in the teenage years because genes that were dormant are now actively expressed. A strategy of statistical control for prior characteristics is also imperfect because it is difficult to measure everything in a child's background. Finally, longitudinal studies often find that there is much constancy in child's characteristics, and also a lot of constancy in how parents behave. Because of this behavioral stability, the amount of change can be small, making a causal analysis inconclusive. Longitudinal studies are certainly better than a single assessment of behavior in a sample of biological families, but they are far from adequate for valid causal inference.

One kind of evidence for child effects comes from observational studies that examine how adults respond to children in a laboratory setting. This approach allows one to infer that a child is an influence on a parent. For example, in lab tests, parents give more attention to physically more attractive infants (not their own children) than they do to less attractive ones (Langlois, Ritter, Casey, & Sawin, 1995). This favoritism is a child effect because appearance elicits parental reactions.

A more complex study reveals the power of children with a psychiatric disorder to elicit different parental treatments (Anderson, Lytton, & Romney, 1986). In this study, parents were asked to play with children who were not their own. Unbeknownst to them, their child partner was either a conduct disordered (CD) child or a normal (N) child. To be explicit, there were four groups in this study, in which no mother was paired with her own biological child: (1) a mother of a CD child paired with a CD child, (2) a mother of a CD child paired with an N child, (3) a mother of an N child paired with a CD child, and (4) a mother of an N child paired with an N child. During the session, the mothers were instructed to oversee the cleanup of a playroom. What made a difference for "compliance to parental requests" was the type of child. Conduct-disordered children complied about 76% of the time, normal children about 96% of the time. Mothers of conduct-disordered children had no problem obtaining compliance—when they had a normal child as partner. In this laboratory setting, the mothers of conduct-disordered children behaved toward their own children much as they did toward conduct-disordered children who were not their own. How nice it must be for a parent to receive 20% more child compliance, which in turn makes the parent look very skilled to other parents, if he or she has an easy-to-socialize child!

Child effects can emanate from the influence of children's genes on their behaviors. Both twin and adoption studies show this process. When genetic child effects are present, siblings who are more genetically alike (e.g., full sibling brothers) should be given more similar parenting than siblings who are less genetically alike (e.g., adoptive sibling brothers). For example, the parenting of an adoptive child with an easy temperament will be different from the parenting of this child's sibling when the sibling has a difficult temperament.

Identical and fraternal twins differ in their level of genetic relatedness. When twins are raised together, they nonetheless report different experiences of parental treatment (Rowe, 1981, 1983). In my first study (Rowe, 1981), adolescent identical and fraternal twins rated their parents using a standardized parenting questionnaire. Fraternal twins reported receiving less equal parental affection than identical twins. Identical twins usually agreed pretty well on how much affection they got from their parents, but fraternal twins often disagreed. One might say that he or she received ample affection, whereas the other might say his or her parents were not at all affectionate. Interestingly, there was no identical versus fraternal twin difference in reports of parental control. Thus, parental control (i.e., the imposition and enforcement of family rules) seemed to be unrelated to the biology of the adolescents. With regard to their reports of parental affection, however, we do not know with certainty whether one twin received more affection than the other because that twin was more cheerful, cooperative, or good-looking, but we do know that fraternal twins differ more in these respects than do identical twins. Also, adolescents' personality qualities may influence how they perceive or rate their parents regardless of the parents' actual behavior. In a second study, using a different measure of twins' perceptions of parental behavior, I obtained similar findings (Rowe, 1983).

My two studies had adolescent twins as subjects. In another study, the twins were adults recollecting their childhoods (Plomin, McLearn, Pedersen, Nesselroade, & Bergeman, 1988). A special feature of this study is that it included twins reared apart and together of both types: identical and fraternal. The adult twins rated their families of origin on several dimensions of family behavior, such as cohesion. Descriptively, in cohesive families, relationships among family members are warm and supportive. The other pole of this parenting dimension is families in which members show little interest in one another. Another family environmental dimension referred to the level of conflict among family members.

Genetic influences existed for the adult twins' perceptions of cohesion and conflict. For example, one comparison was that the reared-together identical twins were more alike in their perceptions of parental treatment than were the reared-together fraternal twins. A further comparison was that of the reared-apart identical and fraternal twins. There are not two parents involved here, but

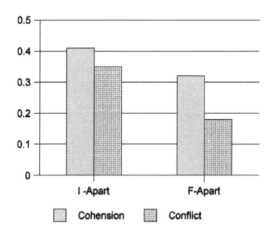

FIG. 2.2. Twin correlations on perception of family cohesion and conflict for identical and fraternal twins reared apart.

four parents, because each twin reports on a separate set of adoptive parents. As shown in Figure 2.2 for cohesion and conflict, the reared-apart identical twins saw their adoptive parents as behaving more similarly than did the reared-apart fraternal twins. The identical twins' resemblance alone is prima facie evidence of genetic influence because genetic similarity is the linking influence on these separated twins raised in different families. But further evidence of genetic influence comes in the observation that the reared-apart identical twins' perceptions were more alike than those of the reared-apart fraternal twins (see bars in Figure 2.2). The separated twins could have elicited different behaviors from their different parents—but even more so when they were genetically more dissimilar.

Or perhaps the identical twins wear more similar "rose-colored glasses" than do fraternal twins, glasses that bias their recollections of childhood. For example, one could imagine that adult successes and failures may color recollections of childhood. An adult who is currently depressed may recollect a disproportionate number of unhappy childhood effects, a bias that might disappear when the depression lifts. Many a blues song catalogs just such a litany of sad stories. Although this rose-colored-glasses effect may hold true, my belief is that the major source of similarity is that the twins elicit similar parental behavior. This is because in observations of children, the power of children to elicit differential adult behavior is readily demonstrated. For example, fraternal twin infants behave more dissimilarly than do identical twin infants. A detailed behavior record on the twin infants and their mothers revealed that fraternal twins elicited more dissimilar parental behavior toward them than did identical twins. A behavioral record keeps track of what each individual does in a social interaction and establishes whose behavior is driving the next behavior, the parent's or the child's (Lytton, 1980; see also Rende, Slomkowski, Stocker, Fulker, & Plomin, 1992).

Children are not born equally easy to raise. Child psychologists talk about difficult infants, who cry and fuss more and do not tolerate separations well. Although colic is a time-limited disorder in most babies, it also stresses parents tremendously. As children become older, many psychiatric disorders of childhood become manifest. Particularly hard on parents are children diagnosed with attention deficit hyperactivity disorder and conduct disorder. Both psychiatric disorders are influenced by genes (Eaves et al., 1997; Slutske et al., 1997; Thapar, Hervas, & McGuffin, 1995). The genes are not completely deterministic in their influence, but children do differ in tendencies toward behaviors that make life easy or difficult for their parents.

Child-to-parent effects can be demonstrated most convincingly in a full adoption study. A full adoption study requires data on both sets of parents of adoptive children: their biological and adoptive parents. Such studies are infrequent because of the difficulty of locating and interviewing biological parents before their children are adopted, or shortly afterwards. This design is even less practical today than previously because of the widespread use of open adoptions that allow contact between the adoptive and biological parents. Furthermore, many children are now placed privately by lawyers working on a fee basis instead of through public and private adoption agencies. One study that does meet all the requirements, however, is the Colorado Adoption Study (O'Connor, Deater-Deckard, Fulker, Rutter, & Plomin, 1998). The study had data on the biological mothers of the adoptive children who were interviewed before they gave their children up for adoption. The adopted children were followed after placement, and multiple assessments were made of the parenting styles of their adoptive parents as the adoptive children grew up.

The Colorado Adoption Project researchers can predict with better than chance accuracy whether children will be easy or difficult to raise on the basis of the characteristics of their biological mothers. The biological mothers completed a short questionnaire about their own externalizing behaviors (e.g., impulsivity, aggression, stealing, lying, and other behaviors that often get people into trouble). Children were divided according to whether their biological mothers scored above the median (higher risk) or below it (lower risk). These classifications did not identify mothers with extreme problems, as those in the high group were neither criminals nor diagnosed with personality disorders; they just reported more minor delinquent and impulsive acts. The presence of a biological correlation between parent and child means that the children of the high-risk biological mothers could be more difficult to raise than those of the low-risk mothers.

Figure 2.3 displays the adoptive parents' discipline style toward their adoptive child and distinguishes the high-(top line) and low-(bottom line) risk children. Assessments were taken at five different ages, starting when the children were 7 years old and ending when they were twelve years old. As shown in Figure 2.3,

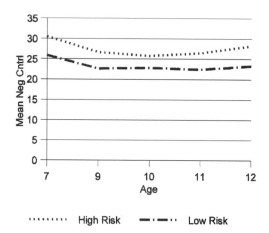

FIG. 2.3.   Negative control of adoptive parents toward biologically low- and high-risk children.

the high-risk children reportedly received more parental negative control than did
the low-risk children. Although not shown in Figure 2.3, the difficult children
also displayed more externalizing behaviors (e.g., aggression, disobedience) than
did the easy children.

The authors of this study conducted some complex analyses in an effort to
decide whether a pathway of effects occurred. The first link is between a high-risk
biological mother and a misbehaving (i.e., externalizing) child. The second link is
between the child's misbehavior and the adoptive mothers' self-report of harsher
discipline (negative control). Mediation implies that the child's misbehavior is a
necessary condition for the harsh discipline. That is, when the biological mother is
high risk and the child does not misbehave, one would not have an adoptive mother who disciplines harshly. This mediational effect did not fully occur. Risk in the
biological mother increased harsh discipline even when the child was well
behaved, at least by one rating scale. Perhaps other child characteristics, not measured, are mediating between risk in the biological mother and a harsher mothering style displayed by the adoptive mother. Alternatively, there may be complex
relationship issues that affect parenting a biological versus an adoptive child, such
as identification and empathy factors.

In summary, the results are impressive because the adoptive mothers did not
know anything about the biological risk status of their adoptive children. The
adoptive parents of both easy and difficult children were equivalent in any tendency to use harsh discipline—but those adoptive parents who had to raise children with more difficult temperaments were significantly more likely to apply a
harsher form of discipline.

TABLE 2.1
SHARED AND NONSHARED ENVIRONMENTAL INFLUENCES

Nonshared Environmental Influences	Shared Environmental Influences
Differential treatment of siblings if causal	Social Class
Birth order	Family warmth insofar as correlated across siblings
Birth traumas	Divorce
Sibling peer pressures	

Child effects also enter into the discussion about shared and nonshared environmental effects. Table 2.1 shows that behavioral geneticists divide environmental effects into those that are common to siblings (shared) and those that are dissimilar for siblings (nonshared environment). A few examples of each type of influence are given.

We have learned that shared environmental influences are generally pretty week (Rowe, 1994). One piece of evidence is that adoptive siblings grow up to have different behaviors despite inhabiting the same family from infancy into adolescence. Because siblings are so different, we are inclined to look for causative environmental influences that differ from one sibling to another. Differential parental treatments qualify as one *potential* within-family environmental influence. For example, if the sibling who is read to more is smarter than a brother or sister, this is perhaps a within-family nonshared environmental effect. But this depends on the direction of causality being from parent to child.

A more subtle critique of nonshared parental treatments—that developmental processes are of one piece—is worth a brief discussion. Variance can be partitioned, but developmental processes cannot. To illustrate this subtle idea, suppose that a certain number of hours of a parent activity with a child is associated with a known IQ gain. A sibling who received this parent activity more than a brother or sister should be a certain number of IQ points smarter than this sibling, after adjusting for baseline differences. If siblings were to receive widely discrepant amounts of this parent behavior, then most of the variance would be "within families." If siblings were treated exactly the same, most of the variance would be "between-families." However, in practical terms, most parental treatments are at neither extreme. Parents who make a great effort to intellectually stimulate their children will give them more stimulation than parents who do attempt this, even when one sibling receives a bit more or less stimulation than the other. This is why I doubt that differential parental treatments have large effects. If these treatments had such strong effects, they would also appear in the similarity of adoptive siblings, because to some extent, siblings would be treated more alike than children in another family. When the occasional family environmental effect has been found, adoptive siblings do tend to be alike (e.g., early childhood IQ, religious affiliation).

THE NURTURE ASSUMPTION

My examples of genetic influence on parenting have established one necessary condition for doubting many studies of socialization: Parenting behaviors are not necessarily independent of genetic influence. These examples accord with the conclusions of much more detailed literature reviews by Robert Plomin (Plomin & Bergeman, 1991; Plomin, 1995).

To reprise, child effects must be considered when evaluating the association between parental behavior and children's behavior to find a better estimate of environmental influence. A parent's harsh discipline may look to be a cause of child behavior because we fail to see how much of that parent's behavior is responsive to the child's. Thus, the association observed between parental treatment and child behavior in families may lead researchers to overestimate the extent to which a change in the parent's behavior would lead to a change in a child's behavior.

The other weakness is that the genes that lead to parental behaviors are often not "factored out" when parent–child associations are examined. Poverty is associated with children's low intelligence. But low parental IQ is associated with their becoming poor. To focus on the one association without considering the other is flawed logic. To give another example, single parenthood is associated with children's sexual precocity. But sexual precocity can also lead to single parenthood in the first place. We cannot derive policy implications by looking at one of these associations and ignoring the other.

The classic example of this problem is the association between social class and children's intelligence; it is stronger in biological families than in adoptive families. The latter families have no biological link between parent and child. Thus, in adoptive families the genes that influence the first association, behaviors in parents leading to their economic success, cannot influence the second association, that between the SES and the adoptive children's IQs. There are both adoptive and (matched) biological families in the *National Longitudinal Study of Adolescent Health* (for a description of this Add Health study, see Rowe, Jacobson, & Van den Oord, 1999). In these biological families, a one-unit (called a standard deviation) increase in income increased children's verbal IQ by about 4.5 IQ points; in adoptive families by only .90 IQ points. The difference for the association between parental education and VIQ was not as great; 5.7 points in the biological families versus 3.3 (statistically significant) in the adoptive families.

This article opened with a mention of Harris' (1998) "nurture assumption." Her definition of the nurture assumption is "the notion that parents are the most important part of the child's environment and can determine, to a large extent, how the child turns out" (p. 15). This nurture assumption is probably wrong because limits exist to the ability of parents to mold particular traits in their off-spring. In some cases, genetic influences can be so strong that, despite parents' best efforts, a child will develop in ways they do not desire, with this child having a psychiatric disorder, a lack of intellectual ability, or simply a poor character (Harris, 1998; Rowe, 1994). Indeed, in many families, typically developing siblings are present in the same family with another sibling who has atypical and undesirable characteristics. Recognition of genetic influence on development will help parents understand their own children as individuals better, and will be a continuing focus of inquiry in the 21st century.

ACKNOWLEDGMENTS

The National Longitudinal Study of Adolescent Health (Add Health) was designed by J. Richard Udry and Peter Bearman and funded by Grant P01-HD31921 from the National Institute of Child Health and Human Development. Data sets can be obtained by contacting the Carolina Population Center, 123 West Franklin St., Chapel Hill, NC 27516-3997; e-mail: addhealth@unc.edu

REFERENCES

Anderson, K. E., Lytton, H., & Romney, D. M. (1986). Mothers' interactions with normal and conduct-disordered boys: Who affects whom? *Developmental Psychology, 22,* 604–609.

Bell, R. Q. (1968). A reinterpretation of the direction of effect in socialization. *Psychological Review, 75,* 81–95.

Bell, R. Q., & Chapman, M. (1986). Child effects in studies using experimental or brief longitudinal approaches to socialization. *Developmental Psychology, 22,* 595–603.

Brown, J. R., Ye, H., Bronson, R. T., & Dikkes, P. (1996). A defect in nurturing in mice lacking the immediate early gene fos B. *Cell, 86,* 297–309.

Burks, B. S. (1938). On the relative contributions of nature and nurture to average group differences in intelligence. *Proceedings of the National Academy of Sciences, 24,* 276–282.

Cohen, D. B. (1999). *Stranger in the nest: Do parents really shape their child's personality, intelligence, or character?* New York: John Wiley & Sons.

Degler, C. N. (1991). *In search of human nature: The decline and revival of Darwinism in American social thought.* New York: Oxford University Press.

Eaves, L. J., Silberg, J. L., Meyer, J. M., Maes, H. H., Simonoff, E., Pickles, A., Rutter, M., Neale, M. C., Reynolds, C. A., Erickson, M. T., Heath, A. C., Loeber, R., Truett, K. R., & Hewitt, J. K. (1997). Genetics and developmental psychopathology: Vol.2. The main effects of genes and environment on behavioral problems in the Virginia Twin Study of Adolescent Behavioral Development. *Journal of Child Psychology and Psychiatry, 38,* 965–980.

Giros, B., Jaber, M., Jones, S. R., Wightman, R. M., & Caron, M. G. (1996). Hyperlocomotion and indifference to cocaine and amphetamine in mice lacking the dopamine transporter. *Nature, 379,* 606–612.

Harris, J. (1998). *The nurture assumption.* New York: Free Press.

Langlois, J. H., Ritter, J. M., Casey, R. J., & Sawin, D. B. (1995). Infant attractiveness predicts maternal behaviors and attitudes. *Developmental Psychology, 31,* 464–472.

Losoya, S. H., Callor, S., Rowe, D. C., & Goldsmith, H. H. (1997). Origin of familial similarity in parenting: A study of twins and adoptive siblings. *Developmental Psychology, 35,* 1012–1023.

Lytton, H. (1980). *Parent-child interaction: The socialization process observed in twin and singleton families.* New York: Plenum Press.

O'Connor, T. G., Deater-Deckard, K., Fulker, D., Rutter, M., & Plomin, R. (1998). Genotype-environment correlations in late childhood and early adolescence: Antisocial behavioral problems and coercive parenting. *Developmental Psychology, 34,* 976–981.

Plomin, R. (1995). Genetics and children's experiences in the family. *Journal of Child Psychology and Psychiatry, 36,* 33–68.

Plomin, R., & Bergeman, C. S. (1991). The nature of nurture: Genetic influence on "environmental" measures. *Behavioral and Brain Sciences, 14,* 373–386.

Plomin, R., McClearn, G. E., Pedersen, N. L., Nesselroade, J. R., & Bergeman, C. S. (1988). Genetic influence on childhood family environment perceived retrospectively from the last half of the life span. *Developmental Psychology, 24,* 738–745.

Plomin, R., Owen, M. J., and McGuffin, P. (1994). The genetic basis of complex human behaviors. *Science, 264,* 1733–1739.

Rende, R. D., Slomkowski, C. L., Stocker, C., Fulker, D. W., & Plomin, R. (1992). Genetic and environmental influences on maternal and sibling interaction in middle childhood: A sibling adoption study. *Developmental Psychology, 28,* 484–490.

Rowe, D. C. (1981). Environmental and genetic influences on dimensions of perceived parenting: A twin study. *Developmental Psychology, 17,* 203–208.

Rowe, D. C. (1983). A biometrical analysis of perceptions of family environment: A study of twin and singleton sibling kinships. *Child Development, 54,* 416–423.

Rowe, D. C. (1994). *The limits of family influence: Genes, experience, and behavior.* New York: Guilford Press.

Rowe, D. C., Jacobson, K. C., & Van den Oord, E. J. C. G. (1999). Genetic and environmental influences on vocabulary IQ: Parental education level as moderator. *Child Development, 70,* 1151–1162.

Slutske, W. S., Heath, A. C., Dinwiddie, S. H., Madden, P. A. F., Bucholz, K. K., Dunne, M. P., Statham, D. J., & Martin, N. G. (1997). Modeling genetic and environmental influence in the etiology of conduct disorder: A study of 2,682 adult twin pairs. *Journal of Abnormal Psychology, 106,* 266–279.

Thapar, A., Hervas, A., & McGuffin, P. (1995). Childhood hyperactivity scores are highly heritable and show sibling competition effects: Twin study evidence. *Behavior Genetics, 25,* 537–544.

Waldman, I. D., Rowe, D. C., Abramowitz, A., Kozel, S. T., Mohr, J. H., Sherman, S. L., Cleveland, H. H., Sanders, M. L., Gard, J. M. C., & Stever, C. (1998). Association and linkage of the dopamine transporter gene and attention-deficit hyperactivity disorder in children: Heterogeneity owing to diagnostic subtype and severity. *American Journal of Human Genetics, 63,* 1767–1776.

Wall, T. L., & Ehlers, C. L. (1995). Genetic influences affecting alcohol use among Asians. *Alcohol Health and Research World, 19,* 184–189.

Wright, W. (1998). *Born that way.* New York: Alfred A. Knopf.

Young, L. J., Roger, N., Waymire, K. G., MacGregor, G. R., & Insel, T. R. (1999). Increased affiliative response to vasopressin in mice expressing the V1a recptor from a monogamous vole. *Nature, 400,* 766–768.

3

Parenting Effects: Issues and Controversies

Eleanor E. Maccoby

Stanford University

This is an opportune time for us to be taking stock of where we stand in our efforts to understand the ways in which parents do or do not influence their children. And it is a time of controversy concerning the nature and strengths of parental influence. Critics are saying that for many years psychologists have overemphasized the role of parents in determining how a child will turn out—that instead, other influences, such as a child's genetic makeup, or experiences with peers, or chance events, have more to do with the trajectory a child's development will take (Harris, 1998; Rowe, 1994).

I would say that these criticisms are partly justified, but certainly not entirely so. For one thing, they are out of date. Under the influence of the learning theories so predominant in the fifties, sixties and seventies, early research on parenting emphasized the role of parents as teachers and disciplinarians in shaping their children's development and their role as models for children to copy. Psychodynamic theory held that children were socialized by internalizing their parents' values and characteristics. Attachment theory argued that the kind of nurturance and responsiveness provided by parents to their infants and toddlers determined the quality of attachment the child formed to the parents, which in turn carried over into a child's subsequent relationships via deep and lasting internal representations. Cognitive theory has more recently added the idea that

Address correspondence to: Eleanor Maccoby, Stanford University, e-mail: maccoby@psych.stanford.edu parents influence the ways in which children interpret the events they experience, and thus influence their subsequent attributions about other people's intent and their own efficacy.

You will note that these traditional points of view are top-down theories, which have indeed fostered a widespread and deep "nurture assumption." And this assumption has surely led many in our field to overemphasize the role of parents in determining how children will turn out. But there's a time-lag problem here. Popular psychology books and elementary textbooks are usually somewhat behind the most recent research, and to some extent critics have been reacting to earlier theories and earlier research. For the past 15 or 20 years, there's been a growing appreciation of bidirectional process, though such processes were by no means ignored at earlier times (e.g., R. R. Sears' APA presidential address in 1950). We now see parenting less in terms of simple parent-to-child influence, and more as a set of interactive processes whereby parents and children react to each other and influence each other from the moment a child is born (e.g., Maccoby, 1992; Bugental and Goodnow, 1998). I would argue, though, that especially when children are young, parents have much more influence on children than children do on parents, in view of parents' control of children's daily lives and the fact that parents are already fully formed persons with mature, established patterns of thought and action, while childhood is a time of rapid learning and great plasticity. The more important question is not whether parents influence children during their day-to-day interactions, but how strongly parents influence the child's future functioning.

Nowadays, no student of socialization claims—if any ever did—that parents are the only important influence on children's development. We now know that there is a network of causal factors that affect children's growth and development. Parenting is only one of them, and not necessarily the most important. Children are influenced by their genetic makeup, the neighborhood they live in, the schools they attend, and the kind of peers they associate with. We should note, though, that parents are implicated in choosing what their children's out-of-home environments will be.

Nonparental influences include what children see on TV and films, and the other cultural currents flowing during their childhood. It matters whether children are growing up during times of war or peace, economic depression or affluence, or a time of stability or rapid change in family structure and social mores. And more or less random events, such as illness or accident, or an unpredictable opportunity, can play their part as well. It has become clear to all of us that there can be no simple one-to-one relationships between a measured aspect of parenting and a child's outcomes. Clearly, we must think in probabilistic terms, seeing parental activities as part of the matrix of risk and protective factors and learning opportunities affecting particular child outcomes.

What are some of the issues and controversies that concern us here? Critics of the traditional research on parenting have drawn heavily on behavior genetics.

They take three basic points from this research, drawing mainly on studies of twins and adopted children:

1. Genetic factors make a substantial contribution to individual differences in children's outcomes.
2. Among environmental factors, it is the factors that are *not shared* by children in the same family that have most influence on children's development. *Shared* factors are unimportant. This means that such things as parental income and education, the neighborhood where the family lives, the amount of conflict between the parents, whether it is a single-parent or a dual-parent family, or any aspect of parenting style that is similarly directed toward all the children in a family—these things matter little, since these all are shared factors.
3. When a correlation is found between parental treatment and a child outcome, this tells us nothing about parental influence. It could reflect an effect of the child upon the parent rather than vice versa.

Thus, a child with a difficult temperament may elicit and experience negative parenting, while an easygoing child is more likely to receive supportive parenting.

Concerning the first point: Behavior geneticists have made their case. Genetic factors do clearly make a significant contribution to individual differences among children in a variety of attributes. I believe there is now general, widespread acceptance of this claim. Let us consider it proven.

Much more controversial is the second claim: that aspects of the environment shared by children growing up in the same household do not affect their outcomes. This conclusion is largely based on the fact that siblings are often so different from one another—no more alike, the behavior geneticists say, than children growing up in different households, except for similarities dictated by their genetic similarity. The idea that a shared household environment does not affect the children growing up in it flies in the face of much of what we know about environmental risk factors. There is a great deal of evidence that such factors as growing up in poverty, or having a teenaged mother who did not finish high school, or having parents who are punitive and coercive, creates risks for children. And, there is also evidence that when children grow up with parents who not only provide support and structure for their children but also set limits and monitor their activities, the children will have a better chance of becoming competent teenagers and adults. If we know these things, how can it be that behavior geneticists continue to report that there are no clear effects of a shared family environment?

In thinking about this issue it is important to remind ourselves that twin and adoption studies are studies of individual variation, not studies of either genetic or environmental main effects. You will remember that in some of the early studies of adopted children, it was found that the IQ's of children adopted in infancy

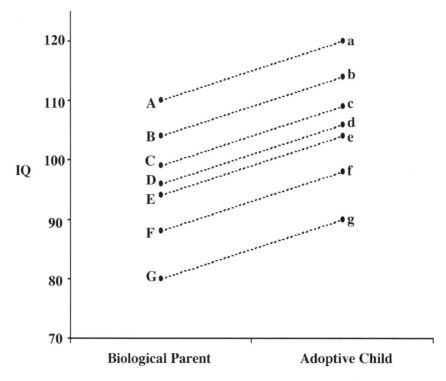

FIG. 3.1. Schematic representation of IQs of adopted children when correlated with IQs of their biological parents.

were correlated with the IQ's of the biological mothers whom they had never seen, and hardly correlated at all with the IQ's of the adoptive parents with whom they had lived throughout their childhood. At the same time, their average IQ was significantly higher than that of the biological mothers. If there were a perfect correlation between the IQ's of the children and their biological mothers, we could graph the situation as in Figure 1:

It is as though the adopted children had all received a bonus from growing up in well-functioning homes, while their initial rank order remained unchanged. It would follow, too, that there would be a zero correlation between the IQ of the adopted child and that of the adopting parent. A behavior genetic analysis of this situation would show a very high h^2 (heritability) and a zero for environmental effects. Of course, children's characteristics are never perfectly correlated with those of their parents—the actual situation might be more as shown in Fig. 2.

We can see that although the rank orders of biological mother and child might not match perfectly, it can nevertheless be true that the entire distribution of adopted children's scores can be moved upward or downward while hardly

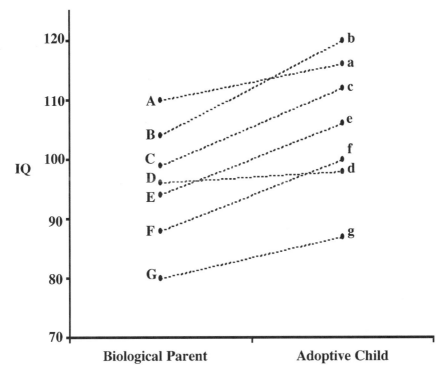

FIG. 3.2. Schematic representation of IQs of adopted children when correlated with IQs of their biological parents.

changing the rank order that would prevail if the child had never been adopted. The correlation with the biological mother remains high, and that with the adoptive parents remains low, while the adoptive environment nevertheless has a substantial effect. This is an effect that goes unreported and undetected in the standard behavioral genetics analysis.

This effect is comparable to the effects found in immigration studies, where, for example, Japanese-American children are substantially taller than their grandparents born and raised in Japan, despite the fact that the heritability coefficient for height is very high indeed—in the .90's. Probably, the American-raised grandchildren also vary in height in ways that correlate with their parents' and grandparents' heights. Some migration effects are not beneficent, as in the case of Pima Indians, who are not obese in their native surround, but almost uniformly become so when they emigrate to America.

What is it about an adoptive environment that can give adopted children a bonus? A recent study done in France by Duyme and colleagues (1999) gives us some clues. This is a study of late-adopted children, all of whom had below-average IQ scores (in the dull–normal range, averaging in the high 70's). The children were tested at about

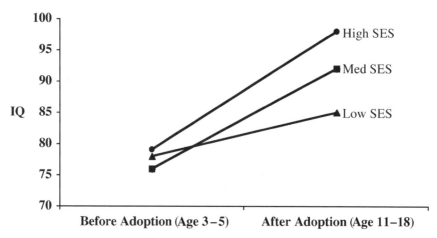

FIG. 3.3. Mean differences in IQ by socioeconomic status of adoptive family (from Duyme, Dumaret, and Tomkiewicz, in press).

the age of four, a year before their adoption at a mean age of 5. They were retested in adolescence, after having lived for about nine years with adoptive families who varied considerably in their socioecnomic level. Fig. 3 shows what they found:

The amount of IQ bonus that the adopted children received depended on the kind of educational and economic advantages—and presumably also on the level of stable supportive parenting (see below)—that their adoptive families were able to provide. When children were adopted into a family of low socioeconomic status (SES) they gained 8 IQ points on the average; in a high SES family, they gained 19½ points. It is notable that the *correlation* between their pre- and postadoption IQ's was quite high. In other words, their initial rank order was not greatly disturbed despite the changes wrought by an improved environment. Their rank order might not match very well with that of their adoptive siblings, and might instead match fairly closely that of their biological parents. If so, this would tell us that children's varying genetic endowments do make a difference, but it tells us little about these powerful environmental effects. The basic point here is that behavior genetic analyses are all correlational, and they are not sensitive to environmental inputs that do not change the rank order of a distribution.

By analogy, we can see that having a black skin in a culture where this elicits hostile or discriminatory reactions from others—while such reactions would be absent or minimal in the culture of racial origin—is like being one of a group of children who are moved from privileged homes to high-risk homes, or immigrants who have moved from a benign environment into a difficult or dangerous one. A mean change would occur that would not be detected in a behavior-genetic analysis. It is for this reason that it is illegitimate to make comparisons on any trait between group averages for blacks versus whites, men versus women, or rich versus poor people and interpret any differences in terms of the heritabilities computed from within-group correlations. It is a fundamentally flawed strategy.

Can we attribute any of the benefits of high parental SES to more supportive or skillful parenting? Recent work in England finds that adopted children do better in school and in later adult life than nonadopted children born in similar circumstances, and that adoptive parents' interest in the children's educational progress is a major factor predicting their success. (Maughan, Collishaw, & Pickles, 1998) We also know (McLoyd, 1990) that poverty, as a generalized risk factor, affects children mainly through the inadequate parenting that occurs under the stresses of uncertain employment, low incomes, crowded housing, and deteriorated, dangerous neighborhoods. McLoyd claims that it is this disordered parenting, more than poverty itself, that is mainly responsible for the children's poor outcomes when they grow up in low-SES households. It is a reasonable inference, then, that in the French study, the high-SES adopting parents were providing parenting of better than average quality, along with an emphasis on educational values and the other advantages their privileged position offered to the children. The main point for our purposes is this: A family's socioeconomic status matters. It is something that all children within a family share, and these findings run counter to the claims that only an unshared environment matters.

I don't wish to make a general case about the benefits of adoption. We all know that some children fare very well in their adoptive homes and some do not. Surely, some of this variation can be accounted for by the genetic qualities children bring with them into adoptive homes. A fascinating Swedish study gives us some insight into the way in which genetics and the adoptive home environment interact. Bohman and colleagues (Bohman, 1996) studied two groups of adopted children. One had a biological parent with a criminal record. The other group carried no such biological risk. The adoptive homes were examined. Some had a characteristic that carried risk for the children: e.g., an alcoholic or mentally ill adoptive parent, divorce, or an adoptive parent with a criminal record. In Figure 3.4 we see how many of the adopted children engaged in some form of petty criminality as they grew into adulthood.

Either a biological risk or a home-environment one elevates the adopted child's risks somewhat, but the important message of the study is that a biological risk factor is seldom manifested unless it is potentiated or triggered by an environmental risk. It is the combination of the two things that substantially elevates the chances that an adopted child will display the problem for which he or she carries a biological risk. The same kind of interaction has also been found for schizophrenia. Interactions of this sort, when they exist, are not revealed in twin studies, and are only revealed in adoption studies when they are specifically looked for and the relevant measures of the adoptive environment are taken. Traditional twin and adoption studies have ignored these kinds of interactions.

Especially strong evidence for gene-environment interactions comes from animal studies. We know that when young monkeys and other young animals are

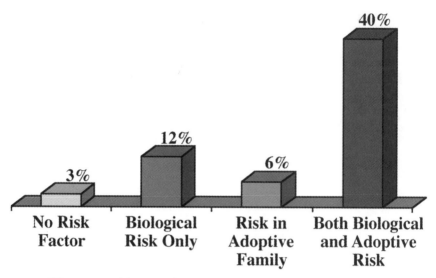

FIG. 3.4. Incidence of petty criminality in adopted children (Bohman, 1996).

deprived of maternal care, their development can be seriously affected. But some animals react more strongly to maternal deprivation than others. We now know that it is the animals most at genetic risk—whose biological mothers were highly emotionally "reactive"—who suffer the severest effects of early maternal deprivation (Suomi, 1997). We have seen, then, that in both human children and nonhuman species, certain aspects of the rearing environment are indeed clear risk factors. However, offspring differ in their vulnerability to these risks.

Nowadays, interactions between parenting styles and possible genetic attributes of children are a matter of active interest in developmental psychology (see, for example, Bates, Pettit, Dodge, & Ridge, 1998). Another excellent example comes from the work of Grazyna Kochanska and her colleagues. They have found that a given parenting style has a different effect on a child who is temperamentally bold and adventurous than it does on a timid, shy child. (Kochanska, 1997). If we were to aggregate the two kind of children together, some of the parenting effects would wash out and we would have only weak parent–child correlations of the sort that have pervaded much of the research literature on childrearing and its effects.

If a given kind of household or a given style of parenting has different effects for children with different predispositions, this means that parenting often functions to make children in the same family different rather than alike (see review by Turkheimer & Waldron, 2000, analyzing "nonshared" environmental effects). In other words, the home environment that children share is indeed having an effect, even though it is a different effect for different children, and would not be computed as a shared effect in a behavior genetics analysis. To call this an unshared environmental effect, as the behavior geneticists do, is to invite misinterpretation.

Much has been said by behavior geneticists concerning how greatly children in the same household differ. They attribute much of this to genetic differences among the children. They speak of "evocative" parent–child correlations, so that, for example, a beautiful or sweet-tempered child will elicit gentler and more positive parenting than an unattractive child with a difficult temperament. If children are "driving" their parents' actions, the argument is that any correlations between what parents do and how their children behave can be safely assigned to the genetic component of the causal equation.

Do children with different temperaments influence how their parents treat them? Of course they do. Does this mean that correlations between what parents do and how their children turn out reflect mainly the child's genetics? Of course not. In any long-standing relationship, it is axiomatic that each partner must influence the other. To assert that the parent–child relationship is a one-way street, with only the child having an influence, is simply bizarre.

There is a recent study that illustrates how the reciprocal influence actually works itself out. The Rutter-Plomin research group in London utilized data from the Colorado Adoption Study (O'Connor, Deater-Deckard, Fulker, Rutter, & Plomin, 1998). They studied two groups of adopted children. One group carried a genetic risk for antisocial behavior (i.e., their biological mothers had a history of such behavior); the other did not. The children at genetic risk received consistently more negative parenting through the age range from 7 to 12 years when parenting was assessed. Here we clearly have an evocative effect. But the parents' negative parenting, in its turn, was independently related to the amount of aggressive, acting-out behavior seen in the child, even after the degree of genetic risk had been statistically partialed out. In short, there were reciprocal effects, whereby something about the children's genes affected parental treatment, but the children were in turn influenced by the way in which their parents reacted.

The point I want to make about gene x environment interactions is that they are present at all levels of the developing organism from the day of conception on, all along the long path from gene to phenotype. A recent very thoughtful book called *Rethinking Innateness*, by Elman, Bates, Johnson, and Karmiloff-Smith (1996), has a chapter called "Interactions All the Way Down." These authors, along with many others, call our attention to the folly of trying to compartmentalize the causes of behavior into two distinct components, G (genes) and E (environment), ignoring their interactions. There is a major problem in assuming, as behavior geneticists do, that the sources of variance in human attributes can be neatly partitioned into two separate components: the genetic and environmental ones, which, when added, will account for 100% of the variance. If we reject this assumption, it becomes evident that we can't estimate environmental effects by first estimating a heritability coefficient and subtracting it from 100%. In fact, when we compute a heritability coefficient from twin or adoption data, it tells us very little about the importance of environmental factors.

In our efforts to identify the contribution of parenting to the matrix of factors that affect children's development, we are handicapped by the fact that we can't experimentally assign children to specifiably different parenting regimes, and we must rely on studies of naturally occurring variations, with all the problems of self-selection this entails. With animal studies it is possible to have better control of both genetic histories and rearing conditions. Most informative are some recent cross-fostering studies, done with both rodents and nonhuman primates. These studies are showing that some females are more genetically predisposed than others to adopt an effective mothering style. However, when offspring are born to a low-nurturant or emotionally overreactive mother, some of them can be put into foster care and be reared by a nurturant or calm mother. Elsewhere in this volume, Suomi provides some details concerning cross-fostering work with Rhesus monkeys (and see also an overview of work with rodents, Anisman, Zaharia, Meaney, & Merali, 1998), but let me now simply summarize by saying: it is clear that the quality of mothering that a young animal receives has a strong impact on its behavioral outcomes, over and above whatever its genetic predispositions may be.

True experiments with human families are extremely difficult to do. If we wanted to demonstrate the impact of parenting, we would have to randomly assign families either to an intervention group or a control group, and then intervene with the parents but not the children, training parents in practices we had prior reason to believe would benefit their children. Then, if the intervention achieved real change in parenting practices, it would have to be shown that children in the parent-intervention group changed in commensurate ways. It would be important to check whether any changes in the child carried over to behavior outside the home context, and to carry on the study long enough to find out how lasting the effects were. This is very difficult, expensive research to do. A few courageous researchers are undertaking such studies—there is some notable current work with single mothers at the Oregon Social Learning Center (Forgatch & DeGarmo, 1999)—and this kind of work is the gold standard when it comes to pinning down the causal role of parenting. Note, however, that almost all randomized controlled trials related to parenting are conducted with low-income, single-parent families that face multiple environmental risks (increased exposure to prenatal teratogens, poor quality housing, and neighborhoods, inferior schools, etc.).

Here are some lessons I think we can take from the current debates about parenting: First of all, some who study family functioning and its effects have gone beyond their data in making grandiose claims about long-lasting parenting effects. We researchers should confine ourselves more closely to what we really know. We still probably do not give enough weight to genetic factors in child development, although we have been moving rapidly toward giving these factors serious attention. We do need to pay more attention to sibling differences and attempt to understand them. But, on the other hand, I believe behavior geneticists have seriously underestimated environmental effects, and this includes shared environmental effects.

Actually, I believe we are making quite good progress in sorting out the role of parenting in the complex mix of factors that influence children's development. Many of us are concerned with such issues as how long do parenting effects last, and in what contexts, inside and outside the home, they appear. I believe the studies I have cited, and the ones reported elsewhere in this volume, will amply illustrate how good the progress is, and also how much remains to be done. Let's get on with it.

ACKNOWLEDGMENTS

I have consulted with many people in assembling reference materials and working out the ideas in this paper. I would like to acknowledge especially the following people: Michael Rutter, Andrew Heath, W. Andrew Collins, E. Mavis Hetherington, Lawrence Steinberg, Marc Bornstein, Steve Suomi, Gerald Patterson, Marion Forgatch, Tom Dishion, Richard Weinberg, Megan Gunnar, and Grazyna Kochanska.

REFERENCES

Anisman, H., Zaharia, M. D., Meaney, M. J., & Merali, Z. (1998). Do early-life events permanently alter behavioral and hormonal responses to stressors? *International Journal of Developmental Neuroscience, 16,* 149–164.

Bates, J., Pettit, G., Dodge, K., & Ridge, B. (1998). Interaction of temperamental resistance to control and restrictive parenting in the development of externalizing behavior. *Developmental Psychology, 34,* 982–995.

Bohman, M. (1996). Predispositions to criminality: Swedish adoption studies in retrospect. In G. R. Bock & J. R. Goode (Eds.), *Genetics of Criminal and Anti-social Behavior, Ciba Foundation Symposium, 194,* (pp. 99–114). Chichester, UK/New York: John Wiley and Sons.

Bugental, D. B., & Goodnow, J. J. (1998). Socialization processes. In W. Damon and N. Eisenberg (Eds.), *Handbook of child psychology* (Vol. 3, 5th ed., pp. 389–462). New York: John Wiley & Sons.

Duyme, M., Dumaret, A., & Tomkiewicz, S. (1999). How can we boost IQ's of "dull children": A late adoption study. *Proceedings of the National Academy of Sciences, 96,* closue 15, 8790–8794.

Elman, J. L., Bates, E. A., Johnson, M. H., Karmiloff-Smith, A., Parisi, D., & Plunkett, K. (1996). *Rethinking innateness: A connectionist perspective on development.* Cambridge, MA: MIT Press.

Forgatch, M. S., & DeGarmo, D. S. (1999). Parenting through change: An effective prevention program for single mothers. *Journal of Consulting and Clinical Psychology, 67,* 711–724.

Harris, J. R. (1998.) *The nurture assumption: Why children turn out the way they do.* New York: Free Press.

Kochanska, G. (1997). Multiple pathways to conscience for children with different temperaments: From toddlerhood to age 5. *Developmental Psychology, 33,* 228–240.

Maccoby, E. E. (1992). The role of parents in the socialization of children: An historical overview. *Developmental Psychology, 28,* 1006–1017.

Maughan, B., Collishaw, S., & Pickles, A. (1998). School achievement and adult qualifications among adoptees: A longitudinal study. *Journal of Child Psychology and Psychiatry, 39,* 669–685.

McLoyd, V. (1990). The impact of economic hardship on black families and children: Psychological distress, parenting, and socioemotional development. *Child Development, 61,* 311–346.

O'Connor, T. G., Deater-Deckard, K., Fulker, D., Rutter, M., & Plomin, R. (1998). Genotype-environment correlations in late childhood and early adolescence: Antisocial behavioral problems and coercive parenting. *Developmental Psychology, 34,* 970–981.

Rowe, D. (1994). *The limits of family influence: Genes, experience and behavior.* New York: Guilford Press.

Suomi, S. J. (1997). Long-term effects of different early rearing experience on social, emotional and physiological development in non-human primates. In M. S. Kesheven & R. M. Murra (Eds.), *Neurodevelopmental models of adult psychopathology* (pp. 104–116). Cambridge, UK: Cambridge University Press.

Turkheimer, E., & Waldron, M. (2000). Nonshared environment: A theoretical methodological and quantitative review. *Psychological Bulletin, 126,* 78–108.

4

The Science and Art
of Parenting

Sharon Landesman Ramey
University of Alabama at Birmingham

Parenting is undeniably one of life's greatest sources of both joy and challenge. Growing up as the child of one's parents is similarly filled with strong, and usually mixed, emotions. An almost universal desire in parents upon the birth of each child is a deep commitment to do everything possible to ensure their child's lasting health, competence, and happiness. And yet most all parents begin their own parenting journey with ideas about how to parent better than their own parents had.

Each child brings a sense of profound responsibility, as well as opportunity and wonder, to his or her parents. Often this sense of responsibility extends to a larger kinship and friendship network and to the community as a whole. The conference sponsored by the National Institute of Child Health and Human Development (NICHD) and the Robert Wood Johnson Foundation, represented a valuable opportunity to reflect on what we as scientists know about parenting practices and the ways in which parents contribute to their children's well-being. Just as importantly, through the process of reviewing major research findings, we have an

Address correspondence to: Civitan International Research Center, University of Alabama at Birmingham, 1719 Sixth Ave., South Birmingham, AL 35294, Phone: 205-975-0299, Fax: 205-975-6530, e-mail: Sramey@uab.edu opportunity to identify promising areas of scientific inquiry for future study and to consider the extent to which current knowledge about parenting and child development can serve as a practical basis for guiding parental behavior and choices for their family. Collectively, this conference provides ample support for the conclusion that parenting in today's world is both science ("facts and principles gained by systematic study") and art ("skill in conducting a human activity").

HOW CHILDREN'S HEALTH AND DEVELOPMENT ARE LINKED TO PARENTAL BEHAVIOR

Children's health and well-being depend on far more than just a healthy pregnancy, a normal birth, and a physician's judgment that "You are the parents of a healthy baby." Literally thousands of diseases, disorders, events, and environments place children at risk for nonoptimal development (Batshaw, 2000; Ramey & Ramey, 1998). Without doubt, infants and young children are especially vulnerable and cannot independently care for themselves. Even older children, adolescents, and young adults, with their increasing array of skills, continue to need and benefit from sound guidance and support from others. The vulnerabilities of older children may differ substantially in kind from those of younger ones, but the potential consequences of risks remain equally grave throughout the developmental period. The extent to which parents provide healthy and supportive environments for their developing children is a critical component in their lifelong well-being.

Throughout the past four decades, the NICHD has sponsored research on the prevention and treatment of childhood conditions that threaten and all too often impair children's healthy development. The NICHD also funds scientific inquiry into the basic processes of development itself, from laboratory and clinical research on genes and brain development to studies of the life course of children and treatment interventions to improve children's outcomes. *Longitudinal research* that traces the development of individual children yields valuable findings about patterns of development and natural associations between parental behavior and child outcomes. *Experimental research* that involves changing parental behavior provides particularly strong evidence about how parents can influence their children's behavior; conversely, child-focused interventions provide a unique opportunity to measure a child's influence on parents. *Laboratory and observational research* about young children's perceptual, cognitive, social, and emotional functioning also offers useful information about the factors associated with individual differences and likely to contribute to children's optimal versus compromised development. These diverse types of research yield findings that are difficult to integrate within a single conceptual framework or theoretical perspective, largely because they rely on such different study designs and methods and because they do not frame their questions in the same way. The situation has led to a large and sound scientific body of evidence, albeit remarkably scattered and uneven, about the multifaceted, multiyear, and multiperson phenomenon of parenting.

WHY THE INCREASED INTEREST IN PARENTING EFFECTS?

Changes in the demography and the dynamics of family life have fueled public interest in the topic of responsible and effective parenting (Ramey & Ramey, 2000). In recent years, much media attention has focused on extreme positions about what parents should or should not do and has been presented in terms of debatelike questions, including "Do parents really matter?" and "Are the first three years of life really important?" Radical proposals about childrearing and sweeping questions about whether parents or early childhood experiences matter have not emerged, however, directly from the scientific community. Rather, the corporations that publish these books and manufacture new child products for parents are the ones that launch vigorous and expensive promotional campaigns to capture prime-time media coverage. Because many of these books and products claim to be based "on scientific evidence," they acquire an air of credibility and legitimacy. At the same time, they usually offer either great hope to parents (such as cures for common or serious childhood problems or the promise of perfectly well-behaved, brilliant, or disease-resistant children) or relief and a sense of freedom from responsibility (such as the claim that parents are not significant in their children's lives and that the early years in life do not matter very much). These three ingredients of (1) apparent scientific backing or breakthrough, (2) potentially sweeping significance, and (3) major controversy or surprise are ideal for media coverage. Unfortunately, all too often these claims seriously misrepresent the scientific findings, often through their presentation of elaborate technical treatises accompanied by an impressive list of publications by some of the field's leading investigators. Such distortions serve to misguide or confuse parents and policymakers and to contribute to a general mistrust of scientists and so-called child experts, especially in the realm of understanding complex human behavior, relationships, and development (Ramey & Ramey, 1999).

The sound knowledge base, accruing from decades of research on typically developing children and children with identified disabilities, alas, does not readily lend itself to a few dramatic headlines, much less conclusions that totally overturn what many parents already think and do. In fact, the breakthroughs in understanding the complex parent–child relationship (e.g., Sroufe, Duggal, Weinfeld, & Carlson, 2000) and the ways in which parenting behavior can, and often does, alter their children's development (e.g., Cowan & Cowan, 1996) are impressive. The chapters in this book comprise only a sampler of the topics in a vast, growing, and important body of evidence about what promotes and hinders children's well-being. There are, indeed, a number of serious, legitimate, and not easily resolved controversies. Exploring the likely reasons for these well-substantiated controversies (in contrast to the superficial popularized controversies) is vital for guiding future inquiry and for informing parents and policymakers about "evidence-based practices"—that is, those parenting practices and decisions (including the absence or lack of certain parenting behavior and actions) that truly promote or hinder children's well-being.

THE FAMILY AS A DYNAMIC, COMPLEX SYSTEM: THE VALUE OF INTERDISCIPLINARY PERSPECTIVES

As a framework for analyzing and integrating major findings from studies about the association between parenting and children's well-being, several scientific perspectives are relevant. *First*, the family creates the context for each child's development and for the enactment of diverse parenting practices (social ecology). *Second*, families are fundamentally dynamic and developmental, exerting complex and reciprocal social and biological influences on their members (systems theory and transactional influences). *Third*, there is a need for both objective and subjective measures of parenting behavior and children's environments, because a child's or parent's experience is not synonymous with mere events and environments (multimethod approaches to studying parenting effects, including children's views on their own lives). *Fourth*, traditional linear causal models and ways of classifying influences on a child's life (e.g., into categories of biological, social and behavioral, and environmental) are woefully inadequate and arbitrary. The application of promising new paradigms, methods, and analytic strategies is likely to provide robust scientific findings that will lead to the development and evaluation of practical approaches to assist parents in fulfilling their responsibilities and desires to ensure their children's health and personal well-being.

In our planning for the NICHD conference, with a large committee to guide us, our greatest challenge was the fact that our time and money were limited, leading to the need to severely limit the number of topics to be addressed and scientists to be invited. The conversations and correspondence generated during the planning process served as a vivid, constant reminder that the topics of parenting, families, and child development have been studied in programmatic and productive ways by demographers, economists, sociologists, developmental psychologists, nurses, pediatricians, social psychologists, educators, child psychiatrists, cognitive psychologists, and ethologists, to name just some of the major disciplines invested in understanding parental influences. Our challenge was further complicated by our recognition of the tremendous relevance of more than five decades of experimental research on the effects of early experience from many different animal models, which is represented only briefly in this volume. What was most surprising to me was the sheer vastness of scope in scientific inquiry funded by the NICHD and the fact that this breadth exceeded what even the "experts' in our field recognized as the "current knowledge base." Remarkably, there are not just a few premier journals where findings about parenting effects are published; nor even a few major scientific meetings where the majority of findings are reported. (Indeed, the first scientific journal dedicated solely to publishing original research as well as reviews about parenting studies—*Parenting*, edited by Marc Bronstein—was not launched until 2000. In contrast, there are scores of popular magazines about parenting, many offering chatrooms for parents' and experts' advice on the Internet as well.) The importance of synthesizing what we know and identifying major gaps in our knowledge thus became highly salient to those of us asked to convene the conference.

THE FAMILY CONTEXT FOR CHILD DEVELOPMENT

Parents create the immediate world in which an individual child develops. For the majority of infants, their parents will be their biological parents. As the months and years go by, the caregiving environment becomes increasingly complex, and increasing numbers of children have experiences with adoptive or foster parents (including informal as well as legal arrangements), one or more stepparents, and even group care with multiple surrogate parents caring for them (Ramey & Sackett, 2000). The configuration of the family can range from the smallest and simplest unit of a biological mother and one child to the most typical of two biological parents and two children to larger and more complex families containing parents who no longer live together, stepparents who have been added to the family, and a combination of full, half, and step siblings.

Acknowledging the entire family unit as the context (primary base) for the developing child, as well as for parenting, is not a small or irrelevant detail. The number of parents and children in a family relates to the demands on parents for resources—economic, time, and psychological resources. The stability of the family's composition, as well as where the family lives and how often and why the family moves, are likely to affect both parents and children in the family. The type of family a child has and where the family lives and spends time further exert influences on the child's broader social network, introducing children to different types of neighborhood influences, schools, and communities that, in turn, afford various combinations of positive and negative experiences. Until recently, however, most studies of parenting behavior did not even consider the composition of the family or the possibility that extrafamilial factors, such as the neighborhood, community, or culture, could serve to moderate the effects of parenting on children.

When considering the family context, it is undeniable that different types of individuals (e.g., in terms of their age, education, income, personal and social competency, intelligence, substance use, social network, and own history of exposure to competent parenting) create and sustain different types of families. This fundamental fact creates a situation in which many events and conditions in a child's life are codetermined or multiply determined. This presents serious problems for those scientists, policymakers, and parents who want to know, in precise quantitative or relativistic terms, how much importance to attach to variables such as parental age, intelligence, or education; infant temperament (e.g., being an easy or difficult baby), birth order, birth weight, or disability status; family income; or parental disciplinary practices, emotional warmth, or teaching style.

Leading investigators routinely recognize that potentially influential factors (often categorized by terms such as *risk conditions* and *environmental affordances*) do not occur in isolation or with equal probability for all children. This recognition leads to efforts to develop increasingly sophisticated and innovative statistical strategies designed to help "control for" or take into account the presence of other naturally correlated variables. Yet we still have no adequate means to estimate or adjust the parameters for many important variables, because they rarely or never exist in nature in a "pure" or completely distributed manner. Some of the most important questions about human development are the "what if" questions that can be answered only through systematically altering children's biology *and* their environments *over time*. (This is clearly an unethical and unfeasible endeavor, except in extreme cases where nonparental care is imperative and critical health risks necessitate biomedical interventions.) Instead, we rely on data from a combination of:

1. Large-scale, population-based, longitudinal studies—as a rich and representative source of descriptive information on parents and children
2. Smaller, more intensive studies of children and family processes—particularly of "at risk" families and children with special needs or identified problems
3. Natural experiments, such as studying children who experience a variety of disruptions or perturbations in their family life (including adoption, divorce, the loss and/or addition of parents, orphanage care)
4. Animal models of development, particularly longitudinal and experimental studies that consider both biological and behavioral outcomes (e.g., Sackett, Novak, & Kroeker, 1999; Suomi, 2000).

Thus, to evaluate with any certainty the extent to which one or more independent variables (such as parenting style, school quality, or peers) influences a child's development necessitates careful documentation of the family context itself—including ascertaining the stability or changes in a child's life over time. An additional layer of complexity derives from the documented evidence that the correlates and consequences of many variables vary as a function of when the study is conducted (cohort effects) and where (cultural, community, and geographic influences). That is, in different times and in different places or cultures, the likely meaning and consequences of having a teen mother, an absent father, divorced parents, or parents who rely on spanking as their primary disciplinary technique can differ tremendously. Thus, considering *context* means that some dimensions of parenting need to be measured in relativistic or normative terms as well as in absolute ones, and to explicitly take into account what is considered acceptable or normative (versus deviant or problematic) parenting within a given community. Studying the reasons why parents endorse or reject certain childrearing practices, for example, has led to valuable insights in cross-cultural research on children's resilience (e.g., Grotberg, 1999).

When apparent discrepancies occur in the scientific findings about parenting effects, a contextual, post hoc analysis often provides plausible reasons for these. Such post hoc analyses can be informed by considering whether similar or different types of families and children were studied; the comparability of the places (neighborhoods, geographical locale) where the families lived in terms of supports for and obstacles to family functioning and children's outcomes; the historical era when the study was conducted and whether any major historical events were likely to impinge on parents' availability, parenting practices, or community resources (e.g., major economic depression, wars, social and political upheaval). Not surprisingly, findings from a well-conducted study can be seriously misrepresented if the major conclusions are reported *out of context.*

This appreciation for the ecological complexity of a young child's world, from the most proximal and tangible environment to the most distal, has been broadly and compellingly articulated by Urie Bronfenbrenner (1979, 1989) and numerous others who endorse a social ecological framework for studying individual development. This framework has led developmental scientists to gather a large array of descriptive variables in an effort to depict the context for the child's development, over time. These rich data sets then propel the development and application of increasingly sophisticated data analyses—analyses that are notably different than the models that dominated the field even a decade or two ago. At the same time, investigators engaged in the study of parental influences continue to reflect the divergent traditions of their disciplinary training (particularly in developmental psychology, sociology, demography, and economics, pediatrics, and maternal and child health) and accordingly show greater (or lesser) attention to the adequacy of certain aspects of theory, measurement, and data analysis about the family as the context for the child's development. This leads to a recognition that efforts to integrate findings across disciplinary boundaries need to consider the levels at which potential parental influences, particularly in combination with other known and hypothesized influences on an identified child outcome (aspect of development), were studied so these can be interpreted within a broader and more integrated social ecological context.

REFINING AND REFORMULATING QUESTIONS ABOUT PARENTING EFFECTS

One of the most lamented limitations in our field is the lack of a sufficiently well-developed theory about the child's environment and the relatively small number of standardized, psychometrically sound tools to capture theoretically important dimensions of the child's environment (e.g., Landesman, 1986; Ramey & Ramey, 2000; Sameroff, 2000). Although extremes in either environments or parenting competency might reasonably be hypothesized to have similar effects on all children (particularly when the environment and parental behavior meet legal criteria for child neglect and abuse in our society), almost all developmental theorists predict a likely "person X environment interaction" or transactional consequences (*cf.* Sameroff, Lewis, & Miller, 2000). In nonjargon terms, this hypothesis states that the consequences of a particular type of environment will not necessarily be the same for all individuals at all ages and stages of development. Practically, this means that particular parenting practices and specific types of family contexts may be more (or less) effective for promoting positive development in different types of children. Theoretically, some children may thrive in a family context that would be nonoptimal for other children, perhaps based on the biological and behavioral propensities of the child, the presence or absence of other environmental supports outside the family, and/or the child's previous history and preparation for a given environment.

The above perspective supports a reformulation of the general question "How much do parents matter?" into a more differentiated query: *What combination and developmental sequence of parental decisions and behavioral practices, in particular types of family and community contexts, increase (or decrease) the probability of different types of children doing well in specified domains of development, both presently and in the future?* If this latter question seems unduly long and detailed, most developmental scientists would respond vigorously by reminding their critics that no one expects physicians or physicists, for example, to reduce their study of multiply determined phenomena, such as cardiovascular disease and the development of cortical neurons or the movement of atoms as well as large bodies within galaxies, to a single, overly simplified question that defies the fundamental nature of the phenomenon under investigation.

Ideally, investment in the intensive and comprehensive study of children within their family contexts would yield a handbook to guide parents and practitioners, specifying more precisely than ever before what types and amounts of parenting behavior, in combination with particular extrafamilial supports, contribute to enhanced developmental outcomes for different types of children at different stages in their lives. The decision within the scientific community to map the human genome provides an inspiring model, wherein scientific leaders and investigators at multiple laboratories participated in identifying the most salient issues to be resolved, the best methodologies, and what critical data were needed to yield a complete map of the human genome. One can only wonder what a comparable concerted, multidisciplinary effort focused on mapping parental behavior could produce in terms of understanding how to enhance children's well-being (human capital).

THE DYNAMIC AND DEVELOPMENTAL NATURE OF FAMILIES

Families have a developmental course of their own, just as individual family members do. Because families are dynamic and change in their structural and functional features over the course of their existence, they are ideally suited to study from a systems theory orientation. The many advantages of a conceptual framework that endorses the principles of biological systems theory (cf. Bertalanffy, 1975; Miller, 1978) have been well articulated and demonstrated in a variety of studies of parent–child relationships and the family since the 1980s (e.g., Hinde & Stevenson-Hinde, 1988; Lewis, 1985).

The fundamental tenets of systems theory, as applied to the parenting process and its potential consequences on a child, include these: that the elements in the system have mutual and interactive effects on one another, as well as the whole system, and that the whole system itself can exert effects that transcend those of the individual elements (i.e., the whole is greater than the sum of its parts). In living systems, systems exist to attain and sustain homeostatis and to continue their existence (including procreation). These outcomes are achieved, more or less successfully, through a variety of specific adaptive mechanisms. In terms of parenting and family life, there is an evolution of parenting behavior that results from the feedback or observed effects that certain parenting actions produce (or fail to produce). Parents' behavior toward their children reflects a difficult-to-specify mix of their knowledge about effective parenting, their understanding of normative child development, their repertoire of parenting skills (obtained through observation, direct experience, and active information seeking), the contribution of external supports and stressors, and undoubtedly many biological influences that are expressed behaviorally over time. The degree to which a parent is highly consistent in his or her parenting approach and practices also may be important, but probably not in any simplistic fashion across the full range of parenting behavior.

WHAT COMPRISES PARENTING BEHAVIOR?

One of the most striking things noted in preparing for the NICHD conference was that there were virtually no definitions of parenting itself, despite numerous lengthy and well-conceptualized treatises about parent–child relationships and the importance of mutual influences (interactions and transactions). Is everything done by a parent to be considered "parenting" because it might have some impact on the child's development? Alternatively, is there a subset of adult behavior that might reasonably be identified as comprising parenting, such as behavior intentionally designed or obviously related to caretaking and the promotion of a child's well-being? In the absence of defining parenting, investigators typically select one or a few aspects of parenting behavior—with seemingly strong face validity—and then proceed to study the association of these with particular domains of child development (e.g., academic achievement, social and emotional competence, psychopathology, intelligence).

The origin of the verb *to parent* means "to bring forth." A content analysis of the most popular tools used to study parenting practices reveals that these instruments tap parental belief systems and attitudes as well as their behavioral practices. Yet there is no readily available taxonomy of parenting behaviors, or universal categories, to describe parenting practices. Recurrent and underlying themes, however, from both observational research on parents and children and self-reports of parents (mostly mothers) include the following dimensions: responsiveness to children's needs and individuality; warmth and expressiveness; explicit teaching and verbal explanation of parental desires and actions; and behavioral control strategies, including traditional disciplinary practices.

Interestingly, the most heated recent controversies concerning the importance of parents in their children's development rely on citing studies that almost never include direct measures of parenting at all. What often is unknown to nonspecialists and the general public is that most of the studies that pit nature against nurture have relied on a few global and static measures of parent characteristics, most notably parental intelligence (often estimated from educational attainment rather than independently tested) and parent personality or psychopathology, with *no direct* evidence of how these parent characteristics or traits are expressed by parents in their interactions with children and the type of environments parents provide for their children. In essence, such research has been guided by the implicit and untested assumption that parents who have higher IQ scores or who lack signs of major psychopathology, for instance, actually treat (i.e., parent) their children in ways that are more similar and presumably more supportive than do parents who have lower IQ scores or who have been diagnosed with major mental health disorders. Further, by limiting the child outcomes to those measured by standardized assessment tools that were developed to tap *stable traitlike qualities* in children (that is, tests that have eliminated those test items that fluctuated in the same individual over time, even if those items measured aspects of "intelligence" or "personality" that theoretically or practically seem important). Thus, many potentially important dimensions of a child's development—including those that are likely to fluctuate with different parenting practices (e.g., knowledge about the world; ability to generate and enact alternative, effective solutions to many real world problems; kindness toward others; health promoting behaviors; family values and spiritual belief systems; and appreciation for culture, art, and citizenship) and to relate to factors classified as nongenetic biological influences (e.g., nutritional status, hormonal status during puberty) and environmental influences (e.g., school quality, neighborhood risks, presence of environmental toxins)—are not measured at all.

These comments are not intended to diminish the scientific integrity or validity of such studies, but rather underscore their limitations when the findings from such research are used to support sweeping conclusions about the extent to which parents matter in their children's lives. What is interesting is that many basic parental decisions and behavior are seldom even included in the deliberations about the extent to which parents influence their children's life course. Whether a child is planned and wanted, for example, relates to a broad array of health and behavioral outcomes for the child yet this is not traditionally considered part of the parenting effects literature. Similarly, parents are the primary people who determine whether children are immunized, receive prompt and appropriate medical care and follow-up treatment for childhood illnesses and injuries, and are cared for in a responsible and healthy manner on a daily basis (e.g., through child care placement decisions, monitoring of before and after school activities, selection of summer activities and programs, monitoring of television viewing and other media exposure, provision of a healthy diet). Although these and many other factors have been investigated and reliably associated with children's risk status and their eventual well-being, rarely are these findings hailed as evidence of parenting influences per se. Even apparently straightforward parental behaviors in the course of caring for a young child, such as the parent's choice of sleep position for a young infant, can be of major significance in terms of survival (see NICHD'S webpage for information on "The Back to Sleep Public Information Campaign). Further, the NICHD has affirmed that cultural, education, and family contextual factors appear to affect this vital parenting practice. To reduce the study of parenting effects to *only* research about the degree to which parents appear to influence their children's intelligence and personality, as measured by a few standardized tests, would be unfortunate and arbitrary.

Philosophically, many parents view their role as parents as one of guiding and assisting their children, knowing full well that each child comes with his or her own individuality and proclivities. This is in marked contrast to those who might seek or hope to shape their children as though they were completely malleable, with no or little inherent direction or shape of their own. In studying parents' beliefs about what contributes to the development of their own exceptionally precocious young children, we found parents who endorsed a wide range of opinions—from accepting almost full responsibility through the stimulation they provided their infants to attributing "good genes' as the cause (Robinson, Dale, & Landesman, 1990).

Although much of this scientific meeting and the chapters in this book concentrate on the evidence concerning more subtle influences of parents and parenting behavior on children's social-emotional development and intelligence, I want to reiterate that what parents *can* do, *actually* do, and *fail* to do for their children encompasses a very broad spectrum and potentially influences many far-reaching aspects of a child's total development. Not a small matter in individuals' lives are the memories they have of their parents and their childhood, which in turn are likely to affect how they parent their own children (e.g., Main, 1989).

PARENTING: MULTIPLE PERSPECTIVES ON A MULTIFACETED, MULTIYEAR SET OF RESPONSIBILITIES

Parents, through their presence or absence, are functionally responsible for creating a family unit for each child in our society. This family unit becomes the child's base at a physical, psychological, and legal or societal level. Multiple activities and opportunities are strongly correlated with the family environment or context. Yet the behavioral consequences of highly similar parenting behavior may differ, at least theoretically, for children who live in different family configurations in different communities at different times in history. As noted above, contemporary theoretical perspectives on children's development invariably take into account multiple levels of simultaneous influence (e.g., Lewis, 2000; Sameroff, 2000); none embrace simplistic notions of only a few important influences or treat the family context as a constant that can be adequately described by measurement at only one or a few times in the course of a child's life.

SELF-REPORT OF PARENTING AND PARENT–CHILD RELATIONSHIPS

When thinking about parenting influences, it is clear that we must rely on markers of parenting and the parent–child relationship, since measuring these phenomena in their totality would be nearly impossible. By far, self-report of parents, almost always mothers, has been the basis for studying what parents do and how these self-reported parenting practices relate to children's developmental outcomes. Direct research on whether parental report is strongly associated with what parents really do, on a day-by-day basis, to varying degrees of consistency, across different situations and with different children in the same family, has simply not been studied in any depth. Given that parental self-report, despite its obvious limitations, does correlate with many child outcomes, there is good reason to continue this tradition. Theoretically, it is valid to posit that parents' perceptions of their own behavior, or how they choose to represent their behavior to others (i.e., scientists), are important to study in their own right. Parents' self-report of parenting practices may reflect their philosophy of childrearing and their beliefs about what constitutes "good," "responsible," "effective," and/or "acceptable" parental behavior toward children. Further, if there is an expansion of scientific inquiry about the efficacy of interventions designed to improve parenting, then it is important to understand parents' initial views about parenting and their own perceptions about what they think they are doing, regardless of the accuracy (validity) of these perceptions. Parents' views on their parenting practices are likely to influence their motivation to change and their willingness to try certain new ways of behaving toward their children.

DIRECT OBSERVATIONS OF PARENTS AND CHILDREN

Investigators who view self-report of parenting practices as inherently a flawed or inadequate way to depict parenting behavior typically reject using these measures altogether. Instead, they proceed to observe parent–child behavior either in naturalistic settings (almost always, the child's home environment) or laboratory environments, where important parent–child exchanges may be elicited through instructions and the provision of appropriate props. The most commonly studied parent–child interactions are in the course of so-called free play, teaching, feeding, caretaking, or structured separations and reunions of the parent and the young child. The majority of observational studies have concentrated on two age periods: the early years of life, with extensive studies of typically developing and "at risk" children under the age of three; and the adolescent years, usually with families that have already experienced serious difficulty with their children. In published results of these observational studies, rarely are parents' own views on their parenting behavior and their child's development integrated with the observed or objectively documented behavior.

METHODOLOGICAL ISSUES
IN INTEGRATING MULTIPLE DATA
SOURCES ABOUT PARENTING

In a population-based study of 400 middle class families, my colleagues and I (e.g., Landesman, Jaccard, & Gunderson, 1991; Wan, Jaccard, & Ramey, 1996; Reid, Ramey, & Burchincal, 1990) discovered that parents' own self-report about many important aspects of family life, including their own parenting practices, showed far more fluctuation within a relatively short period of time (only three to four weeks apart) than we had anticipated. What we learned was that parents' self-reports obtained on the second measurement occasion were much more strongly associated with other measures of parents and children than the first-time measures. We found this perplexing and of great concern, since almost all studies of parents and children obtain one and only one measure at a given stage of a child's development. That is, longitudinal studies seldom have the resources to measure parents and children more than once a year, and most obtain measures on parents, children, and families only every three to five years or so from middle childhood to the adolescent or adult years! Upon reflection and through a series of laborious data analyses, we are able to identify a subgroup of parents who do provide almost the same self-report about parenting behavior and other aspects of family life and child development; and another subgroup that does not. We have postulated that these two groups of parents may differ naturally in how thoroughly and frequently they reflect on their own parenting practices and attitudes. Thus, for those who are naturally more reflective and engage in more self-appraisal, their responses on the first time they complete a questionnaire or respond to an interviewer's queries may be easy to provide and indicative of the perceptions they already hold. In contrast, for parents who are naturally less reflective about these dimensions of life, the questions—upon first exposure—may be truly foreign to their way of thinking and may be more difficult to answer readily and with confidence. When parents then have a second chance to answer these same (or highly similar) questions a few weeks later, the naturally less reflective parents may be more likely to change their answers, in part because participation in the research has led them to notice certain things and to reflect more about their own behavior. Despite the plausibility of our explanation, we have not yet tested this or expanded this finding into ways that could inform future inquiry. The scientific axiom that the process of studying a phenomenon does change the phenomenon (known as the Heisenberg principle in physics) warrants more attention in our research on parenting.

We also have observed families during a typical family event, the family dinnertime (Ramey & Juliusson, 1998). On three occasions within a one-month period, we observed and recorded in detail the social and informational exchanges of all family members ($N = 293$ families) during dinner in their homes. Of particular focus in the analyses was the question of whether school-aged children in single-parent, divorced families showed different types and amounts of interaction than those in two-parent, married families. We also included parents' perspectives on their own family dinnertimes, such as the importance they attach to family mealtimes, their satisfaction with this event, and their report about many objective aspects such as how often the family eats together, what rules they have, and how much time they spend together. We even asked all family members how intrusive the videotape and observational procedure was on each occasion—that is, we queried whether they thought the presence of an observer changed how they behaved, compared to typical evenings when an observer was not there. (By the way, parents reported some self-consciousness or nervousness the first time they were observed, while children reported their mothers cooked fancier meals or their favorite foods and that their parents were a little bit nicer.) Our analyses of the behavioral exchanges, however, showed moderate levels of fluctuation in critical behaviors, such that an average or summary of the observations across the three measurement occasions yielded the most robust estimates of theoretically important parent and child behaviors. Had we relied on only one observation, the data would have been inadequate to detect significant findings concerning the study's guiding hypotheses. What we found was that single parents (all mothers in this study) demonstrated remarkable compensatory behaviors, such that the children received almost the same amounts and types of adult–child social exchanges as did children in two-parent families. To achieve this, however, the mother functionally did "double duty," that is, these mothers displayed the behavior that *both* mothers and fathers together did in the two-parent, married families. Had we studied only the mother–child relationship without coding the exchanges of all family members at the same time, we might have reached very different conclusions than from studying the entire family as a system. Further, had we relied just on mothers' self-report, we might have reported that children in single-parent families experience quite different types of family dinnertimes, because single mothers appeared more self-critical and differed in their ratings about a number of dimensions of family dinnertimes. In these middle-class families, where almost all objective measures of the parent–child relationship and the home environment find few or no significant differences, we also found no negative correlates of the family's marital status on the children's social–behavioral functioning, intellectual status, school adjustment, or peer relationships.

WHOSE PERSPECTIVE ON THE FAMILY IS THE BEST?

In the same study mentioned above, we also confirmed (as many others have) that the self-reports of mothers and fathers rarely showed extremely high agreement or concordance, even when they were asked to report on the same dimensions of parenting and family life at the exact same times. Fathers, compared to mothers, tended to be more optimistic and less critical of many dimensions of family life (particularly their marital relationship, their relationship with their school-age child, and their overall satisfaction with their family), to skip answering more questions, and to report fewer behavioral problems in their children. Although it is easy to spin many plausible explanations for differences in what mothers and fathers report, the phenomenology (subjective experience) of these differences may warrant greater attention than most theories ascribe to such differences. The NICHD has led a national interagency collaboration to synthesize the scientific knowledge about fathers and to promote gathering more information about fathers in routine federally sponsored research and service delivery. Yet even in the expansion of studies that seek to include fathers' perspectives, recognizing the importance of paternal influences as well as maternal ones, this has been challenging. Fathers have been more difficult to locate or schedule to participate in research; single mothers often are reluctant to have investigators contact children's fathers; and many parent tools are not especially "father friendly." Most challenging of all is the sheer complexity faced in data analyses when information is available from both mothers and fathers, but missing disproportionately for fathers from certain types of families.

Besides data provided by the parents and through direct observations of parents, there are other useful sources of information about what parents do. These include teacher reports of parental involvement, administrative and clinical records for families receiving social and health services, ratings by interviewers or observers that provide more summative and subjective impressions than quantitative observational or interview scoring procedures typically provide, and report of others who know the parents. When I entered the field of family research from my own primary specialty of studying exceptional children, often in exceptional residential settings, I was shocked that children's own views on their families and their parents were not included. Admittedly, gathering such sensitive and complex data from very young children might be difficult, but children's perceptions appeared to be essential for full application of systems theory to the study of the family unit, as well as for helping to untangle the thorny issues about how children's individuality (e.g., temperament, personality dimensions, behavioral inclinations, presence or absence of developmental disorders) served to mediate or moderate the effects of different parental behavior.

Our interest in including the perspectives of children younger than adolescents (there were some tools available for use with older children) occupied us for nearly a decade in order to develop a battery of psychometrically sound measurement strategies to gather the same types of information from young children as from older children and from parents (known as "Dialogues About Families'). Through our intensive methodological research, we have learned that children can, in fact, be quite reliable reporters on their own families, their parents, and themselves— particularly when the method used to gather these data take into account the children's cognitive development and establishes a dialogue between the interviewers and the child, rather than direct query or paper-and-pencil techniques that do not consistently engage a child's attention or establish a child's level of understanding for each question asked (*cf.* Reid, Ramey, & Burchinal, 1990; Burchinal, Ramey, Reid, & Jaccard, 1995).

Incorporating children's own developmental perspectives on their lives and their experiences has been fascinating, as well as promising, yet is far from an established approach and has not provided definitive answers to why different children within the same family report different experiences. It is not just grown-up siblings who have different memories of what their parents were like. In the introduction for the conference, however, I pointed out a few fascinating differences that illustrate the profound importance of development and cumulative life experiences in seeking to document the relationships among parenting behavior, family context, and child outcomes.

In selecting these, I chose to emphasize a few points particularly relevant to the conference, in part because they reflected important nuances that often are obscured when seeking simple answers to questions about parental influences on children. *First*, it is clear from our cross-sectional and longitudinal research that children, at different ages, report having different types of relationships with their parents and describe their parents somewhat differently in terms of parental qualities and behaviors. Younger children (6- to 9-year-olds), for example, tend to be more positive than older children (10- to 12-year-olds) in their ratings of parents' qualities such as being loving, eager to learn, responsible, self-confident, honest, or sensitive to the feelings of others. Across the 6- to 12-year-old age range, children's report of satisfaction with the social support provided by their parents is higher than for any other providers (siblings, peers, teachers, and other relatives) in the areas of emotional support, informational support, and instrumental support, with virtually no decline in children's report of the adequacy of parental support over time (Reid, Landesman, Treder, & Jaccard, 1989; Cauce, Reid, Landesman, & Gonzales, 1990). There was one notable exception, namely, children by the ages of 9 or 10 begin to rate their peers as equal or slightly higher than their parents in terms of being able to provide good companionship, as reflected in their ratings of who they have fun doing things with and who they like to hang out with. A finding somewhat surprising to us was that this increase in children's ratings of the role of friends was not accompanied by a decline in how they rated the quality of the companionship support they received from their parents. In fact, children rate their fathers as increasingly more satisfactory social supporters as children become older, including in the area of companionship, while they rate their mothers very highly in all areas during the 5- through 13-year-age period.

When considering parents' roles in their children's social lives, the findings are compatible with an interpretation that parents serve as social support *generalists*, or a core network member who provides a child with many types of support, in contrast to peers, teachers, and siblings, who function as social support *specialists,* being rated as very high in the selective aspects of support they provide to children. As expected, children see teachers as specialists in providing informational support—especially from the third grade on—and they view their

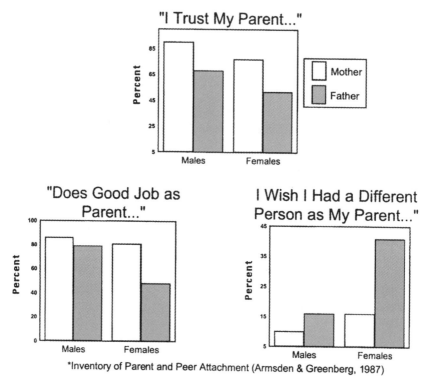

*Inventory of Parent and Peer Attachment (Armsden & Greenberg, 1987)

FIG. 4.1. Gender differences in children's perceptions of their parents.

peers as specialists in providing companionship, rather than serving as reliable providers of information, emotional, or instrumental help and support.

During the adolescent years, however, children become far more critical, and daughters are particularly negative in their appraisals of their fathers' social support and adequacy as a parent (Gaines, Ramey, & Reid, 1996). During the adolescent years, the same girls who had given very positive ratings to both of their parents when they were younger reported much decreased trust in their fathers, lower overall ratings of whether their fathers do a "good job as parent," and "wishing I had a different person as my parent," for example, compared to sons. Adolescent sons, in contrast, held their mothers in about the same high esteem that daughters did and rated their fathers more positively—although fathers were rated much lower in the adolescent years than were mothers—to a much greater extent than during the early and middle childhood years. Figure 4.1 illustrates some of these gender differences in children's perceptions of their parents. These developmental trends warrant careful consideration in studies addressing questions about parental influences. They reflect the dynamic nature of the parent–child relationship; age and gender, to mention just two dimensions, likely contribute to a fluctuations in the extent and ways in which parents influence their children at different ages. Further, we have discovered that not all seemingly negative perceptions by family members lead to negative outcomes or correlates. Theoretically, tensions, distress, and self-criticism may serve as motivating or guiding influences within a family system as long as these are not extreme and may, in turn, produce positive outcomes.

Second, children's perceptions of their relationship with their parents showed significant correlations with their social-emotional adjustment, although some aspects of the parent–child relationship were more important than others. Specifically, children's views of how supportive their parents were in the areas of emotional support (helping the child feel good about who he or she is; understanding how the child really feels and knowing "the real you", helping the child feel better when he or she feels sad or mad; and sharing the child's joy when the child has good news or achievements) and instrumental support (help with getting things done; assistance with homework) related significantly to children's social adjustment and their self-esteem, as rated by parents. In two separate studies with somewhat different types of families, peer social support during the early and midde childhood years (Cauce et al., 1990), and later in the adolescent years (Cauce et al., 1982, 1988), related negatively to children's academic competence and to their curiosity. The majority of 6- to 12-year-old children do not consider their peers to be very good providers of informational support; for the subset of children who do trust their peers in this area, however, there appear to be some negative correlates. Children who are less bright and less curious may be vulnerable to the information provided by age mates; alternatively, children who depend on the generally less accurate or complete information provided by peers may not show the same degree of intellectual advances and continued curiosity about things. As in almost all developmental inquiry, determining causality or a primary reasons for observed relationships among variables is limited—leading to the need for replication of findings and plausible pathways that can be tested in longitudinal studies.

Ideally, investigators will increasingly seek to measure parental influences from multiple perspectives, including the children's own views on their parents and their families, as well as gathering objective data about the types, amounts, and consistency of parenting behavior and monitoring in key areas of interest.

THE VALUE AND LIMITATIONS OF A BROAD CONCEPTUAL FRAMEWORK

When we began our research on family dynamics, we delineated a set of fundamental assumptions (Landesman, Jaccard, & Gunderson, 1991). Over time, the evidence we gathered provided multiple supports for these. Because we found them so useful for informing our own conceptual framework (which focused on

TABLE 4.1

FUNDAMENTAL ASSUMPTIONS ABOUT FAMILIES AND
THE PARENT–CHILD RELATIONSHIPS

1. Events, perceptions, and reports of events are not synonymous.

Objective events that occur in the family and the perception of these events are not identical, for either parents or children. Further, when family members report on what occurs inside their family, further transformations are expected. These transformations reflect factors such as the individual differences discussed in Assumption 3 (below) and to the contexts and timing of the report.

2. Perceptions are important to a family's functioning and to a child's developmental course.

Perceptions can affect the development of individuals and the contexts in which family members operate. Actual events and their perceptions are assumed to influence the (short- and long-term) consequences of these events. In turn, both the events and their perceptions contribute to the developmental course of the family unit. "Perceptions' here are conceptualized broadly to include the particular experiences remembered, the duration and salience of those memories, the meaning given to the events, the emotional connotation of the events and experiences, and supportive details family members provide when reporting on family events and their experiences.

3. Individuals have predispositions that influence their perceptions of what occurs.

In principle, many variables can predispose individual family members to particular biases in how they perceive behavioral events and in how willing they are report to others about their family experiences. These individual variables include developmental ones (e.g., age, prior experience, level of cognitive and emotional maturity) and normative ones (e.g., cohort, gender, and role in the family) as well as person-specific and idiographic elements (e.g., personality or temperamental orientation, intelligence, health status, genetic factors).

4. Perceptions about major dimensions of family functioning are relatively stable, except during periods of disruption and change.

Reports of perceptions held by individual family members, even children as young as 4 years of age, show reasonable stability and cohesion, especially when their families are functioning in ways that family members think are typical and/or desirable.

5. Perceptions can lead to or prevent behavioral events.

When family members' perceptions of their family and one another are shared, these perceptions are particularly likely to be transformed into behavioral events, which then are subject to further perceptions. Family members share their perceptions (views, memories, opinions, judgements) both directly and indirectly with one another, sometimes shortly after an event, at other times far removed from the event. The sharing of family members, experiences becomes an integral part of the family's behavior.

---

the role of parental decision-making abilities and strategies) and for selecting the methods we used to study parents and children, we present these in a summary form in Table 4.1. These assumptions differentiate between objective and subjective events within the family and apply clearly to the realm of parenting behavior.

The challenges in studying parenting influences are, without doubt, immense. The discussion in this introductory presentation is far from complete, and many topics remain unaddressed. In the early stages of planning the NICHD conference, the committee members frequently took paper and pencil to illustrate their views of how to study or represent possible pathways of parental influences. We considered trying to use one or more of these to guide the conference and the summary of findings. In the final analysis, selecting any or even a few of these appeared presumptuous and, more importantly, inadequate for the wide array of findings included in this volume. The phenomena of interest truly defy simple graphic or tabular display in any way that is acceptable to the majority of leading investigators. A broad guiding conceptual framework could be immensely useful to the field if the key elements in this framework were ones for which we had acceptable measurement strategies across the developmental spectrum and different populations. Similarly, if there were analytic tools adequate to integrate the data or even to address select aspects within the large conceptual framework, this would be invaluable. The fact remains, however, in our appraisal, that the present state of our scientific inquiry and understanding about parenting is piecemeal—albeit containing many important facts and conclusions that warrant wide distribution with scientists and the general public, particularly parents themselves.

The NICHD has launched an admirable effort to bring together a small number of family researchers in an ongoing exchange about their own datasets, with the goal of conducting new and promising interdisciplinary analyses. This NIH institute also has been an innovator in designing, conducting, and now analyzing one of the most carefully conduced, large-scale national studies ever of adolescent development, including direct measures of individual biological status along with information about families, peers, and schools. Similarly, the 10-site longitudinal study on early child care represents another NICHD example of commitment to promoting larger-scale, multidisciplinary, and longitudinal inquiry. All of us eagerly await the results of these landmark scientific efforts and hope that in a decade from now many of the unresolved controversies that are of crucial importance to parents and policymakers will be settled. At the same time, we know that there are severe limits imposed on our understanding of the ways parents can, do, and could influence their children in positive ways. A new wave of research that explicitly seeks to study the phenomenon of parenting per se is imperative if we want to know the extent to which parents can, in the future, improve the ways that they help their children realize their full human potential. At the same time that children in high-risk families, with or without identified disorders or disabilities, are studied and new treatments tested, we must also consider the larger societal questions about why so many typically developing children, often with an apparent abundance of resources in their lives, do not achieve happy and healthy adult outcomes.

No one expects that parents can be fully credited or blamed for children's poor outcomes or all the troubles of our society. Yet to ignore the unique role that parents play in their children's lives and their multiple legal and moral responsibilities would be equally wrong. There is an impressive and growing body of scientific literature that unequivocally supports the conclusions that children's cumulative life experiences matter. With little reasonable doubt, "Healthy lifestyles, good mental health, and civility have their roots in early childhood experiences" (Ramey & Ramey, 2000, p. 147). Collectively, we need to expand and improve our efforts to provide parents with useful, reliable information to guide their choices and the ways in which they promote their children's well-being. Lest we forget, those glorious moments at the start of a child's life are not just a promissory note for children or a dream for parents: the inherent reciprocity in parent–child relationships means that parents' own well-being also can be enhanced (or diminished) to a considerable extent by their children's outcomes and, ultimately, the strength of a community and society. The art of parenting will always be an uncertain and individual endeavor to some degree; what science can do is further parents' knowledge and confidence and the effectiveness of how we invest in our children and their future.

REFERENCES

Anastasi, A. (1956). Intelligence and family size. *Psychological Bulletin, 53,* 187–209.

Aylward, G. P. (1992). The relationship between environmental risk and developmental outcome. *Journal of Developmental and Behavioral Pediatrics, 13,* 222–229.

Barnard, K. E. (1978). *Nursing child assessment teaching scale.* Seattle: University of Washington.

Batshaw, M. L. (Ed.). (2000). *When your child has a disability: The complete sourcebook of daily and medical care.* Baltimore: Paul H. Brookes.

Black, M. M., Nair, P., Knight, C., Wachtel, R., Roby, P., & Schuler, M. (1994). Parenting and early development among children of drug-abusing women: Effects of home intervention. *Pediatrics, 94,* 440–448.

Bradley, R. H., & Caldwell, B. M. (1986). Early home environment and the development of competence: Findings from the Little Rock Longitudinal Study. *Children's Environments Quarterly, 3,* 10–22.

Bradley, R. H., & Caldwell, B. M. (1988). Using the HOME inventory to assess the family environment. *Pediatric Nursing, 14,* 97–102.

Bradley, R. H., Caldwell, B. M., & Rock, S. L. (1989). Home environment and cognitive development in the first 3 years of life: A collaborative study involving six sites and three ethnic groups in North America. *Developmental Psychology, 25,* 217–235.

Bronfenbrenner, U. (1979). *The ecology of human development: Experiments by nature and design.* Cambridge, MA: Harvard University Press.

Brofenbrenner, U. (1989). Ecological systems theory. In R. Vasta (Ed.), *Annals of Child Development,* (pp. 187–249). Greenwich, CT: JAI Press.

Burchinal, M. R., Ramey, S. L., Reid, M., & Jaccard, J. (1995). Early child care experiences and their associations with family and child characteristics during middle childhood. *Early Childhood Research Quarterly, 10,* 33–61.

Caldwell, B. M., & Bradley, R. H. (1984). *Home observation for measurement of the environment.* Little Rock: University of Arkansas.

Cauce, A. M., Reid, M., Landesman, S., & Gonzales, N. (1990). Social support in young children: Measurement, structure, and behavioral impact. In I. G. Sarason, B. R. Sarason, & G. R. Pierce (Eds.), *Social support: An interactional view* (pp. 64–94). New York: John Wiley & Sons.

Ceci, S. J., Ramey, S. L., & Ramey, C. T. (1991). Framing intellectual assessment in terms of a person-process-context model. *Educational Psychologist, 25,* 269–291.

Chase-Lansdale, P., & Hetherington, E. M. (1990). The impact of divorce on life-span development: Short- and long-term effects. In P. B. Baltes, D. L. Featherman, & R. M. Lerner (Eds.), *Life-span development and behavior* (Vol. 10, pp. 105–150). New York: Academic Press.

Cirelli, V. G. (1978). The relationship of sibling structure to intellectual abilities and achievement. *Review of Educational Research, 48,* 365–379.

Cole, John D., Miller-Jackson, S., & Bagwell, C. (2000). In A. J. Sameroff, M. Lewis, & S. M. Miller (Eds.), *Handbook of developmental psychology.* (pp. 93–112). New York: Plenum Press.

Coll, C. G., & Garrido, M. (2000). Minorities in the United States: Sociocultural context for mental health and developmental psychopathology. In A. J. Sameroff, M. Lewis, & S. M. Miller (Eds.), *Handbook of developmental psychology* (pp. 177–195). New York: Plenum.

Gaines, K. R., Ramey, S. L., & Reid, M. (1996 June). The developmental origins of social support in adolescence. Poster session presented of the American Psychological Society Meeting, San Francisco, California.

Grotberg, E. N. (1999). *Tapping your inner strength: How to find the resilience to deal with anything.* Oakland, CA: New Harbinger Publications.

Hardy, J. B., & Streett, R. (1989). Family support and parenting education in the home: An effective extension of clinic-based preventative health care services for poor children. *Journal of Pediatrics, 115,* 927–931.

Hetherington, E. M., Cox, M., & Cox, R. (1982). Effects of divorce on parents and children. In M. E. Lamb (Ed.), *Nontraditional families: Parenting and child development* (pp. 233–288). Hillsdale, NJ: Lawrence Erlbaum Associates.

Hinde, R. A. & Stevenson-Hinde, J. (Eds.). (1988). *Relationships within families: Mutual influences.* NY: Oxford University Press.

Hollenbeck, A. R. (1978). Early home environments: Validation of the home observation of the measurement of the environment inventory. *Developmental Psychology, 14,* 416–418.

Hunt, J. McV. (1961). *Intelligence and experience.* New York: Ronald Press.

Johnson, D. L., Swank, P., Howie, V. M., Baldwin, C. D., Owen, M., & Luttman, D. (1993). Does HOME add to the prediction of child intelligence over and above SES? *Journal of Genetic Psychology, 154,* 33–40.

Landesman, S. (1986). Toward a taxonomy of home environments. In N. R. Ellis & N. W. Bray (Eds.), *International review of research in mental retardation* (Vol. 14, pp. 259–289). New York: Academic Press.

Landesman, S., Jaccard, J., & Gunderson, V. (1991). The family environment: The combined influence of family behavior, goals, strategies, resources, and individual experiences. In M. Lewis & S. Feinman (Eds.), *Social influences and socialization in infancy* (pp. 63–96). New York: Plenum Press.

Landesman, S., & Ramey, C. T. (1989). Developmental psychology and mental retardation: Integrating scientific principles with treatment practices. *American Psychologist, 44,* 409–415.

Landesman, S., & Vietze, P. (Eds.). (1987). *Living environments and mental retardation.* Washington, DC: American Association on Mental Retardation.

Lanzi, R. G., & Ramey, S. L. (submitted). Adolescents' perceptions of social support: Individual and family influences. *Child Development.*

Lewis, M. (Ed.). (1984). *Beyond the dyad.* New York: Plenum Press.

Martin, S. L., Ramey, C. T., & Ramey, S. (1990). The prevention of intellectual impairment in children of impoverished families: Findings of a randomized trial of educational day care. *American Journal of Public Health, 80,* 844–847.

McCubbin, H. I., Patterson, J. M., & Wilson, L. R. (1981). *Family Inventory of Life Events.* St. Paul: University of Minnesota.

Miller, J. G. (1978). *Living systems.* New York: McGraw-Hill.

Minuchin, P. (1988). Relationships within the family: A systems perspective on development. In R. A. Hinde & J. Stevenson-Hinde (Eds.), *Relationships with families: Mutual influences* (pp. 7–26). Oxford, UK: Clarendon.

Morrisset, C. E., Barnard, K. E., Greenberg, M. T., Booth, C. L., & Spieker, S. J. (1990). Environmental influences on early language development: The context of social risk. *Developmental Psychopathology, 2,* 127–149.

Norton, D. (1990). Understanding the early experience of black children in high-risk environments: Culturally and ecologically relevant research in regard to support for families. *Zero to Three, 10,* 1–7.

Olds, D. L., Henderson, C. R., & Kitzman, H. (1994). Does prenatal and infancy home visitation have enduring effects on qualities of parental caregiving and child health at 25 to 50 months of life? *Pediatrics, 93,* 89–98.

Ragozin, A. S., Landesman-Dwyer, S., & Streissguth, A. P. (1978). The relationship between mothers' drinking habits and children's home environments. In F. Seixas (Ed.), *Currents in alcoholism: Vol. 4. Psychiatric, psychological, social, and epidemiological studies* (pp. 39–50). New York: Grune & Stratton.

Ramey, C. T., & Ramey, S. L. (1996). Early intervention: Optimizing development for children with disabilities and risk conditions. In M. Wolraich (Ed.), *Disorders of development and learning: A practical guide to assessment and management* (2nd ed., pp. 141–158) Philadelphia: Mosby.

Ramey, C.T., & Ramey, S. L. (1998). Early intervention and early experience. *American Psychologist, 53,* 109–120.

Ramey, C. T., & Ramey, S. L. (1999). *Right from birth: Building your child's foundation for life.* New York: Goddard Press.

Ramey, C. T., Ramey, S. L., & Lanzi, R. (1998). Differentiating developmental risk levels for families in poverty: Creating a family typology. In M. Lewis, & C. Feiring (Eds.), *Families, risk, and competence* (pp. 187–205). Mahwah, NJ: Lawrence Erlbaum Associates.

Ramey, C. T., Ramey, S. L., Gaines, R., & Blair, C. (1995). Two-generation early intervention programs: A child development perspective. In I. Sigel (Series Ed.) & S. Smith (Vol. Ed.), *Two-generation programs for families in poverty: A new intervention strategy: Vol. 9. Advances in applied developmental psychology* (pp. 199–228). Norwood, NJ: Ablex Publishing Corporation.

Ramey, S. L., Dossett, E., & Echols, K. (1996). The social ecology of mental retardation. In J. Jacobson & J. Mulick (Eds.), *Manual of diagnosis and professional practice in mental retardation* (pp. 55–65). Washington, DC: American Psychological Association.

Ramey, S. L., & Juliusson, H. (1998). Family dynamics at dinner: A natural context for revealing basic family processes. In M. Lewis, & C. Feiring (Eds.), *Families, risk, and competence* (pp. 31–52). Mahwah, NJ: Lawrence Erlbaum Associates.

Ramey, S. L., Krauss, M. W., & Simeonsson, R. J. (1989). Research on families: Current assessment and future opportunities. *American Journal of Mental Retardation, 94,* ii–vi.

Ramey, S. L., & Ramey, C. T. (1992). Early educational intervention with disadvantaged children: To what effect? *Applied and Preventive Psychology, 1,* 131–140.

Ramey, S. L., & Ramey, C. T. (1999). *Going to school: How to help your child succeed.* New York: Goddard Press.

Ramey, S. L., & Ramey, C. T. (2000). Early childhood experiences and developmental competence. In J. Waldfogel & S. Danziger (Eds.), *Securing the future: Investing in children from birth to college* (pp. 122–150). New York: Russell Sage Foundation.

Ramey, S. L., Ramey, C. T., & Friedlander, M. J. (Eds.). (1999). Early intervention and early experience [Special issue]. *Mental Retardation and Developmental Disabilities Research Reviews, 5.*

Ramey, S. L., & Sackett, G. P. (2000). The early caregiving environment: Expanding views on non-parental care and cumulative life experiences. In A. Sameroff, M. Lewis, & S. Miller (Eds.), *Handbook of developmental psychopathology,* (2nd ed., pp. 365–380). New York: Plenum Publishers.

Ramey, S. L., Sparling, J., Dragomir, C., Ramey, C., Echols, K., & Soroceanu, L. (1995). Recovery by children under 3 years old from depriving orphanage experiences, Symposium Presentation. Indianapolis, IN: Society for Research in Child Development.

Reid, M., Landesman, S., Treder, R., & Jaccard, J. (1989). "My Family and Friends": Six- to twelve-year-old children's perceptions of social support. *Child Development, 60,* 896–910.

Reid, M., Ramey, S. L., & Burchinal, M. (1990). Dialogues with children about their families. In I. Bretherton & M. Watson (Eds.), *Children's perspectives on their families: New directions for child development* (pp. 5–28). San Francisco: Jossey-Bass.

Robinson, N. M., Dale, P. S., & Landesman, S. J. (1990). Validity of the Stanford Binet IV with linguistically precocious toddlers. *Intelligence, 14,* 173–183.

Robinson, N. M., Weinberg, R. A., Redden, D., Ramey, S. L., & Ramey, C. T. (1998). Family factors associated with high academic competence among former Head Start children. *Gifted Child Quarterly, 42,* 148–156.

Sackett, G. P., Novak, M. F. S. X., & Kroeker, R. (1999). Early experience effects on adaptive behavior: Theory revisited. *Mental Retardation and Developmental Disabilities Research Reviews, 5,* 30–40.

Sameroff, A. J. (2000). Dialectical processes in developmental psychopathology. In A. J. Sameroff, M. Lewis, & S. M. Miller (Eds.), *Handbook of developmental psychopathology* (pp. 23–40). New York: Plenum Publishers.

Sameroff, A. J., Lewis, M., & Miller, S. M. (Eds.). (2000). Handbook of developmental psychopathology (2nd ed.) NY: Plenum Publishers.

Shore, R. (1997). *Rethinking the brain: New insights into early development.* New York: Families and Work Institute.

Sroufe, L. A., Duggal, S., Weinfield, N., & Carlson, E. (2000). Relationships, development, and psychopathology. In A. J. Sameroff, M. Lewis, & S. M. Miller (Eds.), *Handbook of developmental psychopathology* (pp. 75–91). New York: Plenum Publishers.

Suomi, S. J. (2000). A biobehavioral perspective on developmental psychopathology: Excessive aggression and serotonergic dysfunction in monkeys. In A. J. Sameroff, M. Lewis, & S. M. Miller (Eds.), *Handbook of developmental psychopathology* (pp. 237–256). New York: Plenum Publishers.

Terhune, K. W., (1974). A review of the actual and expected consequences of family size (NIH Publication No. 75-779). Washington, DC: U. S. Department of Health, Education, and Welfare, Public Health Service.

Wan, C. K., Jaccard, J., & Ramey, S. L. (1996). The relationship between social support and life satisfaction as a function of family structure: An analysis of four types of support. *Journal of Marriage and the Family, 58,* 502–513.

Zajonc, R. B., Marcus, G. B., Berbaum, M. L., Bargh, J. A., & Moreland, R. L. (1991). One justified criticism plus three flawed analyses equals two unwarranted conclusions: A reply to Retherford and Sewell. *American Sociological Review, 56,* 159–165.

II

Early Influences of Parenting on Achievement and Competence

5

What an Intervention Design Reveals About How Parents Affect Their Children's Academic Achievement and Behavior Problems

Philip A. Cowan and Carolyn Pape Cowan
University of California, Berkeley

Associations between parents' characteristics or behaviors and their children's developmental outcomes have been demonstrated in thousands of studies. One of the points at issue in developmental psychology and family research is precisely what these associations mean. Traditional socialization theories explain correlations between parenting behavior and child outcomes in terms of parent-behavior-driven models: Children are what they are because parents do what they do. This view was supported by theorists from both behaviorist (Watson, 1928) and psychoanalytic traditions (Freud, 1938), which dominated developmental psychology during the first half of the 20th century.

In the second half of the century, the exclusive focus on parenting behavior as a primary determinant of children's development faced a number of challenges. Based on clinical work with troubled families (e.g., Bateson, Jackson, Haley, & Weakland, 1956), theorists from a family systems perspective argued that causality in family relationships is essentially circular in nature: Parents influence children and children influence parents, so adaptation is a joint product of these powerful

Address correspondence to: Philip and Carolyn Pape Cowan, 140 Highland Blvd., Kensington, CA 94708-1023, Phone: 510-526-2586, or 510-693-5608.

bidirectional dynamic forces. The 1970s and 1980s brought behavior genetics to prominence (*cf.* Plomin, 1994), which emphasized the hypothesis that shared genes were responsible for parent–child correlations. These arguments and assumptions pointed away from parents' behavior as the sole influence and toward other within-family and biological sources of influence on children's development.

During the last quarter of this century, it has become clear that at least some of the variations in children's cognitive, social, and emotional development are attributable to forces that operate outside the family. Children's developmental trajectories are affected by their relationships with peers (e.g., Asher & Coie, 1990) and by the quality of their schools, neighborhoods, and other cultural institutions (Parke, Perry & Weinstein, 1998). Explanations of individual differences in children's development that incorporate an interactive, systemic amalgam of the effects of genes, parents, peers, and the larger culture have been central to the contemporary field of child development for some time (*cf.* Damon, 1997). Judith Harris' recent criticism (1998) of developmental psychology's emphasis on parents as the primary shapers of how children become who they are is directed at a single-factor view of developmental theory that has not been prevalent for some time.

Here we examine Harris' claim that the way parents behave toward their children has no important long-term effects on the children's personality. First, because we share Harris' concern that claims about parenting effects may have been overstated by some, we summarize the research designs that a majority of investigators use as they attempt to understand the mechanisms linking parents' behavior with their children's academic and social adaptation between 3 and 10 years of age. We examine simple concurrent designs, retrospective studies, longitudinal prospective studies, and intervention designs with random assignment to experimental conditions. We show that each approach has assets and limitations, but that only intervention designs allow us to draw conclusions about generative causality—whether parents have an impact on their children's developmental course. Even with intervention designs, the inferences that we draw can never be absolutely conclusive. Causality has been a very difficult construct for social scientists to nail down.

To illustrate our theoretical argument, we briefly describe two longitudinal studies of families in transition—during the transition to first-time parenthood and during the first child's transition to elementary school. We present some correlational data linking parents' behavior and their children's adaptation. We then show how the results of an intervention with the parents help us to interpret the complex correlational patterns. From the results of these studies we draw three conclusions. First, parent–child relationships cannot be considered in a vacuum but must be examined in the context of other relationships inside and outside the family. Second, the data support the notion that parents have a significant impact on their children's academic achievement and behavior at school in the early elementary school grades. Third, it is necessary to go beyond a consideration of main effects or the direct impact of parents on children. The overarching questions are concerned with how the quality of parenting combines with biological, psychological, and social factors to shape children's developmental trajectories.

FOUR RESEARCH DESIGNS FOR STUDYING PARENTS AND CHILDREN

Parenting behavior and children's outcomes have been examined with four types of research designs: concurrent correlations, retrospective designs, prospective longitudinal designs, and intervention studies.

Concurrent Correlations

The vast majority of parenting studies use concurrent correlational designs in which the characteristics or behaviors of the parent and the child are assessed at roughly the same time. It is clear from many studies using concurrent data that there are correlations between authoritative parenting (warm, responsive, limit-setting, and encouraging of autonomy) observed in the home or laboratory and children's academic and social competence (Baumrind, 1991). If the data come from the same source (e.g., mother or child), or are obtained in the same assessment situation (e.g., the laboratory), it is legitimate to question whether the resulting correlations are artifacts of the method—inflated by the fact that parent and child have been viewed through the same lens or in the same situation. In the ideal case, seldom achieved in actual studies, parenting behavior and child outcomes would be assessed in different contexts (e.g., home and school), using different informants (parents, observers, and/or children themselves), and different types of measuring instruments (e.g., self-report questionnaires and observations). Even in the ideal case, however, the logic of inference and the assumptions of family systems theorists make it clear that it is impossible to determine the direction of effects from correlational data. The correlations could arise from the parent's effect on the child, the child's effect on the parents, or a combination of the two in which the outcome is a product of the fit between a parent and his or her child (Seifer & Schiller, 1995). Harris' (1988) criticism of studies that draw causal inferences about parenting effects from correlational data, though hardly new, is essentially valid.

Ambiguity concerning the direction of effects does not rule out the utility of all concurrent correlational designs. These designs help us to begin mapping the territory of parent–child relationships, and they serve a useful function in falsifying hypotheses. For example, it becomes much more difficult to support the argument that parents' behavior is causally implicated in a child's adaptation or difficulty if parent and child behavior are not correlated. We want to make another key point about correlations here. It is unwarranted, as Harris often does in both her review article (1995) and her book (1998), to dismiss the findings derived from correlational studies because they do not conclusively establish the nature and direction of parenting effects. To say that the case for parents as nurturers is "not proven" does not mean that the case is false: Correlational studies are consistent with the hypothesis that parents affect children, but they are consistent with other hypotheses as well. It would be equally unwise to dismiss behavior genetic studies because all of the findings are based on correlations since, for example, we have not really "seen" a parent gene influencing a child's behavior.

Retrospective Designs

If single-time measurement confounds cause and effect, why not designate at least two groups (with high and low problems, for example) based on a measure of children's current adaptation and search for assessments of the parents' behavior in the past? Measures of the past could come from children's reports, parents' reports, or earlier written records (e.g., child abuse records). For example, it has been found that harsh physical punishment occurs in the histories of aggressive antisocial children more often than it does in a group of children not classified as antisocial (Bates, Pettit, & Dodge, 1995). We are not raising the problem that retrospective data can be biased by faulty memory or inadequate record keeping (Baumrind, 1983). Even if the data were flawless, retrospective designs can never be used to establish causality because of an inherent problem with the logic of implication. If B implies A (antisocial outcomes imply earlier punitive parenting), it is not necessarily the case that A implies B. It could be that harsh parenting is related to a variety of outcomes, including aggression, depression, academic difficulties, schizophrenia, or successful adaptation.

Prospective Longitudinal Designs

To deal with the inference problems that occur when parents' and children's behaviors are assessed at the same time, or to avoid the problem of making "backward inferences," we can follow families prospectively over time, assessing parenting behavior at Time 1 (point A in Figure 5.1), and child outcomes later, at Time 2 (point E in Figure 5.1).

Parenting Behavior Predicts Child Outcomes

Some investigators claim that the problems of inferring direction of effects can be overcome with prospective longitudinal designs. For example, authoritative parenting when the child is age 3 predicts children's academic and social competence four and seven years later (Baumrind, 1991). In fact, this does not solve the problem of making causal or even directional inferences. Although the measurement of parenting precedes the measurement of children's adaptation, it

1. Concurrent
    e.g., parents' authoritativeness and children's academic and social
competence

2. Longitudinal

(a) Time 1 predicts Time 2
    e.g. parents' authoritativeness (A) at Time 1 predicts children's academic
and social competence (E) at Time 2

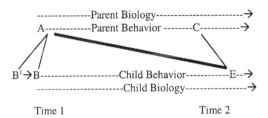

Time 1   Time 2

(b) Change in parents and change in children
    e.g. parents' increasing authoritativeness associated with children's
increasing academic and social competence

3. Randomized intervention design

Parents in intervention → change in parents →change in
                                                    child
No intervention   →less change in parents → less change
                                                    in child

FIG. 5.1.   Parent–child research designs.

is always possible that children's characteristics at B^1—at a point prior to Time 1—influenced the parents' behavior at A and/or played a role in shaping the child's developmental trajectory. It is also possible that biological factors rather than parenting behavior account for the correlations obtained over time.

Furthermore, the A–E correlation that appears to be longitudinal in nature may reflect nothing more than a series of concurrent correlations between parenting behavior and child competence at Time 1 (A–B in Figure 5.1) or Time 2 (C–E in Figure 5.1). That is, there may be a correlation between parental warmth and children's adaptation at age 3, and, because parents are relatively consistent over time, there may also be similar correlations at ages 4, 5, 6, 7, and 8. What looks like predictability over time from early parenting to later child behavior may reflect the result of cumulative interactions between parent and child over five years. In other words, longitudinal designs cannot rule out the possibility that child effects are actually driving the parent–child system.

One way to eliminate the possibility of child effects, using longitudinal designs, is to assess parents before the birth of their child and follow the families to see how their children fare (e.g., Belsky & Kelly, 1994; Cowan et al., 1985;

Cox, Owen, Lewis, & Henderson, 1989; Entwisle & Doering, 1981; Heinicke & Lampl, 1988). In fact, studies using this version of a longitudinal design find substantial predictability on the same measures of parents from mid-to late pregnancy through months and even years later in the life of the child. This design does reduce the possibility of direct effects of the child's behavior on the parents, but it does not rule out biological sources of the pre- to postbirth correlations.

Change in Parenting Behavior Predicts Change in Child Outcomes

In a hypothetical study, it might be found that when parents become more authoritative with their children over time, the children become more academically and socially competent in school. This finding makes the model of parent–child relationships more dynamic and demonstrates parallel shifts in parenting and child domains, but it does not rule out the possibility that a change in the child sets the stage for change in the parents' behavior.

Despite the fact that longitudinal studies cannot be used to establish cause and effect relationships, they have two main advantages over concurrent cross-sectional or retrospective designs. First, by providing data on the same individuals over time, longitudinal studies make it possible to go beyond an examination of differences in means to delineate individual differences in trajectories of development. Second, longitudinal designs allow us to identify statistically some risk and resilience indicators at an early point in a child's development that predict dysfunction and adaptation later on. This means that it is possible to identify children who are more likely to have difficulty in the future even if we cannot establish the causal mechanisms linking early and later measures.

Intervention Designs

The power of intervention designs is derived in large part from the possibility of random assignment of participants to experimental and control conditions. Without a control group, of course, we cannot tell whether intervention participants change more, less, or differently from those who had no intervention. And, without random assignment, it is possible that those who chose the intervention were different from those who did not in ways that affect the outcome. To take one illustrative example, Webster-Stratton (1984, 1992) found that when mothers of young aggressive children, randomly selected, participated in an intervention, the children became less aggressive and more prosocial than the children of parents who were randomly selected to serve as controls. Similar findings come from other carefully assessed intervention studies (cf. Miller & Prinz, 1990). These results provide strong support for the hypothesis that the interventions had a positive impact on children's outcomes. Nevertheless, these results do not *prove* that parents' behavior was the active ingredient affecting their children's behavior. As intervention researchers have begun to recognize, in order to support causal interpretations of intervention effects, it is not enough simply to show that children of parents in the intervention changed in a more positive direction than children whose parents were in the controls. It is also necessary to show that: the intervention affects the family mechanisms hypothesized by the intervenors to be the active ingredients of the intervention; and that when these mechanisms change, the child changes in a positive direction (*cf.* Wolchick et al., 1993).

Intervention research is not infallible with respect to inferring causality. Even with randomized designs, we never know whether the variables that we think we are manipulating are the ones responsible for producing the results. Even if the results demonstrate that it is possible to change parents' behaviors and that parents' changes are followed by improved adaptation in the children, we cannot conclude for certain that the parents' behavior caused the child's problems in the first place. It may be that genetic forces are responsible for the initial correlations or that the parents' behavior was maintaining the child's original behavior. What intervention findings do tell us in the examples we are discussing is whether parents' behavior *can* play a role in children's well-being or distress. In addition to the contribution that intervention studies may ultimately make toward improving the well-being of children, they help us to test conceptual models of the direction of effects from parent to child that are usually based solely on correlational data.

PARENTING BEHAVIOR AND CHILDREN'S ADAPTATION TO SCHOOL: CORRELATIONAL DATA FROM TWO STUDIES

To illustrate our central thesis about how intervention studies can help us to interpret the direction of effects in correlational data, we describe two overlapping longitudinal studies. The first, the Becoming a Family Project (Cowan & Cowan, 2000), followed 96 couples, 72 of whom were expecting a first child, from late pregnancy until the children had completed kindergarten. The couples were recruited in 1980 and 1981 from the practices of obstetrician-gynecologists in the larger San Francisco Bay Area and from newsletters in many of the 28 communities they came from. The expectant fathers in this study were approximately 30 years old, and the expectant mothers were approximately 28 when the study began. Fifteen percent of the sample was African-American, Asian-American, or Latino, and 85% was Euro-American. Family socioeconomic status spanned from working class to upper middle class.

Couples were assessed with interviews and questionnaires in late pregnancy and again when their first child was 6 and then 18 months old. Two further assessments, when the children were 3½ and 5½ in kindergarten included observations of mother and child, father and child, and the whole family as they worked and played together in our laboratory-playroom in three separate 40-minute sessions. During each part of the visit, the child was offered several difficult tasks to solve (puzzles or mazes) and several more playful tasks (storytelling and sand play), and the parents were asked to help the child "as they normally would at home."

School outcomes in kindergarten included academic achievement tests (Peabody Individual Achievement Test [PIAT], Markwardt, 1988) individually administered at the children's homes, and a behavior checklist (the Child Adaptive Behavior Inventory [CABI], Cowan & Cowan, 1995) adapted from Schaefer, Hunter & Edgerton (1987) and completed each child's classroom teacher. Teachers rated the children in their classes without knowing which child was in our study. This method allowed us to assess each study child's adaptation at school relative to the other children in his or her class (Cowan, Cowan, Schulz, & Heming, 1994). The checklist yielded scales indicative of externalizing (antisocial, hostile, oppositional) and internalizing (shy, withdrawn, anxious, depressed) behavior problems.

In the second study, the Schoolchildren and Their Families Project, we recruited 100 new families whose first child was about to enter kindergarten during the next academic year—from daycare centers and preschools throughout the San Francisco Bay Area and from public service announcements in local media. On entering this study, fathers' average age was 34 years and mothers' was 32, with almost exactly the same distribution of ethnicities as the parents in our first study. These families also ranged from working class to upper middle class. As in the first study, the families were assessed with interviews, questionnaires, and laboratory observations during the preschool year, and at the end of kindergarten when the children were 5½. In this study too, we followed families for six years, this time assessing parents and children again at the end of first and fourth grade, when the children were 6½ and 9½ years old. The observational assessments in the laboratory playroom were similar to those in the first study, and most of the questionnaires were identical. Once again, we assessed children's academic competence on the PIAT and an expanded (106-item) CABI completed by the study child's teacher for children in the class.

We have reported the detailed results of the Becoming a Family Project in a number of publications (e.g., Cowan & Cowan, 2000; Cowan et al., 1994), and the longitudinal results of the Schoolchildren and Their Families project are being prepared for publication now. The studies overlap, in that they both include extensive family data from the preschool period and a number of indices of children's adaptation to kindergarten. In Figure 5.2 we present a schematic version of those results in order to convey the general trends from both studies, without focusing on the specific magnitude of each correlational link. We examine the data in stages, showing how correlations between earlier parenting behavior and children's subsequent development (Model 1) are embedded in a matrix of relationships: marital (Model 2), three-generational (Model 3), and outside the family (Model 4).

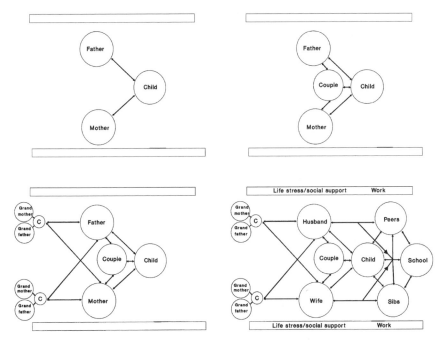

FIG. 5.2. Schematic models of family relationships and children's outcomes.

Parenting Behavior and Children's Outcomes

As many other investigators have shown, our results demonstrated (Model 1) that when mothers or fathers of preschoolers were warmer, more responsive, more structuring, and more encouraging of their child's autonomy—that is, more authoritative—their children were more likely to have higher academic achievement on tests and were less likely to be described by their teachers as having acting out, externalizing problems or shy, withdrawn, depressed, internalizing behaviors in kindergarten and first grade (Cohn, Cowan, Cowan, & Pearson, 1992; Cowan et al., 1994). Providing a counterweight to studies that focus primarily on mothers, our data reveal correlations as high or even higher between fathers' parenting behavior as we observed it and the children's later adaptation to school.

The Marital Context of Parenting Behavior

Recent studies make clear that in two-parent families, whether intact or divorced, parenting takes place within the context of the partners' relationship as a couple. Consistent with the results of other investigations (see Cummings & Davies, 1994), our findings showed (Model 2) that when there is more self-reported or observed tension and unresolved conflict in the marriage, mothers and fathers tended to be less warm, more harsh and structuring, and less likely to encourage their children's autonomy. In turn, the children of more conflicted couples were more likely to have lower achievement test scores and to be described by their teachers as more aggressive or more depressed (Cohn et al., 1992; Cowan et al., 1994).

As Cummings and Davies (1994) and Fincham (1998) and his colleagues have suggested (Fincham, Beach, Arias, & Brody, 1998), there are a number of ways the parents' marital quality can affect the children. A troubled marriage may have a direct impact on the child. The effect of the parents' marital conflict may be filtered through the child's interpretations of the parents' behavior (Ablow, 1994), or parents' marital distress may have indirect effects through its disruption of the quality of one or both parents' relationship with the child.

Transmission of Relationships across the Generations

Consistent with both family systems theory (e.g., Framo, 1992; Minuchin & Fishman, 1981) and attachment theory (Main, 1999), our results suggested that marital and parenting relationships are embedded in a three-generational context (Model 3). Troubled marital and parent–child relationships in the family of origin tend to be repeated in the families of procreation (Caspi & Elder, 1988). Although we did not observe parents interacting with their parents, we did assess the parents' working models of attachment using George's, Kaplan's, and Main's Adult Attachment Interview (AAI, see Hesse, 1999). This 90-minute interview asks interviewees to choose five adjectives to describe their relationships with their mother and with their father, to illustrate why they characterized each relationship that way, and to describe change over time in the quality of both of these attachment relationships. The narratives were coded as indicative of a secure perspective on attachment if the parents in our study described positive or negative relationships in a clear, convincing, and coherent manner and had attained some perspective on the difficulties in the relationships with their parents (the grandparents of the study children). The narratives were coded as indicative of an insecure perspective on attachment if the parents dismissed the importance of early attachment relationships, idealized them and provided no clear examples to support their characterizations, or if the coherence of their narratives was disrupted by preoccupying anger or high anxiety in talking about these early relationships.

Our two transition studies revealed very similar trends using the three-generational data (Cowan, Cohn, Cowan, & Pearson, 1996; Cowan, Bradburn, & Cowan, unpublished manuscript). Fathers coded as having an insecure perspective on attachment from the Adult Attachment Interview (AAI) tended to have higher marital conflict and showed less effective parenting when they worked with their children in our playroom laboratory. In turn, the children of fathers coded as having an insecure perspective on attachment were more likely to be described as aggressive, hostile, and antisocial (externalizing problems) by their kindergarten teachers than children whose fathers were coded as having a secure working model. Similarly, mothers coded as having an insecure perspective on attachment were in more troubled marriages and showed less authoritative parenting; in turn, their children, especially daughters, were more likely to be described as being shy, withdrawn, anxious, and depressed (internalizing problems) than children whose mothers were thought to have a secure perspective on attachment.

The "Full" Family-School Model

In Model 4, the picture is more complex. Consistent with results from many other investigators (e.g., Brody, Stoneman, Flor, & McCrary, 1994; Conger & Elder, 1994; McLoyd, 1990), data from both of our longitudinal studies showed that life stressors elevated the risk of family relationships being more negative, although greater support from parents' networks tended to decrease that risk. Statistical path models following the patterns of Models 3 and 4 (Cowan et al., 1994; Cowan et al., 1996) accounted for a large proportion of the variance in children's adaptation in kindergarten and first grade—from 40% to 70%. Combined data from each of the domains (life stress, social support, and relationship quality in parents' families of origin, marriage, and relationships with their child) predicted significantly greater amounts of variation in children's adaptation to school than did data taken from one domain at a time.

We find it noteworthy that family data obtained one or two years before the children entered kindergarten explained such a large proportion of the variance in their adaptation to the first two years of school. This finding seems all the more compelling because we know from other longitudinal studies that children tend to maintain their rank order of academic and social adaptation as they move through the trajectory of their school careers (Alexander & Entwisle, 1988). In other words, when families had compromised functioning in the preschool period, even in the relatively low-risk families in these two samples, their children were at risk for academic and social difficulties in kindergarten and first grade. We know that these early problems have implications for students' trajectories over the course of their elementary and secondary school careers.

These are "statistical facts." The next question we address has to with the implications of these correlational models for family intervention. Model 1 suggests but does not prove that if we help parents develop more effective parenting strategies, their children are more likely to be make successful academic and emotional adjustments to school. Model 2 suggests but does not prove that if we can help parents develop more effective strategies for dealing with each other, their parenting is more likely to improve and their children are more likely to start their school careers at a more optimal point. Is it the case that the marital relationship has a directional effect on parenting, or are the marital and parenting systems mutually regulating? We can attempt to answer these questions with intervention studies that seek to change the quality of the parents' relationships—as couples or with their children.

A COUPLES GROUP PREVENTIVE INTERVENTION

Rationale and Design

Our ideas about family-based intervention begin with the considerable body of evidence showing that strain in marital or parent–child relationships compromises the effectiveness of men and women as partners and as parents, and places their marriages and their children's development at risk (Erel & Burman, 1995; Cummings & Davies, 1994; Dadds, Schwartz & Sanders, 1987; Katz & Gottman, 1994). In an earlier study we created groups for couples making the transition to parenthood for the first time, meeting weekly for six months, from late pregnancy into the postpartum period (Cowan et al., 1985). Despite the fact that these groups, led by trained mental health professionals, had significant effects on the partners' marriage over the first three years of parenthood, by the time the children entered school six years later, there were no direct effects of intervening with the parents on the children's adaptation to school. With family data from the preschool period through the children's entrance to elementary school, we found that the quality of the parents' marriage and parenting style when the children were preschoolers was correlated with the children's academic achievement levels and problem behaviors in kindergarten two years later. These correlational findings suggest that if working with parents on challenging marital and parenting problems prior to their children's transition to school encouraged positive shifts in the parents, we might see a reflection of those shifts in their children's subsequent adaptation to school. And so we recruited a new set of 100 couples whose first child was four years old and ready to make the transition to kindergarten in the early 1990s. We offered the opportunity to participate in a couples group with mental health professionals as leaders to a randomly chosen two thirds of the couples entering the study.

Our rationale for offering an intervention to couples who are apparently well-functioning and have not sought help for family problems was based on findings from both of our longitudinal studies about strain in the parents. We found more signs of distress in these apparently low-risk families than the literature would have predicted. Despite their educational level, economic status, and minimal use of the mental health system, substantial and almost identical percentages of parents in both the Becoming a Family and Schoolchildren and Their Families studies reported troubling risk indicators in one or several aspects of their lives. For example, 25% of the fathers and mothers had scores above the cut-off for depression on the Center for Epidemiological Studies in Depression scale (CES-D, Radloff, 1977). At some points in both studies, almost 50% of the partners scored in the marital distress range on the short Marital Adjustment Test (MAT, Locke & Wallace, 1959), indicative of the level of marital distress in couples who seek therapy for serious marital problems. A prevention perspective argues that it is better to intervene early, before difficulties reach an overtly distressing level than to wait until the individuals and family relationships have become disorganized by high levels of stress or distress.

The Couples Groups

One staff couple and four couples with a child about to enter kindergarten met every week for 16 weeks, for a total of 32 hours in all. Over time, parents and leaders used a semistructured group format to focus on five aspects of life that research suggests are associated with parents' or children's adaptation. We discussed parents' sense of self, their experience of relationships with one another, with their parents, and with their children, and the life stressors and social support that they experienced in their lives. There was also an open-ended part of each evening during which parents were free to raise any question or problem about an individual, marital, parenting, or family matter.

We offered a group intervention for couples so that both men and women could explore their experiences along with other couples coping with similar circumstances. We found that this context (1) minimized the sense that men and women were failing, (2) maximized the chance that supportive and knowledgeable professionals could encourage partners to make small shifts to address the common stresses of marriage and early parenting, and (3) afforded an opportunity to refer couples for more concentrated help if their difficulties were severe (Cowan & Cowan, 1997, 2000). Including fathers in the intervention had the obvious advantage of engaging men in discussions of key family issues, allowing both spouses' points of view to be heard, and having both partners available for work on parenting and marital issues.

The coleaders of the couples groups were male–female pairs of psychologists, social workers, or marriage and family counselors with whom we met regularly to monitor the issues and problems for either participant or staff couples. Over time, the staff helped parents in the groups focus on their own particular ideas and experiences. In regular weekly discussions over many months, participants and leaders discussed the aspects of life that our preintervention questionnaires focused on. In some groups, it became apparent that there were potential links among these parts of their lives: Parents' conflict as a couple might be affecting their relationships with their child, and their experiences of being parented by their parents might be coloring their ideas, practices, and feelings about parenting their own children. Even though these links may sound obvious to the reader, we found that surprisingly few couples with young children make these connections on their own. It was our belief that if we were able to help parents make these parts of their lives more conscious, they would be more likely to try to modify their painful or destructive relationship patterns.

The staff leaders worked to make the groups a psychologically safe and supportive environment for a group of men and women at the same family life stage so that we could all learn more about what goes on in families. The group leaders tried to help partners (1) listen to one another more sympathetically, (2) be more tolerant of differences between them, (3) regulate their upset and anger more effectively, and (4) begin to experiment with small shifts that might feel more satisfying to both partners. The leaders also encouraged partners to explore how their experiences in their families of origin might be playing a role in their reactions to one another and their children, particularly when they were upset and feeling needy or vulnerable, and become conscious of their expectations for their children's development, to maximize the chance that they would be warm and responsive while providing appropriate amounts of structure and limit setting when their children were having difficulty.

Some couples in each group were willing to bring fresh problems for us to consider. Even couples who were not divulging their own personal difficulties reported that they got ideas from others in the group. What was unusual in these interventions was encouraging men and women in apparently low-risk families to work on unresolved issues together when they were not in the middle of a fight, in a structure that provided for returning to the group every week to evaluate the success of their experiments at making small changes. The group setting became a safe place for spouses to begin some of these discussions. Our aim was not to tell couples how to do things but to help them decide what made sense for them, given their culture, financial resources, and particularly the emotional tone they were striving for in their families.

Two Different Intervention Emphases

Based on our own and others' results showing the importance of both marital and parent–child relationship quality, we created two variations of our couples group intervention. The more structured part of each evening was similar in all groups, but the emphasis of the leaders during the open-ended topics was different in the two sets of groups. We asked the staff couples in half of the groups to place more emphasis on marital issues and to focus more on the parents' relationships with their children in the other half of the groups—during the discussion of problems that the parents brought. This design allowed us to ask whether helping parents improve their relationship as couples also affected the quality of their parenting. Similarly, if we were successful at helping partners become more effective as parents, would we see or would they experience positive shifts in their relationship as a couple?

Intervention Effects

When we compared parents with and without any couples group intervention, using path models similar to those we described above, we found evidence of positive effects of both variations of the couples group intervention on the parents, and subsequently on their children's adaptation to school. School outcomes included teachers' descriptions of internalizing or externalizing behavior (Child Adaptive Behavior Inventory, Cowan et al., 1995), the child's performance on the Peabody Individual Achievement Test (Markwardt, 1988), and the child's view of his or her adaptation to school as described by the Berkeley Puppet Interview (Ablow & Measelle, 1994).

Groups with an Emphasis on Parenting

Parents from the groups that emphasized parenting issues during the open-ended discussions shifted in a positive direction as they worked with their children on difficult tasks one year after the intervention: The fathers were warmer and more responsive with their children, and the mothers were more helpful at structuring difficult tasks for their children than they had been the year before the children entered kindergarten. Although there were effects of these groups on parenting issues, the quality of marital interaction between those parents was not significantly different from that of couples with no group intervention. Nevertheless, there were positive effects on the children. In comparison with the Consultation controls, the children of parents in the groups emphasizing parent–child relationships tended to have a more positive view of their own adaptation to kindergarten and showed a significantly greater decline, according to teacher ratings, in shy/withdrawn/depressed behavior from kindergarten to first grade.

Groups with an Emphasis on Marriage

The parents from the groups in which the leaders emphasized marital issues during the open-ended discussions showed "marital effects"; the parents showed less conflict and hostility as a couple in front of their children one year after the group ended than they had the year before. One bonus here was that when parents in the maritally focused groups were rated by trained observers[1] as more effective and cooperative as couples, they also tended to be rated by another set of observers as more authoritative with their children. They provided more responsive, warm, and structuring assistance when their children were having difficulty than parents with no intervention did with their children. Not surprisingly, the children of these parents had significantly higher academic achievement test

---

[1]Separate coders rated the videotaped marital and parent–child interaction and each team was blind to any other data about the families.

scores in kindergarten and were perceived by teachers as showing less aggressive, acting out behavior than first grade children in the Consultation control groups.

The Magnitude of Intervention Effects

We used latent variable path models to examine the links among marital change, parenting change, intervention effects, and children's adaptation to school (Falk & Miller, 1994). When intervention parents' marital or parent–child relationships shifted in positive ways, their children adjusted better to the challenges of kindergarten: They had higher academic achievement scores and described themselves more positively in terms of academic and social competence on the puppet interview. Furthermore, compared with controls, children of parents in the group interventions showed a greater reduction in aggressive externalizing behavior and shy, withdrawn, depressed, internalizing behavior over the year from kindergarten to first grade.

To get a sense of the size of the intervention effects, we ran the path models with and without the intervention data in the model (see Table 5.1). When the children completed kindergarten, the statistical model predicting academic achievement with both family and intervention data from the year before predicted 40% of the children's scores. Once the intervention data were removed, the model predicted only 28% of their achievement scores—a significant difference of 12%. The model predicting children's self-reports of adaptation that included intervention effects accounted for 30% of the variance; without the intervention effects, it accounted for only 10%. Similarly, when the children were at the end of first grade, the model predicting internalizing behaviors with earlier family and intervention data predicted 36% of the children's internalizing behaviors, but with the intervention data removed the model predicted only 24% of the outcome—a significant difference of 12%. On our fourth outcome, externalizing behavior, the model with family and intervention data predicted 54% of the children's acting out, aggressive behavior, but the model with the intervention data removed explained only 23% of the variation in externalizing behavior—a significant difference of 31%. More traditional multiple regression analyses of children's outcomes confirmed the fact that children whose parents were in one of the couples groups showed higher levels of academic achievement, more positive self-descriptions, and fewer behavior problems in the early years of elementary school.

A Comparison of the Marital and Parenting Interventions

We have shown that the interventions emphasizing the parents' relationships as couples or with their children had some significant effects when intervention families were compared with controls. We also found that despite the fact that the groups emphasizing parenting produced significantly stronger effects on

TABLE 5.1
PLS MODELS: CHILD SEX, MARITAL QUALITY, PARENTING QUALITY, INTERVENTIONS, AND CHILDREN'S OUTCOMES

	Externalizing			Internalizing			Academic achievement			Child's peer problems		
	R^2	F	Fit	R^2	F	Fit	R^2	F	Fit	R^2	F	Fit
Model												
Kg. with int.	.23	5.8**	.08	.13			.40	3.7**	.08	.28	2.22*	.08
Kg. w/o int.	.13	1.9*	.08	.13			.28	2.8*	.08	.07		
Kg. ITT	.15	6.4***	.09	.11			.38			.09		
F (diff.) w–w/o	17.2***			3.9*			5.0**			6.5**		
F (diff.) ITT	34.4***			5.1*			8.1**			ns		
Gr. 1 with int.	.54	5.8**	.08	.36	2.8**	.08	.80	20.0***	.08	.38	3.0**	.08
Gr. 1 w/o int.	.23	1.9*	.08	.24	2.0*	.10	.79	24.3***	.08	.45	4.0***	.08
Gr. 1 ITT	.54	6.4***	.09	.31	3.1**	.09	.80	28.1***	.08	.45	5.6***	.08
F (diff.) w–w/o							ns			ns		
F (diff.) ITT							ns			ns		

*$p < .05$
**$p < .01$
***$p < .001$

91

parenting behavior than did the groups with a marital emphasis, the overall impact of the interventions gave a slight edge to the parents in the maritally focused groups. By contrast, the differential impact of the interventions on the children depended on the outcome measured. The marital groups had significantly stronger effects on academic achievement and externalizing, whereas the parenting groups had marginally stronger effects on the children's reports of their adaptation to kindergarten, and significantly stronger effects on the teachers' reports of the children's internalizing in first grade.

Longer-Term Intervention Effects

We recently completed the follow-up of the same families when the children had finished fourth grade and were 9½ to 10 years old—six years after the intervention with their parents. These analyses revealed that the positive effects of the couples group intervention had been maintained from first grade for the academic, social, and behavioral problem outcomes. That is, the children of parents who shifted toward more effective marital or parent–child interactions following our four-month-long preschool intervention continued to show better adjustment at age 10 than their counterparts whose parents had had no early intervention.

IMPLICATIONS OF INTERVENTION RESULTS FOR UNDERSTANDING THE IMPACT OF PARENTS ON CHILDREN

The intervention data we have presented from the transition to school study speak to the key questions addressed by this volume, namely, whether parents' behavior has measurable effects on their children's development in contexts outside the home. First, we can see that the results of a random assignment, experimental intervention revealed measurable shifts in the quality of most parents' marital and/or parenting relationships. Second, intervention parents' shifts in marital or parenting quality were followed by higher levels of adaptation to kindergarten and improved adaptation between kindergarten and first grade by their children, depending on the outcome measure. It is important to note that the measures of child outcome were obtained one, two, and six years after the intervention with their parents had ended, and that the data were gathered in classroom contexts quite different from those used for gathering data from the parents. These findings suggest that something about parents meeting and talking regularly with other parents and mental health professionals during this family transition resulted in observable marital and/or parenting changes in a positive direction, and that parents' positive shifts were followed by greater positive shifts in their children when change in those families was compared to change in the the no-intervention families. Even when parents without intervention shifted in a positive direction, which some did, those shifts were not systematically related to their children's increasingly successful school adaptation.

The intervention results are helpful in clarifying another aspect of the models of the family system presented in Figure 5.2. The parenting and marital behavior was measured on the same day, though the former was rated from sessions with the child and each individual parent, and the latter was rated from sessions with the whole family present. When we plotted the results and diagrammed the path models, however, we explicitly gave the quality of the parents' marriage a role as an antecedent to parenting behavior by placing it on the left, with arrows to parenting on the right. It could be claimed either that parenting qualities affected the way the parents related as a couple or that the two domains influenced each other mutually. The data on the variations of the intervention suggest that significant reductions in marital conflict in parents from the maritally focused intervention were followed by positive shifts in their parenting quality, but shifts toward a more effective parenting style for couples in the parenting-focused intervention were not followed by reductions in marital conflict.

The design of the study does not allow us to make data-based inferences concerning why children of parents in the marital groups showed higher academic achievement and fewer externalizing behavior problems, while the parenting groups appeared to be more effective in helping children to avoid social rejection and depression, and in fostering a more positive view of their self-competence. It is possible that marital conflict disequilibrates children, provides an inadequate model of problem solving with peers, and distracts children from concentrating on new things, thereby interfering with their ability to learn new material at school. By contrast, the parenting intervention, focusing on children and their inner states, may have helped parents be more sensitive to internalizing issues and to issues relating to self-esteem. These speculations must be tested in future studies.

The decision to provide two kinds of couples groups with different emphases was based on our goal of trying to identify the separate roles of marital and parent–child relationships in affecting the development of the child. The fact that the marital groups had somewhat stronger positive effects on parents does not lead us to conclude that family-based preventive interventions like ours should focus only on the parents' marriage. It is clear from both the correlational and intervention results that if parents can be helped to make positive changes in either if these key family domains their children are likely to benefit.

SUMMARY AND CONCLUSIONS

We have argued that correlations between parents' behavior and children's behavior do not establish causality or direction of effects, even when the studies are longitudinal and measure parents' behavior at Time 1 and children's behavior at

Time 2. Nevertheless, correlations provide important data about family risks that can be used in planning preventive interventions. From our own longitudinal studies, we presented risk models to illustrate that the quality of parents' relationships—as couples and with their children—was associated with how their children adapted academically and in terms of problem behavior between the ages of four and ten.

We then described the schoolchildren and their families study in which couples were randomly assigned to couples groups with an emphasis on either marital or parent–child relationships. These results provided support for the hypothesis that changes in the marital relationship affect the quality of parenting more than changes in parenting quality affect the marital atmosphere. They also provided support for the hypothesis that parents have a direct impact on their children's academic achievement and behavior problems at school.

The results do not prove that parenting behavior is the sole explanation of children's academic competence or problem behavior. Consistent with the correlational data presented by Cummings in this volume, we have shown that parenting behavior is only one of the key family relationship ingredients that affect the child. It is not only what parents do with or to the child that matters, but how the parents behave with each other.

This study does suggest that it is possible to produce change in children's adaptation through helping their parents shift to more positive interactions as a couple or with their children. Since the genetics of mothers, fathers, and children are held constant in these studies, before and after the intervention, we cannot attribute the intervention children's advantage in academic achievement or ability to get along with teachers and peers to genetic effects. The intervention findings, taken together with the correlational models showing continuity across generations and between relationships inside and outside the nuclear family, suggest that arguments about whether parents have an effect on their children are too limited in scope. Given that parents and children exist in a complex network of biological, psychological, and social connectedness, our task is to learn more about how these complex systems work together to affect children's development and adaptation.

ACKNOWLEDGMENTS

The studies and results described here were supported by NIMH grant RO1-31109 to the authors. The chapter is based on a paper given at a conference cosponsored by the National Institute of Child Health and Human Development and the Robert Wood Johnson Foundation held in August 1999. Parenting and the Child's World: Multiple Influences on Intellectual and Social-Emotional Development. Cochairs: John Borkowski and Sharon Landesman Ramey; conference coordinator: Marie Bristol-Power.

REFERENCES

Ablow, J. (1994). *Young children's perceptions and processing of interparental conflict: Predicting behavioral adjustment.* Unpublished master's thesis, University of California, Berkeley.

Alexander, K. L., & Entwisle, D. (1988). Achievement in the first 2 years of school: Patterns and processes. *Monographs of the Society for Research in Child Development, 53,* (2, Serial No. 218),

Asher, S., & Coie, J. D. (Eds.) (1990). *Peer rejection in childhood.* Cambridge, UK: Cambridge University Press.

Bates, J. E., Pettit, G. S., & Dodge, K. A. (1995). Family and child factors in stability and change in children's aggressiveness in elementary school. In J. McCord (Ed.), *Coercion and punishment in long-term perspectives* (pp. 124–138). New York: Cambridge University Press.

Bateson, G., Jackson, D. D., Haley, J., & Weakland, J. (1956). Toward a theory of schizophrenia. *Behavioral Science, 1,* 251–264.

Baumrind, D. (1983). Specious causal attributions in the social sciences: The reformulated stepping-stone theory of heroin use as exemplar. *Journal of Personality and Social Psychology, 45,* 1289–1298.

Baumrind, D. (1991). Effective parenting during the early adolescent transition. In P. A. Cowan & M. E. Hetherington (Eds.), *Family transitions: Advances in family research* (Vol. 2, pp. 111–164). Hillsdale, NJ: Lawrence Erlbaum Associates.

Belsky, J., & Kelly, J. (1994). *Transition to parenthood.* New York: Delacorte Press.

Belsky, J., & Pensky, E. (1988). Marital change across the transition to parenthood. *Marriage and Family Review, 12,* 133–156.

Brody, G. H., Stoneman, Z., Flor, D., & McCrary, C. (1994). Financial resources, parent psychological functioning, parent co-caregiving, and early adolescent competence in rural two-parent African-American families. *Child Development, 65,* 590–605.

Caplan, G. (1964). *Principles of preventive psychiatry.* New York: Basic Books.

Caspi, A., & Elder, G. H., Jr. (1988). Emergent family patterns: The intergenerational construction of poroblem behavior and relationships. In R. A. Hinde & J. Stevenson-Hinde (Eds.), *Relationships within families: Mutual influences* (pp. 218–240). Oxford, UK: Clarendon Press.

Cohn, D.N.A., Cowan, P. A., Cowan, C. P., & Pearson, J. (1992). Mothers' and fathers' working models of childhood attachment relationships, parenting styles, and child behavior. *Development and Psychopathology, 4,* 417–431.

Conger, R. D., & Elder, G. H., Jr. (Eds.). (1994). *Families in troubled times: Adapting to change in rural America.* New York: Aldine de Gruyter.

Cowan, P. A., Cohn, D. A., Cowan, C. P., & Pearson, J. L. (1996). Parents' attachment histories and children's internalizing and externalizing behavior: Exploring family systems models of linkage. *Journal of Consulting and Clinical Psychology, 64,* 53–63.

Cowan, C. P., & Cowan, P. A. (1997). In S. Dreman (Ed.), *The family on the threshhold of the 21st century* (pp. 17–48). Hillsdale, NJ: Lawrence Erlbaum Associates.

Cowan, C. P., & Cowan, P. A. (2000). *When partners become parents: The big life change for couples.* Mahwah, NJ: Lawrence Erlbaum Associates.

Cowan, C. P., Cowan, P. A., & Heming, G. (1988, November). *Adult children of alcoholics: What happens when they form new families?* Paper presented to the National Council on Family Relations, Philadelphia, PA.

Cowan, C. P., Cowan, P. A., Heming, G., Garrett, E. T., Coysh, W. S., Curtis-Boles, H., & Boles, A. J. (1985). Transitions to parenthood: His, hers, and theirs [Special Issue]. *Journal of Family Issues, 6,* 451–481.

Cowan, P. A., Cowan, C. P., Heming, T., & N. Miller. (1995). *The child adaptive behavior inventory [CABI].* Unpublished manual, Institute of Human Development, University of California, Berkeley.

Cowan, P. A., Cowan, C. P., Schulz M., & Heming, G. (1994). Prebirth to preschool family factors predicting children's adaptation to kindergarten. In R. Parke & S. Kellam (Eds.), *Exploring family relationships with other social contexts: Advances in family research* (Vol. 4, pp. 75–114). Hillsdale, NJ: Lawrence Erlbaum Associates.

Cox, M. J., Owen, M. T., Lewis, J. M., & Henderson, V. K. (1989). Marriage, adult adjustment, and early parenting. *Child Development, 60,* 1015–1024.

Cummings, E. M., & Davies, P. T. (1994). *Children and marital conflict: The impact of family dispute and resolution.* New York: Guilford Press.

Dadds, M. R., Schwartz, S., & Sanders, M. R. (1987). Marital discord and treatment outcome in behavioral treatment of child conduct disorders. *Journal of Consulting and Clinical Psychology, 55,* 396–403.

Damon, W. (Ed.). (1997). *Handbook of child psychology* (5th ed.). New York: John Wiley and Sons.

Entwisle, D. R., & Doering, S. G. (1981). *The first birth, a family turning point.* Baltimore: Johns Hopkins University Press.

Falk, R. F., & Miller, N. B. (1992) *A Primer for soft modeling.* Akron, O: U. of Akron Press.

Fincham, F. D. (1998). Child development and marital relations. *Child Development, 69,* 481–493.

Fincham, F. D., Beach, S. R. H., Arias, I., & Brody, G. H. (1998). Children's attributions in the family: The Children's Relationship Attribution Measure. *Journal of Family Psychology, 12,* 481–493.

Framo, J. L. (1992). *Family-of-origin therapy: An intergenerational approach.* New York: Brunner/Mazel.

Freud, S. (1938). *The basic writings of Sigmund Freud* (A. A. Brill, Trans.). New York: Modern Library.

Harris, J. R. (1995). Where is the child's environment? a group socialization theory of development. *Psychological Review, 102,* 485–489.

Harris, J. R. (1998). *The nurture assumption: Why children turn out the way they do.* New York: Free Press.

Heinicke, C. M., & Lampl, E. (1988). Pre- and post-birth antecedents of 3- and 4-year-old attention, IQ, verbal expressiveness, task orientation, and capacity for relationships. *Infant Behavior and Development, 11* (4), 381–410.

Hesse, E. (1999). The Adult Attachment Interview: Historical and current perspectives. In J. Cassidy & P. Shaver (Eds.), *Handbook of attachment: Theory, research, and clinical applications* (pp. 395–433). New York: Guilford Press.

Katz, L. F., & Gottman, J. M. (1994). Patterns of marital interaction and children's emotional development. In R. Parke & S. Kellam (Eds.), *Exploring family relationships with other social contexts: Advances in family research* (pp. 49–74). Hillsdale, NJ: Lawrence Erlbaum Associates.

Main, M. (1999). Epilogue. Attachment theory: Eighteen points with suggestions for future studies. In J. Cassidy & P. Shaver (Eds.), *Handbook of attachment: Theory, research, and clinical applications* (pp. 845–888). New York: Guilford Press.

Main, M., Kaplan, N., & Cassidy, J. (1985). Security in infancy, childhood, and adulthood: A move to the level of representation. In I. Bretherton & E. Waters (Eds.), *Growing points of attachment theory and research. Monographs of the Society for Research in Child Development, 50* (209), 66–106.

McLoyd, V. C. (1990). The impact of economic hardship on Black families and children: Psychological distress, parenting, and socioemotional development. *Child Development, 61,* 311–346.

Locke, H. J., & Wallace, K. M. (1959). Short marital-adjustment and prediction tests: Their reliability and validity. *Marriage and Family Living, 21,* 251–255.

Miller, G. E., & Prinz, R. J. (1990). Enhancement of social learning family interventions for childhood conduct disorder. *Psychology Bulletin, 108* (2), 291–307.

Minuchin, S., & Fishman, H. C. (1981). *Family therapy techniques.* Cambridge, MA: Harvard University Press.

Perry, K. E., & Weinstein, R. S. (1998). The social context of early schooling and children's school adjustment. *Educational Psychologist, 33,* 177–194.

Plomin, R. (1994). *Genetics and experience: The interplay between nature and nurture.* Thousand Oaks, CA: Sage Publications.

Radloff, L. S. (1977). The Ces-D Scale: A Self-Report Depression Scale for Research in the General Population. *Applied Psychological Measurement, 1,* 385–401.

Satir, V. (1972). *Peoplemaking.* Palo Alto, CA: Science and Behavior Books.

Schaefer, E. S., Hunter, W. M., & Edgerton, M. (1987). Maternal prenatal, infancy and concurrent predictors of maternal reports of child psychopathology. *Psychiatry, 50* (4), 320–331.

Seifer, R., & Schiller, M. (1995). The role of parenting sensitivity, infant temperament, and dyadic interaction in attachment theory and assessment. *Monographs of the Society for Research in Child Development, 60* (2–3), 146–174.

Skinner, B. F. (1938). *The behavior of organisms: An experimental analysis.* New York: Appleton-Century.

Watson, J. B. (1928). *Psychological care of infant and child.* London: Allen & Unwin.

Webster-Stratton, C. (1984). Randomized trial of two parent-training programs for families with conduct-disordered children. *Journal of Consulting and Clinical Psychology, 52,* (4), 666–678.

Webster-Stratton, C. (1992). Individually administered videotape parent training: "Who benefits?" *Cognitive therapy and research, 16* (1), 31–35.

Wolchick, S. A., West, S. G., Westover, D., Sandler, I. N., Martin, A., Lustig, J., Tein, J.-Y., & Fisher, J. (1993). The children of divorce parenting intervention: Outcome evaluation of an empirically based program. *American Journal of Community Psychology, 21,* 293–330.

6

Parenting and Family Influences When Children Are in Child Care: Results from the NICHD Study of Early Child Care
NICHD Early Child Care Research Network

In 1989 the National Institute of Child Health and Human Development (NICHD) initiated a multisite prospective study of the effects of early child care on the development of children. The study sought to address fundamental scientific and social policy questions stimulated by the large numbers of very young children receiving care on a routine basis by someone other than their

[1]This study is directed by a Steering Committee and supported by the NICHD through a cooperative agreement (U10) that calls for scientific collaboration between the grantees and the NICHD staff. The participating investigators are listed in alphabetical order with their institutional affiliations designated by number: Mark Appelbaum (18); Dee Ann Batten (18); Jay Belsky (3); Cathryn Booth (16); Robert Bradley (6); Celia Brownell (12); Margaret Burchinal (11); Bettye Caldwell (7); Susan Campbell (12); Alison Clarke-Stewart (8); Martha Cox (11); Sarah L. Friedman (1); Kathryn Hirsh-Pasek (5); Aletha Huston (13); Bonnie Knoke (4); Nancy Marshall (19); Kathleen McCartney (10); Marion O'Brien (9); Margaret Tresch Owen (14); Deborah Phillips (2); Robert Pianta (15); Susan Spieker (16); Deborah Lowe Vandell (17); and Marsha Weinraub (5). The institutional affiliations, in alphabetical order, are the National Institute of Child Health and Human Development (1); National Research Council (2); Pennsylvania State University (3); Research Triangle Institute (4); Temple University (5); University of Arkansas at Little Rock (6); University of Arkansas for Medical Sciences (7); University of California, Irvine (8); University of Kansas (9); University of New Hampshire (10); University of North Carolina, Chapel Hill (11); University of Pittsburgh (12); University of Texas, Austin (13); University of Texas, Dallas (14); University of Virginia (15); University of Washington (16); University of Wisconsin, Madison (17); Vanderbilt University (18); and Wellesley College (19).

Address correspondence to: NICHD Early Child Care Research Network, CRMC, NICHD, 6100 Executive Blvd., 4B05, Rockville, MD 20852.

mothers. Those numbers have shown a steady increase in the past two decades, due primarily to the increase in employment among mothers of young children resulting from both economic conditions and women's changing role in the family and society (Danziger & Gottschalk, 1986; McCartney & Phillips, 1988; Silverstein, 1991). In 1975, 39% of mothers with children less than 6 years of age worked outside the home; currently, 64% of mothers with young children are employed (U.S. Bureau of Labor Statistics, 1997). In 1994, 45% of children in the United States less than one year of age experienced regular nonmaternal care. This figure grew to 54% of children 2 years old and 68% for children 3 years old (National Center for Education Statistics, 1995).

With growing numbers of young children with early nonmaternal and nonparental care experience, are family and parenting influences in children's lives changing too? Many of the prevailing questions and concerns about the effects of early child-care experience on young children's development have focused on the view that the role of the family in young children's lives will be diminished when children spend considerable time in the care of persons other than their parents in their early years. By its design the NICHD study explicitly addresses the family's influence on the development of children who experience child care.

The NICHD Study of Early Child Care was designed as a comprehensive study of two rearing environments—the child-care setting and the family. In its first phase, the study followed the development of a diverse cohort of 1,364 children from across the United States throughout their infancy and preschool years. The children were studied through their first grade year in school in the study's second phase, and we are now following their development in middle childhood in a third phase of the study.

The study has been conducted within the framework of an ecological model of human development and with a holistic view of the developing child. Its fundamental goal has been to assess the development of children in the context of children's day-to-day experiences. In this sense the study has been conducted from a child and family perspective, which differs in many ways from other studies of child care that have focused, first, on the child-care environment, and only secondarily on the individual children who experience the particular child-care settings sampled and studied. As a result, this is much more than a study of child care; it is a study of the role of experience in early development. In framing the focus on children studied prospectively, we gathered extensive information about the varied nature of children's experiences throughout early childhood, in their families and within the child-care settings they experienced. The child-care environment and family environment of the children have been measured repeatedly at the immediate or proximate level of children's experiences and at more distal or indirect levels of experience.

These perspectives provide an examination of parenting and family influences for children within the context of their child-care experiences. The interdependence of children's home environment, child-care environment, and child characteristics is widely acknowledged in the more recent research on child care (Hayes, Palmer, & Zaslow, 1990), and it frames the approach taken in the NICHD study. Thus, we have addressed questions of parent and family influences on young children's development, taking into account their early child-care experiences.

As a natural history study of children's development initiated shortly after their birth, the study's results provide the opportunity to examine family and parenting influences within a large and diverse cohort of children. The study's findings to date address three major questions pertaining to parenting and family influences on children's development:

1. What are the relations between family characteristics and child-care experiences of young children? The use of child care is one of many decisions that parents make about the care of their children in the early years. In this sense, parental choices about the amount and nature of child-care experiences for their children are an important component of parental influence in infancy and preschool. We describe the early child-care experiences received by this large cohort of children and how parent characteristics relate to the amount and nature of child care the children experienced.
2. How are family characteristics and parenting qualities related to children's social, emotional, cognitive, and language development in the first three years after taking into account their child-care experiences?
3. How do family and parenting influences differ for children who predominantly experience maternal care compared to those who experience extensive nonmaternal care?

The study has considered how experiences in child care may modify the influence of family experiences. Primary among such questions has been whether family and parenting influences are weaker or different for children with extensive child-care experience in the early years. Findings from the NICHD Study of Early Child Care will be reviewed in this chapter as they pertain to these questions about parent and family influences.

Evidence from several studies (Egeland & Heister, 1995; Jaeger and Weinraub, 1990; Oppenheim, Sagi, & Lamb, 1988) suggest that nonparental care experience in the early years might attenuate the influence of families and, particularly, the influence of parent–child relationships on children's development. Weinraub, Jaeger, and Hoffman (1988) argued that subtle differences in developmental processes for children with varying amounts of child-care experience might indicate the need to conceptualize maternal employment and child care "as altering not just the *levels* of important . . . variables . . . but their *dynamic relationships* as well" (p. 376).

Howes (1990) provided support for this thesis. She found that parents' management of children's behaviors was a consistently stronger predictor of cognitive and social development of preschool and kindergarten children who did not experience child care in their infancy than for children who experienced infant child care. Similarly, Dunham and Dunham (1992) found that maternal verbal behavior when children were 13 months of age was predictive of children's vocabulary for children who were in exclusive maternal care but not for children in extensive child care. However, in a recent and relatively large sample ($N = 150$), Clarke-Stewart, Gruber, and Fitzgerald (1994) found that family circumstances, as well as specific maternal attributes, attitudes, and behaviors influenced the development of children who were in child care. Results linked family economic resources, maternal education, higher-quality home environments, and sensitive and cognitively stimulating parenting to better psychological outcomes for children with child-care experience initiated in infancy. These findings are similar to many others pertaining to family influences for children who are not in child care or whose child-care experiences are unknown (e.g., Bornstein & Tamis Lemonda, 1989; Friedman & Cocking, 1986; Hart & Risley, 1995; Wachs & Chan, 1986).

Evidence from the NICHD Study of Early Child Care similarly attests to the pervasive influence of families and parenting on the development of young children with early child-care experience. Developmental associations with family and parenting experiences have been found across a wide range of functioning in both the social and cognitive domains. These findings are reviewed in the present chapter and implications are drawn for our understanding of parenting and family influences.

Participants

The study participants come from diverse regions of the United States in urban, suburban, and rural areas. Participants were recruited from 24 designated hospitals at 10 data collection sites. The sites are located in Charlottesville, Virginia; Irvine, California; Lawrence, Kansas; Little Rock, Arkansas; Madison, Wisconsin; Morganton, North Carolina; Philadelphia, Pennsylvania; Pittsburgh, Pennsylvania; Seattle, Washington; and Wellesley, Massachusetts. A total of 1,364 families with healthy newborns were enrolled in the study when the infants were 1 month of age. By 36 months of age 1,216 remained in the study (89% of those originally enrolled). Dyads were eligible for the study if the mother was over 18 and spoke English; the infant was not born with serious medical complications; the mother had no known or acknowledged substance abuse; the mother lived within an hour's distance from the lab site; and the family did not plan to move from the area within three years.

The enrolled families included mothers who planned to work full-time (53%), part time (23%), and not at all during the child's first year (24%). Families came from a wide range of socioeconomic and sociocultural backgrounds (31% low-income families; 24% ethnic minority children; 11% mothers who did not complete high school; 14% single mothers; 16% with extended or augmented family households).

Overview of Procedures

The major face-to-face assessments over the child's first three years occurred when children were 1, 6, 15, 24, and 36 months of age. Measures of the family, parenting, and mother–child relations were collected through interviews, questionnaires, live and videotaped observations conducted in home visits at 1, 6, 15, 24, and 36 months and lab visits at 15, 24, and 36 months. In addition, regular phone calls were made to the families every 3 months between major assessments to update demographic information, including changes in household members and to track child-care arrangements. When children were in regular nonmaternal care 10 or more hours per week, two half-day visits were made to their child-care arrangement at 6, 15, 24, and 36 months to conduct observations of child-care quality, observe child behavior in the child-care context, and collect interview and questionnaire data from the child's caregivers. Measures of the children's social, cognitive, and language development were collected through questionnaires, videotaped observations, and standardized measures.

Research assistants at each site were extensively trained on all procedures and were certified centrally in order to ensure measures were administered reliably and to guard against differences between sites in data collection and measurement procedures. The videotaped observations were shipped to central locations for rating by highly trained rating teams who were blind to other information on the children and families. Details of the constructs and their measurement are described below.

Family Measures

With its basis in an ecological and life-span framework (Bronfenbrenner, 1986; Elder, 1998), the study's measurement of the family has allowed an examination of how parenting and the home environment influence child development, addressing issues such as the quality of parenting and the home environment as well as individual characteristics of the parents and demographic characteristics of the family. Direct measurement of parenting behavior was conducted in naturalistic observations and semistructured videotaped interactions. In addition, measures of the family (e.g., income, household structure) and individual characteristics of the parents (e.g., personality, stresses, attitudes and beliefs) conveyed the family environmental context from a broad variety of viewpoints. Table 6.1 presents an overview of the family constructs and their corresponding ages of assessment.

Structural Characteristics of the Family

In phone and face-to-face interviews, information was collected repeatedly about members of the child's household. This information provides longitudinal measurement of household structure describing whether and when the child lived in a nuclear two-parent family, extended nuclear family, single-parent family,

TABLE 6.1
FAMILY CONSTRUCTS MEASURED IN PHASE 1 OF THE NICHD STUDY
OF EARLY CHILD CARE BY CHILD'S AGE OF ASSESSMENT

	1 Mo.	6 Mos.	15 Mos.	24 Mos.	36 Mos.
Family characteristics					
Household members	X	X	X	X	X
Parent employment	X	X	X	X	X
Income	X	X	X	X	X
Education	X				
Well-being and personality					
Satisfaction with employment	X	X	X	X	X
Depressive symptoms	X	X	X	X	X
Personality		X			
Stress and support					
Social support	X	X	X	X	X
Marital quality	X				X
Financial stress	X	X	X	X	X
Job experiences		X	X		X
Combining work and family		X	X		X
Parenting stress	X	X	X	X	X
Life stress		X	X	X	X
Attitudes and beliefs					
Separation anxiety	X	X	X	X	X
Benefits/costs of employment	X				X
Childrearing	X				
Parenting					
Home environment		X	X		X
Mother–child interaction		X	X	X	X

extended single-parent family, blended two-parent family, and other possible combinations. Thus, the stability and fluidity of the child's household members was obtained.

Employment

Extensive employment information was tracked. Mothers reported on both maternal and paternal employment, including the number of hours, income, times of day worked, and hours of the paid job performed at home. Mothers also rated how satisfied they were with their current employment situation.

Income

Several measures of income were collected repeatedly. We measured maternal income, nonmaternal family income, unearned income and government benefits; and an income-to-needs ratio, measured as the total family income divided by the poverty threshold for the year.

Psychosocial Characteristics of the Mother

Three sets of psychosocial characteristics were measured: maternal well-being and personality, social support and stress, and maternal attitudes and beliefs.

For maternal well-being and personality, depressive symptoms were measured each time using the Center for Epidemiological Studies Depression Scale (CES-D, Radloff, 1977). At 6 months we administered three scales from the Neuroticism Extraversion Openness Personality Inventory (NEO, Costa & McCrea, 1985): extraversion, agreeableness, and neuroticism. An aggregate measure of maternal psychological adjustment was formed by summing the average of repeated CES-D depression scores (reverse-scored) plus neuroticism (reverse-scored), extraversion, and agreeableness.

Support measures included social support from friends and family (Relationships with Other People Scale; Marshall & Barnett, 1993), marital intimacy (Emotional Intimacy subscale of the PAIR, Personal Assessment of Intimacy in Relationships Inventory, Schaefer & Olson, 1981), and the Love, Conflict, and Ambivalence subscales from Braiker's and Kelley's (1979) measure of marital quality. Stress measures addressed parenting stress (Parenting Stress Index, Abidin, 1983) financial stress (NICHD ECCRN, 1997c), job stress and support (Job Role Quality Scale; Barnett & Marshall, 1991), and life stress (Life Experiences Survey; Sarason, Johnson, & Siegel, 1978).

Maternal attitudes toward separation from her child were measured repeatedly (Separation Anxiety Scale; Hock, Gnezda, & McBride, 1983). We used the Attitudes Toward Maternal Employment Questionnaire (Greenberger, Goldberg, Crawford, & Granger, 1988) to measure beliefs about the benefits of maternal employment for child development and beliefs about the risks of maternal employment for child development. Mothers' traditional and progressive beliefs about childrearing were assessed at 1 month using the Modernity Scale (Schaefer & Edgerton, 1985).

Quality of the Home Environment and Parenting

Qualities of the home environment and parenting were assessed using information about observed parental sensitivity, stimulation, and quality of assistance; observed parental involvement; and observed physical characteristics of the home environment.

Maternal sensitivity, stimulation, and quality of assistance were rated from observations of the mother's interaction with the child during 15-minute videotaped mother–child interaction tasks at 6, 15, 24, and 36 months. The tasks provided a context for assessing age-appropriate qualities of maternal sensitivity, supportiveness, intrusiveness, positive regard, hostility, cognitive stimulation, and quality of instruction with the child. (See NICHD ECCRN [1999] for more detailed description.) Father–child interaction was observed in a subset of the research sites in the study's first phase, but these data are not included in the present chapter.

The mother's involvement and responsiveness with her child and various qualities of stimulation in the home environment were measured using the Home Observation for Measurement of the Environment (HOME, Caldwell & Bradley, 1984).

Child-Care Measures

Longitudinal measures of the child-care context included individual experiences of the study child, such as the child-care provider's sensitive responsiveness to the child's needs and stimulation of the child's language. We also measured characteristics of child care that are experienced more indirectly, such as the child-care provider's education level and training. Relations found between the more distal features of care (e.g., regulable features of care such as teacher–child ratio and group size, childrearing attitudes, physical features of the environment) and the children's individual experiences of caregiving quality in child care are described in two reports from the study (NICHD ECCRN, 1996, 2000a), where details of the child-care measures can be found.

Measures of Children's Development

Children's behavior and development were assessed in four major domains: socioemotional, cognitive, language, and physical. Published reports to date have addressed the first three domains. Within these three domains multiple constructs were assessed: temperament, attachment security, self-regulation, social competence, and behavior problems in the socioemotional domain; play complexity, sustained attention, mental development, and school readiness in the cognitive domain; vocabulary, verbal comprehension, sentence complexity, and expressive language in the language domain. The child development measures addressed in the present report and their ages of assessment are listed in Table 6.2.

Infant–Mother Attachment

The Strange Situation was used when the children were 15 months to measure security of infant–mother attachment (Ainsworth and Wittig, 1969). From videotaped observations of the infant's response to brief episodes of increasing stress for the infant, including two separations from the mother, infant attachment behaviors were categorized as secure or insecure. Infants were judged as securely attached if they sought comfort from their mothers when they were distressed or greeted their mothers without ambivalence when they were reunited. Types of insecure attachment coded were avoidant, ambivalent-resistant, and disorganized (Main & Solomon, 1990). Characteristics of infant attachment security in the sample are described in NICHD ECCRN (1997c).

TABLE 6.2

CHILD OUTCOME MEASURES ASSESSED IN PHASE 1 AND CHILD'S AGE AT DATA COLLECTION (MONTHS), THE SOURCE OF DATA (M = MOTHER; CG = CAREGIVER; C = CHILD), AND THE TYPE OF DATA COLLECTED[1]

Name of Instrument	1	6	15	24	36	Data Type	Reference
Social-emotional constructs							
Mother–child interaction		M, C	M, C	M, C	M, C	Observation	NICHD ECCRN, 1997b, 1999
Strange situation (Attachment)			C			Observation	Ainsworth & Wittig, 1969
Child behavior checklist				M, Cg	M, Cg	Questionnaire	Achenbach, Edelbrock, & Howell, 1987
ORCE behavior scales (says "no" to adult, acts defiant)			C	C	C	Observation	NICHD ECCRN, 1998a
ORCE behavior scales (prosocial acts, negative acts [nonaggressive], aggression, complies with adult)				C	C	Observation	NICHD ECCRN, 1998a
ORCE qualitative ratings (positive mood, negative mood, activity level)		C	C	C	C	Observation	NICHD ECCRN, 1996, in press-a
Compliance: Bayley				C		Observation	NICHD ECCRN, 1998a
Compliance: lab cleanup				C	C	Observation	NICHD ECCRN, 1998a
Resistance to temptation/self-control (forbidden toy)					C	Observation	NICHD ECCRN, 1998a
Adaptive social behavior inventory (ASBI)				M, Cg	M, Cg	Questionnaire	Hogan, Scott, & Bauer, 1992
Cognitive Constructs							
Global intellectual functioning							
Bayley MDI			C	C		Child Test	Bayley, 1969, 1993
Knowledge and achievement							
Bracken Test of basic concepts (school readiness)				C	Child Test	Bracken, 1984	
Language development							
MacArthur communicative development inventory				M	M	Questionnaire	Fenson et al., 1994

[1]Additional measures were collected. Table lists outcome measures reviewed in this chapter.

107

Self-control, Compliance, and Problem Behavior

To measure self-control, compliance, sociability, and problem behavior, children were tested and observed in the laboratory and in child care at 24 and 36 months, and mothers and caregivers completed questionnaires (see Table 6.2 for the particular measures). To reduce the number of variables, factor analyses were conducted with the 24-month measures and the 36-month measures. On the basis of factor solutions obtained at the two ages, seven child outcomes were derived at child age 24 months and at 36 months: compliance and cooperation with mother in laboratory observations (24 and 36 months); mother-reported behavior problems (24 and 36 months); mother-reported social competence (i.e., sociability and compliance; 24 and 36 months); defiance and negative affect in laboratory observations (24 and 36 months); caregiver-reported problem behaviors (24 and 36 months); children's observed noncompliant and negative behavior in child care (24 and 36 months); negative mood and inattention in mother–child interaction at 24 months and these negative behaviors plus lack of self control in the laboratory resistance-to-temptation procedure at 36 months.

Cognitive and Language Development

Standardized assessments of language development included the MacArthur Communicative Development Inventory (CDI) at 15 and 24 months (Fenson et al., 1994) and the Reynell Developmental Language Scales at 36 months (Reynell, 1991). Cognitive performance was measured at 15 and 24 months using the Bayley Scales of Infant Development (Bayley, 1969, 1993). School readiness was measured using the Bracken Scale of Basic Concepts (Bracken, 1984) at 36 months.

PARENTING INFLUENCES ON CHILDREN'S EXPERIENCES IN CHILD CARE

We now turn to a review of the study's findings pertaining to family and parenting influences. In this section we first describe the amount, type, and quality of child care used by the families during their children's infancy and convey the characteristics of families related to the use and selection of child care. In the next section we describe findings of the relations of family characteristics and parenting to children's social, cognitive, and language development in the context of children's child-care experience. In the third section we present findings that address whether family and parenting influences are changed or diminished for children in child care.

The use of child care is one of many decisions that parents make about the care of their children in the early years. Parental choices about the amount and nature of child-care experiences for their young children are thus an important component of parental influence. Decisions and choices involve whether and how much nonmaternal child care to use, the type of care arranged, the child's age of entry into a child-care arrangement, quality of the care, and whether and when to change care arrangements.

A large proportion of the families used some child care for their children on a regular, weekly basis beginning in the children's first year of life (NICHD ECCRN, 1997a). By the time they were 12 months of age, 74% of the children experienced at least 10 hours per week of nonmaternal care and 58% experienced 30 or more hours per week. Average age of entry into nonmaternal child care was 3.11 months. Approximately three quarters (72%) of the children entered care before 4 months of age.

Parents choose from among many different types of child care for their children. When infants first began care, for any amount, the most common forms of nonmaternal care were father/partner care (25%), care in a child-care home by a nonrelative (24%), and care by relatives, including grandparents (23%). Care in a child-care center (12%) or in-home care by a nonrelative (12%) were least common. Over the first three years of life, more formal forms of child care (child-care centers and child-care homes) became increasingly common, while care by fathers/partners and relatives decreased (NICHD, 2000a).

Various constraints limit parents' decisions and choices about the use of child care for their children. Their decisions reflect these constraints, but they also relate to their attitudes and beliefs about maternal employment. We examined relations between family characteristics, including economic factors, maternal psychological adjustment, maternal beliefs and attitudes, and features of early child-care experience, including the age of entry into child care, amount of child care, type of care, and quality of care in infancy (NICHD ECCRN, 1997c).

We found that economic factors were most consistently associated with the amount and the nature of children's child-care experience. Maternal personality and beliefs about maternal employment were also related to child-care experience. Higher maternal income and lower total family income predicted the use of more nonmaternal child care in infancy. More nonmaternal infant child care was also related to lower maternal education, longer employment hours, fewer children in the family, and mothers' beliefs in the benefits of maternal employment. Infants who began nonmaternal care between 3 and 5 months of age had mothers who had higher psychological adjustment than infants who had earlier or later entry into child care.

The type of care used for their infants was associated with the family's income, mother's ethnicity, household composition, work schedules, and concerns about the risks of maternal employment for children. Families with more children were more likely to use in-home caregivers and coparental care than those in other types of care. Families using a grandparent's care were more likely to have their relative living in their homes. These families also had the lowest levels of maternal education. When mothers worked nondaytime hours during their child's infancy, fathers/partners were more likely to be primary care providers (50%) than when mothers worked varying schedules (35%) or daytime hours (19%). The highest maternal education was found among those families using in-home caregivers who were not relatives.

Income differences related to the use of different types of care were striking, reflecting the differential costs of child care. Families using care with an unrelated in-home caregiver had average nonmaternal incomes that were $20,000 a year higher than families using any other type of care.

Mothers' beliefs about the effects of maternal employment predicted the age infants entered nonmaternal care and the type of child-care setting parents selected. Beliefs in the benefits of their employment were associated with beginning child care earlier, while concerns about risks of employment were associated with fewer hours of care and the use of more informal types of care arrangements.

For child care in the child's home or in a child-care home, higher family income was associated with higher child-care quality. For care in child-care centers, however, infants from both low- and high-income families received higher quality care than those from moderate income families, reflecting both the parents' ability to choose higher-quality care when they could afford it and the availability of subsidies for child care for some of the lower-income families. These findings are similar to those for preschool children in the National Child-Care Staffing Study (Phillips, Voran, Kisker, Howes, & Whitebook, 1994). They reinforce the conclusion that families in the middle are less likely to receive any federal support for obtaining higher-quality care, either in the form of direct subsidies for low-income families, or child-care tax credit for families with higher incomes (Phillips & Bridgman, 1995).

These findings emphasize circumstances and constraints of families in their choice of child-care arrangements for their infants and young children as well as contributions of their beliefs, particularly regarding the risks and benefits of maternal employment for their children's development. These findings are consonant with the model recently proposed by Pungello and Kurtz-Costes (1999), which identified three types of influences on parents' search and selection of child care: environmental constraints (e.g., the family's need for income, flexibility of work schedule), maternal beliefs, and child characteristics such as age. Other aspects of parents' beliefs, attitudes, and behavior also likely bear upon their children's child-care experiences. Beyond their choices regarding amount, type, and quality of child care their child experiences, families also interface with the child-care setting in how they monitor the child's daily child-care experiences and communicate with the child-care provider regarding the child's behavior and experiences (see Powell, 1989). This aspect of parental influence on children's experiences has received relatively little empirical research.

RELATIONS OF FAMILY CHARACTERISTICS AND PARENTING TO CHILD DEVELOPMENT IN THE SOCIOEMOTIONAL, COGNITIVE, AND LANGUAGE DOMAINS

The findings reviewed in this section come from the various reports and analyses undertaken to date of the children's development in relation to their early child-care experiences. These findings also provide a systematic examination of parenting and family influences on children's development for children with considerable child-care experience in the early years. The general analysis plan for the examination of the effects of child care was similar across the different domains of child development. The plan included covariates addressing characteristics of the family related to choices pertaining to child care ("selection factors") and additional child and family factors broadly considered in the literature to be associated with development within each domain analyzed. Child-care effects were examined controlling for these two groups of factors.

Specific analysis plans differed across domains with respect to the exact set of selection factors included in the analytic models. Family characteristics that were examined for the different domains of child outcomes varied because somewhat different features of the family and home environment were implicated in the research literatures pertaining to the various child outcomes. For example, family income-to-needs and maternal beliefs about the benefits of maternal employment were the selection factors meeting criteria for inclusion in the analyses of the security of attachment in relation to child care, with the criteria being significant relations to the features of child care experienced by the child as well as to secure infant attachment. Family characteristics meeting these criteria for inclusion as selection factors in analyses of children's self control, compliance, and behavior problems were family income-to-needs and the mother's psychological adjustment.

All analytic models included measures of the quality of parenting as assessed from observations of mother–child interaction, naturalistic home observations, or both. Most analyses included measures of the family's income among the selection factors examined, because family income was generally related both to features of child-care experience and to the child outcomes examined. Thus, our examinations of the family and child-care environmental predictors of social-emotional, cognitive, and language development addressed family demographics, maternal individual characteristics, parenting, and child care in multiple regression analyses.

Security of Infant–Mother Attachment

Two formulations of infant–mother attachment security at 15 months were analyzed in logistic regressions. The first was secure (B) versus all types of insecure attachment, avoidant, resistant, and disorganized (A, C, and D). The second type of comparison was between secure attachment classifications and classifications of insecure avoidant attachment. This second comparison was of interest because of past studies which had found an increased likelihood of insecure attachment, particularly with respect to avoidant attachment, when children experienced extensive nonmaternal care in the first year (see the meta-analysis of Belsky and Rovine, 1988). Avoidant attachment is defined as an attachment bond characterized by minimization of attachment behavior, for example, a failure to seek closeness or turning away from the attachment figure when distressed, rarely checking back with the attachment figure when exploring, and/or an absence of overt distress when separated from the attachment figure (Ainsworth, Blehar, Waters, & Wall, 1978).

We examined the prediction of attachment security in logistic regression analyses from family, child, maternal, and child-care variables for the infants who experienced at least 10 hours per week of child care and were observed in that care. (Further details of these analyses can be found in NICHD ECCRN, 1997b) Maternal characteristics and measures of parenting were entered after controlling for selection factors of family income and maternal beliefs about the value of maternal employment for children's development. When mothers were better adjusted psychologically, infant attachment to the mother was more likely to be secure. Maternal sensitivity to the infant also predicted security of attachment, even after controlling for the mother's psychological adjustment. The measure of mothering significant in the prediction of attachment security was the measure of maternal responsiveness and sensitivity derived from the naturalistic HOME observations. Maternal sensitivity rated from the videotaped semistructured mother–child interactions at 6 and 15 months was not a significant predictor of attachment security in the multiple prediction controlling for the selection factors, maternal psychological adjustment, and the naturalistic observation of maternal responsiveness and sensitivity. These findings thus provide support for the role of maternal responsiveness in the development of secure infant–mother attachment as reported in past research. The effect size for maternal sensitivity as measured naturalistically in this study was approximately that found in a recent meta-analysis of infant attachment studies (De Wolff & van IJzendoorn, 1997).

Although not significant in the model predicting secure versus insecure attachment, maternal sensitivity from the semistructured interactions was a significant predictor of attachment security in the model that examined secure versus avoidant attachment. This difference in the parenting factors predicting secure versus all types of insecure attachment, and predicting secure versus avoidant attachment, is informative.

The composite measure of maternal sensitivity from the ratings of the semistructured mother–child interactions was the sum of the ratings of sensitivity to nondistress, intrusiveness (reversed), and positive regard. In the videotaped situation in which mother–child interactions were observed, lower maternal sensitivity ratings from the semistructured videotaped interactions were largely a product of the degree of maternal intrusiveness and lack of child-centeredness in the mother's interactions. Maternal detachment in videotaped mother–child interaction was rarely observed. Maternal intrusiveness has been implicated specifically in the development of insecure avoidant attachment (Belsky & Rovine, 1988) but not in resistant or disorganized insecure attachment. Support for the particular role of maternal intrusiveness and the undermining of child autonomy in the development of avoidant attachment is thus given support in this set of analyses.

Maternal sensitivity also played an important role in understanding the effects of child care on infant–mother attachment. Maternal sensitivity moderated effects of the amount of child care, quality of child care, and number of child-care arrangements. Children whose mothers were low in sensitivity (as measured naturalistically and in videotaped mother–child interactions) were especially likely to be insecurely attached when child care was used for more than 10 hours per week, when child care quality was lower, and when more than one child-care arrangement was used. If maternal sensitivity was not low, features of child care experience were unrelated to infants' attachment security.

Self-control, Compliance, and Problem Behavior

Research on the development of children's self-control, cooperation, and management of aggressive and antisocial impulses has focused on the roles of both temperament and parenting practices. Parenting characteristics that have been studied have included parental sensitivity and warmth in parent–child interaction and secure attachment to the mother (e.g., Kochanska, 1995; Lepper, 1981). In our research on child care and children's compliance, self-control, and problem behavior, we examined various measures of these domains of socioemotional development. Possible associations of child-care experience were examined after selection factors (family income-to-needs and maternal psychological adjustment in these analyses), child temperament and gender, and parenting were first taken into account (NICHD ECCRN, 1998a). We tested for the prediction from parenting qualities after accounting for associations with the selection factors, child factors, and features of child care (amount, quality, stability, and type of child care), and also after accounting only for selection and child factors. Parenting influence examined in the multiple predictions of each of the socioemotional outcomes at 24 and 36 months were infant attachment security and an aggregate measure of maternal sensitivity, formed from ratings of the mother's behavior in semistructured interactions and mother's positive involvement with her child assessed naturalistically by the HOME. Thus, child-care effects were considered in the context of potential child and family influences, and family influences were examined within the context of potential child and child-care influences. A

TABLE 6.3
SUMMARY OF SIGNIFICANT PREDICTORS OF SOCIAL-EMOTIONAL DEVELOPMENT

	Child Functioning—24 Mos.					Child Functioning Outcomes—36 Mos.				
Predictors	Mother-Reported Behavior Problems	Mother-Reported Social Competence	Negative Interaction with Mother	Child-Care Behavior Problems	Child-Care Non-compliance	Mother-Reported Behavior Problems	Mother-Reported Social Competence	Cleanup Com-pliance	Negative, Lack self-control	Child-Care Behavior Problems
Background										
Income-to-needs	−*	+*	n.s.	n.s.	n.s.	n.s.	+*	n.s.	−*	−*
M psych. adjustment	−*	+*	−*	−*	n.s.	−*	+*	+*	−*	−*
Child gender (male)	n.s.	−*	n.s.	n.s.	n.s.	n.s.	−*	n.s.	+*	n.s.
Difficult temp.	+*	−*	n.s.	n.s.	n.s.	+*	−*	n.s.	n.s.	n.s.
Child care[a]										
Amount	n.s.	−*	n.s.	+*	n.s.	n.s.	n.s.	n.s.	n.s.	n.s.
Instability	+*	n.s.	n.s.	n.s.	−*	n.s.	n.s.	n.s.	n.s.	n.s.
Quality	n.s.	n.s.	n.s.	−*	n.s.	n.s.	n.s.	+*	−*	−*
Group Type	n.s.	+*	n.s.	n.s.	−*	n.s.	n.s.	n.s.	−*	−*
Parenting[b]										
Attachment security	n.s.	n.s.	−*	n.s.	n.s.	n.s.	n.s.	n.s.	n.s.	n.s.
Mothering	−*	+*	−*	−*	n.s.	+*	+*	+*	−*	−*
Total R²	.04	.12	.08	.08	.02	.17	.18	.07	.10	.08

*Significant ($p < .05$) beta in multiple regression; + indicates positive prediction, − indicates negative prediction.

[a]Block of predictors tested after background main effects.

[b]Block of predictors tested after background and child-care main effects.

summary of the significance of the predictors of social development at 24 and 36 months from the multiple regression models is displayed in Table 6.3.

Maternal psychological adjustment was a positive predictor of children's compliance and self-control, and a negative predictor of problem behavior for eight of the models examined across 24 and 36 months of age. Among the parenting influences examined, infant attachment security was rarely a unique contributor to these socioemotional child outcomes. Only in the case of the child's negativity with mother in the structured interaction at 24 months did attachment security add to the multiple prediction. Children who were securely attached to their mother at 15 months were less negative with their mothers at 24 months, even after accounting for a mother's sensitivity to her child in the interaction, family income, maternal psychological adjustment, child gender, and child-care experience.

Maternal involvement and sensitivity to the child were significant predictors of 7 of the 11 socioemotional outcomes examined at 24 and 36 months, after controlling for family income, maternal psychological adjustment, child gender and temperament, and child-care experiences. More positive maternal involvement and sensitive mother–child interactions independently contributed at 24 months to the prediction of fewer mother-reported and caregiver-reported problem behaviors, less child negativity in interaction with the mother, and greater compliance and social competence reported by the mother. At 36 months, the mother's positive involvement and sensitivity independently contributed to the prediction of fewer caregiver-reported problem behaviors, more compliant cooperation observed, greater compliance and social competence reported by the mother, and less observed negativity and lack of self-control.

In contrast, there were relatively few significant predictions from child care to children's compliance, self-control, and problem behaviors after adjusting for associations with family characteristics. These findings thus highlight the parent's role in fostering cooperation, compliance, and self-control in early childhood and indicate the generally more consistent and stronger influence of family and parenting than of child care. Similar findings occurred with regard to behavior problems in that lower maternal involvement and lack of sensitive mother–child interaction were associated with problem behaviors in preschool-aged children. These findings are important given that problem behavior at this early age is significantly predictive of future behavior problems (e.g., Richman, Stevenson, & Graham, 1982; Rose, Rose, & Feldman, 1986).

Cognitive and Language Development

In considering how child care relates to cognitive and language development, we examined predictions of children's cognitive and language development at 15, 24, and 36 months from child care, after adjusting for associations with background variables that included family income-to-needs ratio, maternal vocabulary scores, child gender, and parenting influences (see NICHD ECCRN, 2000b). Although designed for the purpose of discerning how child-care experience influences cognitive and language development, these analyses provide important findings

TABLE 6.4
SUMMARY OF SIGNIFICANT PREDICTORS OF CHILD COGNITIVE AND LANGUAGE DEVELOPMENT

	Bayley 15 mos.	Vocabulary Production 15 mos.	Vocabulary Comprehension 15 mos.	Bayley 24 mos.	Vocabulary Comprehension 24 mos.	Sentence Complexity 24 mos.	School Readiness 36 mos.	Expressive Language 36 mos.	Verbal Comprehension 36 mos.
Background									
Income-to-needs	n.s.	n.s.	n.s.	+*	n.s.	n.s.	+*	n.s.	+*
Mother PPVT-R	+*	+*	n.s.	+*	n.s.	+*	+*	+*	n.s.
Child gender (male)	-*	-*	n.s.	-*	n.s.	-*	-*	-*	-*
Child care									
Hours/week	n.s.	n.s.	n.s.	n.s.	n.s.	n.s.	n.s.	n.s.	n.s.
Type care—center	n.s.	n.s.	n.s	+*	+*	+*	+*	+*	+*
Type care—family	n.s.	n.s.	n.s.	+*	n.s.	n.s.	n.s.	n.s.	+*
Quality of care	+*	+*	+*	+*	+*	+*	+*	+*	+*
Parenting									
Maternal stimulation	n.s.	n.s.	n.s.	+*	n.s.	n.s.	+*	+*	+*
HOME total	+*	+*	n.s.	+*	+*	n.s.	+*	+*	+*
Total R²	.14	.07	.05	.30	.08	.13	.33	.18	.41

*Significant ($p < .05$) beta in simultaneous multiple regression; + indicates positive prediction, − indicates negative prediction.

116

regarding parenting influences on children's cognitive and language development when controlling for other characteristics of the family and mother, child gender, and features of child care, including amount of care, type of care experience, and quality of caregiving experience. The parenting influences examined were the overall quality of the home environment as observed using the HOME and maternal cognitive stimulation observed in the semistructured interaction measures, because previous findings in the literature indicate developmental associations of cognitive and language gains with cognitive and language stimulation (Friedman & Cocking, 1986; Hart & Risley, 1995; Hoff-Ginsberg, 1991; Tomasello & Farrar, 1986) as well as an enriching home environment (Bradley, Caldwell, Rock, et al., 1989; Wachs & Chan, 1986). A summary of the significance of the predictors of cognitive and language development from the multiple regression models tested is shown in Table 6.4.

In these multiple predictions of cognitive and language development, maternal vocabulary scores were significant predictors of the 15- and 24-month Bayley mental development scores, sentence complexity at 24 months and expressive language and school readiness at 36 months, controlling for all other predictors. Among the parenting variables, maternal cognitive stimulation was associated with language and school readiness measures at 36 months and Bayley scores at 24 months. The total HOME score, measuring maternal responsiveness and involvement as well as other physical and experiential enrichment provided by parents in the home environment, was a significant predictor of Bayley scores at 15 and 24 months, MacArthur Communicative Development Inventory vocabulary production at 15 and 24 months, Bracken school readiness at 36 months, and Reynell expressive language and verbal comprehension at 36 months. That is, home stimulation was predictive of seven of the nine cognitive and language measures measured across 15, 24, and 36 months, even after controlling for associations with quality of maternal cognitive stimulation, maternal vocabulary, family income, gender, and child care.

Features of child-care experience were also associated with children's cognitive and language development in these multiple prediction models. Overall quality of child care, and language stimulation in child care in particular, were consistently related to cognitive and language outcomes across the three ages assessed in infancy and preschool, even after controlling for multiple family and parent factors.

FAMILY INFLUENCES: ARE THEY WEAKER FOR CHILDREN IN CHILD CARE?

The findings from the NICHD Study of Early Child Care regarding family and parenting influences across cognitive, language, and social and emotional domains of young children's development indicate that children with varied experiences of child care are consistently influenced by the quality of parenting they receive. We have also addressed the compelling question of whether the relation between parenting qualities and children's development are the same or different when children are in exclusive maternal care compared to when they are in relatively extensive child care (NICHD ECCRN, 1998b). Are the influences of the family weaker or different for children in child care?

To answer this question, we compared two groups of children: children in exclusive maternal care and children in extensive (more than 30 hours weekly) nonparental care. The number of children that fit into these two groups was somewhat limited compared to our larger total sample, but yielded 184 children in nonparental care and 164 in exclusive maternal care at 24 months, and 147 in extensive nonparental care and 127 in exclusive maternal care at 36 months. We examined child outcomes in both the cognitive and social domains, including mental development, expressive and receptive language, social competence, and problem behavior. We analyzed whether family predictors were differentially related to these child outcomes when children had extensive experience versus no regular experience of nonmaternal care in the first three years. Family predictors included family income-to-needs, maternal depression, maternal beliefs in the benefits of work, maternal nonauthoritarian childrearing beliefs, infant attachment security, and the parenting variables of maternal sensitivity in mother–child interactions and maternal positive involvement from the HOME. Multivariate comparisons of the matrices of correlations between predictors and outcomes for the group with extensive nonmaternal care and the group without nonmaternal care experience provided no evidence for differences. Overall, the correlations between family demographics, maternal personality and beliefs, and parenting were generally consistent with the findings widely reported in the developmental literature, irrespective of differences in the amount of child care experienced. Moreover, none of the correlations between the measures of mother's observed parenting and children's social and cognitive development were significantly different for the children in the maternal-care and full-time child-care groups.

Despite no evidence at the multivariate level of a difference in relations between family predictors and child outcomes at 24 and 36 months, we took an exploratory approach to determine whether there were significant differences between pairs of correlations that conveyed any pattern associated with differential relations. Two main patterns were found. First, child outcomes were related to marital status in the expected fashion in the maternal-care group but not in the full-time child-care group. Living in a single-parent household was associated with poorer functioning than living in a two-parent household with respect to social competence at 24 and 36 months and school readiness and problem behavior at 36 months, but only when children were reared principally by their mothers, not when they received full-time nonparental care.

A second pattern of differential predictions from family characteristics involved the mother's belief in the benefits of work. Associations with social competence and problem behavior at 24 and 36 months and 36-month school readiness were in opposite directions in the two groups. In the full-time child-care group, beliefs in the benefits of work were related to higher cognitive and socioe-motional functioning; in the maternal-care group, stronger beliefs in the benefits of work were related to lower child functioning. From another perspective, these last differences may in fact portray similar associations for the two groups. If viewed from the perspective of consistencies between mothers' beliefs and their work situation, the pattern of correlations for both groups may be seen to reflect similarly positive benefits for children when the mother's beliefs in the value of employment coincide with her actual employment.

SUMMARY AND CONCLUSIONS

Findings reported here from the NICHD Study of Early Child Care highlight the importance of many aspects of parenting in understanding individual differences in preschoolers' socio-emotional and cognitive development. Further, they indicate that even in the context of various features of child-care experience, parenting and family influences for children with early child-care experience are consistent with reports in the larger literature on family and parenting influences. In particular, qualities of parenting, including maternal sensitivity, responsivity, involvement, and cognitive stimulation were found to be uniquely predictive of young children's socioemotional and cognitive development after taking into account the children's child-care experience over the first three years of life. Contrary to propositions that parenting has minimal effects on children (Harris, 1995; Rowe, 1994), these find-ings attest to relatively strong cumulative influences of parenting and family expe-riences in children's development in their preschool years.

It is also important to note that the qualities of parenting measured in the NICHD study added uniquely to the prediction of children's social and cognitive development after accounting for other family factors predictive of children's development. These family factors included not only demographic characteristics such as family income and maternal education, but psychological adjustment and attitudinal characteristics of the mothers as well.

The results highlight an important role of the parenting features of maternal sensitivity and responsivity and maternal cognitive stimulation of the child. Maternal cognitive stimulation was the particular aspect of mother–child interac-tion included in the prediction of children's cognitive and language development, but the results cannot be used to suggest cognitive stimulation's unique impor-tance for cognitive and language development over other aspects of positive par-enting. Mothers who interacted in a more cognitively stimulating fashion were also more sensitive to their children's needs and supportive of their efforts.

Overall, the findings suggest that the influence of families and parenting is generally not weakened or changed by extensive child-care experience beginning in infancy. The nature of parenting influences discerned throughout the first three years of life in this large and diverse sample of children reinforces the positive associations with positive qualities of parenting—sensitivity, involvement, cognitive stimulation—and young children's development in many domains. In the context of varied child-care experiences, ranging from none to extensive experience of varied types and quality, parenting and family influences on preschoolers' development were prevalent and consistent. Moreover, the pattern of family influences was essentially the same whether children had no child care experience or extensive experience, with remarkably few exceptions.

What are implications of these findings for our understanding of how parenting is associated with children's development? It appears that the significance of children's experiences in the family, and particularly their parenting experiences, is pervasive, regardless of their child-care experience in the early years. Family and parenting characteristics were relatively strong predictors of both social and cognitive development whether or not children spent considerable time in child care. As we follow the development of these children and their families into their middle childhood years, we will continue to address children's experiences of parenting in their families as well as experiences in their rearing environments outside the family, in school, with their peers, and in child-care settings. As individual differences in the children become more consolidated we should become better able to understand how their abilities and behavior may interact with parenting and experiences within their families. The study will continue to examine parenting within the larger contexts of children's lives and address how its influence may change as children mature and their experiences expand and accumulate.

REFERENCES

Abidin, R. R. (1983). *Parenting Stress Index manual*. Charlottesville, VA: Pediatric Psychology Press.

Achenbach, T. M., Edelbrock, C., & Howell, C. T. (1987). Empirically-based assessment of behavioral/emotional problems of 2- and 3-year-old children. *Journal of Abnormal Child Psychology, 15,* 629–650.

Ainsworth, M. D. S., Blehar, M., Waters, E., & Wall, S. (1978). *Patterns of attachment: A psychological study of the Strange Situation.* Hillsdale, NJ: Lawrence Erlbaum Associates.

Ainsworth, M. D. S., & Wittig, B. (1969). Attachment and exploratory behavior of one-year-olds in a strange situation. In B. M. Foss (Ed.), *Determinants of infant behavior* (Vol. 4, pp. 129–173). London: Methuen.

Barnett, R. C., & Marshall, N. L. (1991). The relationship between women's work and family roles and subjective well-being and psychological distress. In M. Frankenhauser, M. Chesney, & U. Lundberg (Eds.), *Women, work, and health: Stress and opportunities.* New York: Plenum Press.

Bayley, N. (1969). *Bayley Scales of Infant Development.* New York: Psychological Corporation.

Bayley, N. (1993). *Bayley Scales of Infant Development* (2nd ed.), San Antonio, TX: Psychological Corporation.

Belsky, J. & Rovine, M. (1988). Non-maternal care in the first year of life and the security of infant-parent attachment. *Child Development, 59,* 157–167.

Bornstein, M. H. (1985). How infant and mother jointly contribute to developing cognitive competence in the child. *Proceedings of the National Academy of Sciences (USA), 82,* 7470–7473.

Bornstein, M. H., & Tamis-LeMonda, C. S. (1989). Maternal responsiveness and cognitive development in children. In M. H. Bornstein (Ed.), *Maternal responsivenes: Characteristics and consequences.* (pp. 49–61). San Francisco: Jossey-Bass.

Bracken, B. A. (1984). *Bracken Basic Concept Scales.* San Antonio, TX: Psychological Corporation.

Braiker, H., & Kelly, H. (1979). Conflict in the development of close relationships. In R. Burgess and T. Huston (Eds.), *Social exchange and developing relationships.* New York: Academic Press.

Bronfenbrenner, U. (1986). Ecology of the family as a contest for human development: Research perspectives. *Developmental Psychology, 22,* 723–742.

Caldwell, B. M., & Bradley, R. H. (1984). The HOME inventory and family demographics. *Developmental Psychology, 20,* 315–320.

Clarke-Stewart, K. A., Gruber, C., & Fitzgerald, L. (1994). *Children at home and in day care.* Hillsdale, NJ: Lawrence Erlbaum Associates.

Costa, P., & McCrae, R. (1985). *The NEO personality inventory manual.* Odessa, FL: Psychological Assessment Resources.

Danziger, S. & Gottschalk, P. (1986). *How have families with children been faring?* Discussion paper No. 801-86. Institute for Research on Poverty, University of Wisconsin–Madison.

De Wolff, M. S., & van IJzendoorn, M. H. (1997). Sensitivity and attachment: A meta-analysis on parental antecedents of infant attachment. *Child Development, 68,* 571–591.

Dunham, P., & Dunham, F. (1992). Lexical development during middle infancy: A mutually driven infant-caregiver process. *Developmental Psychology, 28,* 414–420.

Egeland, B., & Heister, M. (1995). The long-term consequences of infant day-care and mother–infant attachment. *Child Development, 62,* 930–953.

Elder, G. H., Jr. (1998). The life course and human development. In W. Damon & R. M. Lerner (Eds.), *Theoretical models of human development* (pp. 939–992). New York: John Wiley and Sons.

Fenson, L., Dale, P. S., Reznick, J. S., Bates, E., Thal, D. J. & Pethick, S. J. (1994). Variability in early communicative development. *Monographs of the Society for Research in Child Development, 59* (5), v–173.

Friedman, S. L., & Cocking, R. R. (1986). Instructional influences on cognition and on the brain. In S. L. Friedman, K. A. Klivington, and R. W. Peterson (Eds.), *The brain, cognition, and education.* New York: Academic Press.

Greenberger, E., Goldberg, W., Crawford, T. J., & Granger, J. (1988). Beliefs about the consequences of maternal employment for children. *Psychology of Women Quarterly, 12,* 35–59.

Harris, J. R. (1995). Where is the child's environment? A group socialization theory of development. *Psychological Review, 102,* 458–489.

Hart, B., & Risley, T. R. (1995). *Meaningful differences in the everyday experience of young American children.* Baltimore: Paul H. Brookes Company.

Hayes, C. D., Palmer, J. L., & Zaslow, M. J. (Eds.). (1990). *Who cares for America's children?* Washington, DC: National Academy Press.

Hock, E., Gnezda, M. T., & McBride, S. L. (1983). Mothers of infants: Attitudes toward employment and motherhood following birth of the first child. *Journal of Marriage and the Family, 46,* 425–431.

Hoff-Ginsberg, E. (1991). Mother–child conversation in different social classes and communication settings. *Child Development, 62,* 782–796.

Hogan, A. E. Scott, K. G., & Bauer, C. R. (1992). The Adaptive Social Behavior Inventory (ASBI): A new assessment of social competence in high risk three-year-olds. *Journal of Psychoeducational Assessment, 12,* 230–239.

Howes, C. (1990). Can the age of entry into child care and the quality of child care predict adjustment in kindergarten? *Developmental Psychology, 26,* 292–303.

Jaeger, E., & Weinraub, M. (1990). Early maternal care and infant attachment: In search of process. In K. McCartney (Ed.), *Child care and maternal employment; A social ecology approach* (pp. 71–90). San Francisco, Jossey-Bass.

Kochanska, G. (1995). Children's temperament, mothers' discipline, and security of attachment: Multiple pathways to emerging internalization. *Child Development, 66,* 597–615.

Lepper, M. R. (1981). Intrinsic and extrinsic motivation in children: Detrimental effects of superfluous social controls. In W. A. Collins (Ed.), *Minnesota Symposium on Child Psychology* (pp. 155–214). Minneapolis: University of Minnesota Press.

Main, M., & Solomon, J. (1990). Procedures for identifying disorganized/disoriented infants in the Ainsworth Strange Situation. In M. Greenberg, D. Cicchetti, & M. Cummings (Eds.), *Attachment in the preschool years: Theory, research, and intervention* (pp. 121–160). Chicago: University of Chicago Press.

Marshall, N. L., & Barnett, R. C. (1993). Work–family strains and gains among two earner couples. *Journal of Community Psychology, 21,* 64–78.

McCartney, K. & Phillips, D. (1988). Motherhood and child care. In B. Birns & D. Hays (Eds.), *The different faces of motherhood* (pp. 157–183). New York: Plenum Press.

National Center for Education Statistics. (1995). *National Household Education Survey.* Washington, DC: U.S. Department of Education.

NICHD Early Child Care Research Network (1996). Characteristics of infant child care: Factors contributing to positive caregiving. *Early Childhood Research Quarterly, 11,* 269–306.

NICHD Early Child Care Research Network. (1997a). Child care in the first year of life. *Merrill-Palmer Quarterly, 43* (3), 340–360.

NICHD Early Child Care Research Network. (1997b). The effects of infant child care on infant-mother attachment security: Results of the NICHD Study of Early Child Care. *Child Development, 68,* 860–879.

NICHD Early Child Care Research Network. (1997c). Familial factors associated with the characteristics of non-maternal care for infants. *Journal of Marriage and the Family, 59,* 389–408.

NICHD Early Child Care Research Network. (1998a). Early child care and self-control, compliance, and problem behavior at 24 and 36 months. *Child Development. 69,* 1145–1170.

NICHD Early Child Care Research Network. (1998b). Relations between family predictors and child outcomes: Are they weaker for children in child care? *Developmental Psychology, 34* (S), 1119–1128.

NICHD Early Child Care Research Network. (1999). Child care and mother–child interaction in the first three years of life. *Developmental Psychology, 35,* 1399–1413.

NICHD Early Child Care Research Network. (2000a). Characteristics and quality of child care for toddlers and preschoolers. *Applied Developmental Science, 4,* 116–135.

NICHD Early Child Care Research Network (2000b). The relation of child care to cognitive and language development. *Child Development, 71,* 958–978.

Oppenheim, D., Sagi, A., & Lamb, M. (1988). Infant–adult attachments on the kibbutz and their relation to socioemotional development 4 years later. *Developmental Psychology, 24,* 427–433.

Phillips, D. A., & Bridgman, A. (Eds.) (1995). *New findings an children, families, and economic self-sufficiency.* Washington, DC: National Academy Press.

Phillips, D. A., Voran, M., Kisker, E. Howes, C., & Whitebook, M. (1994). Child care for children in poverty: Opportunity or inequity? *Child Development, 65,* 472–492.

Powell, D. R. (1989). *Families and early childhood programs.* Washington, DC: National Association for the Education of Young Children.

Pungello, E. P., & Kurtz-Costes, B. (1999). Why and how working women choose child care: A review with a focus on infancy. *Developmental Review, 19,* 31–96.

Radloff, L. (1977). The CES-D scale: A self-reported depression scale for research in the general population. *Applied Psychological Measurement, 1,* 385–401.

Reynell, J. (1991). *Reynell Developmental Language Scales* (U.S. Edition). Los Angeles: Western Psychological Service.

Richman, N., Stevenson, J., & Graham, P. (1982). *Preschool to school: A behavioural study.* London: Academic Press.

Rose, S. L., Rose, S. A., & Feldman, J. (1986). Stability of behavior problems in very young children. *Development and Psychopathology, 1,* 5–19.

Rowe, D. C. (1994). *The limits of family influence: Genes, experience, and behavior.* New York: Guilford Press.

Sarason, I. G., Johnson, J. A., & Siegel, J. M. (1978). Assessing the impact of life changes: Development of the Life Experiences Survey. *Journal of Consulting and Clinical Psychology, 46,* 932–946.

Schaefer, E., & Edgerton, M. (1985). Parental and child correlates of parental modernity. In I. E. Sigel (Ed.), *Parental belief systems: The psychological consequences for children* (pp. 287–318). Hillsdale, NJ: Erlbaum.

Schaefer, M., & Olson, D. (1981). Assessing intimacy: The PAIR Inventory. *Journal of Marital and Family Therapy, 7,* 640–653.

Silverstein, L. (1991). Transforming the debate about child care and maternal employment. *American Psychologist, 46,* 1025–1032.

Tamis-LeMonda, C. S., & Bornstein, M. H. (1990). Language, play and attention at one year. *Infant Behavior and Development, 13,* 85–98.

Tomasello, M., & Farrar, J. (1986). Joint attention and early language. *Child Development, 57,* 1454–1463.

U.S. Bureau of Labor Statistics. (1997). Current Population Survey. Washington, DC: U.S. Department of Commerce.

Wachs, T. D., & Chan, A. (1986). Specificity of environmental action, as seen in environmental correlates of infants' communication performance. *Child Development, 57,* 1464–1474.

Weinraub, M., Jaeger, E., & Hoffman, L. (1988). Predicting infant outcome in families of employed and nonemployed mothers. *Early Childhood Research Quarterly, 3,* 361–378.

7

Early Educational Interventions for High-Risk Children: How Center-Based Treatment Can Augment and Improve Parenting Effectiveness

Craig T. Ramey, Sharon Landesman Ramey, Robin Gaines Lanzi, and Janice N. Cotton

Civitan International Research Center, University of Alabama at Birmingham

There is a well-established literature documenting the efficacy of early educational interventions for improving children's competencies, particularly related to later school success and positive transitions into young adulthood, from very-low-resources families. This is especially true when the interventions are intensive, multiyear, and theory-based (see reviews by Guralnick, 1997; Ramey & Ramey, 1998a, 1998b; Ramey & Ramey, 1999). For example, by school entry, IQ scores are 10 points higher for children who receive high-quality, intensive, early childhood education programs compared to those that do not. Just as importantly, during the school years, children's rates of grade retention and special education placement can be reduced by as much as 50% or more (Ramey & Ramey, 1999). Similarly, children's performance on standardized tests of reading and math achievement can be raised significantly through high-quality, early childhood educational programs—especially when coupled with good school programs,

Address correspondence to: 1719 Sixth Ave., South Birmingham, AL 35294, Phone: 205-934-8543, e-mail: cramey@uab.edu after school activities, and summer programs (Entwisle & Alexander, 1998; National Transition Study, 2001, Ramey & Ramey, 2000).

What has been less well recognized is that these early educational interventions almost always include a parenting education component, and often attempt to alter parent–child interactions, the life course of young single mothers, and/or the perceptions among parents that they are doing a good job. In this chapter, we will review the findings from two randomized controlled longitudinal studies—the Abecedarian Project and Project CARE—and illustrate some of the actual and theoretical connections between center-based educational treatment and the quality of parenting and the home environment. In addition, results from an eight-site randomized controlled replication trial of early intervention for low birthweight and premature infants will be presented, with special focus on the benefits to the home environment as well as to the child's emerging intellectual and social-emotional skills.

Certain program elements are key to these programs. These program elements include being multidisciplinary, intergenerational, individualized for children and their families, contextually embedded in local service delivery systems, research-oriented, and organized around key concepts undergirding randomized controlled trials (Ramey & Ramey, 1998b). These programs were *multidisciplinary* since they provided a wide range of services, including early childhood education, family counseling and home visits, health services, medical services, nursing services, nutrition services, social work services, special education services, and transportation. The programs were *intergenerational* in that they focused on both the needs of the child and on the needs of the child's caregivers and family members. Since programs sought to meaningfully recognize and address individual and family differences, services for adults and children were *individualized* to meet the unique and changing needs of each family member. To ensure programs were *contextually embedded in local service delivery systems*, cooperation and investment was sought from social, health, and other existing human service agencies in the community. The primary goals of these programs were to better understand how risk factors affect the course of cognitive development and what can be done to minimize the effects of these risk factors. Therefore, they were *research-oriented* and *utilized a randomized controlled trial design* to obtain results that could be generalized to similar populations.

In 1972, the Abecedarian Project was launched at the Frank Porter Graham Child Development Center on the campus of the University of North Carolina. This single-site randomized controlled trial focused on determining if coordinated high-quality services (early childhood education, pediatric care, and family support services) could improve the intellectual and educational competence of participating children. Children were enrolled from birth and were selected for the program based on a 13-item high-risk index (Ramey & Smith, 1977). Basically, the children came from poor and undereducated families but were biologically healthy and had no known genetic or infectious links to mental retardation (Ramey & Campbell, 1992; Ramey & Ramey, 1998b). The conceptual framework for the intervention program was based on developmental systems theory (Bertalanffy, 1975), which articulates how instrumental and conceptual learning is facilitated through a stimulating, positive, and responsive environment (Ramey & Finklestein, 1981). A strong emphasis on conversational language was also emphasized in the program.

There were two phases to this study, both of which had the potential to affect parenting, parent–child attachment and interactions, and child developmental outcomes. Phase 1 covered the first five years of life and educational intervention was provided for a full day each weekday for fifty weeks per year in the child development center. Program features were very similar to those now recommended by the National Association for the Education for Young Children (Ramey & Ramey, 1998b). Teachers who had formal training, teaching experience, and demonstrated skill and competence in working with young children created healthy and stimulating classroom environments. Ongoing professional development for staff was a critical feature of the program, and of particular importance was the language training program that sought to improve teachers' understanding and competence in developing children's language skills through strategies based on response contingency stimulation (Ramey & Campbell, 1992; Ramey, Dorval, & Baker-Ward, 1983). Teachers were trained to develop greater awareness of the significance of children's actions and appropriate methods of responding to their actions and verbal communications. The goal was for the teachers to routinely incorporate positive and appropriate response contingency experiences into the daily curriculum so the children would learn to trust and develop learning, language, and social skills. This was considered to be an important element of the curriculum since it was hypothesized that in the majority of the children's homes, the amount and consistency of positive response-contingency experiences were limited due to high maternal-risk factors.

The curriculum for infants and toddlers was based on the *Partners for Learning* educational program. This program covers 31 skill areas with 265 specific learning activities that are focused on attaining skill goals in four developmental domains. The program has activities appropriate for infants/toddlers and 2-year-olds. The domains and the skill areas for these two age groups can be found in Table 7.1. The learning activities for this program are: presented in a game-like format; integrated into all aspects of the day; focused on specific skills and general principles; and presented in a one-to-one format between teacher and child. There are separate teacher guide sheets for each learning activity, with information listing the goal, how the goal is to be accomplished, and how the activity will benefit the child. In addition to the *Partners for Learning* curriculum, as children grew older they had opportunities to participate in classroom centers where they interacted on a more frequent basis with small groups of children and a teacher (Ramey & Campbell, 1979; Ramey & Ramey, 1998b).

At 3 years of age, the children moved into a classroom that resembled other high-quality developmentally appropriate preschool programs, with learning centers for blocks, art, water play, music, housekeeping, and books. The teaching

TABLE 7.1
PARTNERS FOR LEARNING DEVELOPMENTAL DOMAINS
AND SKILL AREAS

Infant Toddler Skill Areas	Two-year-olds Skill Areas
Domain 1: Cognitive/Fine Motor	
1. Object permanence	2. Number concepts
3. Objects in space	
4. Matching	5. Matching/visual perception
6. Cause and effect	7. Reasoning
8. Sensory awareness	
Domain 2: Social/self	
9. Self-image	
10. Sharing with adult	
11. Children together	
12. Imitating gestures	13. Creative play
14. Self-help	
15. Needs/feelings	
Domain 3: Motor	
16. Rhythm	
17. Balance	18. Balance/motion
19. Throw/pull/push	
Domain 4: Language	
20. Dialogue	
21. Books	
22. Picture–object words	23. Reporting
24. Words as concepts	25. Predicting
26. Action words	27. Imaging
28. Words for things	29. Giving/following directions
30. Position words	31. Sorting/classifying

staff was responsible for planning the program, organizing the environment, assessing the daily progress of the children, and modifying the curriculum based on these assessments. Again, an emphasis was placed on language development, with teachers providing frequent and appropriate verbal exchanges with children that would evoke lengthy conversations leading to developmental competence (Ramey, McGinnis, Cross, Collier, & Barrie-Blackley, 1981). A preliteracy curriculum was also provided for the older preschool children (Wallach & Wallach, 1976).

Families were offered and encouraged to participate in regularly scheduled group sessions in which they were engaged in discussions on a wide variety of topics related to family and child development and parenting. Parents also were supported by project social workers who gave direct and indirect assistance with housing, social services, and counseling on personal and family matters (Ramey & Ramey, 1992). In addition, teaching staff and families communicated daily in the school environment and had regularly scheduled parent–teacher conferences to discuss the child's growth and development.

Assessments were made to determine if participation in the program had an effect on mother–infant interactions, on the family's home environment, and the mother's maternal education and employment. These evaluations were conducted at a time when small numbers of children were enrolled in infant and toddler nonparental care. Therefore, a key question was whether the preschool intervention might be disruptive to the child's primary attachment relationship, even if the child benefited in other ways, such as accelerated language and intellectual development.

Assessments of mother–infant interactions were conducted at 6 and 20 months of age through direct observations in a laboratory resembling a small living room. Comparisons were made with mothers from the experimental group, the control group, and a predominantly middle-class comparison group. Evidence from these observations showed that at 6 months of age there was similarity among all groups. At 20 months of age, however, middle-class mothers communicated and interacted with their children to a greater degree than mothers from the experimental and control groups. Further analyses of exchanges at 20 months showed that experimental group infants were communicating with their mothers at significantly higher levels than control group infants and were comparable to middle-class infants on "requesting" behaviors. This appears to indicate that children in the Abecedarian program were presenting different "demand characteristics" when interacting with their mothers, which may have affected the quality of mother–child interactions. Analyses of laboratory observations at 36 months of age showed that experimental group children were four times as likely as control group children to attempt to change their mothers' behavior (e.g., asking them to read a book or play a game with them). In addition, they played with their mothers twice as long as the control group, which may indicate that the play was more enjoyable to the mothers because of the children's advanced skills. Therefore, it can be concluded that children's participation in the Abecedarian Project may have positively affected the quality of maternal responsiveness (Ramey, Dorval, & Baker-Ward, 1983).

The home environments of experimental and control group children were assessed with the Home Observation for the Measurement of the Environment at 6, 18, 30, and 42 months of age. The HOME measures the:

1. Emotional and verbal responsivity of the child's home environment.
2. Absence of punishment.
3. Physical and temporal organization of the environment.
4. Provision of appropriate toys.
5. Maternal involvement.
6. Opportunity for variety in daily stimulation (Bradley & Caldwell, 1979).

Results showed that there were no differences between the home environments of treatment and control groups. Thus, it was concluded that the child's participation in a high-quality preschool program did not have a positive or negative effect on the child's home environment. Further analyses showed, however, that the total HOME score at 54 months of age was systematically associated with intellectual development at 60 months of age for both treatment and control children. This suggests that home environment has an influence on children's intellectual development, despite their participation in a high-quality preschool program (Ramey, Dorval, & Baker-Ward, 1983).

When the educational levels of mothers were examined, it was found that experimental group mothers had significantly higher educational levels (11.9 years) than control group mothers (10.3 years) despite the fact that the educational levels of mothers were comparable (10.30 and 10.12 for the experimental and control groups, respectively) at the time of the child's birth. Over time the teenage mothers with children in the early childhood educational program derived the greatest educational benefits (Ramey et al., 2000). This seems to indicate that a child's participation in a full-time preschool program gave mothers the time needed to continue their education and that teen mothers benefitted the most. Furthermore, child participation had a positive impact on maternal employment. Mothers of children in the experimental group were more likely to be employed in semiskilled or skilled jobs than control group mothers, possibly due to their increased educational level (Ramey, Dorval, & Baker-Ward, 1983). At age 15, the rates of employment were highest (92%) for teen mothers in the preschool-only experimental group and lowest (66%) for teen mothers in the preschool control group (Ramey et al., 2000).

These positive findings point out the importance of the bidirectional nature of children's interactions with their environments both in the home and school settings. It is also likely that the children's emerging and increased general developmental competence extended to their ability to "bring out" the best in caregivers in settings other than the home.

When the children entered public school, an explicit home–school educational program was added for a three-year period in an effort to help the child meet the educational expectations offered in the school-based curriculum and to determine if early gains might be maintained and/or enhanced by a specific transition-to-school program. Because high-risk children are more likely to learn at a slower than average rate, it was decided that additional tutoring would be beneficial. A tutoring intervention program was created and involved families working directly with their children in the home setting using supplemental educational activities developed by master level home–school resource teachers. Master teachers served as consultants to classroom teachers and provided social and emotional support to the families. In addition, they served as advocates and liaisons between families and schools. Each master teacher had a caseload of 12 families. In a one-year period, the master teacher designed approximately 60 learning activities for each child. They explained the activities to the family, demonstrated how to use them, and encouraged parents to regularly incorporate activities. It was hypothesized that the involvement of master teachers who "taught" the families directly would lead to increased competence and involvement of parents in their child's education, and this would influence both the home and school environments (Ramey & Ramey, 1992; Ramey & Ramey, 1998b). An eight-week summer program consisting of traditional summer camp experiences and enjoyable reading and math experiences was added. The camps were staffed by the master teachers and supplemented by paid and volunteer students and adults.

Parents reported that they averaged working with their child on targeted activities about 15 minutes a day. They were enthusiastic about the activities and stated that overall they found the program to be a very positive experience and would likely continue to participate if the program had lasted longer. Despite these positive reports, the results of the K–2 intervention show short-term and moderate or few benefits for the children's educational outcomes, unlike the five-year preschool intervention, which demonstrated larger benefits. The K–2 program did undergird increased scholastic achievement, but by itself was not as effective as the preschool intervention in preventing school failure and intellectual lags. Nevertheless, the program increased parental involvement in their children's education and had measurable benefits for reading and mathematics achievement that continued to be detected through adolescence.

Accomplishments in reading achievement are particularly striking. Follow-up studies of child participants were conducted at age 15 to measure reading progress at middle adolescence. Effect sizes were computed to determine practical significance. It was found that effect sizes varied from .14 to .87 in proportion to the duration of treatment, with the strongest effect size for the preschool plus K–2 Educational Support Group (see Figure. 7.1). The preschool-only group also had a strong effect size of .68, while the K–2 transition-only group and the control group had effect sizes of less than .25. This highlights the practical and enduring effects of providing intensive preschool plus a K–2 educational program. In addition, children participating in the preschool program were less likely to be retained in grade or placed in a special education program. An especially striking benefit is only 12% of the children in the preschool-only group were placed in special education, as compared to 48% of the control group (Ramey et al., 2000).

These findings indicate the complex interdependencies between parenting and child development and how extrafamilial supports can be beneficial to children and parents, and the dynamic interactions between them. Because many of these mothers were young, undereducated, and had low social and financial resources, there is reason to posit that their parenting skills were also undeveloped and less than optimal. Parenting attitudes and knowledge findings were consistent with what the parenting correctional literature has shown for many other samples.

The second randomized controlled longitudinal study, Project CARE, systematically compared two forms of intervention, a center-based program identical to the Abecedarian Project and a home-based program of weekly home visits for the first three years of life, followed by biweekly visits for the next two years. This project enrolled 63 children that were randomly assigned to treatment or control groups during the first three months of life and followed longitudinally, as in the

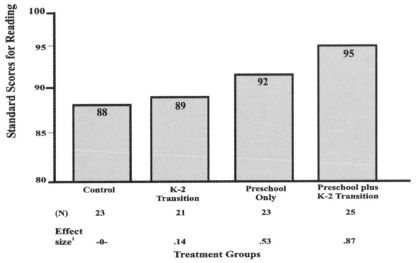

Fig. 7.1.   Abecedarian Project Woodcock-Johnson Age-Referenced reading standard scores at age 15.

Abecedarian Project. The study was conducted in the same community and in the same university-affiliated child development center. It used comparable criteria to determine eligibility for participation (High Risk Index, Ramey & Smith, 1977) and provided similar child care and school-aged treatments as the Abecedarian Project. Additionally, children received a family-based intervention from infancy to school age. Children were randomly assigned to one of three treatment conditions: child care plus home visits, home visits only, or control (see Wasik, Ramey, Bryant, & Sparling, 1990, for more details). All Project CARE children assigned to either the child care plus home visit or home-visit-only groups also received the home-school resource teacher treatment during the first three years of elementary school.

This project was very favorably received by the community, the mothers, and the home visitors (who were community individuals who received extensive training and ongoing support for their work). The child care plus the home visit results replicated those from the Abecedarian Project. We reached the disappointing conclusion, however, that child development outcomes on a wide array of measures did not detect any benefits from the home-visiting-only condition. It is important to consider a number of factors. First, children in the educational child-care program with the home-visiting family education component scored significantly higher on measures of cognitive performance than did other intervention children who did not participate in the educational child-care program. The addition of the home-visiting family education component did not significantly improve the home environment, the parent's attitudes, or the children's or parents' behavior. The results of this study were similar to those found for the Abecedarian Project in terms of the intellectual development of the children up to age three. Consistently over the preschool years, children in the educational child-care program in the Abecedarian Project scored significantly higher than those in the control condition. This, however, was not the case in Project CARE. One major reason this may be the case is that some children in the control condition attended and participated in community child-care programs. Interestingly, children in the control condition that did not participate in a community child-care program scored significantly lower than the children in the educational child-care program by one standard deviation on a measure of cognitive performance at 54 months. These findings cause serious pause and point to the importance of considering the differences in children's environments—whether in the home or in a center. Although the same curriculum materials were available in the home and the center, the use of and delivery of the materials may have varied greatly. The children in the educational child-care setting spent time with well-trained and experienced child-care staff whose main purpose was to provide a stimulating environment. The changes that might have occurred in parenting behavior and in parent–child interactions may not have been early enough and intensive enough (in quantity) to equal what was received in center-based optimal educational care. Unfortunately, follow-up of these families in terms of the development of later-born children did not occur to determine whether there were carryover effects to parental competence.

Another project, the Infant Health and Development Program (IHDP), involved an eight-site randomized controlled trial with 985 low-birth-weight (LBW) and premature infants who varied widely in their social risks (Infant Health and Development Program, 1990; Ramey et al., 1992). Infants were randomly assigned by a computer program, with approximately one third of the sample to the intervention group ($n = 377$) and two thirds to the follow-up group ($n = 608$). The program was similar to Abecedarian and Project CARE. However, IHDP was modified to operate from hospital discharge to three years of age and to use home visits only in the first year, and home visits plus early childhood education in a child development center from one to three years of age. The IHDP was focused more on direct home visiting and parental education around problem-solving for everyday issues. The goals of the home visit program were to:

1. Provide emotional, social, and practical support to parents, as adults.
2. Provide parents with developmentally timed information about their low-birthweight child's development.

3. Help parents learn specific ways to foster their child's intellectual, physical, and social development.
4. Help parents discover ways to cope with the responsibilities of caring for a developing and, initially, vulnerable child.

A major component of the home visiting program were the *Early Partners* (Sparling, Lewis, & Neuwirth, 1992) and the *Partners for Learning* (Sparling & Lewis, 1984) curricula. The *Early Partners* curriculum focused on very young low-birth-weight infants (24 weeks to 40 weeks gestational age) and *Partners for Learning* curriculum focused on infancy and early childhood (birth to 36 months). A series of learning activities that emphasized developmentally appropriate, positive adult–child interactions were used. Home visitors and parents selected activities appropriate to the child's developmental status through discussion and reflection. The choice of activities was based on an educational philosophy that emphasized learning as a natural process.

Each IHDP site established and operated a full-day child development center that exceeded current state licensing requirements for the exclusive use of the children in the intervention group. Children began to attend the centers when they reached their first birthday. Once infants began attending the child development centers, home visitors also helped to coordinate center and home activities. The teacher and assistant teacher in each classroom organized the classroom program by planning and implementing the curriculum, maintaining a developmentally appropriate social and physical environment, and cooperating and coordinating with parents and home visitors in planning educational activities. Parent meetings were conducted every other month during the time the child development centers were operating. These meetings were held to serve as family support groups in which parents could network, provide support for each other, share information and concerns about childrearing, as well as provide parents with information about child-development-related topics and community resources.

The early intervention model of the IHDP was interdisciplinary, representing recommended pediatric practices, family supports, and early childhood education. The intervention content included: parent support, parent problem-solving curriculum, learning curriculum, and play materials. The parent support component of the intervention was an integral part of the home visits, parents groups, and child development centers. The program's goal was to support and to encourage parents by providing informational, instrumental, social, and emotional assistance based on the perceived needs of the parents. These meetings were also used to review with the parents the program's goals of supporting, not supplanting, the parents' roles in their children's growth and development. A parent problem-solving curriculum was developed, known as Problem Solving for Parents (Wasik, 1984). This component was developed to help parents learn to cope effectively with personal issues that they identified as important to their functioning as parents. The approach was designed to help parents consider their own goals, challenges, and problems; set priorities; and develop strategies to solve problems. Seven processes used in interpersonal problem solving were presented to parents in nontechnical language as part of a general model for coping with day-by-day family concerns: (1) problem identification, (2) goal selection, (3) generation of alternative solutions, (4) evaluation of solutions, (5) decision making, (6) actual performance, and (7) evaluation of outcome. Home visitors helped parents identify concerns and goals and to address them using a systematic plan. These plans were concerned with positive parental opportunities as well as "problems" or impediments to personal growth.

The learning activities used in the home and in the child development centers were based on the *Partners for Learning Curriculum*, which was also used in the Abecedarian Project and Project CARE (see page 128 for full description). The educational program was designed to emphasize one-to-one positive interchanges between adults and children rather than group activities, given the needs of very young children. Play materials were also used as a means to facilitate the young child's development. Home visitors took toys and an accompanying guide book to the home and discussed the various ways that the parents could use the toy and how and what the child might learn by playing with it.

A Family Participation Index was created by summing the number of home visits, attendance at parent group meetings, and days attended at the child development centers. Degree of participation was divided into high, medium, and low terciles. The intervention group performed better than did the pediatric follow-up group, and the degree of participation was positively related to cognitive development. The probability of a child's functioning in the borderline intellectual range or lower decreased significantly with increasing terciles of family participation (see Figure. 7.2). The "high participation" intervention group was associated with an 8.9-fold reduction in the number of low-birth-weight children functioning in the retarded range at three years of age, when compared to children who received only high-quality pediatric follow-up services (Ramey et al., 1992). The home environment showed significant improvements, and there were benefits for parent–child interactions. Specifically, children and families participating in the center-based treatment who also received home-based and individualized parenting guidance show marked improvements in their parent–child interactions and home environments. Clearly, these findings indicate that high parental support and involvement and participation in a center-based program helped produce positive outcomes for children.

It is important to note that there was a strong association between maternal education and/or maternal IQ and the magnitude of IQ benefits in children such that lower maternal education and/or IQ was associated with a greater degree of benefits associated with the program (Brooks-Gunn, Gross, Kraemer, Spiker, & Shapiro, 1992, Landesman & Ramey, 1989; Martin, Ramey, & Ramey, 1990). Interestingly, there were virtually negligible or no benefits associated with participating in the

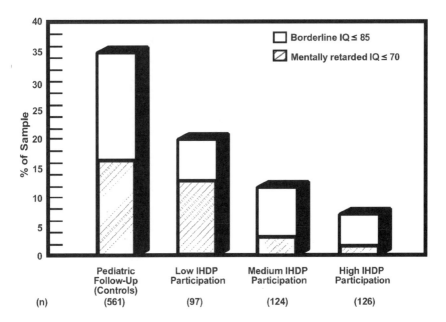

FIG. 7.2. Infant Health and Development Program: Percentage of borderline (IQ ≤ 85) and retarded intellectual performance (IQ ≤ 70).

program for those with college educated parents (see Figure 7.3). It is hypothesized that this may be because these educated parents compensated via increased positive early experiences. In other words, these parents provided additional care for their children in their own homes or the parents obtained other very-high-quality child care and early intervention supports for their premature and low-birthweight infants.

What does this research tell us about parenting and early intervention? What is needed for early intervention programs to augment or improve parenting effectiveness? The evidence from the studies reviewed suggest that there are a number of critical factors that are necessary for early intervention programs to have an impact on parenting effectiveness and the home environment. In a review of the early intervention literature, Ramey and Ramey (1998a) derived six principles pertaining to the impact of early intervention on child and parent functioning. The elements are apparently important in producing significant and positive results for families. These include:

- **Sufficient intensity:** Many home visiting studies have been shown to have few or no effects (Olds & Kitzman, 1990) on the quality of the family environment and parenting skills. This has been largely attributable to the low intensity of programs. A program that is offered once a week often is not

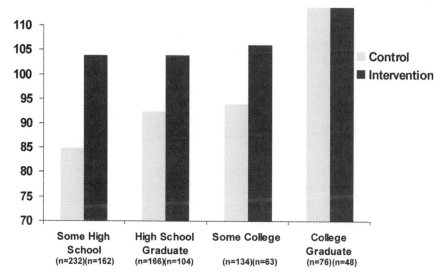

FIG. 7.3. Infant Health and Development Program: Children's IQ at 36 months: Maternal education X treatment group.

intense enough to yield significant improvements in the home. It takes work to make change in a person's actions and practices, it is a daunting task that requires a great deal of rehearsal and repetition.

- **Sufficient duration:** To have long-term benefits, parents and children need more than just an "inoculation" of a program. As with intensity, programs that are shorter in duration have been shown to be less effective in helping address parenting skills and the home environment.

- **Appropriate timing:** Often when we talk about "the right timing" we refer to the child's first three years of life. Clearly, interventions that begin earlier in development and continue longer benefit children the most. The same position can be made for parenting as well—the earlier parent education is provided, the greater the chance the program has to help guide, direct, and mold parents.

- **Direct engagement of parents, children, and the larger family context:** Parenting does not operate in a vacuum. Parents are influenced by their own experiences and histories with their parents and others. Parents are also influenced by their children—their temperament, behavior, and their cognitive, mental, and physical health needs. To adequately address the needs of the home environment and improve parenting skills, early intervention programs must address the bidirectional nature of all the participants in the home and larger family/community context.

- **Diverse supports and services:** Early intervention programs focusing on the whole family are effective in improving parenting and the home environment.

Programs that focus on a single aspect of a parent's family life generally have not been successful (Ramey, Ramey, & Lanzi, 1998).

- **Responsive and individualized programming:** We live in an extremely complex world that is ever changing. To address this, early intervention programs must have at their core an understanding that a "canned" program or service delivery model may not match everyone's needs and may not be the same over time for individuals. Programs must be flexible enough to grow with the parents as they develop new skills and encounter different challenges (Ramey, Ramey, Gaines, & Blair, 1995).

Ongoing longitudinal study and new intervention programs have provided a sound basis for understanding the benefits of early interventions programs on the home environment and parent–child interactions. One clear message is that discussing the controversy about biology versus environment is largely irrelevant—and so is the artificial dichotomy of the child's family or home environment versus other settings where the child spends time. A child's experience of the world is not compartmentalized the way it is for adults. Theoretically, the child experiences his or her life as a continuous series of interactions, opportunities, and events that make more or less sense, more or less stimulate normative development, more or less include exposure to neglect and/or abuse—when children obtain what they need for typical development, regardless of whether it is parent-delivered or delivered from other caring adults. In such cases, the results are highly similar—children thrive and show typical or nearly typical development.

REFERENCES

Bertalanffy, L. V. (1975). *Perspectives on general system theory.* New York: Braziller.

Bradley, R., & Caldwell, B. (1979). Home Observation for Measurement of the Environment: A revision of the preschool scale. *American Journal of Mental Deficiency, 84,* 235–244.

Brooks-Gunn, J., Gross, R. T., Kraemer, H. C., Spiker, D., & Shapiro, S. (1992). Enhancing the cognitive outcomes of low birth weight, premature infants: For whom is the intervention most effective? *Pediatrics, 89,* 1209–1215.

Campbell, F. A., Breitmayer, B. J., & Ramey, C. T. (1986). Disadvantaged teenage mothers and their children: Consequences of educational daycare. *Family Relations, 35,* 63–68.

Campbell, F. A., Goldstein, S., Schaefer, E. S., & Ramey, C. T. (1991). Parental beliefs and values related to family risk, educational intervention, and child academic competence. *Early Childhood Research Quarterly, 6,* 167–182.

Entwisle, D. R., & Alexander, K. L. (1998). Facilitating the transition to first grade: The nature of transition and research on factors affecting it. *Elementary School Journal, 98,* 351–364.

Guralnick, M. J. (Ed.). (1997). *The effectiveness of early intervention.* Baltimore: Paul H. Brookes.

Infant Health and Development Program (1990). Enhancing the outcomes of low birthweight, premature infants. *Journal of the American Medical Association, 263,* 3035–3042.

Landesman, S. L., & Ramey, C. T. (1989). Developmental psychology and mental retardation: Integrating scientific principles with treatment practices. *American Psychologist, 44,* 409–415.

Martin, S. L., Ramey, C. T., & Ramey, S. L. (1990). The prevention of intellectual impairment in chil-dren of impoverished families: Findings of a randomized trial of educational day care. *American Journal of Public Health, 80,* 844–847.

Olds, D. L., & Kitzman, H. (1990). Can home visitation improve the health of women and children at environmental risk? *Pediatrics, 86 (1),* 108–116.

Ramey, C. T. (1980). Social consequences of ecological intervention that began infancy. In S. Harel (Ed.), *The at-risk infant.* Amsterdam: Excerpta Medica.

Ramey, C. T., Bryant, D. M, Wasik, B. H., Sparling, J. J., Fendt, K. H., & LaVange, L. M. (1992). Infant Health and Development Program for low birth weight, premature infants: Program ele-ments, family participation, and child intelligence. *Pediatrics, 3,* 454–465.

Ramey, C. T., & Campbell, F. A. (1979). Compensatory education for disadvantaged children. *School Review, 87* (2), 171–189.

Ramey, C. T., & Campbell, F. A. (1984). Preventive education for high-risk children: Cognitive conse-quences of the Carolina Abecedarian Project. *American Journal of Mental Deficiency, 88* (5), 515–523.

Ramey, C. T., & Campbell, F. A. (1992). Poverty, early childhood education, and academic compe-tence: The abecedarian experiment. In A. Huston (Ed.), *Children in poverty* (pp. 190–221). New York: Cambridge University Press.

Ramey, C. T., Campbell, F. A., Burchinal, M., Skinner, M. L., Gardner, D. M., & Ramey, S. L. (2000). Persistent effects of early childhood education on high-risk children and their mothers. *Applied Developmental Science, 4,* 2–14.

Ramey, C. T., Dorval, B., & Baker-Ward, L. (1983). Group day care and socially disadvantaged fami-lies: Effects on the child and the family. In S. Kilmer (Ed.), *Advances in early education and day care* (pp. 69–106). Greenwich, CT: JAI Press.

Ramey, C. T., Farran, D. C., & Campbell, F. A. (1979). Predicting IQ from mother–infant interactions. *Child Development, 50,* 804–814.

Ramey, C. T., & Finklestein, N. W. (1981). Psychosocial mental retardation: A biological and social coalescence. In M. Begab, H. Garber, & H. C. Haywood (Eds.), *Psychological influences in retarded performance* (pp. 65–92). Baltimore: University Park Press.

Ramey, C. T., McGinness, G., Cross, L., Collier, A., & Barrie-Blackley, S. (1981). The abecedarian approach to social competence. Cognitive and liguistic intervention for disadvantaged preschoolers. Ina K. Borman (Ed.), *The social life of children in a changing society* (pp. 145–174). Hillsdale, NJ: Lawrence Erlbaum Associates.

Ramey, C. T., & Ramey, S. L. (1992). Effective early intervention. *Mental Retardation, 30,* 337–345.

Ramey, C. T., & Ramey, S. L. (1998a). Early intervention and early experience. *American Psychologist, 53,* 109–120.

Ramey, C. T., & Ramey, S. L. (1998b). Prevention of intellectual disabilities: Early interventions to improve cognitive development. *Preventive Medicine, 27,* 224–232.

Ramey, S. L., & Ramey, C. T. (1999). Early experience and early intervention for children "at risk" for developmental delay and mental retardation. *Mental Retardation and Developmental Disabilities Research Reviews, 5,* 1–10.

Ramey, S. L., & Ramey, C. T. (2000). Early childhood experiences and developmental competence. In J. Waldfogel & S. Danziger (Eds.), *Securing the future: Investing in children from birth to college* (pp. 122–150). New York: Russell Sage.

Ramey, S. L., Ramey, C. T., Lanzi, R., Phillips, M., Brezausek, C., Katholi, C., & Snyder, S. (2001). Head start children's entry into public schools: A report on the National Head Start/Public School Early Childhood Transition Demonstration Study. Final report to the US. Department of Health and Human Services, Administration for Children & Families.

Ramey, C. T., Ramey, S. L., Gaines, R., Blair, C. B. (1995). Two-generation early intervention pro-grams: A child development perspective. In S. Smith (Ed.), *Two-generation programs for families in poverty: A new intervention strategy: Vol 9. Advances in Applied Developmental Psychology* (pp. 199–228). Norwood, NJ: Ablex Publishing Corporation.

Ramey, C. T., Ramey, S. L., & Lanzi, R. G. (1998). Differentiating developmental risk levels for families in poverty: Creating a family typology. In M. Lewis and C. Feiring (Eds.), *Families, Risks, and Competence* (pp. 187–205). Mahwah, NJ: Lawrence Erlbaum Associates.

Ramey, C. T., & Smith, B. (1977). Assessing the intellectual consequences of early intervention with high-risk infants. *American Journal of Mental Deficiency, 81,* 318–324.

Sparling, J. J., Lewis, I., & Neuwirths, S. (1992). *Early Partners.* Lewisville, NC: Kaplan Press.

Sparling, J. J., & Lewis, I. (1984). *Partners for learning.* Lewisville, NC: Kaplan Press.

Wallach, M. A., & Wallach, L. (1976). *Teaching all children to read.* Chicago: University of Chicago Press.

Wasik, B. H. (1984). *Problem solving for parents.* Chapel Hill: Frank Porter Graham Child Development Center, University of North Carolina.

Wasik, B. H., Ramey, C. T., Bryant, D. M., & Sparling, J. J. (1990). A longitudinal study of two early intervention strategies. Project CARE. *Child Development, 61,* 1682–1696.

8

Parenting and Academic Achievement: Multiple Paths to Early Literacy

Frederick J. Morrison
Loyola University Chicago

Ramie R. Cooney
Creighton University

For over a decade, concerns have been raised repeatedly in both popular and scientific literatures about the inadequate literacy levels attained by significant numbers of children and adults in American society (Fiske, 1991; Hirsch, 1987; Steinberg, 1996; Stevenson, Chen & Lee, 1993). In the search for possible causes and cures for America's literacy problems, increasing attention is being focused on the early childhood years as a crucial foundation period for later success in school and work. Hence, scientists and educators have renewed interest in understanding the nature and sources of school readiness and the transition to school (Alexander & Entwisle, 1988; Shepard & Smith, 1988; Shonkoff & Phillips, 2000).

Despite growing consensus about the importance of the early years, until recently (Alexander & Entwisle, 1988; Hart & Rislay, 1995; Stepek & Ryan, 1997) surprisingly little solid empirical data had been gathered on the nature and determinants of individual differences among children in skills deemed to be predictive of school readiness and early school success. The vast bulk of the literature has been devoted to the relation between a child's entrance age and

Address correspondence to: Fred Morrison, Loyola University Chicago, Department of Psychology, 1049 DH, 6525 N. Sheridan Rd., Chicago, IL 60626, Phone: 773-508-8684, e-mail: fmorris@luc.edu

141

subsequent academic achievement (Davis, Trimble, & Vincent, 1980), though recent evidence consistently has shown minimal associations between entrance age and achievement during the early school years. (Morrison, Griffith & Alberts, 1997).

GREENSBORO EARLY
SCHOOLING STUDY

Beginning in 1990, we have been studying the nature and sources of cognitive and social development in young American children. A large longitudinal study in the southeast has examined factors in the child, family, and school that predict school readiness and early school success. We began with an interest in when meaningful individual differences became evident and how generalizable they were across literacy and social domains. A total of 500 children were followed longitudinally in three successive cohorts. Testing occurred in the early fall and late spring of kindergarten (Fall K, Spring K) and in the spring of each successive year to third grade. Primary emphasis was placed on the following core set of literacy outcomes: receptive vocabulary (from the Peabody Picture Vocabulary Test—Revised, [PPVT—R], Dunn & Dunn, 1981), reading, mathematics, and general information (from three subtests of the Peabody Individual Achievement Test—Revised, [PIAT—R], Markwardt, 1989). Important predictor variables included child's IQ (Stanford-Binet Intelligence Scale—4th Ed., Thorndike, Hagen, & Sattler, 1986), race, gender, months of preschool experience, age of entry to school, social skills (Cooper-Farran Behavior Rating Scale, [CFBRS], Cooper & Farran, 1991), mother's years of education, single/dual parent status, and quality of the home literacy environment. The latter score was derived from a background questionnaire requesting information such as who reads to the child and how often; ownership and use of a library card; number of newspaper and magazine subscriptions; book reading behavior; possession of stereos, televisions, radios, encyclopedias, and dictionaries, and television viewing habits of the child (Griffin & Morrison, 1997). An extensive battery of information on the child (14 variables), family (11 variables), and school (3 variables) allowed us to investigate the nature and sources or of individual differences in growth of children's early literacy skills.

VARIABILITY IN READINESS

The first question we asked was: What are the nature and extent of individual differences in literacy skills shortly after children start kindergarten? Inspection of scatter plots for all literacy variables revealed that a wide range of variability existed in children's literacy skills at school entry. Although the average age of the children at Fall K testing was approximately 5 years, 4 months of age, the lowest vocabulary score was equal to an age equivalent of 1 year, 9 months whereas the highest score reached 10 years, 8 months. In other words, there was virtually a nine-year spread among children in vocabulary scores at the beginning of kindergarten. A similar picture revealing substantial variation emerged for reading recognition, general information, math, and even alphabet recognition.

Are Individual Differences General or Specific?

The second question of interest was: Is relatively low (or high) performance in one area of literacy associated with comparable levels of performance in other areas? To address this question, correlations were calculated between all pairs of the four outcome variables assessed at Fall K. The results revealed that performance levels across the four literacy domains were strongly and significantly correlated. For example, performance on receptive vocabulary correlated with reading performance .54, with general knowledge .80, and with mathematics achievement .60 (Morrison et al., in preparation). Overall, the pattern of findings revealed that relatively low (or high) performance was not limited to one isolated domain of early literacy. Children who scored relatively low (or high) in one domain tended to score relatively low (or high) across all domains.

What Happens to Individual Differences over Time?

The focus of the third question was "What happens to individual differences as children proceed through the early school years?" The most straightforward hypothesis was that the large individual differences found at school entry would begin to decrease systematically. Since schooling is widely regarded as the great equalizer, we would expect that socially or economically disadvantaged children who had not acquired adequate literacy skills during their preschool years would begin to catch up to their more advantaged peers. Contrary to expectations, however, data from the longitudinal investigation did not reveal uniform reductions in the size of individual differences over time (Morrison et al., in preparation). Individual differences in vocabulary did converge slightly, but on the other measures, variation across individuals was maintained or magnified.

What Factors Predict Literacy Acquisition?

The final question examined a number of child, family, and sociocultural factors that uniquely predicted children's performance at school entry and growth until the end of third grade. A series of forced-entry regressions revealed that a relatively small set of seven factors uniquely contributed to literacy outcomes at school entry and accounted for from 60% to 70% of the variance in outcome measures. Three child factors (IQ, work-related skills, and entrance age), two family factors (literacy environment and maternal educational level), and two sociocultural factors (race and preschool experience) comprised the most powerful predictors at school entry. A child's IQ, age at kindergarten entry, and family literacy environment demonstrated the most pervasive influence across all literacy skills. Most of these factors sustained their influence over the course of the early elementary grades.

PARENTING AND EARLY LITERACY

From the pattern of findings, it was abundantly clear that early experiences before school entry played a crucial role in shaping children's early literacy skills. The family literacy environment in particular and parenting more generally emerges as one major contributor to early development. In recent years we have been examining more closely the nature and impact of early parenting on school performance. It has become increasingly clear that what we call parenting comprises a complex array of skills and beliefs that shape academic growth through diverse pathways of achievement (Collins, Maccoby, Steinberg, Hetherington, & Bornstein, 2000).

Parenting Styles

The concept of parenting styles has dominated theory and research in this area for many years. The study of parenting styles has been significantly shaped by the original triadic configuration developed by Diana Baumrind (1966, 1968, 1971). Her authoritarian, authoritative, and permissive styles were defined by varying levels of parental warmth and control. These delineations were revised by Maccoby and Martin (1983), who claimed that parenting styles could be best understood by exploring the levels of demandingness and responsiveness promoted by parents, yielding four parenting styles: authoritarian, authoritative, indulgent, and neglectful.

Authoritative parenting has been frequently associated with the promotion and maintenance of higher levels of academic competence and school adjustment, while the detrimental effects of neglectful or nonauthoritative parenting on adolescent outcomes, such as poorer classroom engagement and homework completion, appear to accumulate over time (Dornbusch, Ritter, Leiderman, Roberts, & Fraleigh, 1987; Glasgow, Dornbusch, Troyer, Steinberg, & Ritter, 1997; Lamborn, Mounts, Steinberg, & Dornbusch, 1991; Steinberg, Lamborn, Darling, Mounts, & Dornbusch, 1994).

Parental Beliefs

Clark (1983) conducted case studies of ten poor, Black, one- and two-parent families of high- and low-achieving students and found that parents of high achievers promoted strong values, held high expectations for education, fostered children's active participation in school, and felt responsible for their children's performance. In contrast, parents of low achievers communicated a sense of powerlessness over their children's poor academic achievement and behavior, and not only refused to accept responsibility for their children's performance, but viewed academic failure as the fault of the child.

Despite the apparent association between parental beliefs and children's academic achievement, researchers have failed to convincingly establish a direct relation (Okagaki & Sternberg, 1993; Richman & Rescorla, 1995). Further, the association between parental beliefs and children's competence varies across different ethnic groups (Okagaki & Frensch, 1998; Steinberg, Dornbusch, & Brown, 1992; Stevenson, Chen, & Uttal, 1990).

Other work uncovered discrepancies not only between parental beliefs and children's academic outcomes, but also between parental educational beliefs and their literacy-promoting behaviors. Robeson (1997) found that after statistically controlling for the child's IQ, entrance age, gender, maternal education, and amount of preschool experience, parental beliefs about the importance of schooling failed to uniquely predict the quality of the home literacy environment provided by parents. More important, after accounting for the unique variance contributed by background variables and the home literacy environment, parental beliefs failed to predict performance on receptive vocabulary, reading recognition, and mathematics, and contributed roughly 2% of the variance on a measure of general knowledge. Taken together, empirical findings to date have revealed a tenuous relationship between measures of parents' educational beliefs and their children's academic achievement.

Family Learning Environment

Investigators have begun moving from assessing parental beliefs to measuring parenting practices that enhance or inhibit literacy development and academic achievement. Two primary foci of research have included the quality of language stimulation in the home and more explicit literacy-promoting behaviors.

Maternal speech patterns, such as the amount, quality, and kinds of speech produced, have predicted vocabulary growth during the first three years of life (Hart & Risley, 1995) as well as prekindergarten measures of emergent literacy and print-related skills (DeTemple & Snow, 1992; Dickinson & Tabors, 2001). Another facet of parental behavior that has attracted increased attention are deliberate parenting practices that promote children's cognitive and literacy development (Bloom, 1981; Clark, 1983; Morrow, 1989; Stewart, 1995). Researchers have found significant correlations between the home environment measures (including parental reading habits and children's exposure to print) and a number of child outcomes such as IQ scores at one and three years of age (Bradley & Caldwell, 1980), second-grade reading competency (Scarborough, Dobrich, & Hager, 1991), and eleventh-grade reading comprehension (Cunningham & Stanovich, 1997; Cunningham, Stanovich, & West, 1994).

Griffin and Morrison (1997) created a composite measure of the home literacy environment, consisting of assessments of frequency of library card use, number of child and adult magazine subscriptions, number of newspaper subscriptions, how often someone read to the child, the number of books the child owned, the hours of television viewed per week by the child, and how often the father and mother read to themselves. After taking into account a host of other background characteristics (child IQ, maternal education, entrance age, preschool experience, race, and gender), the measure of the home literacy environment uniquely predicted fall kindergarten receptive vocabulary, general knowledge, and reading scores, as well as spring second grade scores in general knowledge and reading. In summary, both aspects of parenting behavior (language and literacy environments) appeared to substantially influence children's cognitive development. Most important, not only were these dramatically significant effects found at very young ages, but these early parenting practices also significantly contributed to children's later academic achievement.

Parental Warmth and Responsiveness

In their reconceptualization of the influence of parenting styles on children's development, Darling and Steinberg (1993) argued that recognition of the emotional climate, which provides the context for socialization, must be assessed in order to understand the relationship between parenting practices and child outcomes. A number of researchers have in fact examined the quality of parent–child interactions, specifically, how parental warmth (displayed in measures of sensitivity, attachment, cooperation, or acceptance) affected different aspects of children's socioemotional development, such as compliance (Maccoby & Martin, 1983), adjustment and coping strategies (Herman & McHale, 1993), academic motivation (Radin, 1971), and self-efficacy (Richman & Rescorla, 1995).

Of particular interest is the role of parental warmth on children's cognitive development. Observations of parental warmth, such as open displays of affection, physical or verbal reinforcement, and sensitivity to children's requests and feelings have been significantly associated with academic achievement and cognitive growth (Clark, 1983; Radin, 1971). Other research also documented a consistent relation over time between the affective quality of mother–child interactions and a number of measures of children's cognitive competence: mental ability scores at age four, school readiness skills at ages five and six, IQ scores at age six, and vocabulary and mathematics performance at age 12 (Estrada, Arsenio, Hess, & Holloway, 1987). Estrada and her colleagues suggested that the affective quality of parent–child interactions influenced children's cognitive development in three ways: through parents' willingness to engage themselves in problem-solving tasks with their children; by regulation of the information shared among adults and children (affecting children's developing social competence); and finally, by encouraging children's exploratory tendencies, thereby enhancing their motivation and persistence in challenging tasks.

Most notable in these studies are the effects of parental influence on social and cognitive domains before kindergarten entry. Not only have patterns of social behavior and cognitive functioning been established before children experience a formal schooling environment, but the affective quality of parent-child relationships apparently contributes to the long-term stability of these effects.

Parental Control

This parenting dimension reflects the "control" aspect of Baumrind's authoritative parenting style. While the "warmth," or emotional climate, of the home is an important component of parenting, setting and maintaining rules, standards, and limits establishes parental authority and creates a supportive, structured context for children's cognitive development. Although this dimension remains somewhat speculative, recent research has suggested an indirect relationship between parental control and children's academic achievement. In our Greensboro study the social skills children developed as a result of parental socialization mediated the relation between parental control and children's literacy skills at the beginning of kindergarten (Cooney, 1998). In summary, while more research is necessary to establish causality, there appears to be an important, if complex, relation between parental rules, standards, and limits and children's cognitive development.

Family Organization

Although not frequently addressed in the literature, there is an additional component of parenting that may influence children's cognitive and literacy development. The effort parents expend to organize the family's schedule into a set of predictable timetables and routines may affect children's school-related social behavior and academic achievement. Family organization refers to the degree of predictability built into a child's schedule. For example, whether and when a family eats together, the consistency of a bedtime routine, and planning for future events or obligations. Family organization also includes creation and maintenance of rituals and traditions surrounding special occasions, holidays, and birthdays. A child who can rely on structured schedules and predictable routines is free to focus energy and time on academic and related pursuits.

While this dimension has also not been heavily investigated, several researchers have studied the role of children's work chores on the development of their behavioral and academic competence. Family rituals and routinized daily household activities aided the formation of a structured environment that fostered responsibility in high-achieving students (Clark, 1983) and may have also benefited children's cognitive functioning through their partnering with others and development of cognitive strategies (Goodnow, 1988). In summary, family organization may play a vital if less direct role in shaping children's social behavior and cognitive growth.

PARENTING AND ACADEMIC
ACHIEVEMENT: MULTIPLE PATHS
TO EARLY LITERACY

Measuring Parenting

A few years ago we set out to measure the dimensions of parenting highlighted in the literature and to relate these dimensions to children's literacy development. To that end, we developed a parenting questionnaire designed to measure five dimensions of parenting: quality of the learning environment; parental warmth and responsiveness; parental control and discipline strategies; parental beliefs about childrearing and qualities in children necessary for success; parental organization and traditions. Since the existing evidence suggested that parental organization and traditions are most important for older children, this dimension will not be discussed further. Items were drawn from several existing instruments. The Home Literacy Environment Scale (HLE$_K$, Griffin & Morrison, 1997), the Parenting Dimension Inventory (PDI, Slater & Power, 1987), and the Home Observation for Measurement of the Environment Inventory (HOME, Caldwell & Bradley, 1984) were particularly influential for development of the instrument.

Table 8.1 provides a brief description of each of the four subscales measured by the parenting questionnaire. First, the quality of the family learning environment subscale (QFLE) was designed to measure parenting behaviors promoting literacy and numeracy knowledge. The learning environment dimension had questions derived from the HLE$_K$ (Griffin & Morrison, 1997) about parent-and child-literacy-related activities and also included additional questions regarding numeracy-based activities with more in-depth probes. Second, the parental warmth and responsiveness subscale (PWR) measured the degree of parental support and the affective climate or warmth in the home for children in early elementary school. The third subscale, parental control (PC), gauged socialization efforts as well as behavioral rules, standards, and limits in the home. Two subcategories—discipline strategy and consistency—were emphasized. Fourth, a

TABLE 8.1
DEFINITION OF PARENTING DIMENSIONS MEASURED
BY THE PARENTING QUESTIONNAIRE

Dimension of Parenting	Definition
Quality of the family learning environment	Elements in the home environment that foster literacy or numeracy skills. These include activities, materials, and child and parental habits that both foster and interfere with learning (e.g. television).
Parental warmth and responsiveness	Parental warmth and the affective climate in the home. The physical affection parents show their children, verbal regard and encouragement given to children, and emotional support in the home.
Parental control	Parental socialization efforts. Rules, standards, and limits in the home Behavior parameters and parental methods used to direct or monitor a child's behavior.
Parental beliefs	Parental beliefs about childrearing, including knowledge of developmentally appropriate practices and aspirations and expectations for their children's educational success.

parental beliefs subscale (PB) assessed knowledge about developmentally appropriate practices, parents' aspirations and expectations for their children's educational success, and parents' beliefs about what qualities they want to develop in their children.

The parenting measures were collected when the children were in second, third, or fourth grade. Therefore, we were not be able to make causal statements about parental influences on children's skills at school entry. Nevertheless, we examined the association between children's academic and social skills at kindergarten entry and parenting dimensions in early elementary school, since the literature strongly suggested that parenting dimensions remain stable throughout elementary school (Baumrind, 1971; Bradley, Caldwell, & Rock, 1988; Gringlas & Weinraub, 1995; Maccoby & Martin, 1983; Power, 1993; Shumow, Vandell, & Posner, 1998).

Factor Analysis of the Parenting Instrument

A principal components analysis (PCA) was conducted on questionnaire responses from 198 families to identify the number of underlying factors to interpret as well as which items load onto each factor. In essence, PCA partitions the total variance for all of 119 original items by finding the combination of items accounting for the maximum amount of variance, the first principal component. Then, the procedure finds the second linear combination of items accounting for the maximum amount of variance after removing the variance associated with the first component. This process continues with each successive factor accounting for the maximum possible amount of variance in the remaining items. Initially, four underlying dimensions were hypothesized; there were strong a priori expectations about which questions would fit into each dimension. A two-part decision-making guideline for identifying the number of factors and dominant item loadings was employed.

Determining How Many Factors to Interpret

The number of eigenvectors, or factors to interpret, was determined using the Kaiser stopping rule (Kaiser, 1960) and scree test (Cattell, 1966). Since four underlying parenting dimensions were expected, it was anticipated that the PCA would extract four initial factors. The Kaiser criterion recommends retaining eigenvectors with eigenvalues ≥ 1. Though only four parenting dimensions were hypothesized, there were seven factors with eigenvalues > 1 in this sample.

In interpreting this result, however, Cattell and Jaspers (1967) claimed the Kaiser criterion could overestimate the number of factors to interpret if the number of items is greater than 30. In this case there were 119 items on the original questionnaire, indicating that the Kaiser criterion could indeed have been inaccurate. Therefore, the scree test, a graphical method proposed by Cattell (1966), was used for deciding the number of factors to interpret. The magnitude of the eigenvalues on the vertical axis is plotted against their number (i.e., first factor, second factor, third factor, etc.). The recommendation is to retain all factors in the sharp descent before the first eigenvector where the graph levels off (Stevens, 1996). Since the eigenvalues in Figure 8.1 level off (to a value of approximately 1) at the fifth factor, results indicated retaining four factors.

Finally, substantive issues concerning parsimony were considered in deciding how many factors to interpret. It was important to retain factors that accounted for a large and distinct amount of the variance on the parenting instrument. The percent of variance contributed by the fourth factor was three times the percent of variance contributed by the next factor, making a clear distinction between the fourth and fifth factors. Further, four factors together accounted for half of the total variance from the parenting questionnaire items.

Interpreting the Four Parenting Questionnaire (PQ) Subscales

Closer examination of the four factors identified by the PCA indicates that they correspond to the four aspects of parenting prevalent in the literature that provided the underlying structure for the original questionnaire. Cronbach's α coefficients were computed for each of the four subscales to assess the internal reliability of the questions. As presented at the bottom of Table 8.2, alpha levels were high for each factor ranging from .75 to .91.

The seven questions that made up the first factor all measure the quality of the family learning environment (QFLE). They include aspects of the physical environment that foster learning (such as how many books the target child owns and the number of board games), as well as an aspect of the environment that inhibits

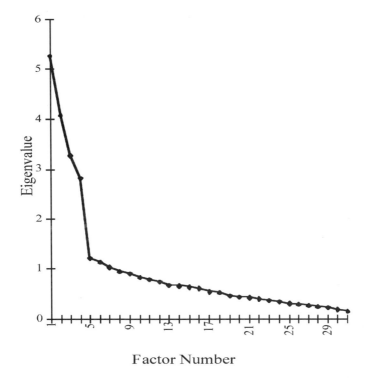

FIG. 8.1. Factor scree plot of the parenting questionnaire.

learning (i.e., amount of TV viewing). All of these questions were grouped in the family learning environment subscale at the outset.

The next dimension represented parental responsiveness and warmth. The group of questions that loaded onto the second factor measure characteristics of parental warmth, support, and the family's affective climate. As such, this second factor was labeled parental warmth and responsiveness (PWR). Like the QFLE, all eight of these PWR questions were created for this subscale at the outset.

The third factor comprised ten questions measuring parental beliefs about childrearing and, in particular, desirable qualities in children (PB). Twenty-one additional items assessing parental beliefs about the importance of schooling and knowledge of developmentally appropriate practices did not hang together with this third factor in the PCA and were eliminated.

Finally, the fourth factor contains questions describing an aspect of parental control. At the outset these six questions were identified as part of the control dimension. However, they appeared to measure a particular area of parental control; namely, parental sensitivity to discipline strategies. It was surprising that questions assessing rule consistency did not load onto this fourth factor. Clearly, further investigation is needed of the nature and consistency of parental control

TABLE 8.2
FOUR-FACTOR PRINCIPAL COMPONENTS ANALYSIS SOLUTION FROM
THE PARENTING QUESTIONNAIRE

	Rotated Using Varimax Criterion				
Variables	Factor 1	Factor 2	Factor 3	Factor 4	h^2
How often mother reads to herself	.62	.02	.08	−.02	.39
How often father reads to himself	.66	−.12	.14	.03	.47
Number of books child owns	.71	.12	.04	−.04	.52
Number of newspapers	.58	.05	−.04	.07	.34
Number of adult magazines	.56	.07	−.02	.02	.32
Hours of TV watched per week	−.66	.03	.23	.07	.50
Number of board games	.58	.09	−.09	−.10	.36
Encourage curiosity, exploration	.24	.57	−.11	.05	.39
Encourage child to express	.02	.73	.05	−.16	.56
Respect child's opinion	−.02	.68	.10	.04	.48
Have warm, intimate moments	.07	.66	.12	.02	.45
Interesting to spend time with	−.03	.70	.13	.01	.50
Typically ask child about their day	.02	.63	.16	−.09	.43
Display child's work in home	.29	.50	−.03	.08	.34
Encourage child to talk about	−.11	.68	.23	−.20	.56
Having good manners important	−.05	−.05	.70	.07	.51
Being honest important for success	.11	.06	.73	−.03	.54
Having self-control important	.13	.23	.59	−.09	.43
Getting along with children	−.09	.20	.70	−.03	.54
Having sound judgment	.05	.06	.58	−.03	.34
Obeying parents	−.34	.07	.71	−.02	.62
Being responsible	.30	.05	.64	−.03	.50
Being considerate	.08	.12	.79	−.08	.65
Being interested	.23	.13	.50	.03	.33
Being a good student important	−.08	−.04	.69	.03	.48
Scold when other children could	.17	−.16	−.03	.70	.54
Scold when child's friends...	.01	.02	−.03	.86	.73
Scold when your close friends...	.01	.01	−.01	.87	.75
Scold when relatives could hear	.01	−.01	.03	.81	.66
Scold when acquaintances could...	−.11	−.04	−.03	.87	.77
Scold in public	−.05	−.03	−.07	.80	.65
Cronbach's α	.75	.81	.87	.91	

and discipline as a component of individual differences in parenting. Since the
six questions that loaded onto the fourth factor measure a particular aspect of
control, the final factor was referred to as parental control/discipline sensitivity
(PC/D).

In order to examine the predictive validity of the PQ, mean summary scores
were computed for each of the four subscales. If parents responded to 75% of
the questions in a dimension, a mean summary score was computed from the

available data. This process maximized the number of cases for analysis and was sensitive to missing information without changing the raw data (as would be done if imputing missing data).

Associations among Parenting Practices and Children's Skills at School Entry

A separate goal of the present chapter is to present findings relating the parenting dimensions to children's academic and social skills. In a structural equation modeling (SEM) analysis, an a priori causal model was constructed and evaluated with LISREL 8.2 (Joreskog & Sorbom, 1996).

Statistical Model

To assess the predictive validity of the parenting questionnaire (PQ), an a priori causal model of how parenting practices influence children's outcomes was tested with SEM analyses. The baseline parental influence model included paths linking four latent predictor variables to two latent outcome variables. Specifically, the model specified that:

1. Parental beliefs about desirable child qualities (PB) would directly influence parental control/discipline sensitivity (PC/D), parental warmth and responsiveness (PWR), the quality of the family learning environment (QFLE), and children's social skills (SS).
2. The influence of PB on academic skills (AS) would be mediated by PWR and QFLE.
3. PC/D would predict SS, but not AS.
4. PR would influence both SS and AS.
5. QFLE would predict AS, but not SS.
6. SS would influence AS and vice versa.

The correlation matrix for the exogenous and endogenous indicator variables included in the baseline parental influence model is shown in Table 8.3. However, as recommended in the structural equation modeling literature (Cudeck, 1989; Joreskog & Sorbom, 1996), the covariance matrix of variable interrelationships was analyzed instead of the correlation matrix.

Goodness-of-fit Indices

Considering Bollen's (1989) recommendations, we relied on the following fit indices to determine how well the baseline model fit the data: maximum likelihood (ML) χ^2, goodness of fit index (GFI), root mean square error of approximation (RMSEA), critical N (CN), comparative fit index (CFI), and parameter estimates.

TABLE 8.3
CORRELATIONS AMONG PARENTING QUESTIONNAIRE
SUBSCALES, CHILDREN'S SOCIAL AND ACADEMIC SKILLS
AT KINDERGARTEN ENTRY

	1	2	3	4	5	6	7	8	9
Parenting dimensions									
1. QFLE									
2. PWR	.16*								
3. PB	.11+	.23***							
4. PC/D	−.00	−.09	−.06						
Academic skills at time 1									
5. Vocabulary	.56***	.18**	.05	.06					
6. Gen. Info.	.47***	.18**	.09	.07	.75***				
7. Reading	.37***	.12+	.04	.14+	.48***	.50***			
8. Math	.48***	.10+	.00	.08	.60***	.57***	.59***		
Social skills at time 1									
9. WRS	.43***	.20**	.20**	.07	.37***	.40***	.28***	.27***	
10. IPS	.48***	.15*	.12 +	.05	.22**	.22**	.12+	.01	.72***

Note: $+.15 > p > .05$; * $p < .05$; ** $p < .01$; *** $p < .001$

Baseline Parental Influence Model Fit

As Figure 8.2 illustrates, a number of indices indicated that the overall fit of the proposed baseline parental influence model was excellent. Namely, the ML χ^2 was nonsignificant, $\chi^2 (19) = 21.11$, $p = .33$, indicating the working model adequately represented the observed data. In addition, the GFI and CFI were both well above the suggested levels for satisfactory fit (.97 and .99, respectively). This indicates that the baseline model explained 97% of the total variance. The RMSEA was also well within the close fit range (RMSEA = .01), and the CN for this model was 242.76. Taken together, these indices indicate that the overall fit of the baseline model was well above satisfactory.

When examining the individual parameter estimates, the same overall pattern emerged (see Figure 8.2). In particular, all but one of the parameter estimates were in the expected direction.[1] Parental beliefs about admirable qualities in children were directly related to parental warmth and responsiveness ($\gamma_{2,1} = .40$, $p < .05$), social skills ($\gamma_{4,1} = .07$, $p < .05$) and the family learning environment ($\gamma_{3,1} = .37$, $p < .05$), but surprisingly not to parental control and discipline strategies ($\gamma_{1,1} = -.17$, $p = $ NS). Further, both the family learning environment and parental responsiveness were associated with academic skills ($\beta_{5,3} = .22$, $p < .05$ and $\beta_{5,2} = .08$, $p < .07$, respectively). Finally, social skills predicted academic skills and vice versa ($\beta_{5,4} = -.48$, $p < .05$ and $\beta_{4,5} = 39$, $p < .05$, respectively).

---

[1] The most conservative critical value of 1.96 was selected to reduce biasing the results in favor of finding a relationship (instead of using the bidirectional CV > 1.64, $p < .05$).

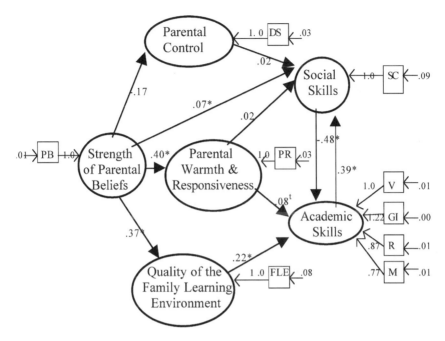

FIG. 8.2. Standardized solution for the baseline parental influence model.

A puzzling finding was the nonsignificant linkage between parental control
and discipline sensitivity and social skills ($\beta_{4,1}$ = .02, p = NS). Discipline sensitivity represents an aspect of the parental control dimension. Originally this subscale also contained questions about rule consistency and control strategies. The
lack of predictability of discipline sensitivity to social skills could reflect a
greater restriction of the range of responses to questions in the dimension.
Alternatively, it could reflect a more complex relation between parental control
and discipline and social skills than is being tapped by our questions. Clearly, further work is needed to flesh out the precise nature and impact of parental control
on children's social development. Nevertheless, results of the SEM analysis
revealed a complex pattern of associations among parenting dimensions and child
characteristics that shape early literacy skills.

Multiple Pathways to Early Literacy

On a broader plane, our conceptualization implies that there are several pathways simultaneously influencing the growth of literacy skills in children. For example, a child's social skills (independence, responsibility, self-regulation, and

cooperation) directly shape growth of academic achievement during the early school years. Likewise, the quality of the family learning environment directly influences growth of literacy skills. In a separate pathway, parental warmth and responsiveness % shape literacy acquisition through their effect on the child's developing social skills. Finally, parental beliefs create another separate path to literacy through their impact on parental warmth and on the family learning environment.

The crucial implication of these findings and the more global framework proposed here is that literacy acquisition is influenced by several factors operating at different levels to directly and indirectly shape the literacy trajectories children follow. The complex pattern of relations produced by parental control, warmth, and the learning environment in combination with important child characteristics like IQ and social skills simultaneously operate to guide the pathways to literacy that children follow.

IMPLICATIONS FOR PARENTING

Finally, it is worthwhile to consider the implication of our work for the task of parenting. We would like to stress the following three points for parents to consider:

1. It is crucial for parents to recognize how early in children's lives meaningful individual differences in important literacy skills can emerge. As a consequence, parents cannot wait until school entry to focus on acquisition of important language, knowledge and prereading and premath skills.

2. Parents need to appreciate the importance of a child's social development for effective growth of literacy skills. As such, parental activities promoting independence, responsibility, self-regulation, and cooperativeness will ultimately benefit early literacy and later academic success. Parents who provide socialization experiences that aid the acquisition of these very important learning related skills will facilitate the growth of children's academic skills, attention, concentration, as well as self-regulation and openness to learning (Bronson, 2000).

3. Effective parenting for literacy in young American children must involve more than providing a rich literacy environment. In reality, all aspects of parenting directly or indirectly shape growth of the child's literacy skills. For example, parental beliefs influence parental warmth and responsiveness, the quality of the learning environment, and aspects of parental control and discipline. Likewise, parental warmth and control contribute to literacy through their impact on social development. Consequently, in promoting literacy acquisition in young children, simply focusing on the learning environment is not sufficient. Multiple parenting dimensions come into play in shaping a young child's growth.

In conclusion, recent research points to parenting as a key element in the development of literacy skills and academic success in young children. Although the relationship between parenting and early literacy acquisition is complex, the conceptualization developed here paves the way for a more complete and detailed understanding of the multiple sources of influence on children's lives and how parents can promote their children's development.

REFERENCES

Alexander, K. L., & Entwisle, D. R. (1988). Achievement in the first 2 years of school: Patterns and processes. *Monographs of the Society for Research in Child Development, 53,* 1–157.

Baumrind, D. (1968). Authoritarian vs. authoritative parental control. *Adolescence, 3,* 255–272.

Baumrind, D. (1971a). Current patterns of parental authority. *Developmental Psychology Monograph, 4,* 1–103.

Bloom, B. S. (1981). *All our children learning: A primer for parents, teachers, and other educators.* New York: McGraw-Hill.

Bollen, K. A. (1989). *Structural equations with latent variables.* New York: John Wiley and Sons.

Bornstein, M. H. (Ed.). (1995). *Handbook of Parenting, 1–4.* Hillsdale NJ: Lawrence Erlbaum Associates.

Bradley, R. H., & Caldwell, B. M. (1980). The relation of home environment, cognitive competence, and IQ among males and females. *Child Development, 51,* 1140–1148.

Bradley, R. H., Caldwell, B. M., & Rock, S. L. (1988). Home environment and school performance: A ten-year follow-up and examination of three models of environmental action. *Child Development, 59,* 852–867.

Bryant, F. B., & Yarnold, P. R. (1995). Principal-components analysis and exploratory and confirmatory factor analysis. In L. G. Grimm & P. R. Yarnold (Eds.), *Reading and understanding multivariate statistics* (pp. 69–136). Washington, DC: American Psychological Association.

Bronson, M. (2000). *Self-regulation in early childhood: Nature and nurture.* New York: Guilford Press.

Caldwell, B., & Bradley, R. (1984). *Home observation for measurement of the environment.* Little Rock: University of Arkansas.

Cattell, R. B. (1966). The meaning and strategic use of factor analysis. In R. B. Cattell (Ed.), *Handbook of multivariate experimental psychology* (pp. 174–243). Chicago: Rand McNally.

Cattell, R. B., & Jaspers, J. A. (1967). A general plasmode for factor analytic exercises and research. *Multivariate Behavior Research Monographs, 67,* 1–211.

Clark, R. M. (1983). *Family life and school achievement: Why poor Black children succeed or fail.* Chicago: University of Chicago Press.

Collins, W. A., Maccoby, E. E., Steinberg, L., Hetherington, E. M., & Bornstein, M. H. (2000). Contemporary research on parenting: The case for nature and nurture. *American Psychologist, 55* (2), 218–232.

Cooper, D. H., & Farran, D. C. (1991). *The Cooper-Farran behavioral rating scale.* Brandon, VT: Clinical Psychology Publishing Company.

Cooney, R. R. (1998, March). *Relations among aspects of parental control, children's work-related social skills and academic achievement.* Poster presented at the biennial Conference on Human Development, Mobile, AL.

Cudeck, R. (1989). Analysis of correlation matrices using covariance structure models. *Psychological Bulletin, 105,* 317–327.

Cunningham, A. E., & Stanovich, K. E. (1997). Early reading acquisition and its relation to reading experience and ability 10 years later. *Developmental Psychology, 33,* 934–945.

Cunningham, A. E., Stanovich, K. E., & West, R. F. (1994). Literacy environment and the development of children's cognitive skills. In E. M. H. Assink (Ed.), *Literacy acquisition and social con-*

text: Approaches, emphases, and questions (pp. 70–90). London, England: Harvester wheat sheaf/ Prentice Hall.

Darling, N., & Steinberg, L. (1993). Parenting style as context: An integrative model. *Psychological Bulletin, 113,* 487–496.

Davis, B. G., Trimble, C. S., & Vincent, D. R. (1980). Does age of entrance affect school achievement? *Elementary School Journal, 80,* 133–143.

De Temple, J. M., & Snow, C. E. (1992, April). *Styles of parent–child book reading as related to mothers' views of literacy and children's literacy outcomes.* Paper presented at biennial Conference on Human Development, Atlanta.

Dickinson, D. K., & Tobors, P. O. (2001). *Beginning literacy with language: Young children's learning at home and school.* Baltimore: Brooks Publishing Company.

Dornbusch, S. M., Ritter, P. L., Leiderman, P. H., Roberts, D. F., & Fraleigh, M. J. (1987). The relation of parenting style to adolescent school performance. *Child Development, 58,* 1244–1257.

Dunn, L., & Dunn, L. (1981). *Peabody picture vocabulary test*—revised. Circle Pines, MN: American Guidance Service.

Estrada, P., Arsenio, W. F., Hess, R. D., & Holloway, S. D. (1987). Affective quality of the mother–child relationship: Longitudinal consequences for children's school-relevant cognitive functioning. *Developmental Psychology, 23,* 210–215.

Fiske, E. B. (1991). *Smart schools, smart kids: Why do some schools work?* New York: Simon & Schuster.

Goodnow, J. J. (1988). Children's household work: Its nature and functions. *Psychological Bulletin, 103,* 5–26.

Glasgow, K. L., Dornbusch, S. M., Troyer, L., Steinberg, L., & Ritter, P. L. (1997). Parenting styles, adolescents' attributions, and educational outcomes in nine heterogeneous high schools. *Child Development, 68,* 507–529.

Griffin, E. A., & Morrison, F. J. (1997). The unique contribution of home literacy environment to differences in early literacy skills. *Early Child Development and Care, 127–128,* 233–243.

Gringlas, M., & Weinraub, M. (1995). The more things change . . . single parenting revisited. *Journal of Family Issues, 16,* 29–53.

Hart, B., & Risley, T. R. (1995). *Meaningful differences in the everyday experience of young American children.* Baltimore: Brookes.

Hayduk, L. (1987). *Structural equation modeling with LISREL: Essentials and advances.* Baltimore: Johns Hopkins University Press.

Herman, M. A., & McHale, S. M. (1993). Coping with parental negativity: Links with parental warmth and child adjustment. *Journal of Applied Developmental Psychology, 14,* 121–136.

Hirsch, E. D. (1987). *Cultural literacy: What every American needs to know.* New York: Houghton Mifflin.

Joreskog, K. G., & Sorbom, D. (1996). *LISREL 8 users reference guide.* Chicago: Scientific Software International.

Kaiser, H. F. (1960). The application of electronic computers to factor analysis. *Educational and Psychological Measurement, 20,* 141–151.

Kaiser, J. (1994). The role of family configuration, income, and gender in the academic achievement of young self-care children. *Early Child Development and Care, 97,* 91–105.

Kearns, D. T., & Doyle, D. P. (1991). *Winning the brain race: A bold plan to make our schools competitive.* San Francisco: Institute for Contemporary Studies Press.

Kline, R. B. (1998). *Principles and practices of structural equation modeling.* New York: Guilford Press.

Kuo, H.-H.-D., & Hauser, R. M. (1997). How does size of subship matter? Family configuration and family effects on educational attainment. *Social Science Research, 26,* 69–94.

Lamborn, S. D., Mounts, N. S., Steinberg, L., & Dornbusch, S. M. (1991). Patterns of competence and adjustment among adolescents from authoritative, authoritarian, indulgent, and neglectful families. *Child Development, 62,* 1049–1065.

Maccoby, E. E., & Martin, J. A. (1983). Socialization in the context of the family: Parent–child interaction. In P. Mussen (Ed.), *Handbook of child psychology* (pp. 1–101). New York: John Wiley & Sons.

Marsh, H. W. (1988). Causal effects of academic self-concept on academic achievement: A reanalysis of Newman (1984). *Journal of Experimental Education, 56,* 100–104.

Markwardt, F. C. (1989). *Peabody individual achievement test—revised.* Circle Pines, MN: American Guidance Service.

Morrison, F. G., Griffith, E. M., & Alberts, P. M., (1997). Nature-nurture in the classroom: entrace age, school readiness and learning in children. *Developmental Psychology, 33*(2), 254–262.

Morrison, F. J., Frazier, J. A., Hardway, C. L., Griffith, E. M., Williamson, G., & Miyazaki, Y. (in preparation). *Early literacy: The nature and sources of individual differences.*

Morrow, L. M. (1989). *Literacy development in the early years: Helping children read and write.* Englewood Cliffs, NJ: Prentice-Hall.

Okagaki, L., & Frensch, P. A. (1998). Parenting and children's school achievement: A multiethnic perspective. *American Educational Research Journal, 35,* 123–144.

Okagaki, L., & Sternberg, R. (1993). Parental beliefs and children's school performance. *Child Development, 64,* 36–56.

Power, T. G. (1993). *Parenting Dimensions Inventory (PDI): A research manual.* Houston, TX: University of Houston.

Radin, N. (1971). Maternal warmth, achievement motivation, and cognitive functioning in lower class preschool children. *Child Development, 42,* 1560–1565.

Richman, E. A., & Rescorla, L. (1995). Academic orientation and warmth in mothers and fathers of preschoolers: Effects on academic skills and self-perceptions of competence. *Early Education and Development, 6,* 197–213.

Robeson, R. A. (1997, May). *Disparity between beliefs about the importance of education and literacy promoting activities.* A poster presented at the annual conference of the Midwestern Psychological Association, Chicago.

Scarborough, H. S., Dobrich, W., & Hager, M. (1991). Preschool literacy experience and later reading achievement. *Journal of Learning Disabilities, 24,* 508–511.

Shepard, L. A., & Smith, M. L. (1988). Synthesis of research on school readiness and kindergarten retention. *Educational Leadership, 44,* 78–86.

Shonkoff J. & Phillips, D. (2000). Neurons to neighborhoods: the source of early childhood development: *** P. C. National Academy of Sciences.

Shumow, L., Vandell, D. L., & Posner, J. K. (1998). Harsh, firm, and permissive parenting in low-income families: Relations to children's academic achievement and behavioral adjustment. *Journal of Family Issues, 19,* 483–507.

Slater, M. A., & Power, T. G. (1987). Multidimensional assessment of parenting in single-parent families. In J. P. Vincent (Ed.), *Advances in family intervention, assessment, and theory* (pp. 197–228). Greenwich, CT: JAI Press.

Sputa, C. L., & Paulson, S. E. (1995). Birth order and family size: Influences on adolescents' achievement and related parenting behaviors. *Psychological Reports, 76,* 43–51.

Steinberg, L. (1996). *Beyond the classroom. Why school reform has failed and what parents need to do.* New York: Simon & Schuster.

Steinberg, L., Dornbusch, S. M., & Brown, B. B. (1992). Ethnic differences in adolescent achievement: An ecological perspective. *American Psychologist, 47,* 723–729.

Steinberg, L., Lamborn, S. D., Darling, N., Mounts, N. S., & Dornbusch, S. M. (1994). Over-time changes in adjustment and competence among adolescents from authoritative, authoritarian, indulgent, and neglectful families. *Child Development, 65,* 754–770.

Stevens, J. (1996). *Applied multivariate statistics for the social sciences* (3rd ed., pp. 362–422). Mahwah, NJ: Lawrence Erlbaum Associates.

Stevenson, H. W., Chen, C. & Lee, S. Y. (1993). Mathematics achievement of Chinese, Japanese, and American children: ten year later. *Science, 259,* 53–58.

Stevenson, H. W., Chen, C., & Uttal, D. H. (1990). Beliefs and achievement: A study of Black, White, and Hispanic children. *Child Development, 61,* 508–523.

Stewart, J. P. (1995). Home environments and parental support for literacy: Children's perception and school literacy achievement. *Early Education and Development, 6,* 97–125.

Stipek, D. J. & Ryan, R. H. (1997). Economically disadvantaged preschoolers: Ready to leave but further to go. *Developmental Psychology, 33,* 711–723.

Thompson, M. S., Entwisle, D. R., Alexander, K. L., and Sundius, M. J. (1992). The influence of family composition on children's conformity to the student role. *American Educational Research Journal, 29,* 405–424.

Thorndike, R. L., Hagen, E. P., & Sattler, J. M. (1986). *Stanford-Binet intelligence scale* (4th ed.) Chicago: Riversdale Publishing.

U.S. Department of Education. (1991). *America 2000: An education strategy.* Washington, DC: U.S. Government Printing Office.

9

The Adolescent as Parent: Influences on Children's Intellectual, Academic, and Socioemotional Development

John G. Borkowski, Toni Bisconti,
Christine C. Willard, Deborah A. Keogh,
and Thomas L. Whitman
University of Notre Dame

Keri Weed
University of South Carolena-Aiken

Despite a dramatic decline of 17% in the rate of adolescent childbearing in the United States during the 1990s, teenage parenting remains a significant problem for millions of young mothers and for society in general. Over three fourths of a million adolescents become pregnant each year, with over one half resulting in live births. Of these births, approximately 90% of first-time mothers choose to assume the responsibilities of parenting rather than placing their children for adoption.

This chapter describes what we know about teenage parenting, drawing heavily from outcomes in the Notre Dame Parenting Project (Whitman, Borkowski, Keogh, & Weed, 2001). This project analyzed a representative sample of adolescent mothers and their children—born in the late 1980s and early 1990s—across

Address correspondence to: John G. Borkowski, Dept. of Psychology, University of Notre Dame, Notre Dame, IN 46556, Phone: 219-631-6549, Fax: 219-631-8883, e-mail: souders.1@nd.edu the first 8 years of life. The focus of the chapter is on describing the sequence of cascading developmental declines in children, especially as they relate to inappropriate parenting practices. Three factors are used to explain why adolescent parenting is often associated with children's developmental delays: (1) inadequate or inappropriate social supports, (2) parental failures to teach cognitive and social self-regulation skills, and (3) parental abuse and neglect. Finally, a dynamical systems approach is proposed to better understand the rapid changes in the quality of adolescent parenting that often occurs within and across days. This "oscillation" in parenting is hypothesized to be unique to adolescence, as an off-timed transitional stage of development, and a potential cause, in its own right, of childhood developmental delays.

ADOLESCENT PARENTING: PROBLEMS AND CONSEQUENCES

Teenage pregnancy presents a set of serious challenges for most first-time young mothers, their families, and society in general. A constellation of problems occur simultaneously with an off-timed pregnancy, often hindering the adolescent mother's progress into adulthood and, simultaneously, compromising her parenting skills, which in turn can adversely influence her child's development (cf. Duncan & Brooks-Gunn, 1997; East & Felice, 1996; Horowitz, Klerman, Kuo, & Jekel, 1991; Whitman et al., 2001). The following factors have been found to be closely associated with adolescent parenting:

- Absence of the biological father and/or unavailability of a reliable and stable male role model
- Insufficient income, which prevents the newly created family from moving out of poverty and into the middle class
- Lack of commitment to postponing additional children until personal and financial problems are resolved
- High levels of stress and socioemotional maladjustment
- A lack of awareness about preparing children emotionally, socially, and cognitively for successful entry into school
- The tendency to use physical punishment and/or to condone emotional neglect
- A changing, and sometimes unreliable, social support system

These individual factors often interact to compromise the formidable parenting task that confronts the typical teen mother, placing both mother and child at risk for a variety of developmental delays. A number of longitudinally based studies have examined the nature and characteristics of maternal and child outcomes following a birth during the teenage years (Apfel & Seitz, 1993;

Furstenberg, Brooks-Gunn, & Morgan, 1987; Dubow & Luster, 1990; East & Felice, 1996; Leadbeater, & Linares, 1992; McKenry, Browne, Kotch & Symons, 1990; Spieker & Bensley, 1994). These projects have revealed much about the lives of adolescent mothers, their parenting practices, and the development of their children. Two of these studies are briefly summarized in the next section.

Major Longitudinal Projects with Adolescent Mothers

Furstenberg et al. (1987) conducted an influential longitudinal study that described outcomes for adolescent mothers and their children from early childhood through early adolescence. The pregnancies occurred in Baltimore in the mid- to late 1960s, a period of optimism for many in poverty, in part because of the promises of the Great Society. The adolescent mothers who enrolled in the Baltimore project during this period experienced a variety of outcomes 17 years following their transition to parenthood. Although the project did not focus intensively on process variables—such as maternal depression, self-esteem, and stress—it did measure important maternal outcomes such as income level, welfare status, and number of subsequent children. Surprisingly, a sizeable number of mothers were not negatively affected by their early pregnancies, and less than one third remained trapped in poverty 10 to 15 years later.

The strongest predictor of welfare status at the follow-up was the education level of the adolescent mothers' parents, independent of her own educational status. Furstenberg et al. (1987) surmised that parents with more education had more effective economic and social resources to assist their daughters in early childrearing. Teens who limited further pregnancies often participated in school and community-based intervention programs; these community supports may have compensated for other less effective support systems in the mothers' lives.

Furstenberg and his colleagues (1987)—evaluating grade retention, academic problems, delinquency, and drug abuse as important outcomes for the children of adolescent mothers in the Baltimore Project—concluded that positive child outcomes were more likely if mothers were married, graduated from high school, had limited their subsequent childbearing, and were not on welfare. It should be emphasized that the children appeared to fare much worse than their mothers, with over 50% experiencing academic and/or adjustment problems during adolescence.

Recently, East and Felice (1996) conducted another important longitudinal project investigating risk and resiliency in the development of Hispanic adolescent mothers and their children across the first 3 years of life. The project was unique in its frequency of assessing the quality of parenting (every six months), use of medical care, repeat pregnancies, and the roles of fathers and grandmothers in parenting. The following factors emerged as predictors or correlates of maternal and parenting outcomes:

1. Older adolescents who had frequent prenatal medical visits and abstained from alcohol and other drugs showed more positive mother–child outcomes.
2. Delayed pregnancies (especially if six months after the first birth) were associated with less alcohol and drug use during the second pregnancy and, not surprisingly, resulted in better child outcomes.
3. Positive parenting and high confidence were associated with good social development in children, and low maternal stress was associated with fewer displays of aggression in children.
4. Hispanic mothers and children were most at risk for developmental problems if they reported less mature parenting values (e.g., unrealistic expectations, less empathy, and greater use of punishment), less confidence in their parenting skills, and lower levels of child acceptance.
5. Adolescents who had more favorable parenting attitudes and skills generally lived apart from their mothers but still received high amounts of child care and support.
6. No clear associations were uncovered regarding father involvement and child outcomes. Although 60% of the fathers were involved with their children at three years, only 30% provided substantial financial supports. Although fathers rarely provided hands-on care, it is likely that the more involved fathers provided more positive role models, especially important to their children's social development.

In short, favorable outcomes were more common in older teens who sought pre- and postnatal care, who learned positive parenting values early during the first year of their children's lives, who were supported by families and partners but who lived apart from their mothers, and who managed to delay a second pregnancy until adulthood (East & Felice, 1996). Although this project describes teenage parenting practices and developmental outcomes in considerable detail during the early years of life, it did not address the negative long-term outcomes in children, as first described by Furstenburg and colleagues (1987). In contrast to these important studies, the Notre Dame Parenting Project provides not only sociological and demographic information but also a detailed psychological picture of children as well as mothers from birth to age 8, thus filling in some of the gaps in existing longitudinal projects.

In the next section, we describe the development of the children of adolescent mothers in the Notre Dame Parenting Project over the first 8 years, suggesting possible associations between a variety of developmental delays and teen parenting practices. In contrast to the aforementioned studies of adolescent mothers and children in large urban settings (Furstenberg's and East's), children in the this project had mothers who were older, less socioeconomically disadvantaged, not significantly involved in drugs and alcohol, and more likely to remain in school until obtaining a diploma.

NOTRE DAME PARENTING PROJECT: CHILDHOOD DELAYS AND PARENTING PRACTICES

Our project differs from previous studies in its comprehensiveness and the intensity of its measurement scheme. The data to be reported were obtained at birth and when children were 1, 3, 5, and 8 years of age. At these various time points we examined intellectual, linguistic, socioemotional, adaptive, and academic development. The portrait that follows shows compromised developmental trajectories for most children with adolescent mothers. In the following sections, we examine these delays in detail and locate their association with inappropriate parenting practices.

Developmental Delays in Children

At the outset of the Notre Dame Parenting Project, we noted that the children of adolescent mothers were physically healthy at birth, as evidenced by their average gestational ages, birth weights, and Apgar scores as well as low incidence of congenital problems. At 6 months and 1 year of age, Bayley IQ scores also suggested that the children were functioning mentally and physically within normal ranges. Moreover, comparative analyses failed to reveal differences in responsivity, activity, and mood between infants of adolescent and adult mothers. Despite this generally optimistic profile of early development, developmental problems began to emerge by the end of the first year of life. These early appearing problems snowballed into more serious developmental delays for many children.

The first problematic outcome we noted involved the intimate relationship between mothers and children: A majority of infants showed disorganized (41%) or other insecure patterns of attachment (22%) at 1 year of age, with only 37% of children classified as securely attached. The proportion of securely attached infants was lower than that typically observed even in low socioeconomic status samples (Vaughn, Egeland, Sroufe, & Waters, 1979) as well as in other studies with children of adolescent parents (Spieker & Bensley, 1994; Ward & Carlson, 1995). Although the infants in the sample appeared physically healthy and developed adequately both mentally and motorically during their first year, they showed signs of risk for later socioemotional problems because of insecure infant attachment (Whitman et al., 2001).

When children reached 3 and 5 years of age, there was additional evidence of emerging developmental problems in four important domains: intellectual-linguistic, socioemotional, adaptive behavior, and preacademic. A large percentage of children performed in the borderline and mentally retarded ranges of intellectual functioning: 45% at three years and 26% at five years, with only a small percentage scoring in the above average category. Even more trouble-some, many children showed serious signs of delayed language development and visual motor integration problems; around 80% were at or below the 10th percentile on the Peabody Picture Vocabulary Test (PPVT-R) at both 3 and 5 years of age, while 57% were in this same range at 5 years of age on the Developmental Test of Visual Motor Integration. Academically, 50% and 34% of 5-year-old children respectively were at or below the 10th percentile on the math and reading portions of the Peabody Individual Achievement Test (PIAT) during kindergarten.

With respect to personal adjustment, a high percentage of children showed either internalizing problems (37% at age three and 24% at age 5) and/or exter-nalizing problems (35% at age 3 and 14% at age five). Children also displayed adaptive behavior deficiencies: By age 5, average scores on the Vineland Adaptive Behavior Scales, which assessed communication, daily living, social-ization, and motor skills, had fallen to one standard deviation below the popula-tion mean. More specifically, children of adolescent mothers generally did not meet age-appropriate expectations for communication or daily living skills (cf. Whitman et al., 2001).

Perhaps the most revealing findings regarding major developmental delays related to the number of children who displayed one or more problems in multi-ple domains: intellectual, socioemotional, adaptive, and academic. At 3 years, 72% of the children had at least one developmental problem, and 44% had more than one. Children at 3 years with multiple problems most commonly displayed cognitive deficiencies and signs of emotional dysfunction. At 5 years, 78% of the children had at least one problem, whereas 48% had multiple problems. At 5 years, children with multiple problems most commonly exhibited deficiencies in cognitive and adaptive behavior domains, although comorbidity was also found with other combinations of developmental delays.

Not surprisingly, at age 8 less than 30% of the children were performing satis-factorily at the end of the second grade, and nearly 40% met traditional criteria for LD or mild MR diagnoses. Despite these learning problems, the majority of children had not been identified as needing special services nor were they receiv-ing special attention in their classrooms. In short, early developmental problems were precursors of more serious academic problems, observed as early as the second grade.

Teen Parenting as a "Cause" of Developmental Delays

It is difficult to determine the precise role of teen parenting as a "unique" causal antecedent of childhood developmental problems because it is confounded with genetic, peer, and environmental variables. Nevertheless, it is important for both theoretical and practical reasons to try to unravel how specific parenting characteristics, as distinct from correlated factors—such as education, SES, or IQ—influence the development of children with adolescent mothers. In the remainder of this section we analyze differences between adult and adolescent parenting. In the next three sections we propose new perspectives on the sources of influence associated with teen parenting that seem to negatively impact children's developmental trajectories. Finally, we suggest the use of dynamical systems analysis as a technique for exploring the importance of "fluctuations" in parenting practices on early child development.

Age-related Parenting Differences

Our contention is that the adolescent mother's personal search for her identity leaves her with little time for, or interest in, new parenting responsibilities (Sommer, Whitman, Borkowski, & Schellenbach, 1993). Whether the adolescent deals successfully or not with her identity crisis—which is a normative, unavoidable event—she most likely will experience some or all of the following developmental problems:

1. Trouble accurately interpreting and learning from her life experiences.
2. A view of herself and her child that is both egocentric and rigid.
3. Poor social problem-solving skills.
4. Stress associated with her relationship with her mother, partner, and new infant.

All of these factors make it likely that an adolescent, who is faced with the dual tasks of identity formation and parenting, will be less prepared and more stressed in responding to her child's needs. From this perspective, it is not surprising that adolescent and adult mothers respond to the challenges of parenting differently.

Adolescent mothers differ from adult mothers on a variety of parenting dimensions. Although some of these differences may be explained by socioeconomic variables, or other contextual and personal factors that often differentiate the two age-related groups (Sommer, Whitman, Borkowski, & Schellenbach, 1993), other differences appear to be associated with the unique status of adolescence as a developmental stage. For instance, Luster and Mittelstaedt (1993) reviewed research comparing adolescent to adult mothers in terms of the quality of the home environment, mother–child interactions, security of infant attachment, and child abuse. They concluded that adolescent mothers provided less supportive home environments than adult mothers as well as less emotional and verbal supports for their children. That is, direct observations of interactions between mothers and infants indicated that adolescent mothers provided less verbal stimulation than adult mothers. Children of adolescent mothers were also less securely attached. However, Luster and Mittelstaedt (1993) hesitated to draw strong conclusions regarding the reasons for these differences, suggesting that once background factors (e.g., socioeconomic status) were considered the distribution of secure attachments in samples of infants with adolescent and adult mothers might be comparable.

Results of research focusing on adolescent versus adult maltreatment have also revealed that children of adolescent mothers are at greater risk for abuse. An extensive analysis based on data from the state of Illinois found that "by age 5, children born to age 17 or younger moms were about 1½ times more likely to be victims than those born to 20- or 21-years-olds, and also 1½ times more likely to be placed in foster care" (Goerge & Lee, 1997, p. 210). The risk for abuse is apparently related to the age of the mother and not to associated factors. Luster and Mittelstaedt (1993) have suggested that high levels of stress and poor developmental histories may contribute to the adolescent mothers' abuse potential.

Data from the Notre Dame Parenting Project also indicate that adolescent and adult mothers differ in many critical aspects of parenting. Adult mothers were more cognitively prepared for the birth of their first child, as indexed by their greater knowledge about child development and important developmental milestones, more empathetic and less punitive attitudes about childrearing, and more realistic attitudes about their maternal role. These differences persisted throughout the first 6 months of life. In addition, direct observations of adolescent and adult mothers with their infants indicated that adult mothers were more involved, attentive, and flexible in their parenting practices (Sommer et al., 1993). Adult mothers were also more likely to be responsive to their infants' behaviors and emotions. They provided more verbal stimulation, more direction, and were more motivating and more positive. Adolescent mothers also reported higher levels of stress related to their parenting roles and perceived their infants as more difficult in their temperaments (e.g., more active and less predictable). Although Sommer et al. (1993) concluded that some of these age-related characteristics disappeared when socioeconomic status and other background factors (e.g., maternal intelligence) were controlled, the impact of many characteristics on the subsequent development of children was nevertheless substantial (Whitman et al., 2001).

To the extent that adolescent mothers possess less accurate and inadequate knowledge about child development and parenting practices, they may be predisposed once they become parents to "miss" the connection between their children's behavior and their parenting practices (Sommer et al., 1993). These mothers often view the source of a child's behavioral problems as residing solely in the child. This type of maternal perception, which was observed during the first months of parenting, can affect the consistency and quality of parent–child interactions and subsequently hinder child development, both emotionally and cognitively. Mothers who perceive their parenting roles as more difficult tend to experience feelings of helplessness and inadequacies about their abilities to parent effectively (Bugental, Blue, & Cruzcosa, 1989), and parents who perceive their parenting role as stressful, are less effective in their parenting practices (Bell, 1976; Crnic, Greenberg, Ragozin,

Robinson, & Basham, 1983; Crnic, Greenberg, & Slough, 1986). In turn, higher levels of reported parenting stress have been associated with a lack of maternal responsiveness to infant cues, lower levels of positive maternal affect, as well as insecure child attachment and child noncompliance (Crnic et al., 1986; Dix, 1991). Finally, inaccurate and negative maternal perceptions regarding children's behaviors have been associated with lower maternal responsiveness, greater interference, and increased irritability in the child (Crockenberg & Smith, 1982; Nover, Shore, Timberlake, & Greenspan, 1984).

Parenting Across the First 5 Years

In the Notre Dame Parenting Project, we hypothesized that problematic parenting among teen mothers would adversely affect the cognitive, adaptive, and socioemotional development of their children. In order to better understand relationships between parenting behavior and early child development, we observed over 100 adolescent mothers interacting with their children in toy play situations when the children were 6 months, 1, 3, and 5 years of age. When infants were 6 months old, mothers were instructed to try to get their infants to reach for, hold and squeeze or shake each of three toys (a squeeze toy, a rattle, and an infant's key ring). The one-year interactive episode was less structured: Mother and child played on the floor, surrounded by a variety of age-appropriate toys; they were given 5 minutes to play "like they normally do at home." Play periods at three and five years were similar: Mothers and children sat at a small table, given a simple puzzle, nesting toy, and shape-sorter to play with for 5 minutes. All episodes were videotaped through a one-way mirror for later coding of parent quality (Whitman et al., 2001).

At each age, observers rated items reflective of Verbal Encouragement (general talkativeness, contingent praise, and positiveness) and Responsiveness (flexibility, over/understimulation, and affectional match). Since Verbal Encouragement and Responsiveness were moderately correlated, the six items comprising the two factors were summed to form an overall measure of parenting quality. Coefficient alphas, based on the intercorrelations of the six items, ranged from .87 to .90 across the four assessment periods.

Parenting skills were often found to undergo significant changes after the birth of the first child. For adolescent mothers, these changes may have been due to growth in their cognitive and emotional maturity, changes in their child, or their parenting experiences. Four patterns of parental changes were observed:

1. High levels of Verbal Encouragement and Responsiveness, which were sustained as infants became toddlers.
2. Initially high levels of Verbal Encouragement and Responsiveness, which declined over time; mothers in this category may have been unable to cope with the growing demands of an active, mobile toddler.

3. Little initial Verbal Encouragement and Responsiveness, but improvements over time; perhaps these teens were cognitively or emotionally unprepared for parenting, but gradually acquired useful skills.
4. Consistently low levels of Verbal Encouragement or Responsiveness across time.

Better cognitive outcomes, such as higher intelligence and better receptive vocabulary, occurred when mothers demonstrated high levels of Verbal Encouragement and Responsiveness at some point during the 5-year period. It did not matter whether positive parenting practices occurred early, late, or consistently. Similarly, children whose mothers failed to demonstrate Verbal Encouragement or Responsiveness, either in infancy or early childhood, scored significantly lower on premath skills at age 5. Internalizing, but not externalizing, problems were related to consistent parenting: Children who received high levels of Verbal Encouragement and Responsiveness across time had significantly fewer internalizing problems than other children. In contrast, children of mothers who consistently failed to demonstrate positive parenting scored significantly lower in intelligence and receptive language.

Regression analyses were used to reveal the importance of early parenting practices at 6 months of age on later development. For each of the child outcomes that showed a relationship with parenting, six-month measures of maternal interactions were included in the regression equations after three-year interactive behavior and maternal intelligence had been entered and thus accounted for. The results showed differential effects associated with the "timing" of the quality of teen parenting practices: Better parenting early in life accounted for significant variations in five-year intelligence scores even after parenting behaviors at three years and maternal intelligence were controlled; this finding suggests the unique importance of early childrearing quality. Maternal interactions at 6 months also explained significant variations in children's communication skills as well as internalizing problems (i.e., depression) at age 5. In contrast, early parenting behaviors failed to account for additional variance, above and beyond that explained by three-year parenting behaviors, in children's premath and receptive vocabulary scores.

In summary, the timing and quality of interactions between adolescent mothers and their children were associated with positive outcomes in three domains: intellectual, adaptive, and socioemotional. Mothers who were responsive to their 6-month-old infants and who exhibited consistent verbal encouragement had children who were more intelligent, better communicators, and with fewer internalizing symptoms. These results held up even after controlling for maternal intelligence, and even when responsiveness and verbal encouragement decreased over time. In the next sections we examine three additional processes that can result in adverse child outcomes: inadequate social supports, parental failures to teach self-regulation, and patterns of abuse and neglect.

THE ROLE OF SOCIAL SUPPORT
IN TEEN PARENTING

There has been extensive research over the last several decades examining the relationship between maternal social support networks and children's development. Broadly defined, social support refers to interpersonal interactions that involve assistance, affect, or affirmation in formal and/or informal contexts (Kahn & Antonucci, 1980). Social support has been shown to help children's cognitive and social development in several ways. First, a positive support network can help a parent to use more appropriate parenting techniques (Bronfrenbrenner & Crouter, 1983). Cognitively and socially stimulating social networks assist mothers by providing appropriate role models and multiple opportunities to engage in productive social problem solving (Salzinger, 1990). Larger and more supportive networks have been also associated with less restrictive and more nurturant parenting (Belsky, 1984), which in turn are predictive of child competence (Roberts & Strayer, 1987). Second, social networks can be viewed as buffers that reduce the impact of stress on parents, thereby reducing its negative effects on the quality of parenting practices (Burchinal, Follmer, & Bryant, 1996). By providing alternative outlets for maternal frustrations and insecurities, a strong support system enables the mother to be more positive, interactive, and encouraging with her infant.

Social support likely influences adolescent parenting in similar ways. Adolescent mothers with more limited social supports have fewer adequate role models to emulate as they develop their own parenting skills. In addition, the degree of parenting stress is often linked directly to the teen's perceptions of social support. Although a direct positive relationship might be expected between amount of social support and adolescent parenting, at times greater social support may be linked to more problematic child outcomes. It is becoming apparent that the effects of social support on parenting practices are different and more complex for adolescent than adult mothers (*cf.* Apfel & Seitz, 1993, 1999).

Three sources of support—partner, friends, and family of origin—serve as potentially important influences on the emerging parenting skills among teen mothers. Each of these sources may contribute to positive parenting by providing appropriate models and by reducing parenting stress. What constitutes an appropriate type of support, however, may change from the prenatal period through the toddler stage. Furthermore, some of these changes or shifts in support may be more problematic in the case of teen mothers.

Partner Support

There are major differences between adolescent and adult mothers in the structure of their social support networks. Adult mothers often draw upon their partners who are experiencing similar parenting stressors and emotions (Belsky, 1984). The spousal supports available to many adult mothers have been found to be more beneficial than both friend and community supports (Crnic et al., 1983). Although the presence of a supportive husband is helpful for effective parenting, a partner's absence does not necessarily handicap the single parent (Cochran & Brassard, 1979). What may be more detrimental to the development of children from single-mother households may not be the absence of a father per se, but rather a lack of consistent appropriate financial and emotional support for the mother (Hetherington, Cox, & Cox, 1985).

In contrast, unmarried teen mothers frequently lack consistent support from a partner and find themselves turning to their families and friends for financial, instrumental, and emotional assistance. The lack of consistent support from the baby's father or a current partner is often unanticipated by adolescent mothers. What the father promised—or what the mother expected—during the prenatal period is often quite different than what is provided after the baby is born. Thus, it is not surprising that support from friends or family is often more important than partner support for maternal attitudes and parenting skills of teen mothers (Colletta, 1981; Nath, Borkowski, Whitman, & Schellenbach, 1991).

Friend Support

Thoits (1986) has suggested that the most effective and beneficial provider of support might be from an individual who is facing similar stressors. In adolescent parenting, "similar others" most often refer to the teen's peer group. In contrast, assistance from dissimilar others (e.g., grandmothers) may be seen as controlling, and consequently may have a negative impact on the teen's adjustment and the development of new parenting skills (Coates & Wortman, 1980). Thus, the impact of support from friends may vary to the extent the adolescent mother considers herself "similar to" her peer group. Some adolescent mothers feel alienated from their peers due to their change to a maternal role. The type of support that is most effective is likely related to the needs of the adolescent at any given moment in her development as a person as well as a parent (Nath et al., 1991). Because many of the adolescent mothers' needs relate to peer group acceptance, friend support is often an important contributor to the adolescent's overall well-being. It should be noted, however, that this type of support may not directly enhance parenting unless the friend is also a competent parent.

Family Support

Although support from a partner and friends can have an important influence on adolescent parenting, family support is considered the most influential source of support for teen mothers. Teens experience less emotional distress and more feelings of positive well-being when social support from their families of origin is available (Unger & Wandersman, 1985). Teens who rely on their families for child care and other types of support also have been found to make easier transitions into their parenting roles (Panzarine, 1986).

Recent research, however, suggests that there are multiple, often conflicting dynamics involved in grandmother-adolescent daughter-infant living arrangements (Apfel & Seitz, 1996, 1999). If the goal for a teenage mother is to become emotionally and financially independent and to provide adequate personal care for her child, this objective may not be achieved if the teen mother relies too heavily on her immediate family and does not accept her own maternal responsibilities (Unger & Cooley, 1992). It has been suggested that support from the grandmother that persists beyond the perinatal period may make it difficult for the young mother and grandmother to renegotiate family responsibilities at a later time and thus hinder the teen mothers' struggle to achieve self-sufficiency. Unger and Cooley (1992) reported that for white adolescent mothers, grandmother contact—including both assistance in child care and home living arrangements—was related to a greater number of childhood behavior problems. For black adolescent mothers, length of time residing with the grandmother was associated with lower maternal responsiveness. In short, teen mothers from both groups appeared to be adversely effected by excessive dependency on grandmother support.

Some grandmothers become the child's primary caregivers, thus assuming the parenting responsibilities of young mothers. Apfel and Seitz (1996) examined how inner-city families adapted to adolescent childbearing. Twelve years after the birth of the first child, 28% of the adolescent mothers were not parenting actively nor living with their children. The major predictor of this outcome was early family support: If the support provided by grandmothers was extreme—either overinvolved in caretaking or providing little or no guidance—the young mother was often not the primary caregiver six years after birth. An overreliance on grandmother support can also negatively impact a teen's completion of standard adolescent developmental tasks as well as her acceptance of maternal responsibilities (cf. Unger, 1985). According to Apfel and Seitz (1996), assistance from family either leads to the adolescent mother's appreciation of support, or resentment if she views the aid as implying that she is an "inadequate" or an incompetent parent.

Family support in the African-American community, especially from the grandmother, is a common response to single motherhood, particularly if the mother is a teenager (Furstenberg et al., 1987). Although shared caregiving between mother and grandmother is traditional in these families—particularly immediately following birth—a weakness of previous research has been its focus on the presence or absence of the grandmother, rather than on exploring the ways in which the grandmother actually facilitates or inhibits the development of her daughter's parenting skills. A family support system that is more moderate and adaptive apparently helps teen mothers gain and/or retain their parenting roles (Apfel & Seitz, 1996, 1999). Researchers need to move beyond an "all or nothing" approach to studying the availability of family supports toward a more multidimensional and process-oriented examination of how supports are delivered and what their impact is on parenting and subsequent child development.

CHILDREN'S ACADEMIC SELF-REGULATION AND TEEN PARENTING

In this section, a second factor that may explain developmental delay in children with teen mothers is discussed: parental failures to teach children to self-regulate. Self-regulation in the classroom involves metacognitive, motivational, and behavioral processes used by students to promote their educational attainment (Zimmerman, 1996). A self-regulatory perspective assumes that academic success depends on constructive efforts by students to understand their experiences—a cognitive process—and to optimize their performance—a motivational process. The latter involves goal setting, self-efficacy, and attributional beliefs, whereas the former involves strategic-based learning necessary for problem solving. Self-regulated students are motivated to learn, set realistic academic goals, choose effective strategies, and monitor their progress (Martinez-Pons, 1996). This type of student activates and sustains cognitive processes and motivational dispositions that help him or her to achieve educational goals. Self-regulated learners have higher levels of strategy use, greater awareness of the effectiveness of their strategies, and higher levels of self-efficacy (Borkowski, Chan, & Muthukrishna, 2000; Schunk & Zimmerman, 1997; Zimmerman, 1996).

Zimmerman (1996) has proposed a model of self-regulation and academic achievement based on social learning theory. Early in children's cognitive development, modeling and imitation serve as important social influences, with children acquiring new skills through: (1) observing learning strategies; (2) imitating the performance associated with those strategies; (3) self-controlled practice of the newly acquired strategies; and (4) adapting and self-regulating strategies to fit immediate goals. This process begins socially, that is, through interactions with adults and peers (Zimmerman, 1998), and later becomes self-directed (Schunk & Zimmerman, 1997). Thus, modeling by parents is the crucial "first step" in the emergence of effective, consistent forms of self-regulation.

Parental inducement of self-regulation occurs through modeling, encouragement, facilitation, and rewarding of self-regulated behavior (Martinez-Pons, 1996). Grolnik and Ryan (1989) investigated how parents influence children's school performance and adjustment, particularly in the areas of self-regulation and school competence. They found that high levels of parental support for autonomy were related to effective self-regulation and low levels of acting out. High levels of parental support were also predictive of subsequent academic achievement. Children of parents who provided environments that facilitate learning and encourage autonomy had higher academic achievement, with children's self-regulation serving as the mediator between parenting and achievement (Grolnik & Ryan, 1989; Martinez-Pons, 1996).

In order for parents to assist their children in learning self-regulatory skills, the parents themselves need to know how to self-regulate their behavior. Because mothers are in large part responsible for teaching their children self-regulation skills, they will be more likely to succeed if they have a history of successful self-regulated learning. Unfortunately, many teenage mothers have not developed mature forms of cognitive and emotional self-regulation. From an academic perspective, they are often not self-motivated; their study skills are frequently unplanned and disorganized; time management skills are not well developed; self-monitoring is not systematic; and they often fail to seek help when needed. Because teen mothers are unaware of the importance and nature of effective self-regulation, it is difficult for them to teach such skills to their children. For these reasons, children with teen mothers likely enter elementary school lacking the self-regulaton processes necessary for achieving success in reading and math. We suspect that future research will reveal that a major characteristic of teenage parents is their inability to promote cognitive, emotional, and social self-regulation in their children.

ABUSE, NEGLECT, AND TEEN PARENTING

We now turn to a discussion of a third factor that likely has critical impact on the development of the children of adolescent parents—parental abuse and neglect. As we have seen, children raised by adolescent mothers are at risk for a variety of developmental problems including deficits in intellectual ability, delays in receptive language, slowed development of adaptive behavior, socioemotional maladjustment, and academic problems. Abused children show many of these same developmental difficulties (Lynch & Roberts, 1982).

For example, Hoffman-Plotkin and Twentyman (1984) found that the average IQ of abused children was approximately 20 points lower than nonabused children. Other researchers have found that by age 9, the reading skills of abused children were severely delayed (Oates, Peacock, & Forrest, 1984). Abused children often lack the skills necessary for school success: They are often impulsive, unable to organize their behavior, and have lower cognitive functioning (Barth, 1998). Neglected children—who often have low cognitive ability, attentional problems, difficulties in understanding their assigned work, and high levels of anxiety, depression, and aggression—sometimes fare even worse in school (Barth, 1998).

Although cognitive and language deficits have been noted in abused and neglected children, problems in behavioral and emotional regulation are generally the critical indicators of maltreatment. Frequently, their behavioral problems include an impaired ability to inhibit aggressive impulses and an outpouring of physical aggression with peers and adults (*cf.* Wolfe, 1987). Egeland and Sroufe (1981) found that maltreated children, as young as 2 years of age, showed more anger, aggression, frustration, and noncompliance when interacting with their mothers than children who were not maltreated. In clinical contexts, abused children—especially boys—have more conduct disorders than is typically observed in the general population (National Research Council, 1993). Abused children are also more likely than nonabused children to be socially withdrawn, depressed, and with feelings of helplessness (cf. Wolfe, 1987).

One obvious explanation for the similarities between the children of adolescent parents and abused-neglected children is that teenage parents are at greater risk for engaging in abusive or neglectful parenting practices than adult parents. Bolton (1990) reported that while 20% of all children are born to adolescent mothers, the proportion of abused children raised by adolescent mothers is estimated to be between 35% and 50%. In a study of adolescent parenting practices, de Lissovoy (1973) found that adolescent parents were more likely than older parents to use physically punitive techniques for gaining child compliance. Furthermore, Connelly and Strauss (1992) showed that the age of the mother at the birth of her first child significantly predicted the occurrence of child maltreatment—even when income, race, education, number of children, and age of the child were controlled. Finally, Dukewich and Borkowski (1996) have suggested that teen mothers who were less cognitively prepared for parenting and who showed a preference during pregnancy for using punishment as a childrearing technique were at greater risk for child abuse.

More recently, Dukewich, Borkowski, and Whitman (1999) found that maternal potential for abuse was significantly related to developmental delays in children of adolescent mothers: Higher abuse potential predicted lower Stanford Binet IQ scores, lower PPVT-R scores, lower adaptive behavior skills (e.g., social skills, communication, living skills, and motor coordination), and higher Internalizing and Externalizing behavior problems on the CBCL. In addition, a unidirectional influence was identified for some of these relationships, suggesting that abuse potential impacted subsequent children's intelligence and adaptive behavior, but that the reverse did not hold. We hypothesize that abuse and neglect negatively impacts development by hindering the emergence of cognitive and emotional self-regulation, thus providing another pathway for explaining developmental delays in children with teen mothers.

FUTURE RESEARCH DIRECTIONS: DYNAMICAL SYSTEMS ANALYSIS

In this chapter, we have suggested that immature and ineffective parenting practices are commonplace among adolescent mothers and often lead to cognitive, socioemotional and academic developmental problems in their children. It was argued that the parenting style is influenced by the availability and quality of the adolescent mother's supports from partner, friends and family, and that ideally family supports should assist but not usurp her parenting responsibilities. Two parenting characteristics of adolescent mothers were proposed as having particularly adverse impact on the development of children—an inability to assist their children in learning self-regulatory skills and an abusive and/or neglectful parenting style. Supportive social networks can assist adolescent mothers in developing a more appropriate and effective parenting style through the provision of effective parenting models, instruction in problem solving, and the teaching of coping techniques as well as emotional and instrumental assistance for mothers who often cope with the multiple stressors associated with parenthood.

In this final section, we conclude with a new hypothesis about a specific link between teen parenting and child development. We suspect that it is not only the quality of teen parenting per se, but also daily fluctuations in parenting practices that influence child development and that may define neglect. We hypothesize that two related variables distinguish adult versus adolescent parents, the *regularity/irregularity and consistency/inconsistency of their instructional approaches to parenting*. To date, within- and across-day variability in the adolescent mothers' parenting styles has not been systematically studied. Dynamical systems analysis can help identify and describe fluctuations in parenting practices across time as well as provide a new base for understanding child outcomes.

The most basic assumption of dynamical systems analysis is that all systems change and evolve in time. The knowledge of a system's current state gives rise to the prediction of the future state of that system (Nowak & Lowenstein, 1994). *Dynamic systems* are made up of dynamic variables, whose values change over time. Changes in these variables characterize the relevant properties of the system. Nowak and Lowenstein (1994) have made distinctions between *order parameters* (which are macroscopic global parameters internal to a system) and *control parameters* (which represent conditions or influences external to the system itself, but that determine to a great extent the character of the dynamics observed).

Dynamical system modeling can be used to examine important developmental outcomes in children with adolescent mothers. An illustration might be helpful. Ramey and Ramey (1999) have identified specific parenting behaviors associated with children's cognitive development and later school success. These "daily essentials" include:

1. Encouraging the child to actively explore his or her environment
2. Mentoring the child in basic concepts and knowledge
3. Rewarding a child's developmental advances
4. Rehearsing and extending the child's newly acquired skills
5. Protecting the child from inappropriate teasing or harsh punishment
6. Stimulating language development and providing a rich child-responsive language environment
7. Guiding and limiting a child's behavior in ways to ensure the child's health and well-being.

Using a dynamical systems approach, we can examine the within and between-person variability in these seven essentials, using data derived from observations, diaries, or phone conversations about the moment-to-moment activities of a mother and her children over a 24-hour period or a 2-week interval. We hypothesize greater fluctuations within and across days in the quality of parenting among adolescent versus adult mothers. Furthermore, we predict that greater variability within a sample of adolescent mothers—perhaps associated with stress, inadequate social supports, or patterns of abuse and neglect—compromises children's cognitive and socioemotional development. A dynamical systems approach could lead researchers to a better understanding of the causal factors in the complex cognitive development of children with teen mothers by focusing on "variability/consistency" as explanatory variables.

An oscillatory (i.e., fluctuating) perspective on teenage parenting might reveal a variety of processes. Some adolescents might manifest consistent parenting techniques, whereas others might display inconsistent parenting because of the nature of their social supports. The former could result from having a grandmother who provides just the "right amount" of support and guidance and the latter due to grandmothers who are intrusive and authoritarian. A "pendulum with friction" model that measures intraindividual disregulation in parenting could be developed and conceptualized. For example, a teen mother who incorporates consistency into her parenting practices across time may be able to be modeled by a *dampened linear model* (i.e., a pendulum with friction). That is, we would anticipate variability in parenting immediately following birth, which would then decrease over time (see Figure 9.1a). In contrast, a teen mother who lacks social support could become neglectful or engage in poor and inconsistent parenting; this behavior would best be described by a *linear oscillatory model* without the

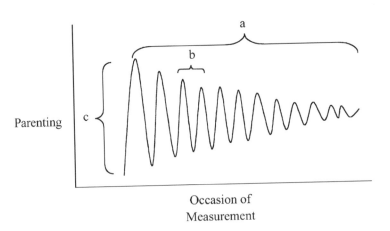

FIG. 9.1a. A dampened linear oscillator model with three parameters: (a) decay rate, (b) 1/frequency, and (c) amplitude.

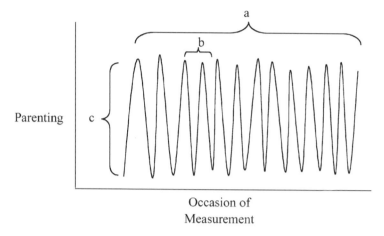

Occasion of
Measurement

FIG. 9.1b.   An undampened linear oscillator model.

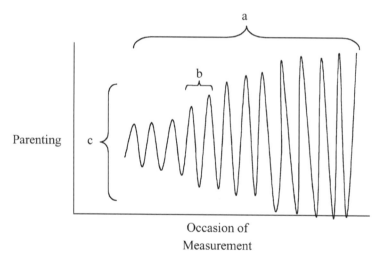

Occasion of
Measurement

FIG. 9.1c.   An increased linear oscillator model.

dampening parameter (i.e., a pendulum without friction). That is, the fluctuations in parenting observed after birth would not decrease with time (see Figure 9.1b), and perhaps might even increase (see Figure 9.1c).

The equation for the dampened linear oscillator is expressed in a regression model in which the acceleration of the pendulum is the outcome variable, and the position and velocity of the pendulum are the predictor variables (Boker, in press). More specific to a developmental perspective, velocity refers to the linear change in the system (e.g., change in a specific parenting behavior or the summed measures of the seven daily essentials) and acceleration describes its curvature (e.g., the speed with which a behavioral change or changes occur). Differential equation models can then be used to express effects within a system in terms of their derivatives (i.e., the instantaneous rates of change of the variables) as well as in terms of the values of the variables themselves (Boker & Graham, 1999).

For example, a differential equation model of parenting behaviors in adolescent mothers might relate the construct (or total score of selected measures) of daily affect to its slope, or first derivative (i.e., changes in parenting behavior). Going back to our example of the seven daily essentials as outlined above, this might include how *consistently* the infant was encouraged to actively explore his or her environment. A more complete model might include effects related to its curvature, or second derivative (i.e., how rapidly behavior was accelerating and decelerating in its change). More specifically, *how quickly* the mother's encouragement to explore the environment changed from considerable encouragement to no encouragement. These three parameters—initial position (e.g., encouraging the child to actively explore his or her environment), velocity (e.g., changes in the encouragement), and acceleration (e.g., the rate at which the mother speeds or slows changes in her encouragement of the child's exploration)—are related as a dynamical system in which the relationships among the components define a central tendency of a family of trajectories that any single mother might have (Boker, in press). After identifying the order parameters of the system that best represents regularity in adolescent parenting, the next step would be to examine factors, or control parameters, that influence the entire system. More specifically, mechanisms such as maternal age, social support variables, cognitive readiness, or self-regulation could be used to predict individual differences in the shape or trajectory of the system.

Understanding the effects of *inconsistent parenting practices*—characteristic of many teenage mothers—represents a new avenue for developmental research. A dynamical systems approach might help to explain the impact of adolescent parenting on children's diverse developmental problems, including the failure to develop self-regulation. Fluctuations in adolescent mothers' parenting practices—whether from day-to-day or over longer time periods—are likely associated with various aspects of social support and their consistency. In the same vein, incidents of abuse or neglect likely constitute extreme examples in the degree of fluctuation or oscillation in parenting: Children who have been maltreated and who develop poor self-regulatory skills are often limited by inconsistent and inadequate modeling of regulation provided by their caregivers and thus constrained by the dynamics of the system in which they are embedded. Alternatively, the development of self-regulation skills allows some children to escape from these constraints.

In short, consistency and regularity in parenting practices may prove to be causal variables in children's developmental outcomes. For a more thorough understanding of the cognitive, academic, emotional, and social outcomes of children with adolescent mothers, it may be necessary to begin to examine in depth the fluctuations that occur in the nature and quality of intimate mother–child interactions within and across days. An exploration of the direct and indirect effects of variability found within and among teenage mothers on child development may be an important next step in the effort to assist young mothers to become more competent parents.

ACKNOWLEDGMENTS

The writing of this paper was supported by the National Institute of Health (grant HD-26456). Christine Willard was supported by a training grant from NICHD (HD-07184).

REFERENCES

Apfel, N. H., & Seitz, V. (1993, November). African-American grandmothers, adolescent mothers, and their firstborns: Their relationship during the first six years. Paper presented at the Society for Research in Child Development Conference, Washington, DC.

Apfel, N. H., & Seitz, V. (1996). African-American adolescent mothers, their mothers, and their daughters: A longitudinal perspective over twelve years. In B. J. R. Leadbeater and N. Way (Eds.), *Urban girls: Resisting stereotypes, creating identities* (pp. 486–506). New York: Cambridge University Press.

Apfel, N., & Seitz, V. (1999, April). Support predicts teen mother's subsequent childbearing and parenting success. Paper presented at the biennial meeting of the Society for Research in Child Development, Albuquerque, NM.

Barth, R. P. (1998). Abusive and neglecting parents and the care of their children. In M. A. Mason, A. Skolnick, & S. D. Sugarman (Eds.), *All our families: New policies for a new century* (pp. 217–235). New York: Oxford University Press.

Bell, R. Q. (1976). Reduction of stress in childrearing. In L. Levi (Ed.), *Social stress and disease* (Vol. 2, pp. 183–207). London: Oxford University Press.

Belsky, J. (1984). The determinants of parenting: A process model. *Child Development, 55*, 83–96.

Boker, S. M. (in press). Differential structural equation modeling of intraindividual variability. In L. Collins & A. Sayer (Eds.), *New methods for the analysis of change*. Washington, DC: American Psychological Association.

Boker, S. M., & Graham, J. (1999). A dynamical systems analysis of adolescent substance use. *Multivariate Behavioral Research, 33* (4), 479–507.

Bolton, F. G. (1990). The risk of child maltreatment in adolescent parenting. *Advances in Adolescent Mental Health, 4*, 223–237.

Borkowski, J. G., Chan, L. K. S., & Muthukrishna, N. (2000). A process-oriented model of metacognition: Links between motivation and executive functioning. In G. Schraw (Ed.), *Issues in the measurement of metacognition* (pp. 1–41). Lincoln: University of Nebraska Press.

Borkowski, J. G., & Dukewich, T. L. (1996). Environment covariations and intelligence: How attachment influences self-regulation. In D. K. Detterman (Ed.), *The environment: Current topics in human intelligence* (Vol. 5, pp. 3–15). Norwood, NJ: Ablex.

Bronfrenbrenner, U., & Crouter, A. C. (1983). The evolution of environmental models in developmental research. In P. H. Mussen (Series Ed.) & W. Kessen (Vol. Ed.), *Handbook of child develop-ment: Vol. 1. History, theories, and methods* (pp. 358–414). New York: John Wiley and Sons.

Brooks-Gunn, J., & Furstenberg, F. F. (1986). The children of adolescent mothers: Physical, academ-ic, and psychological outcomes. *Developmental Review, 6*, 224–251.

Bugental, D. B., Blue, J., & Cruzcosa, M. (1989). Perceived control over caregiving outcomes: Implications for child abuse. *Developmental Psychology, 25*, 532–539.

Burchinal, M. R., Follmer, A., & Bryant, D. M. (1996). The relations of maternal social support and family structure with maternal responsiveness and child outcomes among African-American fam-ilies. *Developmental Psychology, 32*, 1073–1083.

Coates, D., & Wortman, C. B. (1980). Depression maintenance and interpersonal control. In A. Baum & J. Singer (Eds.), *Advances in environmental psychology: Applications of personal control* (Vol. 2, pp. 149–182). Hillsdale, NJ: Lawrence Erlbaum Associates.

Cochran, N. M., & Brassard, J. A. (1979). Child development and personal social networks. *Child Development, 50*, 601–616.

Colletta, N. D. (1981). Social support and the risk of maternal rejection by adolescent mothers. *Journal of Psychology, 109*, 191–197.

Connelly, C. D., & Strauss, M. A. (1992). Mother's age and risk for physical abuse. *Child Abuse and Neglect, 16*, 709–718.

Crnic, K. A., Greenberg, M. T., Ragozin, A. S., Robinson, N. M., & Basham, R. B. (1983). Effects of stress and social support on mothers and premature and full-term infants. *Child Development, 54*, 209–217.

Crnic, K. A., Greenberg, M. T., & Slough, N. M. (1986). Early stress and social support influences on mothers' and high-risk infants' functioning in late infancy. *Infant Mental Health Journal, 7*, 19–33.

Crockenberg, S. B., & Smith, P. (1982). Antecedents of mother–infant interaction and infant irritabili-ty in the first three months of life. *Infant Behavior and Development, 5*, 105–119.

De Lissovoy, V. (1973). Child care by adolescents. *Children Today, 2*, 22–25.

Dix, T. (1991). The affective organization of parenting: Adaptive and maladaptive processes. *Psychological Bulletin, 100*, 3–25.

Dubow, E. F., & Luster, T. (1990). Adjustment of children born to teenage mothers: The contribution of risk and protective factors. *Journal of Marriage and the Family, 52*, 393–404.

Dukewich, T. L., & Borkowski, J. G., (1996). Adolescent mothers and child abuse potential: An evalu-ation of risk factors. *Child Abuse and Neglect, 20*, 1031–1047.

Dukewich, T. L., Borkowski, J. G., & Whitman, T. L. (1999). A longitudinal analysis of maternal abuse potential and developmental delays in children of adolescent mothers. *Child Abuse and Neglect, 23*, 405–420.

Duncan, G. J., & Brooks-Gunn, J. (1997). *Consequences of growing up poor*. New York: Russell Sage Foundation.

East, P. L., & Felice, M. E. (1996). *Adolescent pregnancy and parenting: Findings from a racially diverse sample*. Mahwah, NJ: Lawrence Erlbaum Associates.

Egeland, B., & Sroufe, L. A. (1981). Developmental sequelae of maltreatment in infancy. In R. Rizley & D. Cicchetti (Eds.), *Developmental perspectives in child maltreatment*. San Francisco: Jossey-Bass.

Furstenberg, F. F., Brooks-Gunn, J., & Morgan, S. P. (1987). *Adolescent mothers in later life*. New York: Cambridge University Press.

Goerge, R. M. & Lee, B. J. (1997). Abuse and neglect of the children. In R. A. Maynard (Ed.), *Kids having kids: Economic costs and social consequences of teen pregnancy* (pp. 205–230). Washington, DC: Urban Institute Press.

Grolnik, W. S., & Ryan, R. M. (1989). Parent styles associated with children's self-regulation and competence in school. *Journal of Educational Psychology, 81*, 143–154.

Hetherington, E. M., Cox, M., & Cox, R. (1985). Long-term effects of divorce and remarriage on the adjustment of children. *Journal of American Academy of Psychiatry, 24*, 518–533.

Hoffman-Plotkin, D., & Twentyman, C. T. (1984). A multimodal assessment of behavioral and cognitive deficits in abused and neglected preschoolers. *Child Development, 55,* 794–802.

Horowitz, S. M., Klerman, L. V., Kuo, H. S., & Jekel, J. F. (1991). Intergenerational transmission of school-age parenthood. *Family Planning Perspectives, 23,* 166–172.

Kahn, R. L., & Antonucci, T. C. (1980). Convoys over the life course: Attachment, roles, and social support. In P. B. Baltes & O. Brim (Eds.), *Life-span developmental and behavior* (Vol. 3, pp. 253–286). Boston: Lexington Press.

Leadbeater, B. J., & Linares, O. (1992). Depressive symptoms in black and Puerto Rican adolescent mothers in the first three years postpartum. *Development and Psychopathology, 4,* 451–468.

Luster, T. & Mittelstaedt, M. (1993). Adolescent mothers. In Luster T. & Okagaki, L., (Eds.), *Parenting: An ecological perspective* (pp. 69–99). Hillsdale, NJ: Lawrence Erlbaum Associates.

Lynch, M. A., & Roberts, J. (1982). *Consequences of child abuse.* New York: Academic Press.

Martinez-Pons, M. (1996). Test of a model of parental inducement of academic self-regulation. *Journal of Experimental Education, 64,* 213–227.

McKenry, P. C., Browne, D. H., Kotch, J. B., & Symons, M. J. (1990). Mediators of depression among low-income, adolescent mothers of infants: A longitudinal perspective. *Journal of Youth and Adolescence, 19,* 327–347.

Nath, P. S., Borkowski, J. G., Whitman, T. L., & Schellenbach, C. J. (1991). Understanding adolescent parenting: The dimensions and functions of social support. *Family Relations, 40,* 411–420.

National Research Council. (1993). *Understanding child abuse and neglect.* Washington, DC: National Academy Press.

Nover, A., Shore, M., Timberlake, E., & Greenspan, S. (1984). The relationship of maternal perceptions and maternal behavior: A study of normal mothers and their infants. *American Journal of Orthopsychiatry, 54,* 211–223.

Nowak, A., & Lowenstein, M. (1994). Dynamical systems: A tool for social psychology (pp. 17–53). In R. R. Vallacher & A. Nowak (Eds.), *Dynamical systems in social psychology.* San Diego: Academic Press.

Oates, R. K., Peacock, A., & Forrest, D. (1984). Development in children following abuse and nonorganic failure to thrive. *American Journal of Diseases of Children, 138,* 764–767.

Panzarine, S. (1986). Stressors, coping, and social supports of adolescent mothers. *Journal of Adolescent Health Care, 7,* 153–161.

Ramey, C. T., & Ramey, S. L. (1999). *Right from birth: Building your child's foundation for life.* New York: Goddard Press.

Roberts, W. L., & Strayer, J. (1987). Parents' responsiveness to the emotional distress of their children: Relations with child competence. *Developmental Psychology, 23,* 415–422.

Salzinger, S. (1990). Social networks in child rearing and child development. *Annals of the New York Academy of Sciences, 602,* 171–188.

Schunk, D. H., & Zimmerman, B. J. (1997). Social origins of self-regulatory competence. *Educational Psychologist, 32,* 195–208.

Seitz, V., & Apfel, N. H. (1993). Adolescent mothers and repeated childbearing: Effects of a school-based intervention program. *American Journal of Orthopsychiatry, 63,* 572–581.

Smith, L. B., & Thelen, E. (1993). Can dynamic systems theory be usefully applied in areas other than motor development? In L. B. Smith & E. Thelen (Eds.), *A dynamic systems approach to development* (pp. 151–170). Cambridge, MA: MIT Press.

Sommer, K., Whitman, T. L., Borkowski, J. G., Schellenbach, C. (1993). Cognitive readiness and adolescent parenting. *Developmental Psychology, 29,* 389–398.

Spieker, S. J., & Bensley, L. (1994). Role of living arrangement and grandmother social support in adolescent mothering and infant attachment. *Developmental Psychology, 30,* 102–111.

Thoits, P. A. (1986). Social support as coping assistance. *Journal of Consulting and Clinical Psychology, 54,* 416–423.

Unger, D. G. (1985). The relationship of specific social and psychological coping resources with the adjustment of adolescent primiparas. Unpublished doctoral dissertation, University of South Carolina, Columbia.

Unger, D. G., & Cooley, M. (1992). Partner and grandmother contact in Black and White teen parent families. *Journal of Adolescent Health, 13*, 546–552.

Unger, D. G., & Wandersman, L. P. (1985). Social support and adolescent mothers: Action research contributions to theory and practice. *Journal of Social Issues, 41*, 29–45.

Unger, D. G., & Wandersman, L. P. (1988). The relations of family and partner support to the adjustment of adolescent mothers. *Child Development, 59*, 1056–1060.

Vaughn, B., Egeland, B., Sroufe, L. A., & Waters, E. (1979). Individual differences in infant–mother attachment at twelve and eighteen months: Stability and change in families under stress. *Child Development, 50*, 971–975.

Ward, M. J., & Carlson, E. A. (1995). Associations among adult attachment representations, maternal sensitivity, and infant–mother attachment in a sample of adolescent mothers. *Child Development, 66*, 69–79.

Whitman, T. L., Borkowski, J. G., Keogh, D. & Weed, K. (2001). *Interwoven lives: Adolescent mothers and their children.* Mahwah, NJ: Lawrence Erlbaum Associates.

Wolfe, D. A. (1987). *Child abuse: Vol. 10. Implications for child development and psychopathology.* Newbury Park, CA: Sage.

Zimmerman, B. J. (1996). Enhancing student academic and health functioning: A self-regulatory perspective. *School Psychology Quarterly, 11*, 47–66.

Zimmerman, B. J. (1998). Developing self-fulfilling cycles of academic regulation: An analysis of exemplary instructional models. In D. H. Schunk, & B. J. Zimmerman (Eds.), *Self-regulated learning: From teaching to self-reflective practice* (pp. 1–19). New York: Guilford Press.

III

Parenting Influences on Emotional Development and Socialization

10

From Infant Attachment to Promotion of Adolescent Autonomy: Prospective, Longitudinal Data on the Role of Parents in Development

L. Alan Sroufe

University of Minnesota

For 26 years Byron Egeland, Andrew Collins, and I have been involved in a comprehensive study of individual development beginning before birth. A major focus of this project has been to evaluate the role of caregiving experience age by age in the context of competing and complementary influences. Thus, in addition to parenting variables, we have assessed parent and child IQ, child temperament, cognitive and language development, parent personality and psychopathology, and a host of contextual factors, including life stress and family social support. We also studied child peer relationships at every age. The 175 participants being followed were born into poverty, thus constraining socioeconomic status variation, which can often account for outcomes.

Our findings have revealed that nothing is more important for the child's development than the quality of care received. This has been true for outcomes as diverse as competence with peers, behavior and emotional problems, successful completion of school, and adolescent risk behaviors such as promiscuity. Moreover, the predictive power of parenting variables holds even when other salient influences on development are controlled and when the predictor is

Address correspondence to: Alan Sroufe, 51 E. River Rd., Minneapolis. MN 55455, e-mail: srouf001@tc.umn.edu changing quality of care. When care worsens or improves and child problems respond accordingly, such effects are free from any confounding by potential genetic effects. It is not simply the case that good parents pass along good genes to their children, resulting in good child behavior. What happens to children (and what happens to parents who care for them) matters deeply. Nor is it the case that peer experiences dwarf parenting experiences. Direct study shows that early quality of care strongly predicts peer experiences and that, subsequently, history with parents and history with peers interact in complex ways in shaping later child behavior. All of these issues will be detailed in the overview to follow.

THE PREDICTIVE POWER OF EARLY ATTACHMENT RELATIONSHIPS

Attachment as a Relationship Construct

Variations in attachment using the Ainsworth procedure (Ainsworth, Blehar, Waters, & Wall, 1978) are variations in relationship quality, being specific to the particular parent and being subject to change given changes in parental life stress and caregiving behavior. Such variations are not reflections of genetically based traits of the infant but of the history of interaction with the parent. The most notable evidence for this is that the same child may have a secure relationship with one parent and an anxious relationship with the other, with concordance being significant but only modest in metanalysis (Fox, Kimmerly, & Schafer, 1991). The quality of each of these relationships has been found to be predictable from the quality of care that parent provided (Main & Weston, 1981). Moreover, given changes in parental life stress and quality of care, infant attachment security changes (Vaughn, Waters, Egeland, & Sroufe, 1979). Clearly, the quality of these relationships cannot be based simply in characteristics of the child.

Variations in attachment relationships are predicted by earlier caregiver sensitivity and not at all by infant temperament. This is supported by the large-scale NICHD child-care study (NICHD, 1997) and by numerous other studies (see Weinfield, Sroufe, Egeland, & Carlson, 1999, for a review). Temperamental variation is, of course, revealed in attachment assessments, but shows up in frequencies and intensities of certain behaviors, not in overall organization and quality. Thus, for example, some infants become more upset in the face of the brief separations, but this does not forecast whether they will be readily settled or angry when the caregiver returns. The latter are the hallmarks of the quality of attachment, not the former. Some infants who are secure in their attachment (subtypes B1 and B2) do not become upset by separation; some (B4 and some B3) become quite upset. Likewise, some infants who are secure in their attachments seek a great deal of physical contact; others are content with interacting at a distance. They have in common the capacity to use the caregiver as a ready source of reassurance and as a support for exploration. Those who are anxious in their attachments likewise may have various temperaments.

When relationships are classed as "secure," this means that the infant has confidence in this particular caregiver. Such confidence is shown by behavior such as ease of being settled by this caregiver when distressed, confident exploration in the presence of the caregiver and clear expectations that the caregiver is a willing interactive partner (greetings upon reunion, sharing of discoveries). Anxious attachment relationships take several forms. One pattern, associated with a history of chronic rejection when the infant seeks closeness, is for the infant to actively avoid the caregiver in times of stress. Thus, following the 3-minute separations in the Ainsworth procedure, these infants ignore or turn away from the caregiver upon reunion, doing so more following a second separation, when stress is more greatly activated. This is specific to the caregiver in contrast to a stranger and represents acquired control of the built-in tendency to seek contact when distressed (see below). Members of another group, Anxious/Resistant Attachment, associated with inconsistent care, are palpably wary in the Ainsworth procedure, hovering near the caregiver even before separation and becoming quite distressed when the caregiver leaves. In contrast to distressed secure cases, these infants are unable to be readily settled by contact with the caregiver. They may squirm and angrily resist such contact, even though they sought it. Finally, "disorganized/disoriented attachment" results when caregivers are frightening or confusing. Infants are biologically biased to seek contact with caregivers when frightened. When the caregiver *is the source of fear*, however, they are placed in an irresolvable paradox because they are also disposed to flee from the source of fear. Coherent organization of attachment behavior breaks down; stereotypies, freezing, and oddly sequenced behavior result.

Attachment and Child Adaptation

These characterizations of early primary relationships predict to major domains of later adaptation better than any other assessments from infancy. In our comprehensive data set they consistently outstrip measures of temperament, whether the outcome be peer relationships, school success, or psychopathology. The origins of individual adaptation begin in the caregiving system, even before stable patterns of individual behavior can be discerned outside of this context (Sroufe, 1989).

Some of the specific findings regarding attachment outcomes are especially noteworthy. The relationship between anxious infant attachment and later dependency has been especially strong (e.g., Urban, Carlson, Egeland, & Sroufe, 1991). This holds even for those with avoidant histories who some would argue are simply temperamentally bold. These infants, like those with resistant histories, are later more likely to be on their preschool teacher's laps and more involved with camp counselors at the expense of peers. Bowlby's (1973) specific hypothesis that self-reliance has its roots in early responsive care and effective dependency is amply supported. Genuine independence is not possible in infancy.

A second domain where associations have been quite strong concerns empathic involvement with others and, more generally, competent social relationships. In the presence of an injured or otherwise distressed playmate, preschoolers with histories of secure attachment more likely exhibit concern and effective prosocial behavior (e.g., getting a teacher). Those with avoidant histories often taunt or harass such a child, while those with resistant histories become upset and distraught (Kestenbaum, Farber, & Sroufe, 1989). Similarly, preschoolers with secure histories are more engaged with peers and more effectively positive when initiating or responding to peer contacts (e.g., Sroufe, Schork, Motti, Lawroski, & LaFreniere, 1984). In later years, they continue to show hallmarks of peer competence (Sroufe, Egeland, & Carlson, 1999). In middle childhood they more often form durable friendships, participate actively in the same gender peer group, maintain boundaries with regard to the opposite gender, and smoothly coordinate friendship and group functioning. In adolescence they also are effective in the mixed-gender peer group, consolidating leadership qualities that emerged in childhood (Englund et al., 2000). They have a greater capacity to tolerate vulnerability and intimacy in relationships. As one 11-year-old said in answer to a question about the consequences of an argument for a friendship; "Actually, you would probably be better friends afterwards because you would know each other better." This orientation also appears to be taken forward to the romantic relationships of early adulthood (Hennighausen, 1999). Throughout childhood and adolescence, they are rated as more socially competent by their teachers. Finally, they have more effective relationships with teachers, counselors, and other adults and are more esteemed by them (Sroufe & Fleeson, 1988). In a detailed observational study of a subsample seen in summer camp settings, stability correlations for social competence from infancy through adolescence often are as high as .50.

A third area where relationships have been consistently impressive is in the domain of self-esteem and emotional health (Sroufe, 1983; Urban et al., 1991) or, in more of our reports, psychopathology (Carlson, 1998; Sroufe 1997; Sroufe, Carlson, Levy, & Egeland, 1999). Anxious attachment, especially a history of avoidance and/or disorganized attachment, clearly is a risk factor for disturbance. The combination of avoidant and disorganized attachment variables correlates with a global index of pathology at age $17\frac{1}{2}$ (number plus severity of symptoms on the K-SADS diagnostic interview) in the .40s. Moreover, some specific linkages are noteworthy. Resistant attachment is correlated uniquely and specifically with anxiety disorders (Warren, Huston, Egeland, & Sroufe, 1997); avoidance with conduct disorders; disorganized attachment with dissociative symptoms (Carlson, 1998).

We also have found attachment history to be related to other aspects of competent functioning, including exploration and curiosity in the preschool years

(Sroufe, 1983), agency and purposefulness during middle childhood (Urban et al., 1991), and school success throughout the childhood years (e.g., Carlson et al., 1999; Teo, Carlson, Mathieu, Egeland, & Sroufe, 1996). When infant attachment assessments predict achievement test performance (e.g., .44 with math achievement at age 16; more modest but still significant with IQ controlled) or dropping out of school, such connections obviously are indirect, through links to school attendance, parental involvement with school, and more satisfactory peer relationships. Still, such findings are impressive for an assessment made in infancy.

A final outcome is "resiliency." Children with secure histories show fewer behavior problems in the face of stress (Pianta, Egeland, & Sroufe, 1990) and more likely recover from periods of troubled behavior (Sroufe et al., 1999). One does not leave behind early attachment history even in the face of change (Sroufe, Egeland, & Kreutzer, 1990); rather, behavior is always a product of current circumstances and developmental history.

Interpreting Attachment Findings

None of these findings lead us to a model of linear causality. Attachment variations do not "cause" later outcomes (Sroufe et al., 1999). Rather, they are viewed as initiating developmental pathways, only probabilistically related to particular outcomes. Strong prediction comes only when multiple factors supporting or deflecting individuals from the initial pathway are also considered. For example, quality of care beyond the infancy period enhances our predictions. In our first assessments of the quality of adult romantic relationships, we find a modest but significant prediction (.20) from infant attachment security. The prediction is somewhat better for certain qualities in the relationship, such as hostility (.35). However, these predictions are enhanced when we also consider parenting in the preschool period and at the transition to adolescence (see below).

Moreover, while attachment predicts early peer competence, and predicts later peer competence and other aspects of functioning with earlier peer competence controlled, predictions of outcomes (behavior problems, dropping out) generally are enhanced when both attachment and peer history are considered. Moreover, attachment and peer variables predict best to different outcomes, even in the peer domain. Thus, attachment consistently is a better predictor of intimacy, whereas earlier peer experiences predict better to skill in social interaction (Sroufe, Egeland, & Carlson, 1999).

It is also the case that attachment experiences may interact with other risks, including those considered biological. For example, in an adoption study, Cadoret, Troughton, Merchant, & Whitters, (1990) found that it was not genetic risk (biological mother was depressed) nor attachment history (number of placements or age of permanent placement) that most strongly predicted subsequent depression; rather, it was the combination of both risk factors. In our own study we found that resistant attachment predicted anxiety problems dramatically more strongly for those children who as newborns showed slow habituation to startle (were hyperreactive).

OTHER ASPECTS OF CARE

There is, of course, more to parenting than emotional responsiveness and the building of trust. Parenting also involves discipline, limit-setting, maturity demands, guidance, and supervision. Patterns of stimulation and demands for maturity need to be appropriate to the child's developmental level. We have assessed all of these aspects of parenting and found them to be of importance for the child's development (e.g., Carlson, Jacobvitz, and Sroufe, 1995; Pianta, Hyatt, & Egeland, 1996). As early as 6 months, measures of overstimulating, intrusive care prove to be predictive of behavior problems throughout the childhood years, independent of any endogenous temperament factors.

Patterns of Stimulation and Parent–Child Boundaries

One construct that we have found to be especially powerful, which appears to be relatively independent of attachment, is maintenance or violation of parent–child boundaries. When parents abdicate the parental role, unduly rely on the child for support, or otherwise draw the child into inappropriate roles, development is compromised. In extreme cases this can take the form of seductive parental behavior or frank sexual abuse. At other times it is shown through derision and competitiveness with the child, taunting and teasing, or other "peerlike" behavior (Hiester, 1993; Sroufe, Jacobvitz, Mangelsdorf, DeAngelo, & Ward, 1985). As with physical maltreatment, boundary distortions often are most prominent when the parent becomes tense and the child is already frustrated and losing control. The result is that the child is further stimulated at precisely those times when he or she most needs a settling presence. While in the early years such boundary distortions are most obvious in parental behavior, over time the pattern is internalized and becomes revealed in behaviors of the child (e.g., solicitousness and undo caregiving of the parent; Hiester, 1993).

We have designed and reliably measured this construct from infancy to early adolescence and have demonstrated notable stability in independent assessments. In fact, based on the first 20 cases we obtained a .50 correlation between boundary violations in our original parent–toddler dyads and boundary violation 20 years later in the second generation (Levy, 1999). Moreover, these measures have consistently predicted externalizing problems in boys across ages. Such assessments in the first 3 years are among the best predictors of attention deficit/ hyperactivity problems throughout elementary school, outstripping all early measures of temperament, including infant activity level. They also predict certain problems with peers, especially failure to maintain age-typical gender boundaries in middle childhood and sexual promiscuity and early pregnancy in adolescence.

Parent–child boundary distortion is a complex psychological construct. It cannot be easily reduced to a simple trait of the parent passed along genetically to the child. For example, when a caregiver behaves seductively toward a son, such behavior is negatively correlated with independent measures of warmth or affection. It also is related as predicted to increased derision toward daughters, not to seductiveness with them (Sroufe et al., 1985). These caregivers, having experienced exploitation by adult males in their histories, have learned a complex relational scheme based on generation and gender (Sroufe & Ward, 1980). As another example, it is the pattern of boundary maintenance or violation that is transmitted across generations, not specific behavioral manifestations such as giggling, whispering coyly, or talkativeness.

Another important caregiving feature, especially perhaps during the transition to adolescence, is the parents' support for the child's emerging autonomy. Indeed, one reason boundary distortions may be problematic is that they often compromise autonomy. At age 13 we utilized a laboratory observation procedure to assess boundary issues and more targeted aspects of support for autonomy (see J. Sroufe, 1991, for scale description). Procedures, which were originally developed by Jeanne and Jack Block, tapped into issues of the period by utilizing circumstances where the teen had expertise or a clear viewpoint, challenging the parent to share authority (planning an antismoking campaign together; guiding the blindfolded parent to solve a puzzle; jointly describing the ideal person). In some dyads, the young person was able to freely express positions and stay connected to the parent despite differences. The relationship with the parent supported the teen's exploration, rather than detracted from it. For others, relationship issues, including the parent's difficulty acknowledging the teen's advancing maturity, interfered. These assessments have proven powerful in predicting later social competence with peers and even qualities of romantic relationships in early adulthood (Roisman, Sroufe, Madsen, & Collins, in press). Parent–child boundary problems at age 13 years specifically related to asymmetries in later couple relationships (e.g., one treated the other like a child), to externalizing problems in boys, and to early pregnancy and promiscuity during the later teen years.

Maltreatment

We also have investigated the impact of extremes in poor parenting. Approximately 30% of the children in our high-risk sample experienced some form of maltreatment. This included physical neglect (failure to meet the basic needs of the child for sustenance, protection, or basic care), physical abuse, sexual abuse, and

TABLE 10.1
PERCENT OF K-SADS DIAGNOSES AT AGE 17½ BY PRESCHOOL
MALTREATMENT AND CONTROL GROUP

Maltreatment Groups	Depressed/ Other Mood Disorders	Anxiety/ Phobia/ OCD	Conduct Disorder Oppositional Defiant Disorder	PTSD	Multiple Diagnoses
Physical	40	47	67	13	60
Unavailable	40	53	53	27	73
Neglect	31	62	38	15	54
Sexual	64	64	55	27	73
Control	31	34	19	12	30

"psychological unavailability" (a profound lack of involvement and emotional responsiveness to the child). Our prospective data reveal no causal role for intrinsic child characteristics in generating maltreatment (e.g., prematurity, newborn irritability); rather, maltreatment is associated with parent caregiving history, stress, and certain psychological features, such as failure to grasp that infant needs are independent of parent wishes (Pianta, Egeland, & Erickson, 1989).

Consistent with the extensive literature in this area (e.g., Cicchetti & Lynch, 1995), each of these patterns of maltreatment were associated with negative child outcomes of various sorts (Egeland & Sroufe, 1981; Egeland, 1997). Neglect is a strong predictor of school failure and other signs of incompetence in childhood, even with IQ controlled. Physical abuse predicts diverse problems, including aggression, peer problems and low self-esteem. Psychological unavailability proved to be an especially devastating pattern of care. By 18 months every infant experiencing this form of care in pure form ($N = 18$) manifested avoidant attachment, despite the fact that they generally had been quite robust in the early months of life. In every period following infancy they, as a group, continued to show problems, often showing deterioration in capacities while others were gaining in competence. The legacy of problems shown by these children included adjustment problems at school, poor peer relationships, and conduct disturbances.

Both physical abuse and psychological unavailability were related to psychopathology based on our clinical interview at age 17½ (Egeland, 1997; see Table 10.1). They were especially closely related to general psychological problems and conduct disorders. However, the single strongest predictor of psychopathology was sexual abuse, even though the number of such cases was small ($N = 13$); 73% of these children qualified for two or more psychiatric diagnoses. None were without diagnoses. It should be pointed out that many of these predictions held with other variables controlled. For example, sexual abuse predicted adolescent depression even after taking into account maternal depression, our surrogate for genetic liability (Duggal, Carlson, Sroufe, & Egeland, 2001).

Combined Experiences of Care

It is, of course, the case that a history of nonresponsive care in infancy, anxious attachment and subsequent maltreatment predict more negative outcomes than any single experiential variable. Predictions of psychopathology, for example, commonly go from .30 to .40 when attachment and maltreatment variables are put into multiple regressions together.

We have also obtained evidence for potentiation effects; that is, the presence of certain forms of anxious attachment amplify the impact of later trauma. This is dramatically the case for early avoidant and disorganized/disoriented attachment and later maltreatment (Ogawa, Sroufe, Weinfield, Carlson, & Egeland, 1997; Sroufe, Duggal, Weinfield, & Carlson, 2000). It is well-known that trauma does not produce dissociative symptoms in all individuals (Putnam, 2000). Some individuals, it seems, are more vulnerable. In accord with this, we find that those with histories of avoidance and, especially disorganized/disoriented attachment (postulated to be associated with distortions in the early formation of the self), are dramatically more likely to show dissociative symptoms. The results remain strong (multiple $R = .44$) up to 18 years later on the Putnam Dissociation Experiences scale.

THE RELATIONSHIP CONTEXT OF DEVELOPMENT

Family Violence and Discord

Some effects of the family are more indirect that those described above. Such factors in our study have included tension, discord, and violence between parenting partners. We frequently have found the positive and negative quality of the parental relationship to be a protective factor or a risk factor, respectively (e.g., Pianta et al., 1996). Violence between partners (most commonly abuse of the child's mother by a male partner) is especially powerful. Most noteworthy in our study is the fact that adult–adult violence can be demonstrated to have its impact even after controlling for confounding variables. It is frequently reported in the literature that violence is associated with child behavior problems. Without proper controls, however, such an effect may actually be due to low socioeconomic status, general life stress, or direct abuse of the child, which frequently co-occur with spousal abuse. We control for each of these factors and still find that adult partner abuse predicts externalizing behavior in boys when interparental violence is entered last in regression analyses (Yates, Dodds, Sroufe & Egeland, in press). It should be noted that most of the men contributing to these analyses are not biologically related to our child participants. Therefore, these findings cannot be attributed to shared genetic variance between the violent man and the aggressive, acting-out boy.

Other Influences of Men

Ours has primarily been a study of maternal influences on child development. This was a pragmatic result of studying a sample largely living in poverty. Poor children generally are raised by their mothers, with men often present inconsistently, if at all. Nonetheless, we have been keenly interested in the role of men and have found compelling evidence for both positive and negative influences.

One key variable pointed to by Hetherington, Patterson, Dishion (this volume) and others has been *parental monitoring*—the degree to which the parent is aware of the child's friends, whereabouts, and activities and tracks them. We cannot evaluate adult male monitoring separately, due to the way it would compromise sample sizes for multivariate analyses. We did, however, find that where there was a stable male presence the degree of monitoring was significantly greater than when there was no adult male in the home (Sroufe & Pierce, 1999). Moreover, as in other studies, high monitoring was associated with a lessened likelihood of behavior problems. In general, those families with stable male presence have the lowest frequency of adolescent conduct problems in our sample (only 11% of the boys).

On the other side of the coin, unstable male presence was associated with very negative outcomes (Sroufe & Pierce, 1999). The most unstable situations, with a number of men often moving in and out over short intervals, was associated with a percentage of adolescent male conduct problems of 83%, far higher than the rate for stable single mothers (33%). Thus, while stable male presence operated as a protective factor in our sample, chaotic male involvement increased risk for problems in this already high-risk sample.

Both chaotic male presence and domestic violence, discussed above, showed clear age effects. When such stresses and disruptions were present in the preschool years, consequences were more dramatic. These findings, and others from our project, attest to the special role of early experience. Such findings also call into question simple genetic explanations of the role of parenting variables.

Changing Family Context

Correlations between family variables and child outcomes are, of course, open to a number of interpretations. Even what we consider "nonobvious" relationships, such as the link between responsive care and later compliance and independence, or the link between early parent–child boundary maintenance and child gender–boundary maintenance in middle childhood, can be given post hoc genetic interpretations. Still, the total array of findings outlined above implies a causal role for experiences within the family, especially given the controls for IQ and other possible mediators.

Even more compelling, however, are the data concerning changing family context. For example, the link between maternal depression and child outcomes lends itself to a genetic interpretation, even though the outcomes are diverse and differ for male and female children (Duggal et al., in press). However, we also have found changes in maternal depression to be linked to subsequent changes in child behavior problems (Egeland, Kalkoske, Gottesman, & Erickson, 1990). Clearly, the child's genetic vulnerability does not wax and wane with episodic changes in maternal depression. Likewise, Dawson and Ashman (2000) have found that associations with developmental difficulties are greater when the mother is depressed in the first year of life than when her depressive episode is later or prior to birth. Caregiving experience, as impacted by depression, is implicated.

An even more consistently implicated variable in our study are changes in maternal life stress or social support, age by age. For example, when cases where infants who were anxiously attached at 12 months and secure at 18 months are compared with cases remaining anxiously attached across this period, their mothers independently reported greater reductions in life stress (Vaughn et al., 1979). Moreover, changes in maternal life stress in the early elementary school years also account for changes in attention and hyperactivity problems between kindergarten and third grade (Carlson et al., 1995). From infancy to adolescence, increases and decreases in experienced parental stress predict changing child problems (Sroufe et al., 1999).

Results for social support are quite parallel. Some preschoolers who had histories of anxious attachment did better than we would have expected. When these cases were compared to those with anxious histories who did have behavior problems in preschool, one factor predicted group differences beyond all others: during the intervening years their mothers significantly more often formed a stable relationship with an adult partner (Erickson, Sroufe, & Egeland, 1985). Likewise, in early elementary school increases in social support are associated with decreases in child attentional and activity problems.

DISCUSSION

Demonstrating cause in psychological research is often difficult. No experiments, except those in nature, have been part of our project. This leaves open, as always, that factors not investigated underlie relations described. However, prospective, longitudinal data have certain strengths. Beginning before birth as we did and tracking our participants age by age, we can argue with some confidence that parenting problems were evident earlier in time than child problems, and changes in parenting and parent circumstances preceded changes in child behavior. Our early measures of temperament did not predict parenting quality nor did they, except infrequently and modestly, predict child outcomes. Later measures of temperament, of course, would be substantially confounded with experience.

Effect sizes of individual parenting variables were often small. Almost always the vast majority of variance was left unexplained, even in the case of our robust attachment assessments. Still, the constructs assessed are very challenging to measure and no techniques were utilized to correct for unreliability. Therefore, the correlations reported across years and even decades are impressive. Moreover, when we combined parenting measures, and especially when we combined them with contextual variables such as life stress and cumulated them over time, predictions became much stronger. As one example, a composite measure of early psychosocial support in the first 3½ years (six measures of parenting and the quality of stimulation and organization in the home environment) allowed us to predict dropping out of high school with 77% accuracy. This is stronger than the prediction from child IQ, and even achievement test performance in elementary school does not add to this prediction. Similarly, when we predict to peer relations and psychopathology, cumulating our psychosocial experience variables often allows us to account for 50% of the variance in a given outcome. Properly aggregated, parenting variables show strong relations with important developmental outcomes.

Certainly, one need not pit parent variables against other influences such as temperament, IQ, or peer experiences. We have argued, for example, that parent and peer experiences combine to prepare the individual for adult social relationships. The capacity for close relationships is a developmental construction (Collins & Sroufe, 1999), taking root in early attachment relationships and being sustained throughout by supportive parents, but put into practice and elaborated in the symmetrical relationships of the world of peers (Sroufe, Egeland, & Carlson, 1999). As one example, those with secure histories bring to the world of peers positive expectations concerning the value of relationships, a belief that others will be responsive and that they are worthy of responsiveness, confidence in their effectiveness in eliciting reactions, the capacity for emotional regulation, and a reservoire a exploratory skills nurtured in the secure base of the attachment relationships. All this makes them attractive to peers and able to negotiate the challenges of give-and-take in early peer interaction. At the same time, peer interactions provide opportunities to develop interactive and negotiating skills, arousal modulation, and sustained give-and-take in the midst of conflict that simply aren't available in asymmetrical parent–child relationships. Having enthusiastically engaged such opportunities and given ongoing parental support and only ordinary stress and tension at home, the child is now amply prepared for the close, durable friendships of middle childhood and the new demands to balance relationships. These, then, are the springboard for the more intimate relationships (and relationship networks) of adolescence and beyond.

In such a view it does not make sense to say parent relationships or peer relationships are more important. Both dispositions to be close and skills in interacting are important in social relationships. One certainly should not be misled by appearances. While decades of research (e.g., Brittain, 1963) has shown that teenagers are heavily influenced by peers with regard to dress, mannerisms, music preferences, and other superficial characteristics, the same research also showed more influence of parents regarding basic values. We would also suggest that basic foundations for trust and trustworthiness, valuing of emotional closeness and the capacity to nurture are primary legacies of experience with caregivers. It is noteworthy than in his monkey cross-fostering studies, Suomi (1995) found a strong role for experience in promoting the capacity to nurture offspring and no role for genetics.

At the beginning of this new century, there is abundant evidence for the critical role of caregiving experience for the development of the child, including prospective longitudinal data with other influences well controlled. When this evidence is considered along with family intervention effects (e.g., Dishion, this volume), controlled experiments with monkeys (Fairbanks, 1989; Suomi, this volume), and the natural experiments with eastern European orphans (Gunnar, 2001; Johnson, 2000), the case is compelling. While the evidence two decades ago may have been ambiguous, this is no longer the case.

REFERENCES

Ainsworth, M., Blehar, M., Waters, E., & Wall, S. (1978). *Patterns of attachment.* Hillsdale, NJ: Lawrence Erlbaum Associates.

Bowlby, J. (1973). *Separation.* New York: Basic Books.

Brittain, C. (1963). Adolescent choice and parent–peer cross pressures. *American Sociological Review, 28,* 385–391.

Cadoret, R. J., Troughton, E., Merchant, L. M., & Whitters, A. (1990). Early life psychosocial events and adult affective symptoms. In L. Robins and M. Rutter (Eds.), *Straight and devious pathways from childhood to adulthood* (pp. 300–313). Cambridge, UK: Cambridge University Press.

Carlson, E. (1998). A prospective longitudinal study of attachment disorganization/disorientation. *Child Development, 69,* 1107–1128.

Carlson, E., Jacobvitz, D., & Sroufe, L. A. (1995). A developmental investigation of inattentiveness and hyperactivity. *Child Development, 66,* 37–54.

Carlson, E., Sroufe, L. A., Collins, W. A., Jimerson, S., Weinfield, N., Hennighausen, K., Egeland, B., Hyson, D. M., Anderson, F., & Meyer, S. E. (1999). Early environmental support and elementary school adjustment as predictors of school adjustment in middle adolescence. *Journal of Adolescent Research, 14,* 72–94.

Cicchetti, D., & Lynch, M. (1995). Failure in the expectable environment and their impact on individual development: The use of child maltreatment. In D. Cicchetti & D. Cohen (Eds.), *Developmental psychopathology,* (Vol. 2, pp. 32–71). New York: John Wiley & Sons.

Collins, W. A., & Sroufe, L. A. (1999). Capacity for intimate relationships: A developmental construction. In W. Furman, C. Feiring, & B. Brown (Eds.), *Contemporary perspectives on adolescent romantic relationships* (pp. 125–147). New York: Cambridge University Press.

Dawson, G. & Ashman, S. (2000). On the origins of a vulnerability to depression: The influence of the early social environment. In C. Nelson (Ed.), *The effects of early adversity on neurobehavioral development. Minnesota symposia on child psychology* (Vol. 31, pp. 245–280). Hillsdale, NJ: Lawrence Erlbaum Associates.

Duggal, S., Carlson, E., Sroufe, L. A., & Egeland, B. (2001). Depressive symptomatology in children and adolescents. *Development and Psychopathology, 13,* 143–164.

Egeland, B. (1997). Mediators of the effects of child maltreatment on developmental adaptation in adolescence. In D. Cicchetti & S. Toth (Eds.), *Rochester symposium on developmental psychopathology: Vol. 8: The effects of trauma on the developmental process* (pp. 403–434). Rochester, NY: Rochester University Press.

Egeland, B., Kalkoske, M., Gottesman, N., & Erickson, M. (1990). Preschool behavior problems. Stability and factors accounting for change. *Journal of Child Psychology and Psychiatry, 31,* 891–910.

Egeland, B., & Sroufe, L. A. (1981). Developmental sequelae of maltreatment in infancy. In D. Cicchetti & R. Rizley (Eds.), *New directions in child development: Developmental approaches to child maltreatment.* San Francisco: Jossey-Bass.

Englund, M., Levy, A., Hyson, D., & Sroufe, L. A. (2000). Adolescent social competence: Effectiveness in a group setting. *Child Development, 71,* 1049–1060.

Erickson, M., Sroufe, L. A., & Egeland, B. (1985). The relationship of quality of attachment and behavior problems in preschool in a high risk sample. In I. Bretherton and E. Waters (Eds.), *Growing points in attachment theory and research. Monographs of the Society for Research in Child Development, 50* (1–2, Serial No. 209), 147–186.

Fairbanks, L. (1989). Early experience and cross-generational continuity of mother–infant contact in Vervet monkeys. *Developmental Psychobiology, 22,* 669–681.

Fox, N., Kimmerly, N., & Schafer, W. (1991). Attachment to mother/attachment to father: A meta-analysis. *Developmental Psychology, 62,* 210–235.

Gunnar, M. (2001). Effects of early deprivation: Findings from orphonage-reared infants and children. In C. Nelson & M. Luciana (Eds.), *Handbook of developmental cognitive neuroscience* (pp. 617–629). Cambridge, MA: MIT Press.

Hennighausen, K. (1999). *Developmental antecedents of young adult romantic relationships.* Unpublished doctoral dissertation, University of Minnesota.

Hiester, M. (1993). *Generational boundary dissolution between mothers and children in early childhood and early adolescence.* Unpublished doctoral dissertation, University of Minnesota.

Johnson, D. (2000). Medical and developmental sequelae of early childhood institutionalization in Eastern European adoptees. In C. Nelson (Ed.), *Minnesota symposia on child psychology: Vol. 31. The effects of early adversity on neurobehavioral development* (pp. 113–162). Hillsdale, NJ: Lawrence Erlbaum Associates.

Kestenbaum, R., Farber, E., & Sroufe, L. A. (1989). Individual differences in empathy among preschoolers' concurrent and predictive validity. In N. Eisenberg (Ed.), *Empathy and related emotional responses: No. 44. New directions for child development* (pp. 51–56). San Francisco: Jossey-Bass.

Levy, A. (1999). Continuities and discontinuities in parent–child relationships across two generations: A prospective, longitudinal study. Unpublished doctoral dissertation, University of Minnesota.

Main, M., & Weston, D. (1981). The quality of the toddler's relationship to mother and to father as related to conflict behavior and readiness to establish new relationships. *Child Development, 52,* 932–940.

NICHD Early Child Care Research Network (1997). The effects of infant child care on mother–infant attachment security. *Child Development, 68,* 860–879.

Ogawa, J., Sroufe, L. A., Weinfield, N. S., Carlson, E., & Egeland, B. (1997). Development and the fragmented self: A longitudinal study of dissociative symptomatology in a non-clinical sample. *Development and Psychopathology, 9,* 855–1164.

Pianta, R., Egeland, B., & Erickson, M. (1989). The effects of maltreatment on the development of young children. In D. Cicchetti & V. Carlson (Eds.), *Child maltreatment.* New York: Cambridge University Press.

Pianta, R., Egeland, B., & Sroufe, L. A. (1990). Maternal stress in childrens' development: Predictions of school outcomes and identification of protective factors. In J. E. Rolf, A. Masten, D. Cicchetti, K. Neuchterlen, & S. Weintraub (Eds.), *Risk and protective factors in the development of psychopathology* (pp. 215–235). Cambridge, MA: Cambridge University Press.

Pianta, R., Hyatt, A., & Egeland, B. (1996). Maternal relationship history as an indicator of developmental risk. *American Journal of Orthopsychiatry, 56,* 385–398.

Putnam, F. (2000). Dissociative disorders. In A. Sameroff, M. Lewis & S. Miller (Eds.), *Handbook of psychopathology* (pp. 739–754). New York: Kluwer Academic/Plenum Press.

Roisman, G., Sroufe, L. A., Madsen, S., & Collins, W. A. (in press). The coherence of dyadic behavior across parent-child and romantic relationships as mediated by the internal representation of experience. *Attachment and Human Development.*

Sroufe, J. (1991). Assessment of parent–adolescent relationships: Implications for adolescent development. *Journal of Family Psychology, 5,* 21–45.

Sroufe, L. A. (1983). Infant–caregiver attachment and patterns of adaptation in preschool: The roots of maladaptation and competence. In M. Perlmutter (Ed.), *Minnesota symposium in child psychology* (Vol. 16, pp. 41–83). Hillsdale, NJ: Lawrence Erlbaum Associates.

Sroufe, L. A. (1989). Relationships, self, and individual adaptation. In A. J. Sameroff & R. N. Emde (Eds.), *Relationship disturbances in early childhood: A developmental approach* (pp. 70–94). New York: Basic Books.

Sroufe, L. A. (1997). Psychopathology as an outcome of development. *Development and Psychopathology, 9,* 251–268.

Sroufe, L. A., Carlson, E., Levy, A., & Egeland, B. (1999). Implications of attachment theory for developmental psychopathology. *Development and Psychopathology, 11,* 1–13.

Sroufe, L. A., Duggal, S., Weinfield, N., & Carlson, E. (2000). Relationships, development, and psychopathology. In A. Sameroff, M. Lewis, & S. Miller (Eds.), *Handbook of developmental psychopathology* (pp. 75–92). New York: Kluwer Academic/Plenum.

Sroufe, L. A., Egeland, B., & Carlson, E. (1999). One social world: The integrated development of parent–child and peer relationships. In W. A. Collins & B. Laursen (Eds.), *Relationships as developmental context: The 30th Minnesota syposium on child psychology.* Hillsdale, NJ: Lawrence Erlbaum Associates.

Sroufe, L. A., Egeland, B., & Kreutzer, T. (1990). The fate of early experience following developmental change: Longitudinal approaches to individual adaptation in childhood. *Child Development, 61,* 1363–1373.

Sroufe, L. A., & Fleeson, J. (1988). The coherence of family relationships. In R. A. Hinde & J. Stevenson-Hinde (Eds.), *Relationships within families: Mutual influences* (pp. 27–47). Oxford, UK: Oxford University Press.

Sroufe, L. A., Jacobvitz, J., Mangelsdorf, S., DeAngelo, E., & Ward, M. J. (1985). Generational boundary dissolution between mothers and their preschool children: A relationalships systems approach. *Child Development, 56,* 317–325.

Sroufe, L. A., & Pierce, S. (1999). Man in the family: Associations with juvenile conduct. In G. Cunningham (Ed.), *Just in time research: Children, youth and families* (pp. 19–26). Minneapolis: University of Minnesota Extension Service.

Sroufe, L. A., Schork, E., Motti, E., Lawroski, N., & LaFreniere, P. (1984). The role of affect in social competence. In C. Izard, J. Kagan & R. Zajonc (Eds.), *Emotion, cognition and behavior.* New York: Plenum Press.

Sroufe, L. A., & Ward, M. J. (1980). Seductive behavior of mothers of toddlers: Occurrence, correlates, and family origins. *Child Development, 51,* 1222–1229.

Suomi, S. (1995). Influence of Bowlby's attachment theory on research on nonhuman primate biobehavioral development. In S. Goldberg, R. Muir, & J. Kerr (Eds.), *Attachment Theory* (pp. 185–201). Hillsdale, NJ: Analytic Press.

Teo, A., Carlson, C., Mathieu, P., Egeland, B., & Sroufe, L. A. (1996). A prospective longitudinal study of psychosocial predictors of achievement. *Journal of School Psychology, 34,* 285–306.

Urban, J., Carlson, E., Egeland, B., & Sroufe, L. A. (1991). Patterns of individual adaptation across childhood. *Development and Psychopathology, 3,* 445–460.

Vaughn, B., Waters, E., Egeland, B., & Sroufe, L. A. (1979). Individual differences in infant–mother attachment at 12 and 18 months: Stability and change in families under stress. *Child Development, 50* (4), 971–975.

Warren, S., Huston, L., Egeland, B., & Sroufe, L. A. (1997). Child and adolescent anxiety disorders and early attachment. *Journal for the American Academy of Child and Adolescent Psychiatry, 36,* 637–644.

Weinfield, N. S., Sroufe, L. A., Egeland, B., & Carlson, E. (1999). The nature of individual differences in infant–caregiver attachment. In J. Cassidy & P. Shaver (Eds.), *Handbook of attachment: Theory, research and clinical applications* (pp. 73–95). New York: Guilford Press.

Yates, T., Dodds, M., Sroufe, L. A., & Egeland, B. (in press). Exposure to partner violence and child behavior problems: Controlling for child-directed abuse, child cognitive ability, family income and life stress. *Development and Psychopathology.*

11

Disruptions in Parenting Behavior Related to Maternal Depression: Influences on Children's Behavioral and Psychobiological Development

Lara Embry and Geraldine Dawson
University of Washington

Research has found that maternal depression contributes to the risk of childhood psychopathology. Elevated behavioral disturbances in children of depressed mothers have been observed from infancy through adulthood. Infants of depressed mothers have been found to be less active and more withdrawn, and to display lower levels of positive affect than infants of nondepressed mothers (Field et al., 1985, 1988; Field, Healy, Goldstein, & Guthertz, 1990; Field, 1992). Toddlers whose mothers are depressed have been found to display higher rates of insecure attachment, and to exhibit delays in their acquisition of self-regulation strategies (Cicchetti, Rogosch, & Toth, 1998). The children and adolescents of depressed mothers are more likely to display decreased social competence, increased behavior problems, and decreased self-esteem (Erickson, Stroufe, & Egeland, 1985; Ghodsian, Zajicek, & Wolkind, 1984; Goodman, Brogan, Lynch, & Fielding, 1993; Orvaschel, Welsh-Allis, & Weijia, 1988).

Although it has been established that maternal depression increases the risk for developing emotional and behavioral problems, the mechanisms by which

Address correspondence to: Box 357920, Seattle, WA 98195, Phone: 206-543-1051, e-mail: lembry@u.washington.edu; dawson@u.washington.edu this risk is conferred remain unclear. Several hypotheses have been made as to the mechanisms involved in the transmission of emotional and behavioral difficulties; however, tests of these hypotheses are relatively new. Evidence supports a role of genetic risk factors for depression (Todd, Neuman, Geller, Fox, & Hickok, 1993). There may be heritable traits that predispose children of depressed mothers to developing similar emotional difficulties, such as negative affectivity or low sociability, which indirectly account for the transmission of depression (Goodman & Gotlib, 1999). Furthermore, there is some evidence that prenatal exposure to maternal depression contributes to the development of dysfunctional neuroregulatory mechanisms that may manifest themselves as maladaptive traits or tendencies after birth. Neonates born to depressed mothers tend to be less active, socially less responsive, and fussier than those born to nondepressed mothers (Field et al., 1985; Whiffen & Gotlib, 1989; Zuckerman, Als, Bauchner, Parker, & Cabral, 1990). Hypotheses have also focused on factors affecting child development after birth, particularly the depressed mother's interaction patterns with her child (Field, 1992). It has been suggested that behavioral characteristics of depressed mothers, such as maladaptive cognitions, affect, or behaviors, may place children at increased risk of developing emotional and behavioral problems. Children of depressed mothers may also be more likely to develop emotional and behavioral problems because of shared stressful environmental influences, which increase the risk developing depressive symptoms in both the mother and the child (for a review see Goodman & Gotlib, 1999).

While there is some support for a role of each of these mechanisms, our focus has been on the child's postnatal experiences and, specifically, on the impact of maladaptive parenting on the behavioral and psychobiological development of the child and its relation to risk for psychopathology. Although it is likely that both genetic factors and the intrauterine environment contribute to risk for depression, these factors are unlikely to fully account for the increased risk for emotional and behavioral disorders, including depression, exhibited by children of depressed mothers (Todd, Neuman, Geller, Fox, & Hickok, 1993).

Research examining the behavior of depressed mothers indicates that such mothers often find it difficult to provide contingent responses and optimal levels of stimulation (Field et al., 1985, 1988; Field et al., 1990). Infants may experience such noncontingent interactions with their depressed mothers as stressful and may find it more difficult to learn adequate self-regulation strategies in this context. Depressed mothers also tend to show more negative affect, and less positive affect when interacting with their young infants (Cohn, Matias, Tronik, Connell, & Lyons-Ruth, 1986; Cohn & Tronick, 1989). Indeed, depressed mothers are more likely to share negative states with their infants and are less likely to mimic their infants' positive emotional states (Field et al., 1990). Similarly, toddlers and their depressed mothers have been found to display more mutually negative affect and less mutually positive affect than nondepressed mother–child pairs (Radke-Yarrow & Nottleman, 1989). It may be that infants and toddlers of depressed mothers have increased opportunity to mimic negative affective states, with fewer opportunities and rewards offered for positive affective states. Such opportunities may affect the development of self-regulatory systems involved in the expression of these emotional states.

MATERNAL DEPRESSION AND INFANT BRAIN ACTIVITY AND STRESS RESPONSES

We have been examining differences in early patterns of infant brain activity, as measured by electroencephalographic recordings, which are hypothesized to be related to emotional expression and emotion regulation (Dawson, Grofer Klinger, Panagiotides, Hill, & Spieker, 1992a; Dawson, Grofer Klinger, Panagiotides, Spieker, & Frey, 1992b). Results from our studies indicate that 13-to-15-month-old infants of depressed mothers exhibit reduced electrical brain activity, as measured by EEG power in the alpha frequency range, over the left frontal region. Previous research has shown that asymmetries in brain function related to the expression of specific emotions are localized in the frontal cortex (see Davidson, Ekman, Saron, Senulis, & Friesen, 1990, for a review). In EEG studies, increased left frontal EEG activation has been shown to occur during the expression of emotions involving approach toward the external environment (e.g., joy, interest, anger), while the right frontal region is associated with withdrawal emotions (e.g., distress, sadness, disgust). It has been suggested that resting levels of frontal lobe activation may reflect relatively stable biological differences related to vulnerabilities to express certain negative emotions in stressful situations (Davidson & Fox, 1988). It is possible that resting levels of frontal lobe activation reflect biological differences that develop after birth in response to the social environment (Dawson et al., 1992a, 1992b).

We hypothesize that the early social environment plays a key role in the development of brain systems underlying emotional expression. The central assumption underlying this hypothesis is that repeated stimulation of specific neural systems during early development leads to amplification and stabilization of those neural networks. For instance, when parents respond to their infants with joy and interest, this stimulates the development of neural systems that mediate positive emotions, and the infant more readily experiences positive emotions. Conversely, when parents fail to respond positively and instead are irritable or withdrawn, neural systems that mediate negative emotions such as sadness and distress are stimulated, possibly leading to a lower threshold for the expression of negative emotions. It is likely that the frontal lobe may be particularly sensitive to environmental input because of its very protracted development after birth (Huttenlocher & Dabholkar, 1997; Rakic, Bourgeois, & Goldman-Rakic, 1994).

In addition, we hypothesize that parents play an important role in the development of children's responses to stress. We believe that maternal depression may be a type of early stress for young infants and children. Not only is the mother experiencing depression more often withdrawn and unavailable to her child, when she does interact she may be irritable and insensitive toward the infant (Goodman & Gotlib, 1999). Field (1992) has found that very young infants of depressed mothers show higher stress levels when interacting with their mothers as reflected in higher heart rates and salivary cortisol levels.

There is evidence that individuals who experience stressful events early in life are at greater risk for developing depression (Kendler et al., 1993; Plotsky, Owens, & Nemeroff, 1998). Research in animals has shown that stress early in life, including unpredictable patterns of mothering, affects the functioning of the hypothalamic-pituitary-adrenal system that regulates the stress response (Coplan et al., 1998). Dysregulation of the stress system may be one factor involved in risk for depression (Plotsky et al., 1998).

Our research has sought to explore the effects of maternal depression on the development of children's brain activity, stress responses, and behavior. In 1993 we began a longitudinal study of 159 adult mothers and their 13-to-15-month-old infants. The mothers who participated in this study were generally middle income and were screened for other mental disorders, serious medical conditions, attendance in special education classes, imminent suicide risk, significant pregnancy or birth complications, and contact by Child Protective Services. All of the infants were full-term (not more than 3 weeks late or early), weighed at least 5 pounds at birth, and had no reported history of chronic seizures, central nervous system infection, head injury, sensory motor problems, prenatal drug exposure, foster care, chronic medical condition, surgery or prolonged hospitalization, physical malformations, or current medications. Eighty nine of the infants were female, while 70 were male. The ethnic composition of the sample of mothers who took part in this study was 85% European-American, 1% African American, 1% Hispanic, 1% Native American, and 12% multi-ethnic/other.

Mothers who participated in this study were classified into groups based on information from the Structured Clinical Interview for the DSM-III-R (SCID) and the Center for Epidemiological Studies-Depression Questionnaire (CES-D). Mothers were classified as depressed if they received a diagnosis of major depression ($n = 25$) or double depression ($n = 2$) on the SCID. A subthreshold depression classification was given if mothers received a current SCID diagnosis of subthreshold depression ($n = 9$), dysthymia ($n = 2$), or depression in partial remission ($n = 25$), or if they had a score of 16 or above on the CES-D ($n = 27$). Participants were classified as nondepressed if they had scores lower than 9 on the CES-D and reported no current or lifetime history of depression on the

SCID ($n = 69$). In addition to being assessed for current depression, each participating mother was also administered an adapted version of the Longitudinal Interval Follow-Up Evaluation (LIFE, Keller, Shapiro, Lavori, & Wolfe, 1982; Keller et al., 1987), which was designed to assess, on a month-by-month basis, the longitudinal history of the mother's depression since the infant's conception. There were no significant differences between depressed and nondepressed mothers in age, ethnicity, education level, and socioeconomic level as assessed by the Hollingshead, number of hours spent working outside the home, or biological father's age. Infant groups were not significantly different in their age, gender, birth order, or in how many hours per week they spent in daycare.

The children in this study have been extensively evaluated during laboratory visits at 14 months, 3 years, and most recently at 6 to 7 years of age. In this chapter we report findings from the first two laboratory visits. During these visits we focused on four types of physiological measures. These included two measures of electrical brain activity, salivary cortisol, and autonomic responses (heart rate). The two measures of EEG activity included patterns of frontal EEG asymmetry, which have been shown to be related to the expression of positive versus negative emotions, as well as the overall level of brain activity as reflected in EEG power measured from the right and left frontal and parietal leads. EEG data were collected while the children participated in a variety of conditions that were designed to elicit a range of emotional responses from the infant. The stress response measures included heart rate and salivary cortisol. Heart rate was assessed at both 14 months and 3 years during the same conditions in which EEG was recorded. Salivary cortisol was collected at 3 years only during baseline and a mildly stressful condition. A more complete discussion of the methods used to obtain the EEG data can be found in earlier publications (Dawson, Frey, Panagiotides, Osterling, & Hessl, 1997).

During these laboratory visits we also observed mothers interacting with their infants during a variety of situations designed to elicit mother and infant affective behavior. For the purposes of this chapter, we will be discussing mothers' behavior during a free-play task, in which mothers were asked to play with their baby as they normally would, and a divided attention task, in which mothers were asked to complete a questionnaire while the infants were expected to entertain themselves. The divided attention task was designed to allow for the observation of the mother's ability to help the infant regulate his or her affect and attention. We observed maternal verbal and nonverbal behavior such as affection, praise, sensitivity, negative verbalizations, and affect, among many others. Individual behaviors that were coded in the two interactions tasks were combined to form factors reflecting constructs of interest in the assessment of maternal–child interaction, including warmth, scaffolding, negativity, and insensitivity. Mothers, as well as participating fathers, also completed a variety of questionnaire measures regarding their behavior and that of their child.

Replicating past work with a different sample of todders (Dawson et al., 1992a, 1992b), we found that, at 14 months of age, infants of depressed mothers exhibited atypical frontal electrical brain activity, characterized by reduced activity over the left frontal region (Dawson et al., 1997). Furthermore, analyses revealed a linear relation between maternal depression severity and infant frontal brain activity, with infants of the more severely depressed mothers exhibiting the greater reduction in left frontal activity (Dawson et al., 1997). The atypical pattern of frontal brain activity was found in a variety of conditions, including a baseline condition, and playful interactions with mother and a familiar experimenter (Dawson et al., 1999a).

Consistent with previous studies, we found that mothers who were depressed showed higher levels of "insensitive" behavior as compared to nondepressed mothers. Insensitive behaviors included physically intrusive behaviors such as poking, tickling, as well as responding to infant bids for attention with maternal holding or disengaging behaviors, and initiating physical contact in the absence of bids for attention by the infant. These behaviors reflected mothers' decreased frequency of responding contingently to and following the lead of their infants. Depressed and nondepressed mothers did not differ in terms of behaviors reflecting warmth, engagement, and negativity.

We were interested in examining whether the relation between infant brain activity and maternal depression was mediated by the mothers' behavior. We assessed this question using a subsample of the group of mothers with depression, which consisted of only those mothers who experienced depression during the infant's postnatal life, thus eliminating the potential influence of maternal depression during the prenatal period on infant brain activity. This sample consisted of 115 mothers and their infants, with 69 in the nondepressed group and 46 in the depressed group.

We used path-analysis to address the question of whether mother's behavior mediated the relation between maternal depression and infant brain activity. Results showed that the relation between mothers' depression status and infant brain activity was at least partially mediated by mothers' behavior. Specifically, it was found that infants of depressed mothers whose mothers displayed higher levels of insensitivity were more likely to exhibit reduced left frontal brain activity. In separate analyses, we found that infants who exhibited such patterns of atypical frontal brain activity were also less like to show positive affiliative behaviors when interacting with their mothers (Dawson, Frey, Self, Panagiotides, & Rinaldi, 1999b).

Infants' heart rates were also measured during the baseline condition as well as during two social interaction conditions, one in which the infant interacts with an experimenter and one in which the infant interacts with his or her mother. We found that the heart rates of infants of nondepressed mothers tended to decrease when they were interacting with their mothers or the experimenter. This suggests that the social interaction was helping to regulate the infant's arousal. However, for infants of depressed mothers the pattern was reversed. The heart rates of infants with depressed mothers tended to increase during the social interaction conditions relative to the baseline condition.

PRELIMINARY LONGITUDINAL FINDINGS AT CHILD AGE 3 YEARS

The participants in this longitudinal study returned to the laboratory at the age of 3½ years. Of the 159 mother–child dyads in the original sample, 130 mothers and their toddlers agreed to participate in this visit. In this chapter, we report the results of preliminary analyses of children's brain activity, stress responses, and behavior at age 3 years. At this age children whose mothers were chronically depressed throughout the child's lifetime continued to show atypical brain activity. The pattern at this age was no longer that of lower left frontal activation as displayed in infancy, but rather it was lower activation (higher EEG power) across all brain regions measured, including left and right hemisphere frontal and parietal regions. This finding was consistent across all conditions measured, including baseline and negative and positive affect conditions. Interestingly, children of mothers who were depressed at the time of the first visit but whose depression then went into remission showed normal brain activity patterns at their second visit. This provides additional support for the role of experience in the development of these EEG patterns as well as the early plasticity in these brain activity patterns.

Children of chronically depressed mothers at age 3 years also were found to display higher levels of behavior problems. We found consistent relations between maternal depression as measured by the CES-D and child's symptoms as measured by the mother's report. A mother's report of her depression correlated significantly with her reports of her child's externalizing problems, her child's internalizing problems, and her child's total problems, as well as with combined parent reports from mother and father about children's internalizing problems.

Interestingly, we also found that children with lower levels of frontal brain activity were more likely to be exhibiting behavior problems. Mothers' reports of their child's externalizing symptoms, as well as total problems, were significantly correlated with frontal, parietal, and averaged electrical brain activity, as reflected in measures of EEG power. Mothers' reports of their child's internalizing symptoms were significantly correlated with frontal and total EEG power. Furthermore, children who scored greater than one standard deviation above the mean on mother report of internalizing, externalizing, and/or total problems were found to have significantly lower frontal EEG activity (i.e., higher EEG power).

In order to understand the children's responses to stress, salivary cortisol samples were taken both before and after the children were asked to complete an extremely challenging task in the laboratory. Children who were beginning to show early symptoms of depression and anxiety, i.e., those children with internalizing scores more than one standard deviation above the mean on mother report of internalizing behaviors, were found to have higher salivary cortisol levels during the stressful task.

SUMMARY

In summary, children of depressed mothers have been found to exhibit patterns of brain activity that are atypical both as infants and as preschoolers. In infancy these children display decreased left frontal electrical brain activity, whereas as preschoolers the relative decrease in brain activity was present across the hemispheres and brain regions we measured. The findings from our research with infants support the hypothesis that maternal behavior at least partially mediates the relation between maternal depression and infant brain activity at 14 months of age. We found that depressed mothers were more likely to be insensitive in their interactions with their infant, and level of maternal insensitive behavior was related to a pattern of brain activity characterized by reduced activity over the left frontal brain region. Increases in heart rates during social interactions among the depressed mothers' infants further support the possibility that these infants experience such social interactions as stressful. Preliminary analyses indicated that, at 3 years of age, preschool-age children of mothers who were currently depressed tended to display more behavior problems, and these behavior problems were related to lower levels of electrical brain activity. As would be expected if maternal behavior mediates the relation between depression and child problems, children whose mothers' depression remitted by 3 years of age had patterns of brain activity that were similar to children of mothers with no depression. In addition, results from our preliminary exploration of stress responses as measured by salivary cortisol indicated that children of depressed mothers who were experiencing internalizing symptoms were also exhibiting higher stress responses compared to children who are not experiencing internalizing problems.

While the findings we present in this chapter hopefully offer new insights into the mechanisms of transmission between maternal depression and children's behavior problems, many questions remain. Our findings support the hypothesis that exposure to maternal depression places children at increased risk of developing emotional and behavioral problems and influences the development of cortical and self-regulatory systems. However, there is still much about the relative contributions of behavioral, genetic, and intrauterine influences on the development of child psychopathology that remains to be explored. It is our hope that this research sheds light on the extent to which the developing child incorporates the information in the environment into his or her emerging patterns of social interaction and emotional expression and regulation, and how this contributes to risk for child psychopathology.

ACKNOWLEDGMENTS

The writing of this chapter and the much of the research on maternal depression reported were supported by a grant from the National Institute of Mental Health (No. MH47117). We wish to gratefully acknowledge the women and infants who participated in this research. This chapter is based on a presentation by Geraldine Dawson at a conference on parenting sponsored by the National Institutes of Health, August 1999.

REFERENCES

Cicchetti, D., Rogosch, F. A., & Toth, S. L. (1998). Maternal depressive disorder and contextual risk: Contributions to the development of attachment insecurity and behavior problems in toddlerhood. *Development and Psychopathology, 10* (2), 283–300.

Cohn, J. F., Matias, R., Tronick, E. Z., Connell, D. & Lyons-Ruth, D. (1986). Face-to-face interactions of depressed mothers and their infants. In E. Z. Tronik & T. Field (Eds.), *Maternal depression and infant disturbance* (pp. 31–45). San Francisco: Jossey-Bass.

Cohn, J. F. & Tronick, E. Z. (1989). Specificity of infants' responses to mother'affective behavior. *Journal of the American Academy of Child and Adolescent Psychiatry, 28,* 242–248.

Coplan, J. D.; Trost, R. C., Owens, M. J., Cooper, T. B., Gorman, J. M., Nemeroff, C. B., & Rosenblum, L. A. (1998). Cerebrospinal fluid concentrations of somatostatin and biogenic amines in grown primates reared by mothers exposed to manipulated foraging conditions. *Archives of General Psychiatry, 55* (5), 473–477.

Davidson, R. J., Ekman, P., Saron, C., Senulis, R., & Friesen, W. V. (1990). Approach–withdrawal and cerebral asymmetry: Emotional expression and brain physiology I. *Journal of Personality and Social Psychology, 58,* 330–341.

Davidson, R. J., & Fox, N. A. (1988). Cerebral asymmetry and emotion: Developmental and individual differences. In S. Segalowitz & D. Molfese (Eds.), *Developmental implications of brain lateralization* (pp. 191–206). New York: Guildford Press.

Dawson, G., Frey, K., Panagiotides, H., Osterling, J., & Hessl, D. (1997). Infants of depressed mothers exhibit atypical frontal brain activity: A replication and extension of previous findings. *Journal of Child Psychology and Psychiatry, 38,* 179–186.

Dawson, G., Frey, K., Panagiotides, H., Yamada, E., J., Hessl, D., & Osterling, J. (1999a). Infants of depressed mothers exhibit atypical frontal brain electrical activity during interactions with mother and with a familiar, nondepressed adult. *Child Development, 70,* 1058–1067.

Dawson, G., Frey, K., Self, J., Panagiotides, H., & Rinaldi, J. (1999b). Frontal electrical brain activity in infants of depressed mothers: Relation to variations in infant behavior. *Development and Psychopathology,* 589–605.

Dawson, G., Grofer Klinger, L., Panagiotides, H., Hill, D. & Spieker, S. (1992a). Frontal lobe activity and affective behavior of infants of mothers with depressive symptoms. *Child Development, 63,* 725–737.

Dawson, G., Grofer Klinger, L., Panagiotides, H., Spieker, S. & Frey, K. (1992b). Infants of mothers with depressive symptoms: Electrophysiological and behavioral findings related to attachment status. *Development and Psychopathology, 4,* 67–80.

Dawson, G., Ashman, S., Carver, L., (2000). The role of early experience in shaping behavioral and brain development and its implications for social policy. *Development and Psychopathology, 12,* 695–712.

Erickson, M., Stroufe, L. A. & Egeland, B. (1985). The relationship between quality of attachment and behavior problems in preschool in a high-risk sample. In J. Breatherton & E. Waters (Eds.), *Growing points of attachment theory and research. Society for Research in Child Development Monographs, 50* (1–2), 147–166.

Field, T. (1992). Infants of depressed mothers. *Development and Psychopathology, 4,* 49–66.

Field, T., Healy, B., Goldstein, S., & Guthertz, M., (1990). Behavior-state matching and synchrony in mother–infant interactions of depressed versus nondepressed dyads. *Developmental Psychology, 26,* 7–14.

Field, T., Healy, B., Goldstein, S., Perry, S., Bendall, D., Schanberg, S., Zimmerman, E., & Kuhn, C. (1988). Infants of depressed mothers show "depressed" behavior even with nondepressed adults. *Child Development, 59,* 1569–1579.

Field, T., Sandberg, D., Garcia, R., Vega-Lahr, N., Goldstein, S., & Guy, L. (1985). Prenatal problems, postpartum depression, and early mother infant interactions, *Developmental Psychology, 12,* 1152–1156.

Ghodsian, M., Zajicek, E. & Wolkind, S. (1984). A longitudinal study of maternal depression and child behavior problems. *Journal of Child Psychology and Psychiatry, 25,* 91–109.

Goodman, S. H., Brogan, D., Lynch, M. E., & Fielding, B. (1993). Social and emotional competence in children of depressed mothers. *Child Development, 64,* 516–531.

Goodman, S. H., & Gotlib, I. H., (1999). Risk for psychopathology in the children of depressed mothers: A developmental model for understanding mechanisms of transmission. *Psychological Review, 106,* 458–490.

Huttenlocher, P. R., & Dabholkar, A. S. (1997). Regional differences in synaptogenesis in human cerebral cortex, *Journal of Comparative Neurology, 387,* 167–178.

Keller, M. B., Lavori, P., Freidman, B., Niesen, E., Endicott, J., McDonald-Scott, P. & Andreasen, N. C. (1987). The longitudinal interval follow-up evaluation: A comprehensive method for assessing outcome in prospective longitudinal studies. *Archives of General Psychiatry, 44,* 540–548.

Keller, M. B., Shapiro, R. W., Lavori, P. W., & Wolfe, N. (1982). Recovery in major depressive disorder: Analysis with the life table and regression models. *Archives of General Psychiatry, 39,* 905–915.

Kendler, K. S., Kessler, R. C., Neale, M. C., Heath, A. C., Phil, D., & Eaves, L. J. (1993). The prediction of major depression in women: Toward an integrated etiological model. *American Journal of Psychiatry, 150* (8), 1139–1148.

Orvaschel, H., Welsh-Allis, G., & Weijai, Y. (1988). Psychopathology in children of parents with recurrent depression. *Journal of Abnormal Child Psychology, 16,* 17–28.

Plotsky, P. M., Owens, M. J., & Nemeroff, C. B. (1998). Psychoneuroendocrinology of depression. *Psychiatric Clinics of North America, 21* (2), 293–307.

Radke-Yarrow, M., & Nottelmann, E. (1989, April). Affective development in children of well and depressed mothers. Paper presented at Society for Research in Child Development, Kansas City, MO.

Rakic, P., Bourgeois, J. P., & Goldman-Rakic, P. S. (1994). Synaptic development of the cerebral cortex: Implications for learning, memory, and mental illness. *Progress in Brain Research, 102,* 227–243.

Todd, R. D., Neuman, R., Geller, B., Fox, L. W., & Hickok, J. (1993). Genetic studies of affective disorders: Should we be starting with childhood onset probands? *Journal of the American Academy of Child and Adolescent Psychiatry, 32,* 1164–1171.

Whiffen, V. E., & Gottlib, I. M. (1989). Infant of postpartum depressed mothers: Temperament and cognitive status. *Journal of Abnormal Psychology, 98,* 274–279.

Zuckerman, B., Als, H., Bauchner, H., Parker, S., & Cabral, H. (1990). Maternal depressive symptons during pregnancy and newborn irritability. *Developmental and Behavioral Pediatrics, 11,* 190–194.

12

Mediation, Moderation, and Mechanisms in How Parenting Affects Children's Aggressive Behavior

Kenneth A. Dodge

Duke University

The human infant is born into this world in a more fragile and precarious state than a newborn of any other species. Without an adult to provide shelter, warmth, comfort, and milk, no infant could survive a single day, let alone grow up to become a functioning person. In comparative ethology and evolutionary theory, parenting has been more important to the survival of the human species than to any other species. It is truly ironic that in contemporary American society the importance of parents might even be called into question. On the face of it, the notion that parents might not be important is absurd.

PARENTING AND INDIVIDUAL DIFFERENCES

What is under debate, however, is whether differences across parents matter. When we consider the development of enduring individual differences in the child's behavioral patterns, Sandra Scarr (1992) might well be correct. In a

Address correspondence to: Center for Child and Family Policy, Duke University, Box 90264, Durham, NC 27708, Phone: 919-613-7319, Fax: 919-681-1533, e-mail: Kenneth.Dodge@Duke.edu series of provocative presentations, Scarr has claimed that individual differences in early parenting have little long-term effect on enduring individual differences in cross-situational behavioral traits as long as the rearing environment is within a *limited normal range.* She has argued, instead, that in these circumstances genes play a much more prominent role in child development. Scarr insists that parents can, and should, be relieved of the stress and worry about whether they are adequate as parents. As long as they provide a "just good enough" rearing environment for their child, parents can be relieved of worry about their role in the outcomes to which their child is destined at birth. Scarr uses this argument to support parents' right to work outside the home and suggests that minimal standards for child-care agencies will ensure healthy development for children. What a comfort for anxious parents! There are three problems, though, that they may render Scarr's conclusion irrelevant in contemporary American culture.

The first problem is that it is not at all clear what are the bounds of the normal range of rearing environments. One in four American children is born into government-defined family poverty, and one in three will live in poverty at some time during childhood (Children's Defense Fund, 1997). One in three American children is born to a single mother, and over 50% of all children will live with a single parent at some time before they reach the age of 18. One in six children receives no prenatal care in the first trimester of pregnancy, and 7.5% are born with low birth weight. About 12% of children experience physical abuse (Dodge, Bates, & Pettit, 1990). Estimates of lifetime sexual abuse in girls range up to one in three. Even if these figures suggest that these life experiences are statistically normative, surely no one could include these experiences as "normal." Where are the bounds of "normal" childrearing? Scarr's argument does not apply to over half of American children who are not reared "within normal limits."

In a recent article, Stoolmiller (1999) ingeniously demonstrated that in behavior genetic adoption studies, the statistical estimate of genetic effects will be overestimated and, in contrast, shared family environment effects will be underestimated if the range of environments across individuals is artificially restricted by biased sampling. A restricted range might occur if all children in a sample live in a "normal" relatively homogeneous socialist culture, such as Scandinavia, or if the selection criteria for participation in a study require that there be two financially solvent parents who have been married for a while and who pass tests of parenting adequacy. These, of course, are exactly the criteria for adoption eligibility, and they characterize the families in most twin studies as well. Stoolmiller showed that measures of parenting and family environment such as the Bradley-Caldwell HOME Scale (Bradley, 1994) do, indeed, reveal severely restricted range in outcomes in most major adoption studies, including the Colorado Adoption Project (Plomin & DeFries, 1985). Therefore, the magnitude of estimates for genetic and shared environment effects is largely an artifact of biased sampling and irrelevant for broader conclusions. The value in behavior-genetic studies is still great, but only for demonstrating the presence (versus absence) of a genetic effect on behavior. The estimates of the magnitude of the effect are unreliable and nongeneralizable.

A second problem surfaces when we consider the "optimal measures" of a child outcome. Do socialization theorists really mean to hypothesize that parenting in the first 5 years of life will forever affect personality traits such as agreeableness and introversion, which are general tendency scores that are aggregated across all situations and which, by trait theorist definition, do not change across development? In behavior genetic studies, within-subject differences in scores across situations and across time represent a data nuisance. These differences are called error variance and are eliminated by aggregation. But aggregating yields a score that is fairly useless in predicting anything meaningful. The trait score is akin to the average temperature for a city (Zelli & Dodge, 1999). We are usually more concerned with the temperature tomorrow or at least the average temperature during the month of September for a given city than in the mean temperature for that city for the last century. Furthermore, in order to make precise predictions, the meteorologist is actually concerned with why and how temperature is created.

In developmental psychology, we are concerned not only with average scores in aggressiveness, reaction time, or temperament, but also with within-individual cross-situational variation, developmental trajectories, and the between-individual dynamic processes that affect variations in these measures. In fact, within-individual variations turn out to be anything but random. This discovery is the strongest proof of the importance of environmental effects on behavior. For the most part, environmental effects are narrow and specific to a particular behavior in a certain context at a specific point in development. The behavior-genetic method would treat such effects as error variance, to be eliminated by aggregation across contexts and time in order to derive an "average trait score."

Just as the average temperature trait score for a city has no causal value in predicting tomorrow's weather, so, too, the average aggressiveness trait score may have limited scientific value. The average temperature for a city is a summary score that reflects, rather than drives, the city's weather. It is tautological to say that a city's average temperature causes its temperature every day. So, too, it is tautological to say that a child's aggressiveness trait score causes that child's aggressive behavior. Nonetheless, the goal of behavior genetic studies, and many personality theories such as the Big Five theory, is to predict the life-long, general tendency, behavior trait.

The third problem with Scarr's argument concerns the artificial attempt to isolate a parenting effect from all other influences. Indeed, most researchers attempt to accomplish that task, with regression analyses. However, it is simply unrealistic to expect that individual differences in parenting during the first few years of life will have a unique and life-long enduring effect on a child's general impulsivity level or on an aggregated score for aggressiveness at, say, age 14, after we control for genes and all later parenting and other correlated peer and neighborhood effects at age 14. If, in fact, the environment has an impact on a child's behavior, that environment can act correctively to alter the trajectory of a child's development over time, especially when the child begins to deviate from optimal development. As a species, we have evolved with corrective environmental mechanisms. It is likely that parenting also operates in a largely self-correcting way across time, and most attempts to isolate a parenting factor at one point in life from parenting and other effects prior to, and after, that point lose the real message, which is the complexity of interaction and transaction across development.

As any parent knows, parents continually try to make up for their past errors with their children, and they are generally fairly successful at mid-life corrections. They are constantly responding to their past actions and to their child's current level of adaptation. A child who is getting into trouble will be met with a parent who intensifies her monitoring and restriction of the child, whereas a child's demonstration of responsibility will be met with a parent who grants greater freedom. Because of this responsivity, simple-minded correlational studies will misrepresent the relation between parenting behavior and child behavior as nil, or even counterintuitive (e.g., high parental monitoring leads to child behavior problems). The point is that the parent will titrate her actions in an exquisite manner when the child's behavior begins to deviate. So, too, the child's behavior is just as exquisitely responsive to changes in parenting. To argue that parenting does not matter is to miss this symbiotic interplay. Children do learn from parents, and they alter their behavior accordingly all the time.

WHAT CHILDREN LEARN FROM PARENTS

In this chapter, I wish to posit the general hypothesis that what children learn from parents is how to think and behave in specific situations. The learned behavior is dependent, or contingent, on the situation, and it is continuously being updated. Consider the social situation that has captivated much of my research attention and which, I believe, is crucial to children's aggressive conduct problems. A child is confronted with another person who "disses" him or her, by teasing, knocking into him or her, mockery, or some other disrespectful action. Now consider the implications of the following two different mental stories that a child might learn through socialization: (1) "When dissed, by all means I must fight back because my self-integrity is at stake and is all I've got. In fact, even before I am dissed, I better be ready to fight back;" or (2) "When I am dissed, I won't worry about it. I know that I am not really being dissed at all, because I have me, and I have years of security behind me and years of hope and good fortune ahead of me."

These situationally contingent mental stories—they can be called schemas, scripts, attitudes, or information processing styles (Cervone & Shoda, 1999)—are the "stuff" of socialization by parents. Rather than pit genes versus parenting, or even parents versus peers, it is more fruitful to examine *how* parenting exerts an influence on a child (Collins, Maccoby, Steinberg, Hetherington, & Bornstein, 2000). The most important "how" is through these acquired messages about how the social world operates. These cognitive messages have neurochemical correlates in the brain, are stored as neuronal associations, and drive behavior. Furthermore, children learn the schema of hostility partially from interacting with threat in the form of rejecting and harsh physically assaultive parenting. In contrast, children learn to become nonviolent from interacting with a parent who inspires security, confidence, and hope.

Evidence that is consistent with this hypothesis has been provided by Burks, Dodge, Price, and Laird (1999). They found that children's knowledge structures about the peer social world (structure of peer interactions, accessibility of positive versus negative features, and appropriateness of sequential scripts) in Grade 6 of early adolescence is predictable from children's early experiences with aggression and hostility at Grade 1. Furthermore, these acquired knowledge structures predict the child's level of aggressive behavior in Grade 9 and mediate the effect of early experiences on Grade 9 outcomes.

There is growing evidence from parenting experiments and quasi-experiments that parenting can, indeed, exert a main effect on child outcomes, especially on aggressive conduct problems. Randomized clinical trials in parenting enhancement interventions by Henggeler (Henggeler, Melton, Smith, Schoenwald, & Hanley, 1997), Forehand (Forehand & Long, 1988), Chamberlain and Reid (1991), and the Conduct Problems Prevention Research Group (1999) have revealed positive effects on child conduct problems that are sustained for at least a year.

Even the behavior genetics adoption studies themselves reveal that adoption itself from a low socioeconomic status family into a middle-class family reduces lifetime risk for criminal arrest by one half (Maughan, Collishaw, & Pickles, 1998). As Maccoby (this volume) has noted, adoption can increase the intelligence quotient remarkably, by 8 points when the adoption is made into a lower-socioeconomic-class family and 19 points when the adoption is made into a higher-socioeconomic-class family.

PROSPECTIVE INQUIRY
IN PARENTING EFFECTS

Beginning with the work of Sears, Maccoby, and Levin (1957), a long list of cross-sectional and longitudinal studies has documented a myriad of effects that parenting has on child behavior. This body of work is striking in its robustness, in the multiplicity of different parenting influences (e.g., the effects of harshness of discipline seem to operate independently of the effects of parent–child warmth, Pettit, Bates, & Dodge, 1997), and in the incremental value of cumulating different parenting effects in predicting child outcomes (e.g., Deater-Deckard, Dodge, Bates, & Pettit, 1998). Because of the same problems of bias and artifact that plague behavior-genetic studies, this body of literature has relatively little contribution to make in understanding the absolute magnitude of parenting effects; rather, its merit is in documenting the kinds of main effects that exist in various domains of social–emotional development.

The goal of the research that will be described here is less to evaluate the artificial, isolated main effects of parenting and more to understand how parenting plays a role. The specific problem that will be addressed concerns the role of parents' discipline strategies in child conduct problems.

Findings are drawn from the Child Development Project, a 14-year longitudinal study of the development of conduct problems across childhood and adolescence (Dodge, Bates, & Pettit, 1990). The 585 boys and girls in this study (19% African-American and the remainder white) were drawn at random from each of three communities (Nashville, Tennessee, Knoxville, Tennessee, and Bloomington, Indiana) at the time of kindergarten preregistration in selected schools. Parenting measures were derived from maternal and paternal oral interviews, tests, and in-home observations conducted during the preschool age and annually thereafter. Child conduct problems were derived from annually collected parent, teacher, peer, and self-reports; direct observations; and archival records. Three distinct kinds of statistical parenting effects will be described (moderation, mediation, and mechanism) in order to move closer to discovery of how parenting exerts its influence on children's development.

Moderation

The first way that parenting can operate is by altering the effect of another factor in children's development. For example, Kochanska (1998) has investigated the effect of a child's (presumably) biologically mediated temperament (as gentle or bold) on the development of guilt, morality, and conscience. She found that parents' use of active responsiveness and a close emotional bond with a child are effective in promoting conscience but only for children with a bold, exploratory temperament. In contrast, with children who display a fearful temperament, gentle and emotionally calming childrearing techniques are more effective.

This kind of interaction between biologically driven characteristics and the socializing environment has enormous implications because it alters our examination of parenting effects as well as limits the universality of other effects (such as temperament or biological effects). Collins and colleagues (2000) have highlighted the Gene $\times$ Environment interaction as important in contemporary theories of parenting. Discoveries of interaction effects in field research have been hard to find, mainly because in naturally occurring circumstances variables that might interact are often significantly correlated with each other. When the factors are correlated, the statistical power to detect an interaction effect is minimized because there are fewer "unusual" cases (e.g., cases of mild-temperament children experiencing harsh discipline), which are essential for testing an interaction effect. That is, consider the test of a possible interaction between temperament and harshness of discipline. Also consider that difficult temperament is likely to coincide with harsh discipline. Important to the test of an interaction are those cases in which difficult temperament co-occurs with nonharsh discipline and in which easy temperament co-occurs with harsh discipline. If the factors are correlated, such cases are, by definition, less common, and the statistical power to test this effect is limited. This problem is avoided in experimental studies in which the factors are manipulated and cell sizes are equated. It is not surprising that studies in experimental social psychology more regularly detect interaction effects than do field studies in developmental psychology.

However, recent longitudinal studies have been able to utilize large enough sample sizes that interaction effects can be tested with adequate statistical power. Furthermore, recent theorizing has emphasized interactions, and so these tests have become a high priority in developmental studies. As a result, significant interaction effects have been detected, and they have reshaped developmentalists' theories in numerous ways.

In the Child Development Project, a significant interaction effect has been detected between parenting and children's early temperament, assessed in a standardized way by maternal ratings on the Infant Characteristics Questionnaire (Bates, 1980) in predicting later chronic conduct problems (Bates, Pettit, Dodge, & Ridge, 1998). A child displaying a difficult temperament during the first five years of life is at risk for middle-school conduct problems, as rated by teachers, but only when the child experiences parenting that is inconsistent and nonrestrictive. When these children receive firm, restrictive parental control, their risk is minimized. In contrast, firm control is deleterious to children who had been rated as displaying a calm, easygoing temperament. Thus, the effect of parenting on children's development is striking and significant, but its nature depends on the child's characteristics.

The search for interaction effects also means that the effect of parenting might differ for different types of children. For example, another interaction effect in the Child Development Project has been detected between parenting and child gender (McFadyen-Ketchum, Bates, Dodge, & Pettit, 1996). In response to children's misbehavior, parents often try to intensify their control efforts and use coercive tactics. These coercive parenting tactics were directly observed among families of kindergarteners in the Child Development Project and found to have their desired effect of reducing child misbehavior across time, but only among girls. Among boys, the effect of these coercive parenting tactics was similar to that found by Patterson, Reid, and Dishion (1992), which is to increase child antisocial behavior. Thus, the Patterson coercive model has been replicated in the Child Development Project, but only for boys. For girls, a different model of parenting effects will need to be articulated.

The potential for interaction effects also suggests that the effect of parenting might vary across cultural contexts. In the Child Development Project, the effect of harsh parental discipline has been found to vary significantly across ethnic groups. That is, early harsh discipline was associated with later child aggressive behavior only among white families; among African-American families no such relation was found (Deater-Deckard et al., 1996). An important caveat to this interaction effect is that among the most extremely treated children, that is, those children who have been physically maltreated, the effect of this extremely harsh parenting is universally negative for children from both cultural backgrounds. Within the less extreme range, however, the effect of a harsh, physical discipline style varies as a function of the cultural context in which that parenting is embedded.

Why might the effects of parenting styles vary across these cultural groups? Staples and Johnson (1993) have noted that discipline in African-American families is more often physical than verbal and delivered in response to the transgression's consequences rather than intent. Discipline among African-American families has been described as more harsh and physical, in general, than among white families (Portes, Dunham, & Williams, 1986). Furthermore, physical discipline among African-American families is rarely coupled with withdrawal of love, as is often the case among white families. So, physical discipline practices might be more common, less closely linked to rejection by parents, and therefore less likely to have adverse long-term impact among African-American families. It may be that the relatively unusual nature of harsh physical discipline and its association with the withdrawal of love renders this parenting style as toxic for white children. If so, the interaction effect between parenting and cultural context is extremely important because it offers a more exact description of when, how, and under what circumstances parenting behavior has deleterious effects on any child. This interaction effect affords the opportunity to understand more precisely how parenting might affect children.

A central thesis of this chapter is that socialization by parents operates by teaching children central messages (scripts, stories, schemas) about how the world works. It is quite plausible that the effect of harsh discipline on a child is to teach that child that parents (and the world more generally) are rejecting and harsh and that the child's primary orientation must be defensive. If so, then physical discipline practices will exert a negative impact on children only to the extent that they communicate rejection and harshness. If physical discipline practices are displayed in a way that communicates caring, then the child might learn that adults do care and that the child can be secure. The caveat here is that the child might also learn that physical punishment is an acceptable means of teaching others, and the child might learn to adopt physically coercive strategies to have an impact on others. What the child will not learn, however, is that the world is a cold and harsh place, and the child might not become reactively angry.

Mediation

The concept of interaction is quite different from that of mediation. In addition to modifying the effect of another variable, parenting can also act as a catalyst, or potentiator, of predispositional risk factors, and thus it plays a mediational role in child outcomes.

There is strong evidence that both biological factors such as temperament (Bates, Pettit, & Dodge, 1995) and sociocultural factors such as family poverty (Harnish, Dodge, Valente, & the Conduct Problems Prevention Research Group, 1995), when present at birth, increase a child's risk for later conduct problems. The presence of these statistical relations is not in doubt. Rather, how these factors operate is the controversial question. Findings from the Child Development Project suggest that both of these factors operate at least partially through the mediating role that parenting plays. Consider the young child who is temperamentally impulsive and resistant to control. This child may well elicit harsh disciplinary responses from exasperated parents. In turn, over time, the child may become a chronic conduct problem and grow into a violent adolescent.

Behavior geneticists have been well aware of the fact that inherent child biological factors correlate significantly with the kind of parenting that a child later experiences. The term "evocative" parent–child correlation has been applied to note that the child "evokes" a response from the parent (Plomin, DeFries, & Fulker, 1988). Behavior geneticists have been quick to allocate all of the covarying effects to genetic factors; that is, in a model that attempts to account for 100% of the variance in an outcome, they have assumed that the genetic effect should be subtracted first and only the remaining variance can be available for environmental effects. Certainly, it cannot be the case that a later environmental effect causes a preexisting genetic loading; however, an alternative to the behavior-genetic subtraction model is a mediational or potentiating model. It is quite plausible that a genetic risk will not be realized in a particular outcome unless it is potentiated in a life experience, such as parenting.

In the Child Development Project, we have found that early temperament, assessed by mothers as noted above, predicts conduct problems in middle school with a modest but robust path coefficient of .23. Difficult temperament also predicts the child's experience of harsh physical discipline as rated by home visitors. In turn, this rating of harshness of discipline predicts middle school conduct problems and accounts for the entire relation between temperament and conduct problem outcomes. Thus, the entire effect of temperament is mediated by intervening parenting. What this effect implies is that even though a child may be at risk due to a genetic factor (perhaps operationalized as difficult temperament), that risk operates only indirectly. The more direct effect occurs through the parenting that a child experiences. The genetic risk is potentiated by the parenting experience.

An adoption study by O'Connor, Deater-Deckard, Fulker, Rutter, and Plomin (1998) found a similar pattern of results, although the data were not reported as a mediation effect. In that study taken from the Colorado Adoption Project, children at genetic risk (indicated by having a biological parent with a history of antisocial behavior) were likely to elicit in their adoptive parents more harsh and negative parenting than were children without such genetic risk (i.e., an evocative effect). The adoptive parents' negative parenting, however, exerted an independent and incremental effect on the child's aggressive behaviors, suggesting that at least some of the effect of genes operates through the parenting that a child elicits.

Lest one conclude that this mediating role of parenting is restricted to child factors, a similar finding has been obtained with regard to the effect that family poverty plays in the development of child conduct problems. McLoyd (1990) first generated the interesting hypothesis that poverty should exert its pernicious effects on children by preventing parents from being able to attend adequately to them, by increasing stress that leads parents to act harshly, and by distracting parents from monitoring and supervising their children. In the Child Development Project, family poverty at the time of the child's birth robustly predicted middle-school conduct problems. Likewise, poverty predicted parents' use of harsh discipline (the same measure as described above), which has already been reported to predict conduct problem outcomes. Furthermore, parents' harshness of discipline accounted for half of the statistical effect of poverty on conduct problem outcomes.

Thus, some parenting factors operate by potentiating the effects of other risk factors. A child's genetic predisposition or sociocultural context might well place him or her at risk, but those factors do not operate directly on the child's development. Instead, they operate on the more proximal socialization that a child experiences, which, in turn, has a more direct effect on the child's development. This conclusion offers optimism for those persons interested in prevention and intervention because it suggests that seemingly immutable factors such as genes and family poverty do not have to have an inevitable effect on a child's outcomes. Intervention to alter parenting practices, if successfully implemented, might well have reverberating effects on the child's development.

Mechanisms

It has already been proposed in this chapter that the mechanism through which parenting exerts its influence on child behavior outcomes is likely to be the cognitive messages that the child learns about the social world. A child who has been socialized in a consistent and caring manner is likely to learn the message that the world is safe and there is reason for optimism. The child who has been socialized in a rejecting and harsh manner is likely to learn that the world is hostile and that a defensive, vigilant posture is necessary for self-protection. This thesis is consistent with a variety of theoretical perspectives, including the concept of "working models" of attachment that children acquire as a consequence of interactions with the primary caregiver (Cassidy, 1994).

It is proposed here that two separate kinds of cognitive mechanisms operate. First are the general knowledge structures, schemas, scripts, working models, and mental representations that children acquire and carry around with them as they approach new situations. Burks, Laird, Dodge, Pettit, and Bates (1999) developed instruments for assessing middle-school children's social knowledge structures using sentence completion and memory tasks. They found that measures of social schemas of threat that were derived from these measures predicted the future conduct problem behavior of these adolescents even after previous problem behaviors were controlled. Furthermore, these social knowledge structures were predictable from social experiences five years earlier (Burks, Dodge, Price, & Laird, 1999). Thus, it is plausible that children acquire latent cognitive mental representations of the world through early socialization experiences, and these representations then serve to guide patterns of future social behavior.

The second cognitive mechanism is the set of mental actions that occur online during social interactions, which may be summarized as social information processing. Consider the situation in which a child is confronted by an ambiguously acting peer who shouts a disrespectful remark at the child in front of a group of laughing peers. The child's response—should he or she escalate the situation into a conflict, ignore the remark, or laugh it off?—is a function of a series of cognitive operations that occur online in real time. Following from work in cognitive science, models of social information processing have been formulated to describe the sequence of these actions (e.g., Crick & Dodge, 1994). Processing operations include attention to social cues, perception and mental representation of those cues, experiencing of affect and the setting of goals for responding within the social situation, accessing of one or more possible behavioral responses, evaluating the accessed behavioral responses and selecting one for enactment, and then translating a desire to perform an action into behavior. Individual differences in these operations can be conceptualized as personalitylike characteristics (e.g., the child who regularly makes hostile attributions about others' intentions, Zelli & Dodge, 1999). These characteristics have been correlated with patterns of aggressive conduct problems (Dodge, Pettit, McClaskey, & Brown, 1986).

Furthermore, individual differences in social information-processing patterns have been shown to emerge as a consequence of early experiences with harsh discipline and physical abuse. In the Child Development Project, Dodge Bates, and Pettit (1990) and Weiss, Dodge, Bates, and Pettit (1992) found that children who had experienced physical abuse were more likely than their peers to develop patterns of hypervigilance to hostile cues, hostile attributional biases, and ready access of aggressive responses during problem solving. In turn, these acquired processing patterns not only predict the later development of aggressive behavior patterns but also statistically accounted for significant portions of the effect of early abuse on later child aggression (Dodge, Pettit, Bates, & Valente, 1995). These findings are consistent with a model in which the parenting experience exerts its effect on child behavior through the mechanism of acquired patterns of processing the social world.

An integrated model of the cognitive mechanisms of socialization effects puts together the concepts of latent cognitive knowledge structures with online processing patterns (Dodge, 1993). It is hypothesized that socialization experiences are stored in memory as knowledge structures, which then serve as a proximal guide for the processing of social cues online. The processing actions, in turn, directly result in social behavior. Tests of this multiple mediation path have been few, but preliminary results are consistent with the hypothesis that knowledge structures (in the form of beliefs about aggression) that are acquired during socialization guide the online processing of cues, which in turn guides behavior (Zelli, Dodge, Lochman, Laird, & the Conduct Problems Prevention Research Group, 1999).

CONCLUSIONS FOR PUBLIC POLICY

The findings reviewed here have broad implications for parenting and public policy. In spite of words to the contrary, it appears that parenting experiences, especially during the first 5 years of life but also throughout childhood, do have important and enduring effects on children's development. These effects are sometimes subtle and involve interactions with other factors and may be limited to specific contexts. But the effects endure. The mechanisms of these effects seem to lie in the "storylike" messages that the child receives during socialization. Is the world a hostile place? Can the child trust adults? Will others cooperate, support, and help a child, or will others thwart a child's initiatives? The messages often take the form of context-contingent statements, such as, "If I am initiating play with a group of unacquainted peers, I can count on the peers to accept me (or not)," and "If am provoked by another person, I better defend myself because I will be hurt otherwise." These messages are stored in memory and, in turn, guide the child's future social interactions and outcomes.

In planning socialization practices and policies, it is more important to attend to these basic messages that a child will receive rather than to arbitrary specifics, such as the ratio of adults to children, the activities in which the participants engage, and the amount of time in which adults and children interact. Of course, in order to communicate warm and accepting messages to a child, a parent must be relatively free of stressors and distractions, so policies that help parents attend to their children are likely to have a favorable impact on child development. These policies might include financial supports for parenting, paid leave time for parent workers, child-care subsidies, child health care provision, and other family-friendly provisions.

Another policy implication is to develop practices that will ensure that adults who are likely to abuse or neglect children are not placed into positions in which this outcome could possibly occur. Efforts to enhance parenting skills (e.g., high school classes), to help adults become ready for parenting (e.g., counseling), and to provide support for high-risk parents (e.g., home visiting for young single mothers when they leave the hospital) are all likely to enhance children's chances for successful development.

It may not be possible to extinguish all negative parenting practices, but enormous progress could be made by heightening awareness of the precious role that parents play in children's development. One step toward that goal is achieved by researchers who articulate the ways in which parents have an effect on children. To underestimate the effect that parents play is to undermine children's development.

ACKNOWLEDGMENTS

The author gratefully acknowledges the support of Research Scientist Award K05MH01027 from the National Institute of Mental Health.

REFERENCES

Bates, J. E. (1980). The concept of difficult temperament. *Merrill-Palmer Quarterly, 26,* 299–319.

Bates, J. E., Pettit, G. S., & Dodge, K. A. (1995). Family and child factors in stability and change in children's aggressiveness in elementary school. In J. McCord (Ed.), *Coercion and punishment in long-term perspectives* (pp. 124–138). New York: Cambridge University Press.

Bates, J. E., Pettit, G. S., Dodge, K. A., & Ridge, B. (1998). Interaction of temperamental resistance to control and restrictive parenting in the development of externalizing behavior. *Developmental Psychology, 34,* 982–995.

Bradley, R. H. (1994). The HOME Inventory: Review and reflections. *Advances in Child Development and Behavior, 25,* 241–288.

Burks, V. S., Dodge, K. A., Price, J. M., & Laird, R. D. (1999). Internal representational models of peers: Implications for the development of problematic behavior. *Developmental Psychology, 35,* 802–810.

Burks, V. S., Laird, R. D., Dodge, K. A., Pettit, G. S., & Bates, J. E. (1999). Knowledge structures, social information processing, and children's aggressive behavior. *Social Development, 8,* 220–236.

Cassidy, J. (1994). Emotion regulation: Influences of attachment relationships. *Monographs of the Society for Research in Child Development, 59* (2/3), 228–283.

Chamberlain, P., & Reid, J. B. (1991). Using a specialized foster care community treatment model for children and adolescents leaving the state mental health hospital. *Journal of Community Psychology, 19,* 266–276.

Cervone, D. & Shoda, Y. (Eds.). (1999). *The coherence of personality: Social cognitive bases of consistency, variability, and organization.* New York: Guilford Press.

Children's Defense Fund (Sherman, A., author). (1997). *Poverty matters: The cost of child poverty in America.* Washington, D.C.; author.

Collins, W. A., Maccoby, E. E., Steinberg, L., Hetherington, E. M., & Bornstein, M. H. (2000). Contemporary research on parenting: The case for nature and nurture. *American Psychologist, 55,* 218–232.

Conduct Problems Prevention Research Group. (1999). Initial impact of the Fast Track Prevention Trial for Conduct Problems: I. The high-risk sample. *Journal of Consulting and Clinical Psychology, 67,* 631–647.

Crick, N. R., & Dodge, K. A. (1994). A review and reformulation of social information-processing mechanisms in children's social adjustment. *Psychological Bulletin, 115,* 74–101.

Deater-Deckard, K., Dodge, K. A., Bates, J. E., & Pettit, G. S. (1996). Physical discipline among African-American and European-American mothers: Links to children's externalizing behaviors. *Developmental Psychology, 32,* 1065–1072.

Deater-Deckard, K., Dodge, K. A., Bates, J. E., & Pettit, G. S. (1998). Multiple-risk factors in the development of externalizing behavior problems: Group and individual differences. *Development and Psychopathology, 10,* 469–493.

Dodge, K. A. (1993). Social-cognitive mechanisms in the development of conduct disorder and depression. *Annual Review of Psychology, 44,* 559–584.

Dodge, K. A., Bates, J. E., & Pettit, G. S. (1990). Mechanisms in the cycle of violence. *Science, 250,* 1678–1683.

Dodge, K. A., Pettit, G. S., McClaskey, C. L., & Brown, M. (1986). Social competence in children. *Monographs of the Society for Research in Child Development* (Serial No. 213, Vol. 51, No. 2).

Dodge, K. A., Pettit, G. S., Bates, J. E., & Valente, E. (1995). Social information-processing patterns partially mediate the effect of early physical abuse on later conduct problems. *Journal of Abnormal Psychology, 104,* 632–643.

Forehand, R., & Long, N. (1988). Outpatient treatment of the acting out child: Procedures, long-term follow-up data, and clinical problems. *Advances in Behaviour Research and Therapy, 10,* 129–177.

Harnish, J. D., Dodge, K. A., Valente, E., Jr., & the Conduct Problems Prevention Research Group. (1995). Mother–child interaction quality as a partial mediator of the roles of maternal depressive symptomatology and socioeconomic status in the development of child behavior problems. *Child Development, 66,* 739–753.

Henggeler, S. W., Melton, G. B., Smith, L. A., Schoenwald, S. K., & Hanley, J. H. (1997). Multisystemic therapy with violent and chronic juvenile offenders and their families: The role of treatment fidelity in successful dissemination. *Journal of Consulting and Clinical Psychology, 65,* 821–833.

Kochanska, G. (1998). Mother–child relationship, child fearfulness, and emerging attachment. A short-term longitudinal study. *Developmental Psychology, 34,* 480–490.

Maughan, B., Collishaw, S., & Pickles, A. (1998). School achievement and adult qualifications among adoptees: A longitudinal study. *Journal of Child Psychology and Psychiatry, 39,* 669–685.

McFadyen-Ketchum, S. A., Bates, J. E., Dodge, K. A., & Pettit, G. S. (1996). Patterns of change in early child aggressive-disruptive behavior: Gender differences in predictors from early coercive and affectionate mother–child interactions. *Child Development, 67,* 2417–2433.

McLoyd, V. (1990). The impact of economic hardship on black families and children: Psychological distress, parenting, and socioemotional development. *Child Development, 61,* 311–346.

O'Connor, T. G., Deater-Deckard, K., Fulker, D. W., Rutter, M., & Plomin, R. (1998). Gene-environment correlations in late childhood and early adolescence. *Developmental Psychology, 34,* 970–981.

Patterson, G. R., Reid, J. B., & Dishion, T. J. (1992). *Antisocial boys.* Evgene, OR: Castalin.

Pettit, G. S., Bates, J. E., & Dodge, K. A. (1997). Supportive parenting, ecological context, and children's adjustment. *Child Development, 68,* 908–923.

Plomin, R., & DeFries, J. C. (1985). *Origins of individual differences in infancy.* New York: Academic Press.

Plomin, R., DeFries, J., & Fulker, D. (1988). *Nature and nurture during infancy and early childhood.* Pacific Grove, CA: Brooks/Cole.

Portes, P. R., Dunham, R. M., & Williams, S. (1986). Assessing childrearing style in ecological settings: Its relation to culture, social class, early age intervention, and scholastic achievement. *Adolescence, 21,* 723–735.

Scarr, S. (1992). Developmental theories for the 1990s: Development and individual differences. *Child Development, 63,* 1–19.

Sears, R. R., Maccoby, E. E., & Levin, H. (1957). *Patterns of child-rearing.* Evanston, IL: Row–Peterson.

Staples, R., & Johnson, L. B. (1993). *Black families at the crossroads.* San Francisco: Jossey-Bass.

Stoolmiller, M. (1999). Implications of the restricted range of family environments for estimates of heritability and nonshared environment in behavior-genetic adoption studies. *Psychological Bulletin, 125,* 392–409.

Weiss, B., Dodge, K. A., Bates, S. E., & Pettit, G. S. (1992). Some consequences of early harsh discipline: Child aggression and a maladaptive social information processing style. *Child Development, 63,* 1321–1335.

Zelli, A., & Dodge, K. A. (1999). Personality development from the bottom up. In D. Cervone & Y. Shoda (Eds.), *The coherence of personality: Social cognitive bases of consistency, variability, and organization* (pp. 94–126). New York: Guilford Press.

Zelli, A., Dodge, K. A., Lochman, J. E., Laird, R. D., & the Conduct Problems Prevention Research Group. (1999). The distinction between beliefs legitimizing aggression and deviant processing of social cues: Testing measurement validity and the hypothesis that biased processing mediates the effects of beliefs on aggression. *Journal of Personality and Social Psychology, 77,* 150–166.

13

Parenting and Adolescent Problem Behavior: An Ecological Analysis of the Nurturance Hypothesis

Thomas J. Dishion
Bernadette Marie Bullock
*University of Oregon, Eugene,
and Oregon Social Learning Center*

The nurturance hypothesis asserts that pervasive attention, emotional investment, and behavior management of adult caregivers are critical to a child's social and emotional development. Adult caregivers have important direct and indirect influences on children's socioemotional development, in general, and problem behavior, in particular. Using an ecological framework for studying the development of problem behavior (Dishion, French, & Patterson, 1995b), the question becomes: Under what conditions are parenting practices influential in the development, maintenance, and reduction of problem behavior?

The term parent, used loosely, refers to an adult caregiver who assumes the long-term responsibility for a child's socioemotional development. The constellation and characterization of parents vary in important ways across cultures and settings.

One approach to studying the impact of parenting on problem behavior is to build models specifying pathways of direct and indirect influence (see Fig. 13.1). The concept of model-building is embedded within a pragmatic philosophy of behavior science, where the primary goal is to build and test models that potentially

---

Address correspondence to: Thomas J. Dishion, Ph.D., Child and Family Center, 195 West 12th Ave., Eugene, OR 97403-3408, e-mail: tomd@darkwing.uoregon.edu

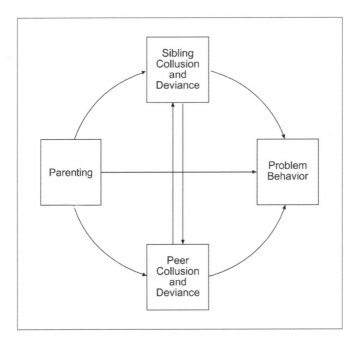

FIG. 13.1. A summary model for the direct and indirect influences of parenting on child and adolescent problem behavior.

guide prevention and intervention (Dishion & Patterson, 1999). The assumption is that to fully understand developmental processes and the range of influences it is necessary to model direct and indirect influences (Reid, 1993). Intervention studies, in turn, provide an experimental test of various links in a developmental model, thereby leading to further model revisions. Linking models to experimental manipulation provides a basis for establishing what is often referred to as "causality" (Cook & Campbell, 1979).

The model shown in Figure 13.1 poses parenting practices as having direct effects on problem behavior through two pathways: coercive limit-setting and poor monitoring (Patterson, Reid, & Dishion, 1992). The indirect effects of parenting are those that are mediated through the influence of sibling and peer interaction on problem behavior. That is, how parents structure and manage behavior in the home can lead to collusion and deviance among siblings; parents' poor management of peer environments affects exposure to deviant peers.

In this chapter, we review literature on the direct and indirect influences of parenting on problem behavior. We also review key developmental and experimental intervention research that address the direct and indirect effects of parenting specified in Figure 13.1. Finally, we examine the variability in parenting strategies and influence in diverse communities.

DIRECT EFFECTS OF PARENTING

Coercive Process

Social development researchers have come to conceptualize parenting as a bi-directional process (Bell, 1968). Quantitative genetic models of family processes suggest that family processes can be affected by children's temperament to the extent that a child experienced as difficult is often treated with greater negativity and less positivity (Deater-Deckard, 2000; Rothbart & Bates, 1998). Several stud-ies have provided support for this evocative gene-environment correlation in rela-tion to observed parenting behavior (Goodman & Stevenson, 1991; Leve, Winebarger, Fagot, Reid, & Goldsmith, 1998; O'Connor, Hetherington, Reiss, & Plomin, 1995). While an analysis of evocative gene-environment correlations in parenting behavior is beyond the focus of this chapter, models of social develop-ment must consider this potential dynamic.

The coercion model describes how a bidirectional process between the parent and child can lead to escalation in aggressive, antisocial behavior in children (Patterson, 1982; Patterson et al., 1992). For adults who care for children, it is often necessary to set limits and request cooperation from those youngsters. A microsocial analysis of these parenting episodes has proven instructive. When the parent–child interactions turn into aversive interchanges, the probability of the child being negatively reinforced for antisocial behavior increases. This pattern of escalation in limit-setting conflicts characterizes parent–child interac-tions in aggressive children compared to nonaggressive children (Snyder & Patterson, 1995).

Careful observation work by Gardner (1989) reveals that parents of problem children handle 43% of the limit-setting situations inconsistently, compared to parents of nonproblem children, who were inconsistent only 5% of the time. Generally, parents of problem children tended to relinquish demands in the face of limit-setting conflict. When this pattern unfolds frequently, the data suggest that children usually will be uncooperative and antisocial in other situations. This traitlike characteristic of the child seriously interferes with the ability to develop positive peer relations (Coie & Kupersmidt, 1983; Dishion, 1990; Dodge, 1983), academic skills (Patterson et al., 1992), and positive friendships (Dishion et al., 1995b).

Correlational and longitudinal research on the coercion model itself does not preclude the possibility that adults' reactions are evoked by some aspect of the child. Therein lies the bidirectional influence. From an ecological perspective, parenting skills may significantly reduce these coercive interchanges, improving the long-term developmental outcomes of children and adolescents, especially for those who are perceived as difficult from a caregiver's perspective.

Family management was introduced by Patterson (1982) as a set of constructs that formulated what these parenting skills might be. The constructs emerged from observations in clinical work with families of aggressive children and consist of some version of the following: limit-setting, positive reinforcement, problem-solving, and monitoring; relationship quality can also be conceptualized as a family management skill (see Dishion & McMahon, 1998).

There is ample evidence that such family management skills in childhood are prognostic of adolescent problem behavior (Baumrind, Moselle, & Martin, 1985; Block, Block, & Keyes, 1988; Loeber & Dishion, 1983). A model linking parent-monitoring and discipline to child antisocial behavior has been tested and replicated on several samples (Conger, Patterson, & Ge, 1995; Forgatch, 1991; Patterson et al., 1992). In the analysis of the developmental course of antisocial behavior, Patterson (1993) tested a model that poor family management skills accounted for childhood onset and persistence of antisocial behavior, whereas deviant peer association accounted for escalation in adolescent problem behavior.

Increasingly, it becomes clear that the impact and nature of parenting varies as a function of family context. We conceptualized the impact of context as mediated through parenting practices and peer influence (Dishion et al., 1995b). Parenting, however, may function as a protective factor in high-risk social contexts.

Wilson (1980), for example, found that parent supervision was more predictive of delinquency in high-risk neighborhood compared to low-risk neighborhoods. Investigators have examined parent-monitoring in inner urban settings in the United States and found it to be predictive of early-onset substance use across ethnic groups (Chilcoat, Dishion, & Anthony, 1995; Chilcoat & Anthony, 1996). Additionally, parental efforts in behavior management were critically important (i.e., a statistically reliable interaction) in reducing increases in African American adolescents' future problem behavior (Mason, Cauce, Gonzales, & Hiraga, 1996).

These findings are supportive of the hypothesis that parenting is a protective factor in high-risk settings. Research on protective factors in developmental psychopathology is especially informative to the design of effective interventions (Cicchetti & Toth, 1992).

Clearly, correlational and longitudinal research are promising, but not convincing in confirming that parents make a difference. Parenting behavior observed in these studies could be evoked simply by child characteristics that are relatively predetermined and resistant to change (Harris, 1995). Clinical research with families of problem children, however, suggests the opposite at each developmental stage.

In early childhood, random assignment studies to parenting interventions that emphasize family management practices produce significant (clinically and statistically) reductions in young children's behavior at home and school (e.g., Webster-Stratton, 1990). In middle childhood, a focus on family management skills resulted in statistically reliable reductions in antisocial behavior at home and school (e.g., Patterson, 1974).

Although adolescents are often considered beyond parental control, several studies document that a focus on family management skills and family structural dynamics result in reduced delinquency (Henggeler, Schoenwald, Borduin, Rowland, & Cunningham, 1998) and substance use (Liddle, 1999). Moreover, random assignment of repeat offenders (10 offenses) to treatment foster care versus group home care revealed reductions in official and self-reported delinquency (Chamberlain & Moore, 1998). Literally hundreds of studies document the effectiveness of mobilizing adult caregivers to attend and better manage children with problem behavior. Reviews of the child clinical literature invariably conclude that interventions targeting parenting practices are the most promising for effecting clinically significant change (Dumas, 1989; Kazdin, 1987; McMahon & Wells, 1989; Patterson, Dishion, & Chamberlain, 1993).

The use of intervention science to infer developmental processes has limitations, the major one being that the processes linking the intervention to change in the dependent variable are often unspecified (Kazdin, 1999). More recently, there has been an effort to specify mediation in intervention studies (Dodge, 1993; Reid, 1993). From a model-building perspective, it is important to document that change occurred as expected in both the outcomes, as well as in the variables indirectly related to the outcome. For example, parenting interventions would presumably reduce parent–child coercive interactions, which in turn are related to reductions in antisocial behavior.

In our own work, we found that families with high-risk adolescents who were randomly assigned to an intervention focusing exclusively on family management practices (the child did not attend sessions) produced reductions in mother–adolescent coercion and teacher ratings of antisocial behavior at school (Dishion & Andrews, 1995). More importantly, for those families participating in the parenting interventions, we found changes in coercive parent–child interactions (see Figure 13.2) to be correlated with changes in teacher ratings of antisocial behavior (Dishion, Patterson, & Kavanagh, 1992).

The data suggesting that there are biological factors relevant to the onset of children's problem behavior does not preclude the possibility that there are also important direct effects for parenting. Correlation, longitudinal, and intervention data converge in support of the idea that parent–child coercion is etiologically significant, and focus on family management practices can have a significant positive effect on reducing child and adolescent problem behavior.

INDIRECT EFFECTS OF PARENTING

Siblings

The sibling context is influential in the development and escalation of problem behavior. Not only do longitudinal studies on the development of adolescent problem behavior simply document large family size as a predictor (Loeber & Dishion, 1983), but a minority of families produce a disproportionate number of

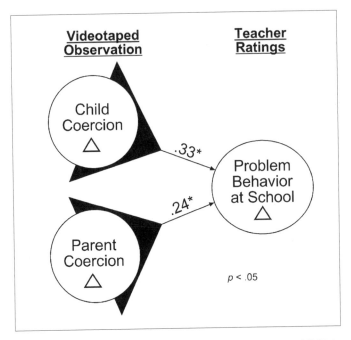

FIG. 13.2. Zero order correlations in change in parent–child interactions and teacher ratings of externalizing behavior.

the crimes in a community (West & Farrington, 1973). We hypothesize that a significant proportion of this variance is attributable to parenting practices, which set
up processes among siblings that contribute to the development of problem
behavior. Furthermore, interventions that effectively improve family management
would reduce problem behavior in the child and sibling environment.

Conflict, coercion, and collusion among siblings have been directly linked to
an association with deviant peers, poor peer relations, substance use, aggressive
behavior, and academic difficulty in children and adolescents (Bank, Patterson, &
Reid, 1996; Bullock & Dishion, 2001; Hetherington, 1989; Loeber & Tengs,
1986; Patterson, 1982; Patterson, Dishion, & Bank, 1984; Stormshak, Bellanti, &
Bierman, 1996). Theories regarding sibling interaction suggest that aversive sibling exchanges are representative of the collective family dynamic, with both parents and their children engaging in coercive processes (Patterson, 1982). A
critical feature of family management in large families, therefore, is the management of the sibling environment.

Research regarding parental discipline practices demonstrates that ineffectual
parental discipline increases the prospect of conflict escalation between siblings
(Bank, Burraston, & Snyder, 2001; Garcia, Shaw, Winslow, & Yaggi, 1998).
Ineffectual parental discipline and a lack of attention to negative sibling interac-

tion, then, may elevate the likelihood of a hostile sibling environment, thus increasing the risk for synchronous and impending child antisocial problem behavior.

Studies reveal that siblings at risk for problem behavior are often participants in a coercive, distressed family system. In particular, siblings in families characterized by elevated levels of aversive family interaction have been reported to be more coercive than siblings in nondistressed families and more likely to engage in protracted coercive exchanges. High levels of coercion among siblings, in turn, are determinants for future antisocial conduct (Patterson, 1984, 1986).

Observation studies of negative patterns of sibling interaction during middle childhood are predictive of boys' future adjustment and psychopathology in adolescence and early adulthood (Bank, Patterson, & Reid, 1996; Patterson, 1982; Snyder & Patterson, 1986). Coercive and negative interactions among siblings have also been found to contribute significantly to the escalation of an aggressive child's concurrent and future antisocial behavior, and to consistently predict adult arrests and the severity of criminal history for clinically-referred and nonreferred boys.

Seemingly positive exchanges between siblings may lead to maladaptive adolescent outcomes as well. Sibling collusion is a process in which siblings cooperate secretly, conspire, and connive to engage in problem behavior and undermine parent leadership and efforts to socialize. The collusion process is predicated on positive reinforcement for rule-breaking talk (Bullock & Dishion, 2001) similar to the "deviancy training" process identified in peer groups (Dishion, Andrews, Kavanagh, & Soberman, 1996).

In a recent study of early adolescents (Bullock & Dishion, 2000), we compared the sibling dynamics of young adolescents and identified them as successful (B average, no discipline contacts) and high risk (teacher ratings of problem behavior at school), and found that sibling collusion was virtually absent among the successful students and prevalent in the families of high-risk students.

Because collusion among siblings is embedded in positive affect, we also found that sibling communications among high-risk siblings were more positive and more negative than those of the successful adolescents. As expected, sibling collusion was uniquely predictive of deviant peer association and concurrent problem behavior (substance use and delinquency). Moreover, sibling collusion significantly predicted young adolescent problem behavior, controlling for the influence of deviant peers.

These data suggest that siblings in high-risk families are collusive and such processes are associated with deviant peer group involvement and problem behavior. Changes in parental management of coercive and collusive sibling interactions would improve children's long-term adjustment.

Intervention research suggests that the correlation between parenting and sibling coercion and collusion is more than correlational. Arnold, Levine, and Patterson (1975) examined the outcomes of clinical cases randomly assigned to parent training to determine the impact on the behavior of the siblings. These investigators found that a focus on parenting skills not only improved the behavior of the target child, but also produced a statistically reliable reduction in the observed coercive behavior among the siblings. Studies are currently underway that address the specific intervention needs of families with siblings to determine the link between improved family management and changes in the sibling interaction system (e.g., L. Bank, personal communication, 1999).

Peers

Peer influence on delinquency and substance use is undoubtedly powerful (Elliott, Huizinga, & Ageton, 1985), leading some theorists to conceptualize adolescent problem behavior as a team activity (Gold, 1970). The compelling evidence for peer influence has suggested a group socialization theory: The majority of environmental influences on child and adolescent social development comes from the impact of group affiliation with peers (Harris, 1998).

We have spent considerable time studying the dynamics of peer influence through direct observations. In our Oregon Youth Study research, we asked the boys in our longitudinal study to bring in their best friend for a videotaped problem-solving task. In this task, the adolescent boys planned activities, planned a party, and discussed problems they had experienced with parents and peers. These interaction sequences were relatively simple and involved selective reinforcement (by laughter and positive affect) rule-breaking discourse.

When these interactions were coded, we examined the extent to which the boys engaged in a process we called deviancy training. We related the boys' friendship interactions with their subsequent social development. Surprisingly, the 30 minutes of videotaped interaction predicted escalations in substance use and delinquency by middle adolescence (Dishion, Capaldi, Spracklen, & Li, 1995a; Dishion et al., 1996). More surprising, the adolescent boys' tendency to engage in these discussions on videotape uniquely predicted their involvement in serious violent offenses (e.g., rape, assault), after controlling for history of harsh discipline and their own history of antisocial behavior (Dishion, Eddy, Haas, Li, & Spracklen, 1997).

Generally, it is true that parenting constructs will not compete with deviant peer constructs in a model predicting adolescent problem behavior. One advantage of the ecological approach to modeling is that indirect influences are as important as direct influences. The literature is consistent in finding that parent-monitoring practices are prognostic of deviant peer involvement (Dishion & Loeber, 1985; Dishion & McMahon, 1998; Dishion, Patterson, Stoolmiller, & Skinner, 1991; Patterson & Dishion, 1985). As seen in Figure 13.3, within the Oregon Youth Study sample, the correlation between parent-monitoring and deviant peer involvement in early adolescence was above .70 ($p < .001, n = 206$; Dishion et al., 1995a). Covariation of this magnitude among predictors in the

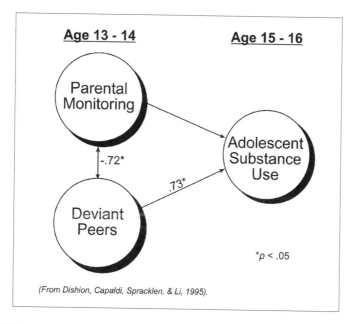

FIG. 13.3. Parent monitoring, deviant peers, and subsequent drug use.

same equation is what is referred to as the multicollinearity problem: It simply does not make sense to infer that one predictor is more important than another because of the massive indirect effect.

We hypothesize that the above estimates are probably underestimates of the parents' role in their children's exposure to peer influence. Parents are truly managers of the children's peer environments, and much of their effort is planful and future-oriented. They often engineer a social world for their offspring that precludes contact with deviant peers. Given the economic resources, parents will place children in positive sports activities as early age 5 or 6 to promote the development of prosocial skills and the connection to other families with similar concerns. Also true is that parents lose control of their adolescents if they become involved in a deviant peer group—at such a time, the adolescent actively disengages from the family and directly undermines parental efforts to monitor. Stoolmiller (1994) studied and nicely described this process of "wandering."

A particularly poignant example of the powerful role adults play in exposing young adolescents to negative peer influence is found in the literature and pertains to iatrogenic effects associated with interventions that aggregate high-risk youth. Of published interventions aimed to improve delinquent behavior in adolescence, 29% actually have negative effects (Lipsey & Wilson, 1993). Recently, two random-assignment longitudinal studies were reported that revealed aggregating high-risk youth to interventions with other adolescents was associated with escalations in substance use and delinquency and 30-year negative life outcomes (Dishion, McCord, & Poulin, 1999).

In the Adolescent Transitions Program study, random assignment to a 12-week cognitive behavioral intervention, which focused on goal-setting, resistance skills, and problem-solving did result in positive outcomes, such as improved parent–child interaction. However, it also resulted in iatrogenic growth in tobacco use and teacher-reported delinquent behavior at school (Poulin, Dishion, & Burraston, in press). Similarly, in a reanalysis of a prevention experiment conducted over 50 years ago (see McCord, 1992), we found that elevated rates of negative life outcomes in the intervention group were almost entirely due to the youth being sent to summer camps. The odds ratio was 10:1 for experiencing a negative life outcome, compared to a matched control group, if the youth was sent more than twice to a summer camp.

Correlational, longitudinal, and observational research converge on the conclusion that peer group affiliation is central to escalations in problem behavior, especially in adolescence. Young people select friends similar to themselves and find common ground, engaging in deviancy training. Random assignment intervention research indicates that strategies placing high-risk adolescents in peer group settings can have an iatrogenic effect on problem behavior. These findings can be seen as supportive of models that emphasize parental indirect effects. Parents often work at managing their child's exposure to peer influences through supervision or structuring activities involving peers (see Dishion & McMahon, 1998). Unfortunately, these efforts can be inadvertently undermined by well-meaning professionals.

VARIABILITY OF PARENT EFFECTS

It is unlikely there are family management strategies that are universal across cultures. To suggest that all cultures manage families and parenting in the same way is a form of European colonialism (Duran & Duran, 1995) and underestimates the complex diversity of socialization (Whiting & Whiting, 1975).

The very structure and cross-generation involvement of adults in caregiving varies dramatically across ethnic groups. For example, from an epidemiological perspective, grandmother–daughter dyads are prevalent and effective in African American families (e.g., Kellam, 1990).

Historically, Native American families were also known to have quite an effective strategy for socializing young children into the norms and behaviors of the tribe, in a system in which the biological parents did very little direct limit-setting (as would be described in families of European descent). Such issues where handled differently at the group level. As a result of colonizing Native American tribes through policies of mandatory boarding schools, the strengths of these cultural traditions were nearly lost (Duran & Duran, 1995).

A study of the effects of harsh discipline among European American and African American elementary school-aged children also supports the cultural relativity hypothesis (Deater-Deckard, Dodge, Bates, & Pettit, 1996). Interviewers carefully assessed parenting practices in both these family types. Deater-Deckard and colleagues reported that elevated levels of physical punishment were associated with increased levels of child aggression and externalizing only among European American children. African American children receiving harsh physical punishment had lower externalizing and aggression scores compared to their European American children. It was also true that African American children reported physical punishment as fair, whereas children of European descent did not.

Similar conclusions were reached in large-sample survey studies of the impact of authoritative versus authoritarian parenting in American children of diverse ethnicities. Authoritative (i.e., firm but democratic) parenting, identified in studies of educated middle-class families as related to competence and low rates of problem behavior (e.g., Baumrind, 1985), did not predict achievement in African American families (Steinberg, Dornbush, & Brown, 1992).

Family Observations

In our study of successful and high-risk students living in an urban setting, we directly observed family management in the home (Kavanagh, Dishion, Medici Skaggs, & Schneiger, 1998). Each family participated in a series of seven videotaped conversations designed to directly assess family management practices on drugs (relationship quality, limit-setting, positive reinforcement, parent-monitoring, problem-solving, and norm-setting).

Scales were derived to assess the parents' skills in each of the above domains. Coders (blind to the family's risk status) watched the videotapes and made macro ratings on at least five items describing parenting skills. Ratings were made on a 9-point scale (9 = very high, 0 = very low). Minimum internal consistency for the reported scores was greater than .70. Coders were trained until they obtained agreement above 80%, using a 2-anchor-point window for agreement and disagreement.

Table 13.1 provides the summary of the results on the extent to which the family management skills differentiated the families of successful from high-risk students. Inspection of Table 13.1 reveals that, indeed, parent-monitoring and norm-setting differentiated the two groups, in the expected direction. It is interesting to note, however, that almost all family management skills, when considered individually, showed statistically reliable ethnicity by risk interactions. In addition, parent-monitoring and relationship quality showed significant gender by ethnicity by risk status interactions.

TABLE 13.1

MEAN DIFFERENCES IN SUBSCALE AND TOTAL SCORES FROM THE
FAMILY ASSESSMENT TASK FOR NORMATIVE AND HIGH-RISK YOUTH

Observed	Normative ($N = 120$) Mean (*SD*)	High-Risk ($N = 70$) Mean (*SD*)	Univariate Effects
Relationship quality	6.72 (1.20)	6.42 (1.47)	R × E × G
Positive reinforcement	4.24 (1.29)	4.48 (1.62)	R × E
Monitoring	6.13 (1.03)	5.71 (1.14)	R, E
Limit-setting	5.94 (1.46)	5.94 (1.46)	R × E
Problem-solving	5.88 (1.62)	5.39 (1.56)	R × E
Family drug-use norms	6.28 (1.01)	5.65 (1.45)	R
Family management—total score	6.48 (0.93)	6.10 (0.98)	R

Note. E = ethnicity main effect; R × E = risk by ethnicity interaction; R × E × G = risk by ethnicity by gender interaction.

Inspection of the trends for the subgroups on parent–child relationship quality
(Figure 13.4) and limit-setting (Figure 13.5) suggest complexity in the study of
parenting effects across cultural groups. In Figure 13.2, the distribution of relationship quality across the four groups is shown using box plots. The pattern of
findings is as expected from the social developmental literature for European
American boys and African American girls, with lower relationship qualities
associated with high-risk status. However, in contrast, high-risk African
American boys were rated as having the most positive parent relationships of all
groups. This was much higher than the successful students. European American
girls were rated as having positive relationships with parents, regardless of their
risk status.

The distribution of observed scores on limit-setting is summarized by ethnicity
in Figure 13.5, as gender interactions were not statistically reliable. Limit-setting
was rated high (if parents did not use physical discipline), consistent, contingent,
and provided rationales for consequences. As with previous research, we found
that this definition of limit-setting described successful students in families of
European descent, but failed to discriminate between successful and high-risk
groups in families of African descent.

Of note, the Total Family Management score discriminated the successful and
high-risk students, despite the variability of patterns in its constituent scores (i.e.,
limit-setting, parent-monitoring, problem-solving). Aggregating diverse parenting practices into a total score obscured the richness of variability across groups
as a function of gender and ethnicity. Aggregating improves reliability, thereby
reducing variation due to "error." Perhaps, in general, groups vary in the parenting strategies they use, but they manage nonetheless, and that is the critical issue
in understanding parent influences.

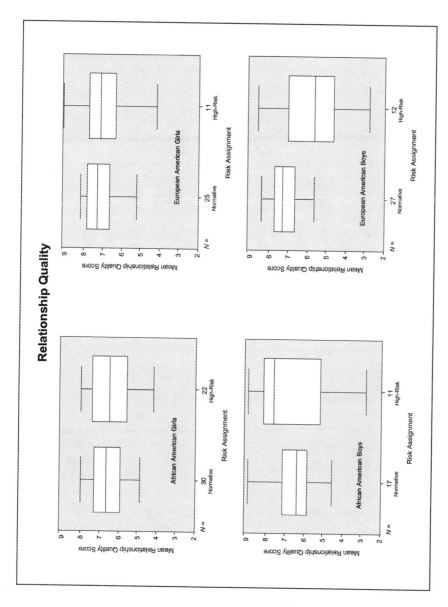

FIG. 13.4.   Parent–child relationship quality as a function of risk, ethnicity, and gender.

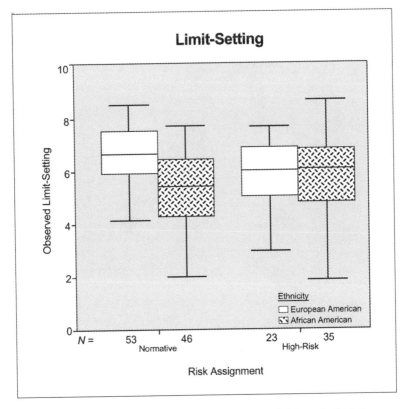

FIG. 13.5.   Parent limit-setting as a function of risk and ethnicity.

To test this hypothesis, we used the Total Family Management score to predict future self-reported drug use; for externalizing behaviors, we used the Parent Form of the Child Behavior Checklist (PCBC, Achenbach, 1991) one year later. First, the risk status of the child was entered, then family management. We found that for both outcomes, family management reliably ($p < .05$) accounted for future problem behavior, controlling for the risk status of the child one year earlier. In fact, the zero order effect of risk status on future problem behavior became nonsignificant in the presence of observed family management practices.

CONCLUSION AND IMPLICATIONS

Maccoby (2000) provides a review of the methodological and theoretical gaps in questions that pit nature versus nurture in the attempt to set statistical parameters to those broad questions. Model-building provides an alternative to addressing this question. In this respect, we attempt to build a model that specifies processes, which in turn specify the conditions under which parenting has an effect, eventually integrating biological and social constructs into the process models (Dishion & Patterson, 1999).

The coercion model provides a basis for understanding bidirectional effects between the parent and child in social development and also guides effective intervention practices. The evidence suggests that intervening with parents reduces negative outcomes of young children, those in middle childhood, and adolescents, as measured by objective criteria outside the home.

One advantage of model-building is the formulation of indirect effects in development. With respect to parenting, indirect effects may be the most powerful. The parents' management of the sibling and peer environment over the formative years can have dramatic effects on eventual family deviance and group socialization processes. In fact, a parent's willingness to allow a child to repeatedly participate in summer camps, alternative schools with other high-risk children, or treatment programs with high-risk children can have a large effect on their eventual rates of problem behavior.

Clearly, despite the evidence for both direct and indirect effects of parenting, we are increasingly aware that more work is needed to understand the variability of these effects in diverse developmental, geographical, and cultural contexts. Models that aggregate across heterogeneous contexts, or that study parenting within the normal range, may underestimate parenting effects (Stoolmiller, 1994). Moreover, the exclusive study of disruptive environments may lead to an underestimation of biological factors. The general principle is that biology and environment are inextricably linked in such as way that the best we can do is understand relative influences in specific ecological conditions.

We especially appreciate the variability in which diverse cultures organize socialization and approach parenting and the variety of ways adults achieve socialization of children. Our data, as well as those of others, suggest universal family management strategies do not exist. Working collaboratively with parents in diverse situations will present a fuller appreciation of the universal investment, formidable challenges, and adaptive integrity of caregivers in raising children.

ACKNOWLEDGMENTS

This project was supported by grant DA 07031 from the National Institute on Drug Abuse to Thomas J. Dishion, Ph.D., by grant MH 37940 from the National Institute of Mental Health to Deborah Capaldi and by grant MH 46690 from the National Institute of Mental Health to John B. Reid. This work would not have been possible without the persistent dedication of the Portland Project Alliance staff, supervised by Dr. Kate Kavanagh. We also express our appreciation to Ann Simas for her skillful work in editing this manuscript.

REFERENCES

Achenbach, T. M. (1991). *Manual for the Child Behavior Checklist/4–18 and 1991 profile.* Burlington: University of Vermont, Department of Psychology.

Arnold, J., Levine, A., & Patterson, G. R. (1975). Changes in sibling behavior following family intervention. *Journal of Consulting and Clinical Psychology, 43,* 683–688.

Bank, L., Burraston, B., & Snyder, J. (2001). The sibling amplifier model: Unskilled parenting and sibling conflicts as predictors of adolescent and early adult antisocial behavior and peer relations. (Manuscript under review.)

Bank, L., Patterson, G. R., & Reid, J. B. (1996). Negative sibling interaction patterns as predictors of later adjustment problems in adolescent and young adult males. In G. H. Brody (Ed.), *Advances in applied developmental psychology. Sibling relationships* (pp. 197–229). Norwood, NJ: Ablex.

Baumrind, D. (1985). Familial antecedents of adolescent drug use: A developmental perspective. In C. L. Jones & R. J. Battjes (Eds.), *Etiology of drug abuse: Implication for prevention* (pp. 13–44). National Institute on Drug Abuse Research Monograph 56. Washington, DC: Superintendent of Documents, U.S. Government Printing Office.

Baumrind, D., Moselle, K., & Martin, J. A. (1985). Adolescent drug abuse research: A critical examination from a developmental perspective. *Advances in Alcohol Substance Abuse, 4,* 41–67.

Bell, R. Q. (1968). A reinterpretation of the direction of effects in studies of socialization. *Psychological Review, 75,* 81–94.

Block, J., Block, J. H., & Keyes, S. (1988). Longitudinally foretelling drug usage in adolescence: Early childhood personality and environmental precursors. *Child Development, 59,* 336–355.

Bullock, B. M., & Dishion, T. J. (2001). Sibling collusion and problem behavior in early adolescence. (Manuscript under review.)

Chamberlain, P., & Moore, K. J. (1998). A clinical model of parenting juvenile offenders: A comparison of group versus family care. *Clinical Child Psychology and Psychiatry, 3,* 375–386.

Chilcoat, H. D., & Anthony, J. C. (1996). Impact of parent monitoring on initiation of drug use through late childhood. *Journal of the American Academy of Child and Adolescent Psychiatry, 35,* 91–100.

Chilcoat, H., Dishion, T. J., & Anthony, J. (1995). Parent monitoring and the incidence of drug sampling in multiethnic urban children. *American Journal of Epidemiology, 141,* 25–31.

Cicchetti, D., & Toth, S. L. (1992). The role of developmental theory in prevention and intervention. *Development and Psychopathology, 4,* 489–493.

Coie, J. D., & Kupersmidt, J. B. (1983). A behavioral analysis of emerging social status in boys' groups. *Child Development, 54,* 1400–1416.

Cook, T. D., & Campbell, D. T. (1979). *Quasi-experimentation: Design and analysis issues for field settings.* Boston: Houghton Mifflin.

Conger, R. D., Patterson, G. R., & Ge, X. (1995). A mediational model for the impact of parents' stress on adolescent adjustment. *Child Development, 66,* 80–97.

Deater-Deckard, K. (2000). Parenting and child behavioral adjustment in early childhood: A quantitative genetic approach to studying family process. *Child Development, 71,* 468–484.

Deater-Deckard, K., Dodge, K. A., Bates, J. E., & Pettit, G. S. (1996). Physical discipline among African American and European American mothers: Links to children's externalizing behaviors. *Developmental Psychology, 32,* 1065–1072.

Dishion, T. J. (1990). Peer context of child and adolescent troublesome behavior. In P. Leone (Ed.), *Understanding troubled and troublesome youth.* Beverly Hills, CA: Sage.

Dishion, T. J., & Andrews, D. W. (1995). Preventing escalation in problem behaviors with high-risk young adolescents: Immediate and 1-year outcomes. *Journal of Consulting and Clinical Psychology, 63,* 538–548.

Dishion, T. J., Andrews, D. W., Kavanagh, K., & Soberman, L. H. (1996). Preventive interventions for high-risk youth: The Adolescent Transitions Program. In B. McMahon & R. DeV. Peters (Eds.), *Childhood disorders, substance abuse and delinquency: Prevention and early intervention approaches* (pp. 184–214). Newbury, CA: Sage.

Dishion, T. J., Capaldi, D., Spracklen, K. M., & Li, F. (1995a). Peer ecology of male adolescent drug use. *Development and Psychopathology, 7,* 803–824.

Dishion, T. J., Eddy, J. M., Haas, E., Li, F., & Spracklen, K. (1997). Friendships and violent behavior during adolescence. *Social Development, 6,* 207–223.

Dishion, T. J., French, D. C., & Patterson, G. R. (1995b). The development and ecology of antisocial behavior. In D. Cicchetti & D. Cohen (Eds.), *Manual of developmental psychopathology* (pp. 421–471). New York: John Wiley and Sons.

Dishion, T. J., & Loeber, R. (1985). Male adolescent marijuana and alcohol use: The role of parents and peers revisited. *American Journal of Drug and Alcohol Abuse, 11,* 11–25.

Dishion, T. J., McCord, J., & Poulin, F. (1999). When interventions harm: Peer groups and problem behavior. *American Psychologist, 54,* 755–764.

Dishion, T. J., & McMahon, R. J. (1998). Parental monitoring and the prevention of child and adolescent problem behavior: A conceptual and empirical formulation. *Clinical Child and Family Psychology Review, 1,* 61–75.

Dishion, T. J., & Patterson, G. R. (1999). Model-building in developmental psychopathology: A pragmatic approach to understanding and intervention. *Journal of Clinical Child Psychology, 28,* 502–512.

Dishion, T. J., Patterson, G. R., & Kavanagh, K. (1992). An experimental test of the coercion model: Linking theory, measurement, and intervention. In J. McCord & R. Trembley (Eds.), *The interaction of theory and practice: Experimental studies of interventions* (pp. 253–282). New York: Guilford Press.

Dishion, T. J., Patterson, G. R., Stoolmiller, M., & Skinner, M. (1991). Family, school, and behavioral antecedents to early adolescent involvement with antisocial peers. *Developmental Psychology, 27,* 172–180.

Dodge, K. A. (1983). Behavioral antecedents of peer social status. *Child Development, 54,* 1386–1399.

Dodge, K. A. (1993). The future of research and the treatment of conduct disorder. *Development and Psychopathology, 5,* 311–319.

Dumas, J. E. (1989). Treating antisocial behavior in children: Child and family approaches. *Clinical Psychology Review, 9,* 197–222.

Duran, E., & Duran, B. (1995). *Native American postcolonial psychology.* New York: State University of New York Press.

Elliot, D. S., Huizinga, D., & Ageton, S. S. (1985). *Explaining delinquency and drug use.* Beverly Hills, CA: Sage.

Forgatch, M. S. (1991). The clinical science vortex: Developing a theory for antisocial behavior. In D. J. Pepler & K. H. Rubin (Eds.), *The development and treatment of childhood aggression* (pp. 291–315). Hillsdale, NJ: Lawrence Erlbaum Associates.

Garcia, M. M., Shaw, D. S., Winslow, E. B., & Yaggi, K. E. (1998). Destructive sibling conflict and the development of conduct problems in young boys. *Developmental Psychology, 36,* 44–53.

Gardner, F. E. M. (1989). Inconsistent parenting: Is there evidence for a link with children's conduct problems? *Journal of Abnormal Child Psychology, 17,* 223–233.

Gold, M. (1970). *Delinquent behavior in an American city.* San Francisco: Brooks and Coleman.

Goodman, R., & Stevenson, J. (1991). Parental criticism and warmth toward unrecognized monozygotic twins. *Behavioral and Brain Sciences, 14,* 394–395.

Harris, J. R. (1995). Where is the child's environment? A group socialization theory of development. *Psychological Review, 102,* 458–489.

Harris, J. R. (1998). *The nurture assumption: Why children turn out the way they do.* New York: Free Press.

Henggeler, S. W., Schoenwald, S. K., Borduin, C. M., Rowland, M. D., & Cunningham, P. B. (1998). *Multisystemic treatment of antisocial behavior in children and adolescents.* New York: Guilford Press.

Hetherington, E. M. (1989). Coping with family transitions: Winners, losers, and survivors. *Child Development, 60,* 1–14.

Kavanagh, K., Dishion, T. J., Medici Skaggs, N., & Schneiger, A. (1998, March). *Prediction of parent participation in a tiered model of assessment and intervention for early adolescent problem behavior.* Paper presented at Sixth Annual Meeting of the Society for Prevention Research, Park City, UT.

Kazdin, A. E. (1987). Treatment of antisocial behavior in children: Current status and future directions. *Psychological Bulletin, 102,* 187–203.

Kazdin, A. E. (1999). Current (lack of) status of theory in child and adolescent psychotherapy research. *Journal of Clinical Child Psychology, 28,* 533–543.

Kellam, S. G. (1990). Developmental epidemiological framework for family research on depression and aggression. In G. R. Patterson (Ed.), *Depression and aggression in family interaction* (pp. 11–48). Hillsdale, NJ: Lawrence Erlbaum Associates.

Leve, L. D., Winebarger, A. A., Fagot, B. I., Reid, J. B., & Goldsmith, H. H. (1998). Environmental and genetic variance in children's observed and reported maladaptive behavior. *Child Development, 69,* 1286–1298.

Liddle, H. A. (1999). Theory development in a family-based therapy for adolescent drug abuse. *Journal of Clinical Child Psychology, 28,* 521–532.

Lipsey, M. W., & Wilson, D. B. (1993). The efficacy of psychological, educational, and behavioral treatment: Confirmation from meta-analysis. *American Psychologist, 48,* 1181–1209.

Loeber, R., & Dishion, T. J. (1983). Early predictors of male delinquency: A review. *Psychological Bulletin, 94,* 68–99.

Loeber, R., & Tengs, T. (1986). The analysis of coercive chains between children, mothers, and siblings. *Journal of Family Violence, 1,* 51–70.

Maccoby, E. E. (2000). Parenting and its effects on children: On reading and misreading behavior genetics. *Annual Review of Psychology, 51,* 1–27.

Mason, C. A., Cauce, A. M., Gonzales, N., & Hiraga, Y. (1996). Neither too sweet nor too sour: Problem peers, maternal control, and problem behavior in African American adolescents. *Child Development, 67,* 2115–2130.

McCord, J. (1992). The Cambridge-Somerville Study: A pioneering longitudinal-experimental study of delinquency prevention. In J. McCord & R. E. Tremblay (Eds.), *Preventing antisocial behavior: Interventions from birth through adolescence* (pp. 196–206). New York: Guilford Press.

McMahon, R. J., & Wells, K. C. (1989). Conduct disorders. In E. J. Mash & R. A. Barkley (Eds.), *Treatment of childhood disorders* (pp. 73–132). New York: Guilford Press.

O'Connor, T. G., Hetherington, E. M., Reiss, D., & Plomin, R. (1995). A twin-sibling study of observed parent-adolescent interactions. *Child Development, 66,* 812–824.

Patterson, G. R. (1974). Interventions for boys with conduct problems: Multiple settings, treatments, and criteria. *Journal of Consulting and Clinical Psychology, 42,* 471–481.

Patterson, G. R. (1982). *A social learning approach: III Coercive family process.* Eugene, OR: Castalia.

Patterson, G. R. (1984). Siblings: Fellow travelers in a coercive system. In R. J. Blanchard & D. C. Blanchard (Eds.), *Advances in the study of aggression* (Vol. 1, pp. 173–215). New York: Academic Press.

Patterson, G. R. (1986). The contribution of siblings to training for fighting: A microsocial analysis. In D. Olweus, J. Block, & M. Radke-Yarrow (Eds.), *Development of antisocial and prosocial behaviors* (pp. 235–260). Orlando, FL: Academic Press.

Patterson, G. R. (1993). Orderly change in a stable world: The antisocial trait as a chimera. *Journal of Consulting and Clinical Psychology, 61*, 911–919.

Patterson, G. R., & Dishion, T. J. (1985). Contributions of families and peers to delinquency. *Criminology, 23*, 63–79.

Patterson, G. R., Dishion, T. J., & Bank, L. (1984). Family interaction: A process model of deviancy training [Special issue] *Aggressive Behavior, 10*, 253–267.

Patterson, G. R., Dishion, T. J., & Chamberlain, P. (1993). Outcomes and methodological issues relating to treatment of antisocial children. In T. R. Giles (Ed.), *Effective psychotherapy: A handbook of comparative research* (pp. 43–88). New York: Plenum Press.

Patterson, G. R., Reid, J. B., & Dishion, T. J. (1992). *A social interactional approach: IV Antisocial Boys.* Eugene, OR: Castalia.

Poulin, F., Dishion, T. J., & Burraston, B. (in press). Long-term iatrogenic effects associated with aggregating high-risk adolescents in preventive interventions. *Applied Developmental Science.*

Reid, J. B. (1993). Prevention of conduct disorder before and after school entry: Relating interventions to development findings. *Journal of Development and Psychopathology, 5*, 243–262.

Rothbart, M. K. & Bates, J. E. (1998). Temperment. In W. Damon (Series Ed.) & N. Eisenberg (Vol. Ed.), *Handbook of child psychology: Vol 3. Social, emotional and personality development* (5th ed.). New York: John Wiley and Sons.

Snyder, J., & Patterson, G. R. (1986). The effects of consequences on patterns of social interaction: A quasi-experimental approach to reinforcement in natural interaction. *Child Development, 57*, 1257–1268.

Snyder, J. J., & Patterson, G. R. (1995). Individual differences in social aggression: A test of a reinforcement model of socialization in the natural environment. *Behavior Therapy, 26*, 371–391.

Steinberg, L., Dornbusch, S. M., & Brown, B. B. (1992). Ethnic differences in adolescent achievement: An ecological perspective. *American Psychologist, 47*, 723–729.

Stoolmiller, M. (1994). Antisocial behavior, delinquent peer association and unsupervised wandering for boys: Growth and change from childhood to early adolescence. Multivariate *Behavioral Research, 29*, 263–288.

Stormshak, E. A., Bellanti, C. J., & Bierman, K. L. (1996). The quality of sibling relationships and the development of social competence and behavioral control in aggressive children. *Developmental Psychology, 32*, 79–89.

Webster-Stratton, C. (1990). Long-term follow-up of families with young conduct problem children: From preschool to grade school. *Journal of Clinical Child Psychology, 19*, 144–149.

West, D. J., & Farrington, D. P. (1973). *Who becomes delinquent? Second report of the Cambridge Study in Delinquent Development.* New York: Crane, Russak.

Whiting, B. B., & Whiting, J. M. (1975). *Children of six cultures: A psychocultural analysis.* Cambridge, MA: Harvard University Press.

Wilson, H. (1980). Parental supervision: A neglected aspect of delinquency. *British Journal of Criminology, 20*, 203–235.

14

Interparental Relations as a Dimension of Parenting

E. Mark Cummings
Marcie C. Goeke-Morey
Marybeth A. Graham
University of Notre Dame

Developmental psychologists have focused on the effects of qualities of parent–child interactions on children's development. The chapters in this volume demonstrate the developmental significance of parenting conceptualized in this way. Parenting in this sense comprises two broad dimensions of parental behavior: parenting as the qualities of the emotional relationships and communications between parents and children; and parenting as control, including discipline practices and child management strategies (Cummings, Davies, & Campbell, 2000). On the other hand, these traditional notions about the dimensions of parenting, while tapping issues and matters that, in our estimation, profoundly influence children's socialization, underestimate the effects of the parents' behavior in the home on the children by failing to consider the entire spectrum of parental behavioral influences on children's development. Specifically, the parents' behavior in interaction with each other constitutes an additional important dimension of parenting. Thus, these additional parent-related influences must also be considered in order to understand and account for the full effects of parenting on child development. These effects are in addition to or in interaction with parental influences

Address correspondence to: E. Mark Cummings, 215 Haggar Hall, Notre Dame, IN 46556, Phone: 219-631-3404, e-mail: Cummings.10@nd.edu

251

that may be due to genetic transmission or parental influences over the children's social environment, for example, relationships with peers (Harris, 1995).

Put another way, parenting has not been defined broadly enough to include interparental relations, so that the full extent of parenting as a factor in child development has often not been considered. Relatedly, notions about the origins and bases of parenting practices are similarly too narrow, especially given the associations reported between marital functioning and parent–child interactions (Erel & Burman, 1995). In many studies the consideration of parenting is restricted to various dimensions of parent–child interactions, failing to consider the impact of other potentially significant dimensions of how parents behave outside of the parent–child relationship. Nonetheless, children are affected by these other classes of parental behaviors, regardless of whether these behaviors are directed at the children or are in any way intended by the parents to influence the children's functioning. In particular, interparental relations merit consideration as another dimension of parenting behavior since such behaviors involve a volitional choice by the parents with regard to how to behave, and these behaviors have effects and implications for children's functioning and development.

Evidence that the parents' behavior in the context of marriages is a significant influence on child development is examined below. In particular, we focus on the implications for children's functioning of how parents work through their everyday disagreements and problems, that is, interparental conflict behavior. Conflict behavior is a predictor of marital happiness and risk for divorce (Gottman, 1994), and marital distress is by some reports the most common reason why adults seek psychological help (Bradbury & Fincham, 1990). In recent years considerable evidence has also accumulated to indicate that the qualities of interparental conflict predict children's adjustment (Grych & Fincham, 1990). Thus, an accumulating literature supports the thesis of this report: Marital functioning merits inclusion as a dimension of parenting.

MARITAL CONFLICT AND CHILD ADJUSTMENT

Among the components of marital relations, marital conflict has emerged as a particularly significant aspect of interparental relations with regard to effects on children's development. The publication of a landmark review by Emery (1982) called particular attention to the significance of this matter. However, evidence for relations between marital discord and child development has been accumulating for decades. Moreover, recent work identifies marital conflict as a mediator of relations between marital functioning and child adjustment. Marital conflict is a better predictor of a wide range of children's difficulties than is general marital distress, and relations between marital hostility and child adjustment remain after statistically controlling for general marital distress (Cummings & Davies, 1994a).

Associations between child problems and conflict between the parents are typically modest to moderate in magnitude. Thus, across studies focusing on community samples, marital conflict accounts for 4% to 20% of all of the differences in psychological adjustment problems between children (Grych & Fincham, 1990). However, while relations with childhood problems may be modest in relatively well-functioning families, few family problems are more closely related to children's adjustment than marital conflict, even in "happy" marriages. In distressed families, marital conflict is even more closely associated with children's adjustment than in nondistressed families. Thus, approximately 40% to 50% of children exposed to severe marital hostility exhibit behavior problems, a considerably higher rate of behavior problems than is found in the general population (Cummings & Davies, 1994a).

Marital conflict has been most consistently associated with children's externalizing problems (e.g., aggression, conduct problems). On the other hand, improved measurement of children's covert feelings and anxieties has resulted in increasing evidence for relations between marital conflict and children's internalizing disorders (e.g., anxiety, depression; Davies & Cummings, 1998; Grych, 1998). Evidence has also been found for associations between high levels of marital discord and children's lower social competence with peers, and with children's behavioral and academic problems (e.g., poor grades, problems in intellectual achievement; Cummings & Davies, 1994a; Grych & Fincham, 1990).

However, a caveat is that this literature almost certainly underestimates the negative impact of hostile, unresolved marital disputes on the children, and, at the same time, overestimates the negative effects (if any) of more positive forms of interparental conflict behaviors. Notably, standardized assessments of marital conflict have not included fine-grained distinctions with regard to how marital conflict is handled by the parents. Measurement of marital conflict at a global level of analysis is simply not an adequate approach given the current state of knowledge regarding the importance of precisely how parents handle their disputes (Cummings & Davies, 1994a; Fincham, 1998).

Moreover, the impact of interadult conflict on children is not limited to instances of intact marriages (see Stoneman, Brody, Churchill, & Winn, 1999). Risk for children's adjustment problems increases as the number of family stressors increases (Cummings, Davies, & Campbell, 2000), and children raised in single-parent homes are faced with multiple sources of adversity (McLanahan & Sandefur, 1994). Thus, interpartner or interadult disputes may pose even more severe problems for children raised in such homes. Unfortunately, standardized instruments for assessing interadult conflicts in families without intact marital relationships are a gap in the literature. Thus, systematic study of the effects of conflicts in homes that lack stable marital relationships and corresponding innovations in the development of measurement strategies and approaches to these issues are urgently needed, especially given the potential significance for understanding children's development in lower-income families and families from diverse ethnic and cultural backgrounds.

Finally, while stable, harmonious marital relationships undoubtedly often provide a highly positive and supportive context for parenting for many adults and their children, there has been relatively little systematic study of the positive side of marital relations as a dimension of parenting. Obviously, a misleadingly negative picture of the effects of marital relationships on children is likely to emerge when only the negative effects of a dimension of parenting are considered. Thus, this constitutes another important direction for future research on interparental relations and their effects on the children.

MARITAL CONFLICT AND FAMILY DYSFUNCTION: THE EFFECTS ON CHILDREN OF DIVORCE, MATERNAL DEPRESSION, ABUSE, AND ALCOHOLISM

Marital conflict is also a factor in the effects of other family processes on children's adjustment. Notably, the role of marital conflict in these influences on child development may not be widely recognized. For example, how marital conflict is handled has been shown repeatedly to be a significant factor in children's adjustment before, during, and after divorce, including the effects of custody arrangements following divorce (Amato & Keith, 1991; Emery, 1994). The effects of divorce appear to be minimized if parents are able to handle conflicts well despite divorce, whereas the occurrence of violence or other intense, chronic forms of conflict between the parents increases the negative effects of divorce.

Interparental conflict has also been identified as a factor in the effects of parental depression on the children (Cummings & Davies, 1994b). Interparental conflict and parental depression are highly associated with each other, with evidence for causal relations between high marital conflict and parental depression (Whisman, 2001). Children of depressed parents have been found to be two to five times more likely to develop behavior problems than children of nondepressed parents (Beardslee, Bemporad, Keller, & Klerman, 1983). Moreover, marital conflict associated with depression is a significant predictor of negative outcomes in children, with some longitudinal studies finding that marital conflict is a stronger predictor of adjustment problems than is parental depression (see Cox, Puckering, Pound, & Mills, 1987). Thus, Downey and Coyne (1990) concluded that marital conflict is more closely associated with some forms of adjustment problems in children from these families than parental depression per se.

Parental physical abuse of children is associated with interspousal conflict and aggression (Jouriles, Barling, & O'Leary, 1987). In community samples, the co-occurrence rate is estimated at about 6%, but in clinical samples the percentage overlap in published research ranges as high as 100% (Appel & Holden, 1998).

Marital abuse increases the negative effects of parent–child abuse, and some reports indicate that witnessing abuse has effects similar to experiencing abuse (Jaffe, Wolfe, Wilson, & Zak, 1986). Moreover, children with disabled siblings are more reactive to marital conflict and other forms of family conflict, perhaps reflecting a general sensitization to family problems experienced by children growing up in these challenging family environments (Nixon & Cummings, 1999). Notably, children with disabled siblings are at increased risk for adjustment problems as well. Finally, alcoholism is a disorder marked by high levels of anger expression and marital conflict (El-Shiekh & Cummings, 1997). Some studies suggest that children are particularly disturbed and affected by the marital conflict associated with alcohol abuse. In summary, there is considerable evidence from literatures on diverse family dysfunctions indicating that problems in how the parents handle their conflicts may underlie or contribute to children's adjustment problems in these families.

MARITAL CONFLICT AS PARENTING I: DIRECT EFFECTS ON CHILDREN'S FUNCTIONING

While it may be recognized that marital problems negatively impact on parenting, it is less often understood that children may be negatively affected simply by exposure to marital conflict. Nonetheless, the stressful effects of exposure to interparental conflict have been repeatedly documented, with effects reported in children as young as six months of age. Literally dozens of studies, with the findings converging on the same conclusions even when based on multiple and different types of home- and laboratory-based methodologies, have consistently shown that children react with distress as bystanders to conflict (Cummings & Davies, 1994a). Distress responses include motor inhibition and freezing; self-reported anger, distress, and fear; behavioral responses of anger, distress, and aggression; physiological indices of stress reactions (e.g., blood pressure); and active mediation in the parents' disputes, indicating that children are highly concerned about the parents' conflicts. Negative representations and expectations about interparental relations are also associated with marital conflict (Davies & Cummings, 1998; Grych, 1998). Moreover, children react more negatively to marital conflict than to other forms of family conflict (e.g., parent–child; sibling–sibling; El-Sheikh, 1997; Hall & Cummings, 1997).

Notably, children's distressed reactions to marital conflict, including the disposition to intervene, increase as a function of conflict histories (i.e., sensitization), and such reactions to marital conflict are associated with adjustment problems (Cummings & Davies, 1994a). Exposure to negative marital conflict styles also provides a negative role model for children's own conflict behavior.

Some evidence implicates children's learning of parental behavioral and attributional styles regarding conflict in children's own adjustment problems (Beach, 1995) although, surprisingly, this matter has been little examined. In sum, various and multiple lines of evidence implicate children's exposure to marital conflict in the development of children's adjustment problems, particularly in families with high marital conflict.

MARITAL CONFLICT AS PARENTING II: EFFECTS ON OTHER FORMS OF PARENTING (PARENT–CHILD INTERACTIONS)

A perhaps less surprising finding is that marital conflict is associated with differences in terms of parent–child relationships. A rather substantial literature supports relations between marital conflict and negative changes in parenting. Conflict between parents may drain them of the necessary emotional resources to operate effectively, or anger between parents may translate directly into angry interactions with children (Kerig, Cowan, & Cowan, 1993). Relationships marked by the presence of violence or a high frequency of overt conflict have been linked to inconsistent childrearing (Holden & Ritchie, 1991) and disciplinary problems (Stoneman, Brody, & Burke, 1989). Marital conflict has also been associated with increased parental negativity and intrusive control (Belsky, Youngblade, Rovine, & Volling, 1991) and low levels of parental warmth and responsiveness (Cox, Owen, Lewis, & Henderson, 1989). Parental rejection has been identified as a factor underlying the effects of marital conflict on children's externalizing and internalizing problems (Fauber, Forehand, Thomas, & Wierson, 1990). Specifically, parental behaviors such as withdrawal and hostility have been associated with social withdrawal, depression, and anxiety in children (Denham, 1989) in addition to externalizing problems (Sternberg et al., 1993). Marital conflict can thus be viewed as an important contributor to disruptions in the parenting process, which impacts a variety of indices of relevant parenting behavior and influence.

Marital relations are also predictive of the quality of the emotional bond or attachment that forms between parents and children, that is, the emotional security of the attachment between parents and children (Davies & Cummings, 1994). Studies show that increases in marital conflict during the first 9 months, or even prenatally (Cox & Owen, 1993), are linked to insecure attachment at one year of age. Another study found that high marital conflict when children were one year of age predicted insecure attachment at age 3 (Howes & Markman, 1989). Finally, children's relationships with their parents may also change because of the negative effects on their sense of trust or high regard for parents due to watching them behave in mean or hostile way toward each other. Thus, the impact of marital conflict on parenting may be quite direct (Owen & Cox, 1997).

To synthesize the information from studies of marital relations and parent–child relations, Erel and Burman (1995) performed a meta-analysis of 68 pertinent studies. The results indicated a moderately large relationship between marital conflict and parenting. Furthermore, significant relations were found between marital conflict and multiple forms of problems in parenting, and no evidence was found for a compensatory hypothesis, that is, that parents improved parenting to make up for the distress induced by marital problems. Moreover, the effects were uniform across 13 variables examined as potential moderators of these relations (e.g., gender of child or parent, child's age, child's birth order), suggesting relative homogeneity in this relationship regardless of differences in various types of child or family context. Based on this extensive meta-analysis, the authors concluded: "These findings suggest that, regardless of causality, positive parent–child relations are less likely to exist when the marital relationship is troubled" (pp. 128–129).

However, as Erel and Burman (1995) indicate, it is not yet clear why the relations between marital functioning and parent–child relations, and their subsequent effect on children, are found. One notion is that anger and hostility between the parents spills over into interactions with the child, particularly in distressed families (Margolin, Christensen, & John, 1996). This anger and hostility between the parent and child may increase the likelihood of abuse or alienating interactions, and ultimately result in the development of adjustment problems in kids. On the other hand, it may be that marital conflict is emotionally draining and causes parents to be less available emotionally for their children (Emery, 1982). Parents' preoccupation with their own marital problems may render them less able to recognize and respond to their children's needs and signals (Margolin, 1988). Children may perceive their parents' unavailability as a sign of personal rejection, which may contribute in various ways to the development of internalizing and/or externalizing problems (Fauber, Forehand, Thomas, & Wierson, 1990). Yet another possibility is that the disruption associated with marital discord causes parents to be ineffective or inconsistent in discipline (Mann & MacKenzie, 1996) and other parenting practices (Fauber & Long, 1991), increasing the likelihood of the development of behavior problems in the children.

In summary, while the research to date establishes that this is an intriguing area for family research pertinent to a broader concept of parenting as well as to an understanding of the influences on why parents behave as they do toward their children, there is much to learn, especially with regard to the particular psychological processes that underlie the relations between marital functioning and parent–child relationships.

INTERPARENTAL CONFLICT AS PARENTING: IT'S NOT WHETHER BUT HOW THE PARENTS FIGHT THAT MATTERS

A differentiation between marital conflict styles in terms of their effects on children is central to the perspective of interparental relations as parenting. Just as there are more optimal and less optimal ways for parent–child interactions to occur, it might be presumed that there are optimal and nonoptimal ways for parents to handle conflicts from the perspective of the children. In fact, evidence emerging in recent years indicates that some forms of marital conflict can be regarded as destructive from the child's perspective, whereas other forms can be regarded as constructive. Typically, these determinations have been based on children's emotional reactions in response to interparental conflict and/or links found between conflict behaviors and children's adjustment.

Cummings (1998) surveyed the evidence for constructive versus destructive conflict. At the time of that review, the evidence for this distinction was based on relatively loose and multiple criteria. The classification of marital conflict as destructive was based on links with children's distress and/or adjustment problems. Table 14.1 shows the behaviors that were identified as destructive. As the table indicates, these behaviors ranged across a broad spectrum, from physical aggression to withdrawal. Much less was known about the characteristics of constructive conflict. The classification of marital conflict behavior as constructive was based, again rather loosely, on links with non-negative emotional responses by children to these forms of conflict, or a reduction in negative responding to conflict with the introduction of these forms of conflict. The relatively recent finding of the highly ameliorative effects of the resolution of conflict

TABLE 14.1
CURRENT EMPIRICAL EVIDENCE OF DESTRUCTIVE AND
CONSTRUCTIVE FORMS OF MARITAL CONFLICT

Destructive Forms	Constructive Forms
Interpersonal aggression	Mutual respect
Aggression with objects	Emotional modulation
Verbal aggression	Positive communications
Threatening statements	Resolution of conflict
Intense anger	Progress toward resolution
Escalation	Resolution behind closed doors
Nonverbal anger or silent treatment	Later explanation of resolution
Withdrawal	Agreeing to disagree
Child-blaming conflicts	
Lack of resolution of conflict	

on children's functioning was an exciting result, suggesting one clear direction toward how the parents might handle conflicts better for the sake of the children. However, as Table 14.1 shows, the identification of constructive conflict has focused on instances of conflict resolution or various ways of communicating conflict resolution or progress toward resolution. Many questions remained, including questions about how conflicts could be more constructive from the children's perspective *during* the conflicts.

Notwithstanding the exciting nature of these findings, the listing of forms of constructive and destructive marital conflict behaviors from the perspective of the children compiled by Cummings (1998) was undoubtedly an incomplete one. The identification of the distinction between constructive and destructive conflict from the children's perspective is vital because it informs parents how to better parent in terms of this dimension of parenting. Given the repeated links of marital problems with children's problems, this matter has implications for children's mental health. Moreover, a likely bonus of handling conflicts better for the sake of the children is that parents will learn how to handle conflicts better for their own sake as well. A recent, rather hopeful, finding is that parents, even when undergoing the process of divorce, can be successfully educated to handle conflicts better (Shifflett & Cummings, 1999).

Accordingly, a major focus of ongoing research at our family studies laboratory at the University of Notre Dame is to further understand the distinctions between constructive and destructive marital conflict from the children's perspective. A conceptual advance that overcomes theoretical imprecision regarding the bases for this distinction is to define the relative constructiveness of marital conflict behaviors in terms of children's emotional reactions to the conflicts. From the perspective of the emotional security hypothesis, children's emotional reactions provide an index of the relative constructiveness versus destructiveness of conflict from the children's perspective (Davies & Cummings, 1994). Interestingly, recent work suggests that a dichotomy between constructive and destructive conflict may oversimplify matters, and that a more appropriate classification system is to distinguish between constructive, destructive, and productive conflicts (Goeke-Morey, 1999).

Ongoing prospective, longitudinal research studies at our laboratory are further advancing the study of these distinctions. A particular concern is with testing how different forms of marital conflict patterns, and children's responses to these interparental conflict behaviors and patterns, predict child, marital, and family functioning over time. This research will permit the confirmation (or disconfirmation) of the distinctions made on the study of children's reactions to analogue presentations of conflict stimuli. In addition, these studies also include comprehensive assessments of the other dimensions of parenting (e.g., attachment, parent–child discipline, control practices), which will permit a comparison of the relative effects of these different dimensions of parenting on children's development over time, as well as a thorough test of the interrelations among these various dimensions of parenting in predicting child development.

FUTURE DIRECTIONS

An important gap in terms of the big picture on research in this area is the need for relatively easy-to-administer, self-report measures (e.g., questionnaires) that easily allow investigators to differentiate between the occurrence of different forms of marital conflict behaviors in the home. That is, research to date is generally based on relatively labor-intensive laboratory, observational, or parental diary methodologies (Cummings, Goeke-Morey, & Dukewich, 2001). The limitation of such methodologies is that they are not readily accessible and may not be feasible for many researchers primarily concerned with other problems (e.g., parental abuse of children, parent–child attachment), and who simply wish to include an adequate assessment of interparental relations as one among several indices of parenting. As we have seen, children's reactions to marital conflict vary tremendously as a function of how parents handle their disputes and, in fact, some forms of marital conflict behaviors may even increase children's emotional security about family functioning (Cummings, Goeke-Morey, & Papp, 2001). Thus, it is essential that the measurement of marital conflict be sufficiently sophisticated. Advances in survey methodologies are particularly needed, since the availability of such methodologies would increase the potential currency of the assessment of marital functioning for large-scale studies of the effects of multiple dimensions of parenting on child development. Inadequate assessment approaches that blur important distinctions with regard to the nature of marital interactions will minimize the extent to which light can be shed on relations between this dimension of parenting and children's adjustment. In particular, no effects, or misleading effects, may result when assessments are too global or are imprecise for methodological or other reasons due to measurement problems or limitations.

Another gap is that relatively little is known about the effects of specific constructive, destructive, or productive marital conflict behaviors on parent–child relations. As we have shown, a case for the general relationship between marital conflict and parenting is well established (Erel & Burman, 1995). However, many questions remain about the details. That is, directions toward distinguishing between different marital conflict behaviors have focused on children's responding to conflict stimuli, but little is known about the carryover from marital conflict to specific parent–child interactions (for example, emotionality or parental control practices). There are multiple pathways by which specific marital conflict behaviors or patterns may have effects by causing changes in parent–child relationships. Notably, while the pathways between marital conflict, parenting, and child outcomes have been explored to a significant degree in terms of relatively global definitions of marital conflict as discord, little is known about this matter in terms of more differentiated distinctions between marital conflict behaviors. This matter is a significant question toward fuller understanding of the distinctions between constructive, destructive, and productive marital conflict behaviors in terms of child, parent–child, and family functioning.

CONCLUSION

The present paper makes a case for the parents' capacity to engage in effective conflict management and resolution as an important component of parenting. As we have seen, exciting and new directions toward more sophisticated and inclusive models of marital conflict and other aspects of parenting hold promise for a more comprehensive understanding of the role of the parents' behavior in influencing children's functioning and development over time. Future research on parenting also requires broader conceptualization and measurement of the broad range of environmental, biological, and genetic variables, and their interaction within the context of prospective, longitudinal research designs. The goal of the present paper has been to chart current progress and future directions towards understanding one particular piece of the puzzle regarding how parents influence children's development.

ACKNOWLEDGMENTS

Preparation of this paper was supported in part by a grant from the National Institute of Child Health and Human Development (HD 36261) to E. Mark Cummings.

REFERENCES

Amato, P. R., & Keith, B. (1991). Consequences of parental divorce for children's well-being: A meta-analysis. *Psychological Bulletin, 110*, 26–46.

Appel, A. E., & Holden, G. W. (1998). The co-occurrence of spouse and physical child abuse: A review and appraisal. *Journal of Family Psychology, 12*, 578–599.

Beach, B. (1995). *The relation between marital conflict and child adjustment: An examination of parental and child repertoires.* Unpublished manuscript.

Beardslee, W., Bemporad, J., Keller, M. B., & Klerman, G. L. (1983). Children of parents with a major affective disorder: a review. *American Journal of Psychiatry, 140*, 825–832.

Belsky, J., Youngblade, L., Rovine, M., & Volling, B. (1991). Patterns of marital change and parent–child interaction. *Journal of Marriage and the Family, 53*, 487–498.

Bradbury, T. N., & Fincham, F. D. (1990). Attributions in marriage: Review and critique. *Psychological Bulletin, 107*, 3–33.

Cox, A. D., Puckering, C., Pound, A., & Mills, M. (1987). The impact of maternal depression in young people. *Journal of Child Psychology and Psychiatry, 28*, 917–928.

Cox, M., J., & Owen, M. T. (1993, March). Marital conflict and conlfict negotiations: Effects on infant–mother and infant–father relationships. In M. Cox & J. Brooks-Gunn (Chairs), *Conflict in families: Causes and consequences.* Symposium conducted at the meeting of the Society for Research in Child Development, New Orleans, LA.

Cox, M. J., Owen, M. T., Lewis, J. M., & Henderson, V. K. (1989). Marriage, adult adjustment, and early parenting. *Child Development, 60*, 1015–1024.

Cummings, E. M. (1998). Children exposed to marital conflict and violence: Conceptual and theoretical directions. In G. W. Holden, R. Geffner, & E. N. Jouriles (Eds.), *Children exposed to martial violence: Theory, research, and applied issues* (pp. 257–288). Washington, DC: American Psychological Association.

Cummings, E. M., & Davies, P. T. (1994a). *Children and marital conflict: The impact of family dispute and resolution.* New York: Guilford Press.

Cummings, E. M., & Davies, P. T. (1994b). Maternal depression and child development [Annual research review]. *Journal of Child Psychology and Psychiatry, 35,* 73–112.

Cummings, E. M., Davies, P. T., & Campbell, S. B. (2000). *Principles, research and practice directions of developmental psychopathology: Applications for the study of childhood disorders and families.* New York: Guilford Publications.

Cummings, E. M., Goeke-Morey, M. C., & Dukewich, T. L. (2001). The study of relations between marital conflict and child adjustment: Challenges and new directions for methodology. In J. H. Grych & F. D. Fincham (Eds.), *Interparental Conflict and Child Development* (pp. 39–63). Cambridge, MA: Cambridge University Press.

Cummings, E. M., Goeke-Morey, M. C., & Papp, L. M. (2001). Couple conflict, children, and families: It's not just you and me, Babe. In A. Booth, A. Crouter, & M. Clements (Eds.), *Couples in Conflict* (pp. 117–147). Mahwah, NJ: Lawrence Erlbaum, Associates.

Davies, P. T., & Cummings, E. M. (1994). Marital conflict and child adjustment: An emotional security hypothesis. *Psychological Bulletin, 116,* 387–411.

Davies, P. T., & Cummings, E. M. (1998). Exploring children's emotional security as a mediator of the link between marital relations and child adjustment. *Child Development, 69,* 124–139.

Denham, S. A. (1989). Maternal affect and toddlers' socioemotional competence. *American Journal of Orthopsychiatry, 59,* 368–376.

Downey, G., & Coyne, J. C. (1990). Children of depressed parents: An integrative review. *Psychological Bulletin, 108,* 50–76.

El-Sheikh, M. (1997). Children's responses to adult–adult and mother–child arguments: The role of parental marital conflict and distress. *Journal of Family Psychology, 11,* 165–175.

El-Sheikh, M., & Cummings, E. M. (1997). Marital conflict, emotional regulation, and the adjustment of children of alcoholics. In K. C. Barrett (Ed.), *The communication of emotion: Current research from diverse perspectives. New directions for child development, no. 77* (pp. 25–44). San Francisco: Jossey-Bass.

Emery, R. E. (1982). Interparental conflict and the children of discord and divorce. *Psychological Bulletin, 92,* 310–330.

Emery, R. E. (1994). *Renegotiating family relationships.* New York and London: Guilford Press.

Erel, O., & Burman, B. (1995). Interrelatedness of marital relations and parent–child relations: A meta-analytic review. *Psychological Bulletin, 118,* 108–132.

Fauber, R., Forehand, R., Thomas, A. M., & Wierson, M. (1990). A mediational model of the impact of marital conflict on adolescent adjustment in intact and divorced families: The role of disrupted parenting. *Child Development, 61,* 1112–1123.

Fauber R. L., & Long, N. (1991). Children in context: The role of the family in child psychotherapy. *Journal of Consulting and Clinical Psychology, 59,* 813–820.

Fincham, F. D. (1998). Child Development and Marital Relations. *Child Development, 69,* 543–574.

Goeke-Morey, M. C. (1999). *Children and marital conflict: Exploring the distinction between constructive and destructive marital conflict behaviors.* Unpublished doctoral dissertation, University of Notre Dame, Notre Dame, IN.

Gottman, J. (1994). *Why marriages succeed or fail.* New York: Simon & Schuster.

Grych, J. H. (1998). Children's appraisals of interparental conflict: situational and contextual influences. *Journal of Family Psychology, 12,* 437–453.

Grych, J. H., & Fincham, F. D. (1990). Marital conflict and children's adjustment: A cognitive-contextual framework. *Psychological Bulletin, 108,* 267–290.

Hall, E., & Cummings, E. M. (1997). The effects of marital and parent–child conflicts on other family members: Grandmothers and grown children. *Family Relations, 46,* 135–144.

Harris, J. R. (1995). Where is the child's environment? A group socialization theory of development. *Psychological Review, 102*, 458–489.

Holden, G. W., & Ritchie, K. L. (1991). Linking extreme marital discord, child rearing, and child behavior problems: Evidence from battered women. *Child Development, 62*, 311–327.

Howes, P., & Markman, H. J. (1989). Marital quality and child functioning: A longitudinal investigation. *Child Development, 60*, 1044–1051.

Jaffe, P., Wolfe, D. A., Wilson, S. K., & Zak, L. (1986). Family violence and child adjustment: A comparative analysis of girls' and boys' behavioral symptoms. *American Journal of Psychiatry, 32*, 793–810.

Jouriles, E. N., Barling, J., & O'Leary, K. D. (1987). Predicting child behavior problems in maritally violent families. *Journal of Abnormal Child Psychology, 15*, 497–509.

Kerig, P. K., Cowan, P. A., & Cowan, C. P. (1993). Marital quality and gender differences in parent–child interaction. *Developmental Psychology, 29*, 931–939.

Mann, B. J., & MacKenzie, E. P. (1996). Pathways among marital functioning, parental behaviors, and child behavior problems in school-age boys. *Journal of Clinical Child Psychology, 25*, 183–191.

Margolin, G. (1988). Marital conflict is not marital conflict is not marital confect. In R. De, V. Peters, & R. McMahon (Eds.), *Social learning and systems approaches to marriage and the family* (pp. 193–216). New York: Brunner/Mazel.

Margolin, G., Christensen, A., & John, R. S. (1996). The continuance and spillover of everyday tensions in distressed and nondistressed families. *Journal of Family Psychology, 10*, 304–321.

McLanahan, S., & Sandefur, G. (1994). *Growing up with a single parent: What hurts, what helps.* Cambridge, MA: Harvard University Press.

Nixon, C. L., & Cummings, E. M. (1999). Sibling disability and children's reactivity to conflicts involving family members. *Journal of Family Psychology, 13*, 274–285.

Owen, M. T., & Cox, M. J. (1997). Marital conflict and the development of infant–parent attachment relationships. *Journal of Family Psychology, 11*, 152–164.

Shifflett, K., & Cummings, E. M. (1999). A program for educating parents about the effects of divorce and conflict on children. *Family Relations, 48*, 79–98.

Sternberg, K. J., Lamb, M. E., Greenbaum, C., Cicchetti, D., Dawud, S., Cortes, R. M., Krispin, O., & Lorey, F. (1993). Effects of domestic violence on children's behavior problems and depression. *Developmental Psychology, 29*, 44–52.

Stoneman, Z., Brody, G. H., & Burke, M. (1989). Sibling temperaments and maternal and paternal perceptions of marital, family, and personal functioning. *Journal of Marriage and the Family, 51*, 99–113.

Stoneman, Z., Brody, G. H., Churchill, S. L., & Winn, L. L. (1999). Effects of residential instability on head start children and their relationships with older sibling: Influences of child emotionality and conflict between family caregivers. *Child Development, 70*, 1246–1262.

Whisman, M. (2001). The association between depression and marital dissatisfaction. In S. R. H. Beach (Ed.), *Marital and family processes in depression: A scientific foundation for clinical practice* (pp. 3–24) Washington, DC: American Psychological Association.

15

Parents, Peers, and the Process of Socialization in Primates

Stephen J. Suomi

National Institutes of Health

INTRODUCTION

An apparent paradox concerning the importance of parenting for the development of the child has emerged over the past decade. On the one hand, recent findings from neurobiological research with animals have emphasized the critical role that early rearing experiences, particularly those provided by parents, can play in shaping brain development, ultimately influencing a wide range of biological and behavioral systems throughout the life span and perhaps beyond (e.g., Francis, Champagne, Liu, & Meaney, 1999). At the same time, an increasing number of developmental researchers and practitioners have come to accept the basic principles underlying the theory of attachment formulated by Bowlby (1969, 1988), especially the perceived importance of an infant's initial attachment relationship with his or her mother (*cf.* Cassidy & Shaver, 1999).

On the other hand, the basic assumption that parenting *per se* is important for a child's development has itself come under increased scrutiny on a variety of fronts. Behavioral geneticists have provided one source of criticism, pointing to

Address correspondence to: Stephen J. Suomi, Phone: 301-496-9550, Fax: 301-496-0630, e-mail: ss148k@nih.gov consistent findings of generally unimpressive contributions of "shared" (i.e., family) environmental influences for many developmental phenomena. Some advocates of this position have also suggested that most (if not all) of the so-called "parenting effects" previously reported in the literature may in fact be more a product of the parents' genes than a result of their actual interactions with their children (e.g., Bouchard, 1997). Others, reviewing the extant socialization literature, have concluded that with respect to the social behavior, attitudes, and personality characteristics of adolescents and young adults, parents have far less influence on their offspring than do peers and/or other extrafamilial agents (e.g., Harris, 1995, 1998). On another front, several studies with animals have recently demonstrated considerable "plasticity" in neuronal growth and synaptic connectivity well into adulthood, suggesting that early experiences may not always have permanent or even lasting consequences for adult central nervous system functioning (e.g., Greenough, Cohen, & Juraska, 1999).

These new findings and criticisms of previous socialization research have led to a vigorous debate among developmental scientists, practitioners, and even the public at large around the question "Do parents matter?" (e.g., Gladwell, 1998). The protagonists typically have pitted parents against peers as competing forces in the socialization process, with arguments centering largely around the relative influence—or lack thereof—of each. Indeed, this either-or argument readily brings to mind previous debates about the relative roles of nature and nurture in shaping a child's development—debates that have been ongoing since the time of Aristotle. Today, it is widely recognized that development is ultimately the product of both nature and nurture and, more importantly, the complex and dynamic ways in which they interact to shape individual ontogeny (cf. Cairns, Elder, & Costello, 1996).

In a similar vein, most primatologists who study development in general and the socialization process in particular would likely view the "parents vs. peers" debate as largely missing the point. Instead, extensive data from both laboratory and field studies of many primate species have consistently supported the notion that both parents and peers play crucial roles in socializing infants, juveniles, adolescents, and even adults. Indeed, these roles, while clearly distinctive, appear to complement each other in shaping an individual monkey's or ape's social—and even biological—development.

SPECIES-NORMATIVE DEVELOPMENT OF MATERNAL AND PEER RELATIONSHIPS IN MACAQUE MONKEYS

For the vast majority of primate species, parenting largely boils down to mothering, inasmuch as in these species the primary caregiver is almost always the biological mother, and males appear to play minimal roles in the initial rearing of their offspring. Interestingly, the exceptions to this general primate pattern of primary maternal responsibility for childrearing are largely limited to the relatively few species in which monogamy is also the species-normative pattern. The more typical pattern and sequence of relationship development is for infants to establish an initial, highly specific relationship with their biological mother and subsequently to develop separate relationships with multiple peers, relationships that are fundamentally different from that with their mother. Some of the most comprehensive data documenting these phenomena have come from longitudinal studies of rhesus monkeys (*Macaca mulatta*), a highly adaptive species of macaque monkeys.

Rhesus monkeys in their natural habitats typically reside in large, distinctive social groups ("troops") that can range in size from two dozen to two hundred or more individuals. Every troop is composed of several female-headed families each spanning three or more generations of kin, plus numerous immigrant adult males. This form of social group organization derives from the fact that all rhesus monkey females spend their entire life in the troop in which they were born, whereas virtually all males emigrate from their natal troop around the time of puberty and eventually join other troops (Lindburg, 1971). Rhesus monkey troops are also characterized by multiple social dominance relationships, including distinctive hierarchies both between and within families, as well as a hierarchy among the immigrant adult males (Sade, 1967).

In these social settings, rhesus monkey infants begin life completely dependent on their mother for survival, receiving from her all nourishment, physical warmth and other basic biological support, and psychological comfort derived from tactile contact, not to mention protection from the elements, potential predators, and even other troop members (*cf.* Harlow, Harlow, & Hansen, 1963; Hinde, Rowell, & Spencer-Booth, 1964). Infants spend virtually all of their first month of life in physical contact with or within arm's reach of their mother. During this time a strong and enduring social bond inevitably develops between mother and infant, recognized by Bowlby (1969) to be basically homologous with the mother–infant attachment relationship universally seen in all human cultures.

Rhesus monkey infants are inherently curious (Harlow, 1953), and like human infants, once they have become attached to their mother they quickly learn to use her as a secure base from which to organize the exploration of their immediate environment, beginning as early as their second month of life. Shortly thereafter, they start to spend increasing amounts of time engaging in social interactions with other troop members. Because rhesus monkeys are generally seasonal breeders (i.e., most conceptions within any given troop typically occur within the same 2- to 3-month period every year, a likely product of seasonal variability in male sperm counts), most infants grow up with numerous same-age peers readily available as potential interaction partners. Seasonal breeding also effectively guarantees that the siblings of young infants (and their siblings' peers) will always be at least 1 (or even 2) years older, an age gap roughly equivalent to 4 (or 8) years in human developmental terms. Therefore, perhaps it is not surprising that young rhesus monkeys soon come to prefer to interact with others their age, related or not, than to interact with older relatives or nonrelatives, and by the time of weaning most rhesus monkey youngsters typically spend several hours each day playing with same-age peers. Indeed, peer interactions continue to increase in both frequency and complexity throughout the rest of the young monkeys' first year of life. In contrast, the amount of time youngsters spend interacting with their mother declines substantially after weaning, and this decline typically accelerates if the mother becomes pregnant again (Berman, Rasmussen, & Suomi, 1993).

Interactions with multiple peers continue at high and essentially stable rates until the onset of puberty (Ruppenthal, Harlow, Eisele, Harlow, & Suomi, 1974). During this time peer play becomes increasingly gender-specific, sex segregated (i.e., males tend to play more with males and females with females), and involves behavioral sequences that appear to simulate virtually all adult social activities, including courtship and reproductive behaviors as well as dominance–aggressive interactions. By the end of their third year, rhesus monkey juveniles have had ample opportunity to develop, practice, and perfect behavioral routines that will be crucial for normal functioning when they become adults. At the same time, juveniles retain unique social ties with their mother, even as she becomes increasingly involved with their younger siblings. They continue to use her as a secure base, routinely seek physical contact with her under stressful circumstances, and actively solicit her participation (and respond to her solicitations) in agonistic exchanges with other monkeys both inside and outside their troop (Suomi, 1998).

The onset of puberty, usually during the fourth year for rhesus monkeys growing up in the wild, is associated with major transitions in social relationships for both genders. Although females remain in their natal troop throughout adolescence and thereafter, their postpubertal interactions with peers decline dramatically as they redirect most of their social activities toward matrilineal kin, including both their mothers and the offspring they subsequently bear and rear. Nevertheless, females do retain some aspects of previous relationships with female peers throughout their adult lives, although their mutual activities tend to be greatly diminished in frequency and largely limited to grooming bouts and (paradoxically) agonistic encounters rather than play.

Pubertal males, by contrast, leave both their family and their natal troop permanently, typically joining all-male "gangs" for varying periods before attempting to enter a different troop. In doing so, these young males effectively terminate their relationship with their mother and all other female relatives, inasmuch as they are not permitted to reenter their natal troop once they have emigrated, although some males are able to reunite with older brothers by joining troops into which the older brothers previously immigrated. Adolescent males also effectively terminate their relationships with most of their natal group peers, including all females. A few of these males may continue to interact with male peers from their natal troop if those males also join the same all-male gang or immigrate into the same troop as themselves, but most lose all contact with both family and familiar peers. Not surprisingly, this period of transition represents a time of major stress for adolescent and young adult males, with a mortality rate that approaches 50% in some wild monkey populations (Dittus, 1979). Some surviving males remain in their new troop for the rest of their lives, whereas other males may transfer from one troop to another several times during their adult years, although they never go back to their natal troop (Berard, 1989).

In summary, rhesus monkey infants develop distinctive social relationships with their mothers and with same-age peers during their initial weeks and months of life, respectively, and these specific relationships are maintained at least until puberty for males and throughout the life span for females. However, the relationships differ substantially from one another in several fundamental ways. An infant's attachment relationship with its mother is firmly established long before it begins any interactions with peers. The resulting attachment is specific to its mother, whereas the infant typically develops multiple relationships with several different peers. The infant's frequency and duration of interactions with its mother are greatest during its first month of life and decline steadily thereafter, especially following the birth of younger siblings. By contrast, its frequency and duration of interactions with peers increase steadily throughout the first year and remain at relatively high levels until puberty. The specific behaviors that comprise mother–infant relationships are very different from those that are typically seen in peer interactions, and they tend to change more over time in both form and relative reciprocity in the former than in the latter type of relationship (Suomi, 1979). Finally, the attachment relationships that male and female monkeys develop with their mothers tend to be far more similar to each other, at least until puberty, than are the relationships they develop with their respective peers, which typically become increasingly sex-segrated over the same period of development (Harlow & Lauersdorf, 1974).

On the other hand, it can be argued that despite (if not because of) these fundamental differences, a young monkey's relationships with its mother and its peers actually serve to complement, rather than compete with, each other in shaping its overall course of biobehavioral development. The two types of relationships emerge sequentially rather than simultaneously, with the first subsequently declining in relative frequency and duration of interactions over the very same chronological period that the second is increasing. Each type of relationship provides the young monkey with specific stimulation that the other either can not (e.g., nursing) or typically does not (e.g., extended ventral contact with mother, play with peers). As infant monkeys grow older their interactions with the mother increasingly take place in different physical settings and social contexts than their interactions with peers. This is not to say that the two sets of relationships are completely independent of one another; to the contrary, mothers can clearly influence the nature of their offspring's interactions with peers, if not vice versa, as will be discussed below.

The distinctive social relationships that rhesus monkeys develop with their mother and with their peers, including the characteristic features of each, can be found in all other macaque species (Lindburg, 1991), if not in most other old-world monkeys and apes as well. To be sure, there are species differences in some aspects of the respective relationships, especially those involving mothers. For example, bonnet macaque (*Macacca radiata*) mothers are generally more likely to share some aspects of infant caregiving with females from other matrilines than are rhesus or pigtail macaque (*Macaca nemestrina*) mothers (Rosenblum, 1971), while Barbary macaque (*Macaca silvana*) mothers are more likely to permit adult males to handle their newborn infants (Deag & Crook, 1971). Stumptail macaque (*Macaca arctoides*) juvenile and adolescent males are more likely to engage in reconciliation behavior following a bout of physical aggression with peers than are their rhesus monkey counterparts (deWaal & Johanowicz, 1993). Nevertheless, these species differences seem relatively minor in comparison, with the obvious similarities seen in mother–infant relationships on the one hand, and in patterns of peer interaction on the other, across all species of macaques, if not most other advanced primates. Indeed, such cross-species similarity in the differential yet complementary development of maternal and peer relationships suggests that they are in large part a product of primate evolution.

DEVELOPMENTAL CONSEQUENCES OF VARIATION IN MONKEY MOTHER–INFANT RELATIONSHIPS

Although there is strong consistency both between and within macaque monkey species in the general pattern of mother–infant and peer relationships, there is also considerable interindividual variability in many specific aspects of these respective relationships. For example, numerous studies carried out in both field and captive environments have found that monkey mothers tend to spend more time in ventral contact with their firstborn infants, wean them later, and punish them less often during weaning than they do with their subsequent offspring (e.g., Berman, 1982; Mitchell, Ruppenthal, Raymond, & Harlow, 1966). One consequence of this differential maternal treatment is that first-born infants spend less time interacting with peers during their first year of life than will their subsequent siblings. Other studies have consistently shown that mothers who rank relatively high in their troop's female dominance hierarchy typically develop maternal styles that are laissez-faire in nature, permitting their infants to explore and engage their physical and social environment essentially at will, whereas low-ranking mothers typically are much more restrictive of their infant's exploratory efforts and attempts to play with peers. The standard interpretation of these findings is that low-ranking mothers risk reprisal from others if they attempt to intervene whenever their infant is threatened, so they minimize such risk by restricting its exploration and opportunities for interaction with peers (e.g., Altmann, 1980). Perhaps as a result, their offspring typically become low-ranking themselves within their peer group. Additional studies carried out in both field and captive settings have reported that mothers generally become more restrictive and increase their levels of infant monitoring when their immediate social environment becomes less stable, such as when major changes in adult female dominance hierarchies take place or when new males attempt to join the social group (Suomi, 1999).

Some recent laboratory studies have demonstrated that even relatively short-term environmental perturbations can influence the relationship between a mother and her offspring, with striking long-term behavioral and even physiological consequences for the offspring. Rosenblum and his colleagues studied the effects of systematically manipulating ease of access to food for bonnet macaque mothers and their infants in a captive setting by providing some groups of mothers and infants with essentially an *ad libitum* supply of food (low-foraging demand—LFD). Other groups were provided with a food supply that was switched back and forth biweekly from *ad libitum* availability to a high-foraging-demand situation, in which mothers had to spend several hours each day foraging in order to maintain their normal dietary intake (variable foraging demand—VFD). These differential feeding schedules were maintained for a total of 14 consecutive weeks, beginning when the infants were approximately 3 months old. The researchers found that when LFD and VFD mother–infant dyads were subsequently challenged by brief introductions into a novel playroom, VFD infants left their mothers to explore less frequently and engaged in less social play than LFD infants, reflecting less "secure" attachments to their mothers (Andrews & Rosenblum, 1991).

Surprising long-term consequences of the 14-week period of VFD treatment during infancy emerged when the offspring of VFD and LFD were 3 years old and underwent two pharmacological challenges. The VFD monkeys were behaviorally and physiologically hyperresponsive to injections of yohimbine, a noradrenergic probe, and were hyporesponsive to injections of mCPP, a serotonergic probe, relative to the LFD juvenile-age monkeys. Moreover, at 4 years of age VFD monkeys exhibited persistently elevated cerebrospinal fluid (CSF) concentrations of corticotropiin-releasing factor (CRH) relative to those of LFD adolescents (Coplan et al., 1996). Presumably, these long-term effects resulted from the differential treatment of infants by VFD and LFD mothers during the 14-week period of differential foraging, rather than differential foraging by the infants themselves, who during that period had not yet been weaned, i.e., "a consequence of less secure attachment" (Andrews & Rosenblum, 1991, p. 686). These findings thus demonstrate that seemingly minor environmental pertubatrions can have significant, indeed dramatic, behavioral and physiological consequences that become apparent only later in life.

The extent to which mothers' rearing styles can affect not only their offspring but also their troop as a whole can be seen in a long-term study of free-ranging rhesus monkey troops undergoing steady population growth (Berman, Rasmussen, & Suomi, 1997). These investigators found that mothers living in small troops tended to be laissez-faire in their maternal style relative to mothers living in larger troops. Small-troop mothers rarely restricted their infants' early exploratory efforts, seldom intervened in their subsequent interactions with peers, and spent relatively little time monitoring their behavior after weaning. Their infants, in turn, usually established strong, positive relationships with their nonkin peers prior to puberty, and those positive relationships tended to be maintained among the females throughout adolescence and into adulthood. Berman et al. (1997) found these small troops to be quite cohesive and relatively peaceful.

However, as each troop expanded its population, mothers began to change their basic style of infant care in terms of increasing restriction, intervention, and monitoring of offspring. Their infants consequently had fewer opportunities to interact with age-mates from other families, and those interactions were often truncated by their mothers' active interventions. The play bouts that did occur tended to be less frequent, briefer in duration, and less affectively positive than had been the case when the troop was smaller. These young monkeys thus did not have the same opportunities to develop extensive social relationships with peers from other families prior to puberty as did cohorts from previous years. Moreover, their interactions with nonkin peers did not improve much with age, remaining infrequent and often hostile throughout adolescence and into adulthood. Not surprisingly, the general atmosphere within these now-larger troops became increasingly tense and involved less cooperation between matrilines than in previous years when the troops had been smaller (Suomi, 1999).

Over time these large troops eventually broke up, usually splintering after a long episode of particularly intense interfamily aggression. The breakups typically occurred along matrilines, resulting in several small "splinter" troops that quickly developed their own distinctive identity. Of special interest was the finding that mothers in these new small troops tended to be laissez-faire in their respective maternal styles, and once again their offspring developed extensive positive play partnerships with peers from other families. However, as the splinter groups started expanding in population themselves, the mothers once again began restricting their infants' social world, thus beginning the cycle anew.

The findings of the Berman et al. (1997) study provide compelling evidence that rhesus monkey mothers are capable of adjusting their maternal style to deal with changes in their troop's social demographic characteristics. But the larger lesson from this study is that the mothers' adaptations had long-term consequences not only for their offspring and their larger family but also for their offsprings' relationships with peers and other troop members—indeed, for the basic identity of the troop as a whole. This case demonstrates that while changes at the "community" level can affect how a mother raises her infants, changes in those individual dyadic relationships can ultimately influence the very nature of the troop itself. Thus, relationships between individual mothers and their infants, family allegiances, and troop characteristics appear to be inextricably linked in a system involving long-term reciprocal feedback.

The research cited above clearly suggests that how a mother rears her infant can influence not only its own behavioral and physiological development but also the nature of other social relationships it develops throughout its childhood years. A much less extensive literature suggests that variation in experience with peers can likewise influence a young monkey's emerging social-behavioral repertoire. For example, individual female monkeys exposed only to peer groups that were otherwise exclusively male developed play repertoires that had much higher frequencies of male-like rough-and-tumble play than female monkeys provided with at least one female playmate (Goldfoot, Wallen, Neff, McBrair, & Goy, 1984). Rhesus monkey juveniles introduced to peer groups of slightly older stumptail macaques subsequently exhibited a more "stumptail-like" pattern of aggressive and reconciliation behavior than rhesus monkey juveniles introduced to comparable groups of slightly older conspecifics (deWaal & Johanowicz, 1993). In both of these studies, however, the young rhesus monkey subjects were no longer living with their mothers, so it was not possible to determine whether these sorts of experiences with atypical peer groups could influence their relationship with their mother as well.

SHORT- AND LONG-TERM CONSE-QUENCES OF PEER AND MATERNAL DEPRIVATION ON RHESUS MONKEY BIOBEHAVIORAL DEVELOPMENT

A very different issue concerns the possible developmental consequences of being reared in the **absence** of an established relationship with one's mother or with peers. A few experimental studies carried out in the 1960's addressed this issue with respect to peer relationships by having rhesus monkey mothers rear their infants in dyad cages for varying periods of time (e.g., 4 vs. 8 months) before giving the infants the opportunity to interact with peers (Alexander & Harlow, 1965; Harlow & Harlow, 1969).

The results of these "mother-only" rearing experiments were relatively clear-cut: Monkeys whose first exposure to peers was delayed tended to be contact-shy and engaged in significantly less social play and significantly more physical aggression toward age-mates than control subjects who had access to peers from birth onward. Moreover, the longer the duration of initial peer deprivation, the greater in magnitude were these behavioral differences from the control subjects. Unfortunately, these studies did not include any long-term follow-up beyond the first year of life, nor were any measures of physiological activity obtained from either the peer-deprived or control monkeys.

Much more is known about the consequences of rearing rhesus monkey infants away from their mothers (and other adults) but with continuous exposure to peers from their first month of life onward. In several studies of peer-only rearing, infants have been separated from their biological mothers at birth, hand-reared in a neonatal nursery for their first month of life, housed with same-aged, like-reared peers for the rest of their first 6 months, and then moved into larger social groups containing both peer-reared and mother-reared age-mates. During their initial months, these infants readily develop strong social attachment bonds to each other, much as mother-reared infants develop attachments to their own mothers (Chamove, Rosenblum, & Harlow, 1973; Harlow, 1969). However, because peers are not nearly as effective as typical monkey mothers in reducing fear in the face of novelty or in providing a "secure base" for exploration, the attachment relationships that these peer-reared infants develop are almost always "anxious" in nature (Suomi, 1995). As a result, while peer-reared monkeys show completely normal physical and motor development, their early exploratory behavior is somewhat limited. They seem reluctant to approach novel objects and tend to be shy in initial encounters with unfamiliar peers (Suomi, 2000).

When peer-reared youngsters interact with their same-age cage mates in familiar settings, their emerging social play repertoires are usually retarded in both frequency and complexity. One explanation for their relatively poor play performance is that their cage mates have to serve both as attachment figures and playmates, a dual role that neither mothers nor mother-reared peers have to fulfill; another is that they face difficulties in developing sophisticated play repertoires with basically incompetent play partners. Perhaps as a result of either or both of these factors, peer-reared youngsters typically drop to the bottom of their respective dominance hierarchies when they are grouped with mother-reared monkeys their own age (Higley et al., 1996). Moreover, peer-reared monkeys consistently exhibit more extreme behavioral, adrenocortical, and noradrenergic reactions to social separations than their mother-reared age-mates even after they have been living in the same social groups for extended periods. Such differences in prototypical biobehavioral reactions to separation persist from infancy to adolescence, if not beyond (Higley & Suomi, 1989).

Other studies have found that early peer-rearing tends to make monkeys more impulsive, especially if they are males. Peer-reared males initially exhibit aggressive tendencies in the context of juvenile play; as they approach puberty, the frequency and severity of their aggressive episodes typically exceeds those of mother-reared group members of similar age. Peer-reared females tend to groom (and be groomed by) others in their social group less frequently and for shorter durations than their mother-reared counterparts and, as noted above, usually stay at the bottom of their respective dominance hierarchies. These differences in aggression, grooming, and dominance remain relatively robust throughout the preadolescent and adolescent years (Higley, Suomi, & Linnoila, 1996). Peer-reared monkeys also consistently show lower cerebrospinal fluid (CSF) concentrations of 5-hydroxyindoleacetic acid

(5-HIAA), the primary central serotonin metabolite, than their mother-reared counterparts. These group differences in 5-HIAA concentrations appear well before 6 months of age and remain stable at least throughout adolescence and into early adulthood (Higley & Suomi, 1996).

Other laboratory studies utilizing peer-reared monkeys have disclosed additional differences with their mother-reared counterparts as they mature. For example, peer-reared adolescent and adult males require larger doses of the anesthetic ketamine to reach a comparable state of sedation. They also exhibit significantly higher rates of whole-brain glucose metabolism under mild isoflurane anesthesia, as determined by positron emission tomography (PET) imaging, than mother-reared controls (Doudet et al., 1995). Additionally, peer-reared adolescent monkeys consistently consume larger amounts of alcohol under comparable *ad libitum* conditions than their mother-reared age-mates (Higley, Hasert, Suomi, & Linnoila, 1991). Recent follow-up studies have demonstrated that the peer-reared subjects quickly develop a greater tolerance for alcohol; this can be predicted by their CNS serotonin turnover rates (Higley et al., in press), which in turn appear to be associated with differential serotonin transporter availability (Heinz et al., 1998). Other recent studies have demonstrated an interaction between allelic variation in the serotonin transporter gene (5-HTT) and early attachment experience for CSF 5-HIAA concentrations on the one hand, and neonatal measures of visual orienting capabilities on the other, such that the "short" 5-HTT allele is associated with deficits in both measures for peer-reared, but not mother-reared, rhesus monkey adolescents and infants, respectively (Bennett et al., in press; Champoux et al., 1999).

An additional risk that peer-reared females carry into adulthood concerns their maternal behavior. Peer-reared mothers are significantly more likely to exhibit neglectful and/or abusive treatment of their firstborn offspring than are their mother-reared counterparts, although their risk for inadequate maternal care is not nearly as great as is the case for females reared in social isolation; moreover, their care of subsequent offspring tends to improve dramatically (Ruppenthal, Arling, Harlow, Sackett, & Suomi, 1976). Nevertheless, most multiparous mothers who experienced early peer-rearing continue to exhibit nonnormative developmental changes in ventral contact with their offspring throughout the whole of their reproductive years (Champoux, Byrne, Delizio, & Suomi, 1992).

As an aside, several studies of monkeys reared by their mothers in naturalistic social groups have demonstrated strong continuities between the type of attachment relationship a female infant develops with her mother and the type of attachment relationship she develops with her own infant(s) when she becomes a mother herself. In particular, the pattern of ventral contact a female infant has with her mother (or mother substitute) during her initial months of life is a powerful predictor of the pattern of ventral contact she will have with her own infants during their first 6 months of life (e.g., Fairbanks, 1989). In addition, laboratory studies have found that this predictive cross-generational relationship is apparently as strong in females who were foster-reared from birth by unrelated multiparous females as it is for females reared by their biological mothers, strongly suggesting that cross-generational transmission of at least one fundamental component of mother–infant attachment—patterning of mutual ventral contact—necessarily involves non-genetic mechanisms (Suomi & Levine, 1998). What those nongenetic mechanisms might be, and through what developmental processes they might act, are questions at the heart of ongoing investigations.

To summarize, early rearing by peers seems to make rhesus monkey infants both more highly reactive to environmental challenges and more impulsive, and their resulting developmental trajectories tend to persist in that vein long after their period of exclusive exposure to peers has been completed and they have been living in more species-typical social groups. Indeed, some effects of early peer rearing may well be passed on to the next generation via aberrant patterns of maternal care, as appears to be the case for both highly reactive and impulsive mothers rearing infants in their natural habitat. As noted by Bowlby and other attachment theorists for the human case, the effects of inadequate early social attachments may be both life-long and cross-generational in nature. For monkeys, the type of attachment relationship an infant establishes with its mother (or mother substitute) can markedly affect its biobehavioral developmental trajectory, even after its interactions with her have ceased.

SUMMARY

Throughout this chapter it has been argued that the process of socialization for rhesus monkeys and other primate species inevitably and importantly involves both mothers and peers throughout development. Three sets of evidence have been presented in support of this argument. First, normative studies of longitudinal development in these species consistently have found that monkey infants characteristically establish strong attachment bonds with their biological mothers in their initial weeks of life and subsequently develop distinctively different relationships with multiple peers that flourish throughout their juvenile years. These relationships appear to complement, rather than compete with, one another with respect to the specific behaviors that characterize each type of relationship, the physical and social contexts in which each type of relationship is expressed, and the manner in which each type of relationship changes as the monkeys mature. Second, both laboratory and field studies have demonstrated that how a mother rears her infant can significantly influence not only its own behavioral development and physiological functioning from infancy to adulthood but also the nature of relationships it develops with other members of its social group, including peers. A less extensive set of findings suggests that exposure to particular groups of peers can also influence a monkeys emerging behavioral repertoire. Finally, numerous laboratory studies have found that rearing monkeys from birth in the absence of the opportunity to establish relationships with either mothers or peers can have profound consequences across a wide range of behavioral and physiological domains. The findings are particularly striking for monkeys reared without mothers or appropriate foster mother substitutes. Indeed, to paraphrase Gladwell's (1998) previously cited question "Do parents matter?" the answer, at least for monkeys, seems obvious: Mothers clearly matter . . . but so do peers.

REFERENCES

Alexander, B. K., & Harlow, H. F. (1965). Social behavior of juvenile rhesus monkeys subjected to differential rearing conditions during the first 6 months of life. *Zoologische Jahrbuche Physiologie, 60,* 167–174.

Andrews, M. W., & Rosenblum, L. A. (1991). Security of attachment in infants raised in variable- or low-demand environments. *Child Development, 62,* 686–693.

Arling, G. L., & Harlow, H. F. (1967). Effects of social deprivation on maternal behavior of rhesus monkeys. *Journal of Comparative and Physiological Psychology, 64,* 371–377.

Altmann, J. (1980). *Baboon mothers and infants.* Cambridge, MA: Harvard University Press.

Bennett, A. J., Lesch, K. P., Heils, A., Long, J., Lorenz, J., Shoaf, S. E., Champoux, M., Suomi, S. J., Linnoila, M., & Higley, J. D. (in press). Early experience and serotonin transporter gene variation interact to influence primate CNS function. *Molecular Psychiatry.*

Berard, J. (1989). Male life histories. *Puerto Rican Health Sciences Journal, 8,* 47–58.

Berman, C. M. (1982). The ontogeny of social relationships with group companions among free-ranging rhesus monkeys: I. Social networks and differentiation. *Animal Behavior, 30,* 149–162.

Berman, C. M. (1992). Immature siblings and mother–infant relationships among free-ranging rhesus monkeys on Cayo Santiago. *Animal Behavior, 44,* 247–258.

Berman, C. M., Rasmussen, K. L. R., & Suomi, S. J. (1993). Reproductive consequences of maternal care patterns during estrus among free-ranging rhesus monkeys. *Behavioral Ecology and Sociobiology, 32,* 391–399.

Berman, C. M., Rasmussen, K. L. R., & Suomi, S. J. (1997). Group size, infant development, and social networks: A natural experiment with free-ranging rhesus monkeys. *Animal Behavior, 53,* 405–421.

Bouchard, T. (1997). Experience Producing Drive theory: How genes drive experience and shape personality. *Acta Paediatrica Supplement, 422,* 60–64.

Bowlby, J. (1969). *Attachment.* New York: Basic Books.

Bowlby, J. (1988). *A secure-base.* New York: Basic Books.

Cairns, R. B., Elder, G. H., & Costello, E. J. (Eds.). (1996). *Developmental science.* Cambridge, UK: Cambridge University Press.

Cassidy, J., & Shaver, P. R. (Eds.). (1999). *Handbook of attachment: Theory, research, and clinical applications.* New York: Guilford Press.

Chamove, A. S., Rosenblum, L. A., & Harlow, H. F. (1973). Monkeys (*Macaca mulatta*) raised only with peers. A pilot study. *Animal Behavior, 21,* 316–325.

Champoux, M., Bennett, A. J., Lesch, K. P., Heils, A., Nielson, D. A., Higley, J. D., & Suomi, S. J. (1999). *Society for Neurosciences Abstracts, 25,* 69.

Champoux, M., Byrne, E., Delizio, R. D., & Suomi, S. J. (1992). Motherless mothers revisited: Rhesus maternal behavior and rearing history. *Primates, 33,* 251–255.

Coplan, J. D., Andrews, M. W. Rosenblum, L. A., Owens, M. J., Friedman, S., Gorman, J. M., & Nemeroff, C. B. (1996). Persistent elevations of cerebrospinal fluid concentrations of corticotrophin releasing factor in adult nonhuman primates exposed to early-life stressors: implications for the pathophysiology of mood and anxiety disorders. *Proceedings of the National Academy of Sciences, 93,* 1619–1623.

Deag, J., & Crook, J. (1971). Social behavior and "agonistic buffering" in the wild Barbary macaque (*Macaca silvana*). *Folia Primatologia, 15,* 183–200.

DeWaal, F. B. M., & Johanowicz, D. L. (1993). Modification of reconciliation behavior through social experience: An experiment with two macaque species. *Child Development, 64,* 897–908.

Dittus, W. P. G. (1979). The evolution of behaviors regulating density and age-specific sex ratios in a primate population. *Behaviour, 69,* 265–302.

Doudet, D., Hommer, D., Higley, J. D., Andreason, P. J., Moneman, R., Suomi, S. J., & Linnoila, M. (1995). Cerebral glucose metabolism, CSF 5-HIAA, and aggressive behavior in rhesus monkeys. *American Journal of Psychiatry, 152,* 1782–1787.

Fairbanks, L. A. (1989). Early experience and cross-generational continuity of mother–infant contact in vervet monkeys. *Developmental Psychobiology, 22,* 669–681.

Francis, D. D., Champagne, F. A., Liu, D., & Meaney, M. J. (1999). Maternal care, gene expression, and the development of individual differences in stress reactivity. *Annals of the New York Academy of Science, 896,* 66–84.

Gladwell, M. (1998, August 17). Do parents matter? *New Yorker,* 54–64.

Goldfoot, D. A., Wallen, K., Neff, D. A., McBrair, M. C., & Goy, R. W. (1984). Social influences on the display of sexually dimorphic behavior in thesus monkeys: Isosexual rearing. *Archives of Sexual Behavior, 13,* 395–412.

Greenough, W. T., Cohen, N. J., & Juraska, J. M. (1999). New neurons in old brains: Learning to survive? *Nature Neuroscience, 3,* 203–205.

Harlow, H. F. (1953). Mice, monkeys, men, and motives. *Psychological Review, 60,* 23–35.

Harlow, H. F. (1969). Age-mate or peer affectional system. In D. S. Lehrman, R. A. Hinde, & E. Shaw (Eds.), *Advances in the study of behavior,* (Vol. 2., pp. 333–383). New York: Academic Press.

Harlow, H. F., & Harlow, M. K. (1969). Effects of various mother–infants relationships on rhesus monkey behaviors. In B. M. Foss (Ed.), *Determinants of infant behaviours* (Vol. 4, pp. 15–36). London: Metheun.

Harlow, H. F., Harlow, M. K., & Hansen, E. W. (1963). The maternal affectional system of rhesus monkeys. In H. L. Rheingold (Ed.), *Maternal behavior in mammals* (pp. 254–281). New York: John Wiley and Sons.

Harlow, H. F., & Lauersdorf, H. E. (1974). Sex differences in passions and play. *Perspectives in Biology and Medicine, 17,* 348–360.

Harris, J. R. (1995). Where is the child's environment? A group socialization theory of development. *Psychological Review, 102,* 458–489.

Harris, J. R. (1998). *The nurture assumption: Why children turn out the way they do.* New York: Free Press.

Heinz, A., Higley, J. D., Gorey, J. G., Saunders, R. C., Jones, D. W., Hommer, D., Zajicek, K., Suomi, S. J., Weinberger, D. R., & Linnoila, M. (1998). In vivo association between alcohol intoxication, aggression, and serotonin transporter availability in nonhuman primates. *American Journal of Psychiatry, 155,* 1023–1028.

Higley, J. D., Hasert, M. L., Suomi, S. J., & Linnoila, M. (1991). A new nonhuman primate model of alcohol abuse: Effects of early experience, personality, and stress on alcohol consumption. *Proceedings of the National Academy of Sciences, 88,* 7261–7265.

Higley, J. D., Hommer, D., Lucas, K., Shoaf, S., Suomi, S. J., & Linnoila, M. (in press). CNS serotonin metabolism rate predicts innate tolerance, high alcohol consumption, and aggression during intoxication in rhesus monkeys. *Archives of General Psychiatry.*

Higley, J. D., King, S. T., Hasert, M. F., Champoux, M., Suomi, S. J., & Linnoila, M. (1996). Stability of individual differences in serotonin function and its relationship to severe aggression and competent social behavior in rhesus macaque females. *Neuropsychopharmacology, 14,* 67–76.

Higley, J. D., & Suomi, S. J. (1989). Temperamental reactivity in nonhuman primates. In G. A. Kohnstamm, J. E. Bates, & M. K. Rothbard (Eds.), *Handbook of temperament in children* (pp. 153–167). New York: John and Sons Wiley.

Higley, J. D., & Suomi, S. J. (1996). Reactivity and social competence affect individual differences in reaction to severe stress in children: Investigations using nonhuman primates. In C. R. Pfeffer (Ed.), *Intense stress and mental disturbance in children* (pp. 3–58). Washington, DC: American Psychiatric Press.

Higley, J. D., Suomi, S. J., & Linnoila, M. (1996). A nonhuman primate model of Type II alcoholism? Part 2: Diminished social competence and excessive aggression correlates with low CSF 5-HIAA concentrations. *Alcoholism: Clinical and Experimental Research, 20,* 643–650.

Hinde, R. A., Rowell, T. E., & Spencer-Booth, Y. (1964). Behavior of socially living monkeys in their first six months. *Proceedings of the Zoological Society of London, 143,* 609–649.

Lindburg, D. G. (1971). The rhesus monkey in north India: An ecological and behavioral study. In L. A. Rosenblum (Ed.), *Primate behavior: developments in field and laboratory research* (Vol. 2, pp. 1–106). New York: Academic Press.

Lindburg, D. G. (1991). Ecological requirements of macaques. *Laboratory Animal Science, 41,* 315–322.

Mitchell, G. D., Ruppenthal, G. C., Raymond, E. J., & Harlow, H. F. (1966). Long-term effects of multiparous and primiparous monkey mother rearing. *Child Development, 37,* 781–791.

Rosenblum, L. A. (1971). Ontogeny of mother–infant relations in macaques. In H. Moltz (Ed.), *Ontogeny of Vertebrate Behavior* (pp. 28–56). New York: Academic Press.

Ruppenthal, G. C., Arling, G. L., Harlow, H. F., Sackett, G. P., & Suomi, S. J. (1976). A 10-year perspective on motherless mother monkey mothe ring behavior. *Journal of Abnormal Psychology, 88,* 341–349.

Ruppenthal, G. C., Harlow, M. K., Eisele, C. D., Hawlow, H. F., & Suomi, S. J. (1994). Development of peer interactions of monkeys reared in a nuclear family environment. *Child Development, 45,* 670–682.

Sade, D. S. (1967). Determinants of social dominance in a group of free-ranging rhesus monkeys. In S. Altmann (Ed.), *Social communication among primates* (pp. 91–114). Chicago: University of Chicago Press.

Suomi, S. J. (1979). Differential development of various social relationships by rhesus monkey infants. In M. Lewis & L. A. Rosenblum (Eds.), *Genesis of behavior: The child and its family* (Vol. 2, pp. 219–244). New York: Plenum Press.

Suomi, S. J. (1995). Influence of Bowlby's attachment theory on research on nonhuman primate biobehavioral development. In S. Goldberg, R. Muir, & J. Kerr (Eds.), *Attachment theory: Social, developmental, and clinical perspectives* (pp. 185–201). Hillsdale, NJ: Analytic Press.

Suomi, S. J. (1998). Conflict and cohesion in rhesus monkey family life. In M. Cox & J. Brooks-Gunn (Eds.), *Conflict and cohesion in families* (pp. 283–296). Mahwah, NJ: Lawrence Erlbaum Associates.

Suomi, S. J. (1999). Developmental trajectories, early experiences, and community consequences: Lessons from studies with rhesus monkeys. In D. Keating & C. Hertzman (Eds.), *Developmental health: The wealth of nations in the Information Age* (pp. 185–200). New York: Guilford Press.

Suomi, S. J. (2000). A biobehavioral perspective on developmental psychopathology: Excessive aggression and serotonergic dysfunction in monkeys. In A. J. Sameroff, M. Lewis, & S. Miller (Eds.), *Handbook of Developmental Psychopathology* (2nd ed, pp. 237–256). New York: Plenum.

Suomi, S. J., & Levine, S. (1998). Psychobiology of intergenerational effects of trauma: Evidence from animal studies. In Y. Danieli (Ed.), *International handbook of multigenerational legacies of trauma* (pp. 623–637). New York: Plenum Press.

IV

Contextual–Cultural Influences on Parenting Nondisabled and Disabled Children

16

The Role of Parenting in Shaping the Impacts of Welfare-to-Work Programs on Children

Sharon M. McGroder, Martha J. Zaslow,
Kristin A. Moore, Elizabeth C. Hair,
and Surjeet K. Ahluwalia

Child Trends

INTRODUCTION

Evaluations of the effects of welfare-to-work programs have generally focused on adults, with only secondary consideration for the children in families that receive welfare. This reflects both the fact that the primary goals of the programs are economic (e.g., to increase rates of employment and earnings and to decrease welfare receipt), and the fact that most welfare-to-work programs do not include explicitly child-centered components, such as early childhood intervention or developmental screening. However, it has increasingly been suggested that features of welfare reform may have implications for children to the extent that these programs have impacts on outcomes that are important to children's development (McGroder, Zaslow, Moore, & LeMenestrel, 2000; Moore, Zaslow, Coiro, Miller, & Magenheim, 1995; Wilson & Ellwood, 1993; Zaslow, Moore, Morrison, & Coiro, 1995).

For example, welfare-to-work programs seek to increase earnings, decrease receipt of public assistance, and increase overall family income, and there is

Address correspondence to: Sharon M. McGroder, Child Trends, 4301 Connecticut Ave., NW, Suite 100, Washington, DC 20008, Phone: 202-362-5580, e-mail: smcgroder@childtrends.org evidence that maternal employment in low-income families is associated with positive outcomes in children (Vandell & Ramanan, 1992; Zaslow & Emig, 1997) and that parental income level is positively associated with the cognitive development, behavior, and physical health and safety of children (Duncan & Brooks-Gunn, 1997; Hill & Sandfort, 1995; Huston, 1991; Korbin, 1992). Thus, if welfare-to-work programs succeed in changing "targeted" outcomes, such as maternal employment and total family income, this could have implications for children. In addition, welfare-to-work programs are likely to lead to increased use of child care—if not by program design, then as a derivative of program impacts on participation in work preparation activities and employment. Research has shown a small but consistent association between the quality of child care and young children's developmental outcomes, (NICHD Early Child Care Network, 1998; NICHD Early Child Care Network, 2000) and there is emerging evidence that type of care (e.g., formal versus informal) may be important to cognitive outcomes in children from low-income families (Zaslow, Oldham, Magenheim, & Moore, 1998).

In addition, welfare-to-work programs may have impacts on aspects of family life beyond their targeted outcomes, and such impacts could affect children either directly or through their impacts on targeted outcomes. An example of a direct effect, the mandate to participate in work preparation activities may enhance mothers' psychological well-being (if, for example, mothers view it as an opportunity to improve their economic well-being) and translate into more positive parenting and child outcomes. Nontargeted outcomes may also be affected indirectly, through the programs' impacts on targeted outcomes. For example, if welfare-to-work programs do not lead to adequate improvements in economic self-sufficiency, then families and children may suffer. Research has shown that families who struggle with insufficient economic resources tend to experience more stress than more economically secure families (Conger & Elder, 1994; McLoyd, 1990), which may lead low-income parents to become more depressed (McLoyd, 1990) and/or irritable (Elder, 1974) and to use harsher parenting practices (McLoyd, 1990) compared to higher-income families. As a result, children may exhibit more behavior problems (McLoyd, 1990; Rothbaum & Weisz, 1994), immaturity (McGroder, 2000), and demonstrate lower school readiness (Estrada, Arsenio, Hess, & Holloway, 1987; McGroder, 2000). Figure 16.1 portrays our conceptual model for how welfare-to-work programs may lead to impacts on children.

Thus, parenting is hypothesized to be a key pathway through which welfare-to-work programs may affect children. However, if "parents don't matter" (as has been suggested by Harris, this volume), then such program-induced changes in parenting would not be expected to lead to changes in children's development and well-being. This chapter uses experimental data from a welfare-to-work evaluation to examine whether assignment to a particular welfare-to-work program did indeed affect children's developmental outcomes and, if such changes came about, whether they are explained, at least in part, by changes in parenting.

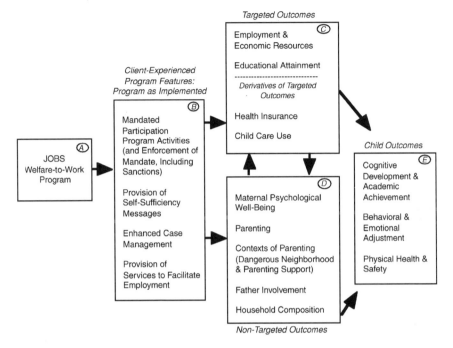

FIG. 16.1.   Conceptual framework.

Analytic Approaches to Examining the Role of Parenting in Shaping Children's Developmental Outcomes

The importance of parental influences for children has been strongly challenged in recent years (see Rowe, this volume, and Harris, this volume). Indeed, it has been argued that, apart from imparting genetic potential and, perhaps, their potential influence on the peers to which their children are exposed (for example, in their choice of neighborhoods in which to live), parents have little important long-term effects on their children (Harris, 1995, 1998). For example, although Harris acknowledges that parental abuse or neglect can be harmful to children, she contends that, in general, parenting has little effect on children's personality and social development. Rather, Harris places primary importance on children's peer groups. Few contest the importance of peer influences (Bearman & Brückner, 1999b; Brown & Theobald, 1999), and there is general agreement that more research is needed on the positive as well as negative implications of peers for the development of children and adolescents (Dunn, 1988; Dunn & Kendrick, 1982; Bearman and Brückner, 1999a). However, the contention that parents do not matter has been highly controversial, both in the press (Begley, 1998) and among researchers of children's development (Maccoby, 1999).

It is difficult to assess the importance of parenting for children's development for a variety of reasons. One reason is that the only definitive methodology for assessing causality—an experimental design—would require random assignment of children to parents with differing parenting skills, and this is ethically unacceptable for studies with human subjects. However, such studies have been undertaken with nonhuman primates, and results indicate the importance of maternal nurturance for keeping young monkeys' excessive aggression in check, which is critical for these monkeys' very survival (Suomi, 1999). This important work notwithstanding, the debate over parenting effects for human children continues.

This has led many researchers to use adoption studies involving twins as an approach to examining the influence of parents (Rowe, 1994; see review in Lykken, 1995). This approach, employed by behavioral geneticists, consists of calculating *heritabilities*—that is, the proportion of variance in a child outcome measure (such as IQ) accounted for by the degree of genetic relatedness—in order to assess the strength of the genetic component of this child outcome measure. Environmental influences are then partitioned into "shared" components (those experienced by children in the same family) and nonshared components (those that vary for children in the same family). Behavioral geneticists assign the variance associated with parenting to the "shared" environment. Because research has shown that the variance accounted for by the "shared" environment is relatively small, these researchers conclude that, at best, there are limits to families' influence on children (Rowe, this volume; Rowe, 1994) and that, at worst, "parenting doesn't matter" (Harris, this volume; Harris, 1998).

However, critics argue that this behavioral genetics approach is flawed. One criticism is that it assumes that all children in a family share the same experiences and/or that the effect of these experiences is identical for all children. To the extent that children in the same family experience different effective environments—for example, if parents treat siblings differently—then the importance of parenting is underestimated (Dunn and Plomin, 1991). Critics have also questioned the underlying assumption that genetic and environmental influences operate independently of each other (which is necessary in order for the variance accounted for by each of these influences to be effectively "partitioned") and thus have questioned the very legitimacy of calculating a heritability coefficient (Wahlsten, 1994). Finally, others argue that calculating heritabilities fails to address the question of whether *changes* in a child's environment can elicit *changes* in a developmental outcome (Bronfenbrenner & Ceci, 1994; Lykken, 1995).

Another approach to assessing the influence of parents on children is to examine the effects of experimentally induced changes in parenting on the developmental outcomes of children. The null hypothesis in this case is that experimentally induced changes in parenting will have no effect on children's development. Such a hypothesis can be examined in experimental evaluation studies of programs that had components explicitly seeking to improve parenting with the goal of enhancing children's development, such as the Infant Health Development Program (this volume) or in nurse home visiting models (Olds et al., 1999). However, testing such a hypothesis need not be limited to experimental evaluations of programs that explicitly seek to improve parenting. Programs that do not explicitly target parenting outcomes, such as welfare-to-work programs, may nevertheless affect enrollees' parenting if, for example, these programs have impacts on aspects of family life that, in turn, have implications for parenting (see Conceptual Framework, Fig. 16.1). Finding that aspects of parenting mediate, or help to explain, the impact of welfare-to-work programs on children would provide compelling evidence that parents *do* matter to their children's development.

There are, however, several reasons to be cautious in our expectations that welfare reform policies and programs might affect children's developmental outcomes through effects on parenting. First, as we have noted, these programs are generally focused on adults' economic outcomes and make little or no attempt to affect children, nor do they provide services directly to children. Consequently, such programs would have to affect those environments and/or adult outcomes that would, in turn, be expected to affect children. Second, program impacts would have to be of sufficient magnitude to affect children's outcomes. Third, these programs may affect nontargeted adult and family outcomes, such as parenting, but these hypothesized intervening mechanisms could be found to have no effect on children's development. That is, in a careful experimental study in which parents are randomly assigned to a program and there are documented program impacts on parenting, these impacts might not translate into impacts on children either because parenting does not matter, or does not matter enough, to bring about changes in children's development and well-being.

STUDY BACKGROUND

The Job Opportunities and Basic Skills Training (JOBS) Program

The Job Opportunities and Basic Skills Training (JOBS) Program was authorized under the 1988 Family Support Act. The programs implemented under JOBS had four key components:

1. Mandated participation in education, training, and/or employment activities
2. Messages about the importance of such activities for securing employment
3. Enhanced case management services to direct and monitor clients' progress
4. Services (such as child care and transportation) to facilitate employment.

Programs implemented under JOBS adopted one of two approaches for moving clients off welfare and into jobs: a labor force attachment (LFA) approach that emphasized a rapid transition to employment, and a human capital development (HCD) approach that focused on education and training with an emphasis on building the parents' employability. (See Hamilton, Brock, Farrell, Friedlander, and Harknett, 1997, for a more detailed description of these program approaches.) These approaches represent differing views on how best to foster the economic self-sufficiency of families receiving welfare. The LFA approach presumes that working is the best way to learn work behaviors and skills, while the HCD approach assumes that building human capital and skills related to employment will enhance earnings and increase job stability in the long run.

The National Evaluation of Welfare-to-Work Strategies (NEWWS)

The National Evaluation of Welfare-to-Work Strategies (NEWWS), being conducted by the Manpower Demonstration Research Corporation (MDRC), assesses the economic impacts of a set of programs implemented under JOBS and is being carried out in seven sites across the country. In three of the seven sites (Atlanta, Georgia; Grand Rapids, Michigan; and Riverside, California), families in the evaluation were randomly assigned to either one of the two program groups (the human capital development group or the labor-force-attachment group), or to a control group. Corresponding to exemptions from the requirement to participate in the JOBS Program, the NEWWS did not include families in which the recipient was ill or incapacitated, caring for a household member who was ill or incapacitated, pregnant past the first trimester, living in an area where program services were unavailable, or had a child younger than age three (or age one at state option—an option taken by three states with sites in the NEWWS, but affecting only one of the study sites in the Child Outcomes Study: Grand Rapids).

Program mothers continued to be eligible to receive payments under Aid to Families with Dependent Children (AFDC). In addition, for mothers assigned to either the LFA group or the HCD group, JOBS was mandatory. It is important to note, however, that the experimental evaluation of JOBS does not examine the effects of participating in JOBS per se, because the program groups included individuals who did not actually participate in any JOBS activities for at least a day, since random assignment. Nevertheless, these clients still attended the JOBS orientation and, therefore, received messages regarding the most effective ways to become self-sufficient, as well as the message that participation in JOBS activities was mandated and that failure to participate could result in sanctioning (a reduction in welfare benefits). Consequently, the experimental evaluation assesses the impact of having been assigned to one of the JOBS program approaches, and thus, at the very least, reflects the impact of exposure to program messages and the participation mandate, even if clients never received enhanced case management or employment preparation services.

By contrast, mothers in the control group also remained eligible for AFDC benefits, but they were not required to participate in any JOBS activities. Control group members were, however, free to seek out education and training programs in their communities at their own volition and were guaranteed child care while participating in such approved activities, as required by the Family Support Act provisions.

The Child Outcomes Study

Because the JOBS Program represented the first time that a federal welfare program implemented nationally required participation in welfare-to-work activities by mothers with preschool-age children, a substudy focusing on the developmental outcomes of these young children was funded. The Child Outcomes Study is being conducted by Child Trends. Families in the Child Outcomes Study are from three sites—Atlanta, Georgia; Grand Rapids, Michigan; and Riverside, California—and were eligible for inclusion in the Child Outcomes Study if they had a child between about three and five years old at the time of enrollment. This child was the "focal" child, or the child focused on in interviews and who received the cognitive assessments. (Where there was more than one child in this age range in the family, one was selected randomly to be the focal child). This focal child had to be the biological or adoptive child of the mother participating in the evaluation. All eligible families had applied for or were receiving AFDC at the time of enrolling in the evaluation, which occurred between September 1991 and January 1994.

The Child Outcomes Study offers a rare opportunity to examine the importance of parenting in an experimental context. If a distal influence such as a mandate to participate in work preparation activities can affect parenting, and if there is evidence that program impacts on parenting help to explain program impacts on children, this would provide evidence against the hypothesis that parenting does not matter.

METHOD

Sample

Across the three Child Outcomes Study sites, 3,670 eligible families were selected to be interviewed at the two-year follow-up. Overall, a total of 3,194 (or 87%) of selected families completed the two-year follow-up survey, with response rates ranging from 80% (in Riverside) to 91% (in Atlanta and Grand Rapids). Families were dropped from the sample if they had moved 100 or more miles away or if the focal child no longer lived with the respondent at the two-year follow-up. As a result, 3,018 (or 82%) of the families selected to be interviewed were both administered the in-home survey and retained for the present analyses.

Table 16.1 notes characteristics of the families in each of the three study sites at baseline. As can be seen in the table, the mean age of the focal child ranged from about 50 months (in Riverside) to 53 months (in Atlanta). The mean age of the mother at baseline ranged from about 27 years (in Grand Rapids) to about 29 years (in Atlanta and Riverside). The majority of mothers in the sample in Atlanta were black/non-Hispanic (95%), whereas mothers in the other two sites were more racially and ethnically diverse: In the Grand Rapids site, just over half of the sample mothers were white/non-Hispanic, and about 40% were black/non-Hispanic. In the Riverside site, just under half of the sample mothers were white/non-Hispanic, about 20% were black/non-Hispanic, and almost one third were Hispanic. Three fourths of households in Grand Rapids and nearly two thirds of households in the other two sites had only one or two children living in the household at baseline. In Atlanta and Grand Rapids, the majority of mothers had never been married (71% and 59%, respectively), but in Riverside, the majority had been married (58%). In all, three sites, over half of mothers had a high school diploma or General Education Development (GED) degree at study enrollment.

Procedures

Demographic and background data, as well as attitudinal information, were obtained for all of the sample members in the NEWWS during the JOBS orientation session just prior to random assignment. Immediately prior to random assignment, recipients were also given an assessment of reading and math skills. In addition, administrative data are available for each of the families in the sample from county and state Aid to Families with Dependent Children records and from state unemployment insurance records. Two years after enrollment, the families were visited by carefully trained interviewers. Participants in the NEWWS Child Outcomes Survey received both the "core" interview given to all those receiving the 2-year follow-up client survey in the full evaluation sample and a 20-minute interview specific to the Child Outcomes Study. Mothers were interviewed about work and family topics and about their children, with more detailed information obtained about the focal child, who was between the ages of about 5 and 7 years at the 2-year follow-up. In addition, developmental assessments of focal children's cognitive school readiness were conducted.

Data quality was monitored intensively during the first months of fielding, and then periodically during the course of fielding, through detailed review of completed surveys (including assessments and ratings) in each of the three sites by staff from Child Trends, Manpower Demonstration Research Corporation, and the fielding organization, Response Analysis Corporation. Interviewers were contacted

TABLE 16.1
SELECTED MATERNAL AND FAMILY CHARACTERISTICS OF THE
2-YEAR SAMPLE AT BASELINE, BY RESEARCH SITE

Characteristics	Atlanta	Grand Rapids	Riverside
Sociodemographic			
Mean age of focal child (in months)	53.0	52.1	50.2
Gender of focal child (%)			
Male	50.5	50.3	51.2
Female	49.5	49.7	48.8
Mean age of mother (in years)	29.0	26.7	29.3
Ethnicity of mother (%)			
White, non-Hispanic	3.6	52.7	46.3
Hispanic	0.7	6.0	31.4
Black, non-Hispanic	95.2	39.1	19.6
Black Hispanic	0.1	0.2	0.0
American Indian/ Alaskan	0.2	1.1	1.3
Asian /Pacific Islander	0.1	0.2	1.5
Other	0.1	0.8	0.0
Number of children in household (%)			
Only one child	29.3	25.3	33.6
Only two children	35.6	50.8	31.7
Three or more children	35.1	23.9	34.7
Marital status (%)			
Never married	71.3	58.9	42.5
Married, living with spouse	0.9	2.1	2.2
Separated	16.1	22.7	31.4
Divorced	11.4	15.9	22.0
Widowed	0.3	0.3	1.9
Education and Basic Skills			
Highest degree earned (%)			
GED	5.7	8.1	9.6
High school diploma	54.0	51.1	40.9
Tech. AA/ 2-yr.	6.0	3.6	3.9
Four yr + college	1.3	0.6	0.2
None of the above	33.0	36.4	45.4
Sample Size	1422	646	950

Note: Total sample sizes in each site are noted in the bottom row; descriptive statistics are presented for the available sample for each measure. In the Riverside site, the Private Opinion Survey was not administered to mothers during the first months of the evaluation; consequently, information on mothers' psychological well-being, social support, and attitudes toward work and welfare were not available for this "early cohort" ($N = 212$). Fortunately, the characteristics of this early cohort did not differ statistically from the characteristics of the later cohort ($N = 738$), with one exception: focal children in the early cohort were somewhat younger than focal children in the later cohort (46 vs. 51 months, respectively). Consequently, we chose to impute missing baseline data—even for the 22% of families in the early cohort in Riverside—for subsequent analyses, and we are confident that in doing so we are not biasing the sample.

directly regarding any problems in their administration of the follow-up. Data quality appears to be excellent, with very little missing or inconsistent information.

Measures

Child Outcome Measures

Children's development and well-being have been categorized in varied ways (Moore, Evans, Brooks-Gunn, & Roth, 1998; Zill & Coiro, 1992). In this study, the developmental status of the children was assessed across three domains: cognitive development and academic achievement, behavioral and emotional adjustment, and physical health and safety. The possibility of program impacts on children is examined in detail through the use of multiple child outcome measures for each of the three domains (see McGroder et al., 2000, for a detailed description of the full set of measures and a complete description of program impacts on all child outcome measures). In this chapter, we focus on one measure from each of these three developmental domains in our investigation of parenting as a mediator of child impacts: the Bracken Basic Concept Scale/School Readiness Composite (Bracken, 1984); the Antisocial Subscale of the Behavior Problems Index (Peterson & Zill, 1986; Zill, 1985); and a global health rating (Adams & Marano, 1995) (see Table 16.2).

Measures of Mediators

Table 16.2 also provides definitions of the variables that emerged in statistical analyses as mediators of at least one of the five selected program impacts on children (see below for description of these selected impacts). (See McGroder et al., 2000, for a complete description of program impacts on all targeted and nontargeted adult and family outcomes examined, regardless of their role in mediating selected child-impact findings.) These mediators fell into the following categories: employment and economic resources; program participation and perceptions of the welfare office; maternal psychological well-being; parenting; and father involvement.

RESULTS

Brief Overview of "Aggregate" Impacts on Child Outcomes

The first question explored is whether any of the six JOBS programs studied (the HCD and the LFA program approaches in each of the three study sites) had impacts on measures of children's development and well-being. Whereas the full report (McGroder et al., 2000) also presents child impact findings for subgroups of families (based on initial characteristics of children and families at baseline), we focus here on the "aggregate" impact findings—that is, impacts that occurred, on average,

TABLE 16.2
DESCRIPTION OF MEASURES/SOURCES OF ITEMS

Category/Measure	Description	Alpha
1. Child Outcome Measures		
Bracken Basic Concept Scale/ School Readiness Composite (Bracken, 1984)	This direct assessment of cognitive school readiness administered at T2[3] to the focal child uses the five subtests comprising the School Readiness Composite and assessed the focal child's knowledge of colors, letters, numbers/ counting, comparisons, and shapes. Interviewers received special training to complete this assessment, which requires about 15 minutes to administer, as part of the 2-year follow-up. In previous research with children born to mothers receiving welfare, this measure was found to be significantly correlated with teachers' assessments of children's academic progress (Polit, 1996).	.97
Antisocial Behavior Problems Subscale of the Behavior Problems Index (see Peterson & Zill, 1986; Zill, 1985)	The Behavior Problems Index (Zill, 1985) asks mothers to indicate whether descriptions of children's behavior are not true, sometimes true, or always true of the focal child. The antisocial subscale, developed based on earlier work by Peterson and Zill (1986), as well as factor analyses using the present dataset, is a subset of five items from the Behavior Problems Index that tap antisocial problems: • Bullies or is cruel or mean to others • Cheats or tells lies • Is disobedient at home • Is disobedient at school • Does not seem to feel sorry after she or he misbehaves	.61
Child Health Rating (Adams & Marano, 1995)	Mothers rated the focal child's overall health in response to the single interview question: "Would you say that your child's health in general is (1) excellent, (2) very good, (3) good, (4) fair, or (5) poor?" Validation work indicates that this health rating reflects primarily physical health problems (Krause and Jay, 1994).	NA
2. Measures of Economic Self-sufficiency		
Current employment status	Maternal report at T2 of employment status in month prior to 2-year follow-up survey	NA
3. Measures of Perceptions of the Welfare Office		
Perceptions that the welfare department makes people go to school or get training	Mothers rated the statement: "The welfare department tries hard to make people go to school or get training" on a scale of 0 (do not agree) to 10 (agree completely).	NA
Beliefs re: fairness of sanctioning	Mothers responded to the question: "Some welfare agencies require people on welfare to go to an education, training, or employment program. These agencies can reduce the amount of money in people's welfare checks if they don't go and don't	NA

TABLE 16.2   (Continued)

Category/Measure	Description	Alpha
	have a good excuse. What do you think about reducing a person's welfare checks for this reason?" Mothers answered: , very fair fair, mixed feeling, unfair, very unfair, or don't know (CT).	

4. Maternal Psychological Well-being Measures

Category/Measure	Description	Alpha
Depressive symptomatology	Maternal report at T2 on 12 items from the 20-item CES-D (Radloff, 1977), asking how often (0) rarely, (1) some/a little, (3) moderate amount, (4) most or all days "During the past week. . ." "I felt sad." "I felt lonely." "I felt depressed." "I felt that I could not shake off the blues, even with help of family and friends." "I was bothered by things that usually don't bother me." "I did not feel like eating; my appetite was poor." "I had trouble keeping my mind on what I was doing." "I felt that everything I did was an effort." "I felt fearful." "My sleep was restless." "I talked less than usual." "I could not get going."	.90
Time stress	Maternal report at T2 on item developed by Child Trends, asking the degree to which they (1) agree a lot, (2) agree, (3) disagree, (4) disagree a lot with the statement: "I always feel rushed even to do the things I have to do."	NA

5. Parenting Measures[4]

Category/Measure	Description	Alpha
Maternal warmth (maternal report)	On a scale from 0 ("none of the time") to 10 ("all of the time"), the mother reported how often: (1) she feels that the focal child likes her and wants to be near her (PSI), (2) she shows the focal child a lot of love, even when in a bad mood (CT), and (3) she and the focal child have warm times together (PACR).	.55
Index of maternal warmth (interviewer rating)	Interviewers reported on five maternal behaviors relating to mothers' warmth toward the focal child as observed during the course of the 2-year follow-up home interview. Three items (developed by Child Trends)—mothers' warmth (versus hostility), pride, and warm tone of voice–were rated on an 11-point scale and dichotomized into yes/no, with responses at the ends of the distribution (i.e., 7–10 or 0–3, depending on the direction of the wording) coded as yes. These items were summed along with affirmative responses to a dichotomous item ("Did mother kiss, caress, or hug focal child at least once?" HOME-SF) and an item recoded to reflect whether the mother	NA

TABLE 16.2 (Continued)

Category/Measure	Description	Alpha
	spontaneously praised the focal child at least once (HOME-SF), yielding a summary score ranging from 0 to 5.	
Index of the amount and complexity of maternal verbal interactions with focal child (interviewer ratings)	Four interviewer ratings comprise a summary index of the amount and complexity of the mother's verbal interactions with the focal child. One item using an 11-point scale—and relating to the degree to which the mother spoke to the focal child in complex sentences (0) or used single words or gestures (10)—was dichotomized, with responses of 0 to 3 given a 1 (CT). This item was summed along with affirmative responses to three dichotomous items—relating to whether the mother introduced the interviewer to the focal child (HOME-SF), explained to the focal child what was going on (CT), or conversed with the focal child at least twice (HOME-SF). Summary scores ranged from 0 to 4.	NA
Index of harsh maternal discipline (interviewer ratings)	Interviewers noted whether the mothers yelled at the focal child in a "harsh or hostile manner" and rated the mother from 0 ("extremely hostile, cold, harsh to child") to 10 ("extremely warm, loving, affectionate to child") (CT). A score of 1 on this measure indicates that the mothers screamed or yelled at the focal child at least once during the visit and/or that the interviewer rated the mothers at the "hostile" end (i.e., 0–3) of that scale.	NA
Summary index of favorable parenting	A point was given if: (1) mothers' warmth score (maternal report) was at the higher end of the scale (i.e., between 7 and 10); (2) interviewers rated mothers as warm on all five indicators; (3) mother's cognitive stimulation scores indicated more frequent engagement in cognitively stimulating activities (i.e., at least once a week), or (4) interviewers rated mothers favorably on each of the four indicators of mothers' verbal interactions with the focal child. Thus, this summary index could range from 0 to 4.	NA

6. Measures of Father Involvement

Number of informal supports from father	Biological fathers who do not reside with the focal child may still be involved in the child's life. This three-item measure sums the number of affirmative responses to a question asking whether in the previous 12 months the focal child's biological father had: (1) bought clothes, toys, or presents, (2) bought groceries, or (3) baby-sat for the focal child, yielding a score from 0 to 3.	NA

[3]T2 refers to measures from the 2-year follow-up survey.

[4]Key to abbreviations: PSI = Parenting Stress Index (Abidin, 1986); PACR = parental attitudes toward childrearing (Easterbrooks & Goldberg, 1984); HOME-SF (Baker & Mott, 1989); CT = developed by Child Trends for the Child Outcomes Study.

across all families in the program or the control group. Note that aggregate impacts presented here may or may not reflect impacts found for key subgroups of families.

Overall, these six JOBS welfare-to-work programs had both favorable and unfavorable aggregate impacts on children. These impacts were generally small in magnitude (i.e., effect sizes of .20 or smaller; Cohen, 1988) and were not found for all outcomes examined. Nevertheless, there were impacts in each of the three developmental domains studied, and impacts were found more often than would be expected by chance (McGroder et al., 2000).

The pattern of favorable and unfavorable impacts differed by child outcome domain. Specifically, impacts in the domain of cognitive development and academic achievement were all favorable, impacts on maternal ratings of focal children's overall health were unfavorable, and both favorable and unfavorable impacts were found for children's behavioral outcomes.

Particular Impacts Selected for Mediational Analyses

For the full report (McGroder et al., 2000), we conducted a modest investigation of the pathways through which particular JOBS programs led to impacts in each of the three domains of child development by selecting five of the child impact findings for mediational analyses. These impacts—a favorable cognitive impact, one favorable and one unfavorable behavioral impact, and two unfavorable health impacts—were selected because they are among the largest impacts in each child outcome domain and because they reflect the general pattern of overall program impacts on children. Specifically, the following aggregate impacts on focal children were selected for mediational analyses:

1. The favorable impact of Atlanta's LFA program on cognitive school readiness scores
2. The favorable impact of Atlanta's LFA program on reports of antisocial behavior problems
3. The unfavorable impact of Grand Rapids' LFA program on reports of antisocial behavior problems
4. The unfavorable impact of Riverside's HCD program on maternal ratings of general health
5. The unfavorable impact of Riverside's LFA program on maternal ratings of general health.

Overview of Mediational Analytic Strategy

Figure 16.2 portrays the mediational model employed in these analyses, which is adapted from the model presented in Baron and Kenny (1986). The experimental impact of a given JOBS program on a given child outcome measure is represented

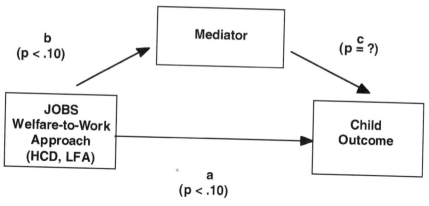

Baron and Kenny (1986). Copyright by the American Psychological Association. Model adapted and used with permission of the authors.

FIG. 16.2. Mediation model.

by path *a*. In order for a particular aspect of family life to be a mediator of a program impact on a child outcome, it must first have been affected by the given JOBS program. This experimental impact is represented by path *b*. Finally, path *c* represents the nonexperimental "effect" of the mediator on the child outcome (controlling for the program impact on the child outcome). If path *c* is statistically significant, and the statistical significance of path *a* is reduced or eliminated, then this aspect of family life does, indeed, statistically mediate the particular child impact being examined.

Multivariate regression analyses proceeded in two steps. First, we identified variables that, when considered individually, mediated the given child impact. Next, we included all variables that individually mediated the child impact into a final, "full" model. This model indicates which variables continue to mediate the program impact, controlling for other mediators. If, in this full model, one or more of the mediators remain(s) statistically significant, and the magnitude of the experimental impact on the given child outcome is reduced and is no longer statistically significant, then we conclude that the variables *completely* mediate this particular child impact. If one or more of the mediators remains statistically significant, and the magnitude of the experimental impact on the given child outcome is reduced but remains statistically significant, then we conclude that these variables *partially* mediate this particular child impact. When a given child impact is only partially mediated, this suggests that additional pathways not in the model are also important.

Mediators that *decrease* the size of the experimental impact of JOBS help to explain how the program impact came about. However, it is also possible that including mediators in the statistical model serves to *increase* the magnitude of the experimental impact of JOBS on the child outcome. In this case, the mediator has a buffering effect, indicating that the program impact on the given child outcome measure would have been even more pronounced if not for this mediator's counteracting effect.

Findings Regarding Parenting as a Mediator of Program Impacts on Children

As noted, in order for a variable (e.g., a particular measure of parenting) to act as a mediator of program impacts on children, it must first have been affected by the given welfare-to-work program. With respect to the unfavorable health impacts in Riverside, we found that neither of Riverside's JOBS programs had aggregate impacts on any of the 11 measures of parenting examined in this study. Consequently, parenting cannot serve as a pathway through which either of Riverside's JOBS programs had its unfavorable impact on ratings of focal children's health.

For the remaining three child impact findings selected for mediational analyses, aggregate impacts on measures of parenting were found for the particular JOBS programs in which these cognitive and behavioral impacts were found (i.e., Atlanta's LFA program and Grand Rapids' LFA program). Thus, parenting is at least a potential pathway through which these two JOBS programs led to these three impacts on children. Below we describe the degree to which measures of parenting did, in fact, mediate these three impacts on measures of focal children's cognitive functioning and behavior.

Mediators of the Favorable Impact of Atlanta's LFA Program on Focal Children's Mean Cognitive School Readiness Scores

Children whose mothers were assigned to Atlanta's LFA program had significantly higher scores on the Bracken Basic Concepts Scale/School Readiness Composite than children whose mothers were in Atlanta's control group. Specifically, focal children of these program mothers understood, on average, almost 49 concepts relating to colors, letters, numbers/counting, comparisons, and shapes, whereas control group children understood only about 47 concepts, on average.

In terms of program impacts on targeted and nontargeted adult and family outcomes (see McGroder et al., 2000), Atlanta's LFA program successfully increased participation in job search and work experience activities. Assignment to Atlanta's LFA program also resulted in some small gains in educational attainment and employment, reductions in AFDC receipt, increases in child care use, and improvements in parenting. The program also led to greater feelings of time stress among mothers. Although fewer of these program families were living in "deep poverty" (i.e., below 50% of the poverty line) two years after enrollment in JOBS, their average total incomes did not differ significantly from those of control group mothers.

Mediational analyses reveal that four variables individually mediated the impact of Atlanta's LFA program on focal children's mean cognitive school readiness scores. Maternal verbal interactions with the focal child, "favorable" parenting, and current maternal employment each predicted higher cognitive school readiness scores, and perceptions that the welfare office tries to make clients go to school or get training functioned in an opposing direction, that is, predicted lower cognitive school readiness scores. Controlling for all four of these variables, only the maternal employment and the two parenting variables continued to partially mediate this favorable program impact (noted in bold in Table 16.3, column 1), whereas mothers' perceptions of the welfare office no longer diminished this favorable impact. In addition, there still appears to be a direct effect of Atlanta's LFA program on children's cognitive school readiness that is unexplained by the targeted and nontargeted adult and family outcomes examined in the full report. That is, while maternal employment and parenting helped to explain this program impact on children, there is still something unexplained about the program's effects on families that contributed to this favorable impact on focal children's cognitive school readiness.

Mediators of the Favorable Impact of Atlanta's LFA Program on Focal Children's Antisocial Behavior Problems

Compared to control group mothers, mothers assigned to Atlanta's LFA program reported significantly less frequent antisocial behavior problems for their focal children. On a scale from 0 to 2, these program mothers reported a mean frequency of .41, whereas control group mothers reported a mean frequency of .45, indicating that the five antisocial behaviors happened, on average, between "some of the time" and "none of the time" in both groups, but slightly though significantly less often in the LFA group.

To reiterate briefly the impacts on targeted and nontargeted adult and family outcomes, Atlanta's LFA program increased participation in job search and work experience activities, improved educational and employment outcomes, decreased AFDC receipt, decreased the proportion of families living in deep poverty, increased used of nonmaternal child care, and improved some aspects of parenting, but it also led to greater feelings of time stress among mothers. Accordingly, these variables represent, once again, candidate

TABLE 16.3

MEDIATORS OF THE (FAVORABLE) IMPACT OF ATLANTA'S LFA PROGRAM ON FOCAL CHILDREN'S COGNITIVE SCHOOL READINESS SCORES, THE (FAVORABLE) IMPACT OF ATLANTA'S LFA PROGRAM ON FOCAL CHILDREN'S ANTISOCIAL BEHAVIOR PROBLEM SCORES, AND THE (UNFAVORABLE) IMPACT OF GRAND RAPIDS' LFA PROGRAM ON FOCAL CHILDREN'S ANTISOCIAL BEHAVIOR PROBLEM SCORES[5]

Atlanta LFA: Mediators of the Impact on Cognitive School Readiness Scores

LFA (1=yes; 0=control group)	1.21+
Amount and complexity of maternal verbal interactions (0–4)	**1.20*** **
"Favorable" Parenting (0–4)	**1.12** **
If employed in month prior to survey (1=yes)	**1.24+**
Perceives that the welfare office tries to make people go to school/training (0–10)	–.13
adj R²	.28***
d.f.	27, 791

Atlanta LFA: Mediators of the Impact on Antisocial Behavior Problem Scores

LFA (1=yes; 0=control group)	–.04
Interviewer rating of maternal warmth (0–5)	–.01
"Favorable" Parenting (0–4)	**–.05** **
Harsh parenting (1=yes)	.06
Time stress: feeling rushed (0–10; higher=agree)	.009*
Perceives that the welfare office makes people go to school/get training (0–10: higher=agree)	.007+
Participation in job club (1=yes)	.05
adj R²	.19***
d.f.	30, 677

Grand Rapids LFA: Mediators of the Impact on Antisocial Behavior Problem Scores

LFA (1=yes; 0=control group)	.04
Depressive symptomatology at 2-year follow-up (0–36)	**.01*** **
Maternal Report of Warm Parenting (0–10)	**–.03** **
Beliefs regarding fairness of sanctioning (1=fair, .5=unfair)	.01
Number of informal supports from father (1–3)	–.02
adj R²	.15***
d.f.	28, 362

Note: $+p < .10$; $*p < .05$; $**p < .01$; $***p < .001$

[5]**Bolded** coefficients indicate mediators that helped to explain the program impact when considered simultaneously in the full model. Coefficients in *italics* indicate mediators that operate in an opposing direction; that is, the program impact would have been more pronounced if not for the presence of these mediators. In addition to the program dummy variable and the mediator(s) being examined, the regression models included the following baseline covariates: marital status, number of children, race, mother's age, average AFDC benefit per month, number of months received AFDC in prior year, focal child's age and gender, high school diploma or GED, literacy, numeracy, time on welfare, work history, depressive symptoms, locus of control, source of support, family barriers, and number of baseline risks, if employed in prior year, if received AFDC in prior year, earnings in prior year, and prior year earnings squared. Because we relied on maternal reports of children's behavior and health (but not of focal children's cognitive school readiness), we controlled for the number of depressive symptoms reported by the mother at the 2-year follow-up in all mediational analyses of child behavioral and health impacts to control for possible response bias due to the respondent's subjective state during the 2-year interview. Thus, results are net of any significant effect of concurrent depressive symptoms.

300

mediators of this favorable program impact on focal children's antisocial behavior problems.

Mediational analyses reveal that six variables individually mediated the impact of Atlanta's LFA program on the reported frequency of focal children's antisocial behaviors: Interviewer ratings of maternal warmth, the summary measure of "favorable" parenting, interviewer ratings of harsh parenting, feeling rushed (a measure of time stress) each predicted children's antisocial behaviors in the expected direction, whereas perception that the welfare office tries to make clients go to school or get training and participation in job club each predicted more frequent antisocial behavior. Controlling for all six of these variables, only the summary index of "favorable" parenting remained a significant mediator (noted in bold in Table 16.3, column 2). In fact, this summary index of favorable parenting *completely* mediated this favorable program impact. In addition, mothers' feelings of time stress and perceptions that the welfare office tries to make clients go to school or get training continued to diminish this program impact (noted in italics in the table), indicating that the impact on reports of focal children's antisocial behavior would have been even *more* favorable if not for the counteracting influences of these two variables. In the end, however, the negative effect of these feelings and perceptions was outweighed by the positive effect of parenting such that the net effect for focal children's antisocial behavior was favorable.

Mediators of the Unfavorable Impact of Grand Rapids' LFA Program on Focal Children's Antisocial Behavior Problems

Compared to control group mothers, mothers assigned to Grand Rapids' LFA program reported significantly more frequent antisocial behavior problems for their focal children: On a scale from 0 to 2, these program mothers reported a mean frequency of .49, whereas control group mothers reported a mean frequency of .43, indicating that the five antisocial behaviors happened, on average, between "some of the time" and "none of the time" in both groups, but slightly though significantly more often in the LFA group.

Consistent with the labor force attachment philosophy, mothers assigned to Grand Rapids' LFA program were more likely than control group mothers to participate in job search activities and were less likely to have received a high school diploma, GED, or trade degree since random assignment. Despite modest employment gains since random assignment, these program mothers did not have greater incomes and were somewhat more likely than control group mothers to be living in poverty at the 2-year follow-up. Grand Rapids' LFA program also had significant impacts on nontargeted outcomes: Compared to those in the control group, mothers assigned to this program reported somewhat greater informal support from the focal child's biological father, and they reported feeling less warmth toward the focal child and more depressive symptoms—to levels suggestive of clinical depression—at the 2-year follow-up point.

Mediational analyses reveal that four of those variables individually mediated the impact of Grand Rapids' LFA program on the reported frequency of focal children's antisocial behaviors: Depressive symptomatology, mothers' reports of warmth, and the number of informal supports from the focal child's biological father each predicted children's antisocial behavior in the expected direction; beliefs that sanctioning is unfair predicted more frequent antisocial problems. Controlling for all four of these variables, only maternal depressive symptomatology[6] and less warm parenting as reported by the mother continued to mediate the impact of Grand Rapids' LFA program on focal children's antisocial behaviors (noted in bold in Table 16.3, column 3). In fact, these two variables *completely* mediated this program impact on children. In addition, the tendency to believe that sanctioning is unfair no longer exacerbated this unfavorable impact, and the number of informal supports from the focal child's nonresidential biological father no longer buffered this unfavorable impact.

SUMMARY AND CONCLUSION

To what extent is parenting implicated as a pathway through which these JOBS programs had impacts on selected measures of children's development and well-being? This paper addresses this question by examining the extent to which experimentally induced changes in selected measures of children's cognitive development, behavior, and physical health can be explained by experimentally induced changes in parenting. The underlying premise is that if "parents don't matter," then experimentally induced changes in parenting would not serve as a pathway through which welfare-to-work programs had impacts on children.

We selected five child impact findings to explore in greater detail with mediational analyses. Results indicate, first, that parenting could not serve as a pathway through which the two JOBS programs in Riverside led to lower health ratings in focal children, because these programs had no significant impacts on parenting in the first place.

---

[6]That concurrent depressive symptomatology is predictive of focal children's antisocial behavior problems may, in part, reflect a subjective bias in this maternal report measure. However, because Grand Rapids' LFA program had an impact on depressive symptomatology, we suspect that these mediational results do not (entirely) reflect subjective bias in maternal reports of behavior problems and that the impact on depressive symptomatology and, thus, the apparent implications for children, are real.

On the other hand, experimentally induced changes in parenting did help to explain the one cognitive and two behavioral impacts selected for further study. Specifically, maternal verbal stimulation and a summary index of "favorable" parenting, along with mothers' current employment, partially mediated the favorable impact of Atlanta's LFA program on focal children's mean cognitive school readiness scores. In addition, "favorable" parenting completely mediated this program's favorable impact on maternal reports of focal children's antisocial behavior problems. Finally, less warm parenting, along with maternal depressive symptoms, completely mediated the unfavorable impact of Grand Rapids' LFA program on maternal reports of focal children's antisocial behavior problems. It is worth noting that the same program approach (the labor force attachment strategy) resulted in both favorable and unfavorable impacts on children's antisocial behavior problems in two different sites, and the role of parenting in helping to explain these impacts is implicated in both cases.

This study demonstrates that parenting did not always serve as a pathway through which these welfare-to-work programs had impacts on children (note the health impact findings), and that other aspects of family life (maternal depressive symptomatology and employment) were also important. Nevertheless, this study provides evidence that parenting was important in explaining selected impacts of particular welfare-to-work programs on children's cognitive functioning and behavior and thus supports the view that parenting matters to children's developmental outcomes.

DISCUSSION

One of the factors motivating welfare reform in 1996 was the relatively modest effect of previous efforts to move welfare recipients from welfare to work and economic self-sufficiency. The Family Support Act of 1988 replaced the earlier WIN (Work Incentive) Program and has since been supplanted by the Personal Responsibility and Work Opportunity Reconciliation Act of 1996. During the early 1990s, the increased value of the Earned Income Tax Credit has provided a further incentive to individuals—including single mothers—to initiate employment. The strong economy, combined with the 1996 welfare reform, has accelerated this movement (Moffitt, 1999). Although most evaluations of these efforts have focused on impacts for the parents, several studies are now yielding information about the implications of welfare reform for the children in families that receive welfare. Because studies of welfare reform in the early 1990s tended to employ an experimental methodology, the data from these studies lend themselves to further nonexperimental analyses in an experimental context.

Given decades of research conducted in nonexperimental contexts indicating that aspects of parenting are associated with children's development, measures of parenting were included in the Child Outcomes Study to examine their role as potentially important pathways through which JOBS programs might affect children. Given the evolving debate on whether parents matter for children's development, the data generated by this study provide an important and rare opportunity to explore whether and how a public policy such as the JOBS Program might affect children by affecting parenting.

This study provides evidence that parenting was important in explaining selected impacts of specific welfare-to-work programs on children's cognitive functioning and behavior. Specifically, impacts of Atlanta's LFA program and Grand Rapids' LFA program on mothers' warmth and/or engagement in cognitively stimulating activities with the focal child largely explained the respective impacts on children's cognitive school readiness scores and antisocial behavior problems. These results are in accord with the parenting literature, which indicates that mothers' warmth and cognitively stimulating behavior are associated with more favorable cognitive outcomes in young children, including in low-income samples (Greenstein, 1995; McGroder, 2000; Moore et al., 1995), and which documents the association between less emotionally supportive parenting and antisocial behaviors in children (e.g., Weinfield, Egeland, & Ogawa, 1998). In addition, the finding that increased maternal depressive symptomatology also played a major role in explaining the unfavorable impact of Grand Rapids' LFA program on focal children's antisocial behavior problems is in accord with literature documenting the positive association between maternal depression and antisocial behaviors in children (see Downey and Coyne, 1990, for a review).

Limitations and Future Research

Whereas experimental analyses provide strong causal evidence regarding the existence of program impacts on children, they cannot address the question of how these impacts came about. Analyses attempting to model the pathways through which a program had its impacts are necessarily nonexperimental. As such, they do not allow firm causal inferences to be made regarding the pathways through which impacts came about. Nonexperimental analyses must contend with the possibility of selection bias. The mediational analyses reported on here and in the full report (as well as the experimental impact analyses that preceded them) did not control for children's prior developmental and behavioral outcomes; however, they did control for numerous other variables representing prior characteristics of the child, mother, and family at baseline that have been shown, in this sample, to serve as selection factors into employment (Zaslow, McGroder, Cave, & Mariner, 1999), child care (Zaslow et al., 1998), and parenting pattern (McGroder, 2000). Thus, we are likely to have controlled for many, though not all, possible selection effects.

The mediational analyses conducted for this paper rely on information about mediators and child outcomes measured at the same point in time and used a relatively modest statistical approach in modeling pathways[7]; consequently, results should be considered preliminary. Nevertheless, given the limited knowledge about the ways in which welfare-to-work programs affect children and families, it is important to begin to address this issue, statistically, even with contemporaneous measures of intervening mechanisms and child outcomes and using a relatively modest statistical approach. Our future research will use five-year data from the Child Outcomes Study to test explicit hypotheses using more complex statistical approaches (e.g., structural equation modeling, instrumental variables).

Finally, the reader should keep in mind that, in the present study, a relation between parenting and a child outcome was reported *only* in cases where there was both an experimental impact on a child outcome measure and an experimental impact on a parenting measure. This amounts to a relatively narrow test of whether parenting matters to children, for it is possible (and, given findings from decades of such research, likely) that associations between parenting and child outcomes exist in this sample even in the absence of program impacts. Indeed, other research on families receiving welfare provides evidence of such associations (Zaslow & Eldred, 1998; Zaslow et al., 1999). Thus, for example, our findings indicate that parenting could not serve as a pathway through which Riverside's JOBS programs led to lower health ratings of focal children because these programs had no significant impacts on parenting. However, this does not mean that what parents do has no bearing on their children's health. Recent research indicates that many parents engage in health-compromising behaviors (Zill, 1999) that could have implications for their children's health.

---

[7]There is debate among researchers on the "best" way to model pathways of influence. The multivariate regression mediational analyses conducted in this study are standard practice in the field of developmental psychology (see, e.g., Brooks-Gunn, Berlin, & Fuligni, 1998; Burchinal, Campbell, Bryant, Wasik, & Ramey, 1997), and researchers are increasingly including measures hypothesized to capture selection effects (see, for example, Zaslow et al., 1999; Zaslow et al., 1998; and McGroder, 2000). Developmentalists are also increasingly using structural equation modeling to explore mediators of program effects, once specific hypotheses regarding multiple pathways have been articulated (see, e.g., Bradley et al., 1993). Others, mainly economists, favor instrumental variables modeling, in which a less endogenous estimate of the mediating variable is included in the explanatory model in an effort to control for selection effects. Ogawa and his colleagues have compared the OLS regression approach to the instrumental variables approach, and they conclude that OLS-based regression methods tend to undercontrol for endogeneity, whereas an instrumental variable approach tends to overcontrol for endogeneity (Ogawa, Weinfield, & Egeland, 1999). Still others rely on nonstatistical methods, juxtaposing program impact findings for adults and for children and inferring pathways of influence (see Bos et al., 1999).

Policy Implications

Quite different policy implications are suggested if impacts are transmitted via maternal employment, parenting, child care, or maternal depression. The goal of mediational analyses of program impacts is to identify pathways through which the program being evaluated had its impacts. If net impacts are favorable, then pathways helping to explain these favorable impacts are sought; if impacts are unfavorable, then the focus is on the pathways explaining these unfavorable impacts. However, attention must also be given to mediators that operate in the opposing direction and thus serve to buffer either favorable or unfavorable impacts. Thus, to maximize favorable program impacts on children, policymakers can strengthen the pathways (e.g., "favorable" parenting, maternal employment) leading to favorable impacts, but also strengthen pathways (potentially, the number of informal support from nonresidential fathers) that serve to buffer unfavorable program impacts. Similarly, policymakers may want to consider ways of weakening the pathways (e.g., maternal depressive symptomatology) that lead to unfavorable impacts, as well as weakening the pathways (e.g., maternal time stress) that serve to diminish otherwise favorable impacts on children.

ACKNOWLEDGMENTS

This research would not have been possible without the permission of officials at the U.S. Department of Health and Human Services and the U.S. Department of Education, which funded the Manpower Demonstration Research Corporation (MDRC) to conduct the National Evaluation of Welfare-to-Work Strategies, and Child Trends to conduct the Child Outcomes Study (contract no. HHS-100-89-0030).

We would like to thank Howard Rolston (from the Administration of Children and Families in the U.S. Department of Health and Human Services), Martha Moorehouse, and Audrey Mirsky-Ashby (both from the Office of the Assistant Secretary for Planning and Evaluation in the U.S. Department of Health and Human Services) for their careful review and feedback on an earlier draft of this manuscript.

The authors would also like to thank Fanette Jones for assisting with figures.

REFERENCES

Aber, J. L., Brooks-Gunn, J., & Maynard, R. A. (1995). Effects of welfare reform on teenage parents and their children. *Future of Children, 5* (2), 53–71.

Abidin, R. R. (1986). *Parenting Stress Index Manual* (2nd ed.). Charlottesville, VA: Pediatric Psychology Press.

Adams, P. F., & Marano, M. A. (1995). Current estimates from the National Health Interview Survey, 1994. National Center for Health Statistics. *Vital Health Statistics, 10* (193). Washington, DC: U.S. Department of Health and Human Services.

Baker, P. C., & Mott, F. L. (1989). *NLSY child handbook 1989: A guide and resource document for the National Longitudinal Study of Youth 1986 child data.* Columbus: Center for Human Resource Research, Ohio State University.

Baron, R. M., & Kenny, D. A. (1986). The moderator–mediator variable distinction in social psychological research: Conceptual, strategic, and statistical considerations. *Journal of Personality and Social Psychology, 51* (6), 1173–1182.

Bearman, P., & Brückner, H. (1999a). *Peer potential: Making the most of how teens influence each other.* Washington, DC: National Campaign to Prevent Teen Pregnancy.

Bearman, P., & Brückner, H. (1999b). *Power in numbers: Peer effects on adolescent girls* = sexual debut and pregnancy. Washington, DC: National Campaign to Prevent Teen Pregnancy.

Begley, S. (1998, September 7). The parent trap. *Newsweek,* 52–59.

Bos, H., Huston, A., Granger, R., Duncan, G., Brock, T., & McLoyd, V. (1999). *New hope for people with low incomes: Two-year results of a program to reduce poverty and reform welfare.* New York: Manpower Demonstration Research Corporation.

Bracken, B. A. (1984). *Bracken Basic Concept Scale: Examiner's Manual.* Psychological Corporation, Harcourt Brace Jovanovich.

Bradley, R. H., Whiteside, L., Caldwell, B. M., Casey, P. H., Kelleher, K., Pope, S., Swanson, M., Barrett, K., & Cross, D. (1993). Maternal IQ, the home environment, and child IQ in low–birth weight, premature children. *International Journal of Behavioral Development, 16,* 61–74.

Bronfenbrenner, U., & Ceci, S. J. (1994). Nature–nurture reconceptualized in developmental perspective: A bioecological model. *Psychological Review, 101* (4), 568–586.

Brooks-Gunn, J. B., Berlin, L. J., & Fuligni, A. S. (1998). Early childhood intervention programs: What about the family? In J. P. Shonkoff & S. J. Meisels (Eds.), *Handbook of early childhood intervention* (2nd ed). New York: Cambridge University Press.

Brown, B. B., & Theobald, W. (1999). How peers matter: A research synthesis of peer influences on adolescent pregnancy. In *Peer potential: Making the most of how teens influence each other.* Washington, DC: National Campaign to Prevent Teen Pregnancy.

Burchinal, M. R., Campbell, F. A., Bryant, D. M., Wasik, B. H., & Ramey, C. T. (1997). Early intervention and mediating processes in cognitive performances of children in low-income African-American families. *Child Development, 68,* 935–954.

Chase-Lansdale, P. L., & Vinovskis, M. (1995). Whose responsibility? An historical analysis of the changing roles of mothers, fathers, and society in assuming responsibility for U.S. children. In P. L. Chase-Lansdale & J. Brooks-Gunn (Eds.), *Escape from poverty: What makes a difference for poor children?* (pp. 11–37). Cambridge, UK: Cambridge University Press.

Cohen, J. (1988). *Statistical power analysis for the behavioral sciences* (2nd ed). Hillsdale, NJ: Lawrence Erlbaum Associates.

Coiro, M. J. (1999). *Depressive symptoms among women receiving welfare.* Manuscript submitted for publication.

Conger, R. D., & Elder, G. H., Jr. (1994). *Families in troubled times: Adapting to change in rural America.* New York: Aldine de Gruyter.

De Temple, J., & Snow, C. (1998). Mother–child interactions related to the emergence of literacy. In M. J. Zaslow & C. A. Eldred (Eds.), *Parenting behavior in a sample of young mothers in poverty: Results of the New Chance Observational Study* (pp. 114–169). New York: Manpower Demonstration Research Corporation.

Downey, G. & Coyne, J. C. (1990). Children of depressed parents: An integrative review. *Psychological Bulletin, 108,* 50–76.

Duncan, G. J., & Brooks-Gunn, J. (Eds.). (1997). *Consequences of growing up poor.* New York: Russell Sage Foundation.

Dunn, J. (1988). *The beginnings of social understanding.* Cambridge, MA: Harvard University Press.

Dunn, J., & Kendrick, C. (1982). *Siblings: Love, envy, and understanding.* Cambridge, MA: Harvard University Press.

Dunn, J., & Plomin, R. (1991). Why are siblings so different? The significance of differences in sibling experiences within the family. *Family Process, 30* (3), 271–283.

Easterbrooks, M. A., & Goldberg, W. A. (1984). Toddler development in the family: Impact of father involvement and parenting characteristics. *Child Development, 55,* 740–752.

Elder, G. (1974). Children of the Great Depression: Social change in life experience. Chicago: University of Chicago Press.

Estrada, P., Arsenio, W. F., Hess, R. D., & Holloway, S. D. (1987). Affective quality of the mother–child relationship: Longitudinal consequences for children's school-relevant cognitive functioning. *Developmental Psychology, 23,* 210–215.

Freedman, S., Friedlander, D., Hamilton, G., Rock, J., Mitchell, M., Nudelman, J., Schweder, A., & Storto, L. (1999). *Evaluating alternative welfare-to-work approaches: Two-year impacts for eleven programs.* Washington, DC: U.S. Department of Health and Human Services, Administration for Children and Families and Office of the Assistant Secretary for Planning and Evaluation, and U.S. Department of Education.

Friedlander D., & Burtless, G. (1995). *GAIN: Two-year impacts in six counties.* New York: Russell Sage Foundation.

Goldberger, A. S., & Kamin, L. J. (1998, November). *Behavior-genetic modeling of twins: A deconstruction.* Social System Research Institute Working Paper 9824.

Greenstein, T. N. (1995). Are the "most advantaged" children truly disadvantaged by early maternal employment? *Journal of Family Issues, 16* (2), 149–169.

Hamilton, G., Brock, T., Farrell, M., Friedlander, D., & Harknett, K. (1997). *National Evaluation of Welfare-to-Work Strategies: Evaluating two welfare-to-work program approaches: Two-year findings on the labor force attachment and human capital development programs in three sites.* Washington, DC: U.S. Department of Health and Human Services, Administration for Children and Families and Office of the Assistant Secretary for Planning and Evaluation.

Harris, J. R. (1995). Where is the child's environment? A group socialization theory of development. *Psychological Review, 102* (3), 458–489.

Harris, J. R. (1998). *The nurture assumption: Why children turn out the way they do.* New York: Free Press.

Hill, M. S., & Sandfort, J. R. (1995). Effects of childhood poverty on productivity later in life: Implications for public policy. *Children and Youth Services Review, 17,* 91–126.

Huston, A. C. (Ed.). (1991). *Children in poverty: Child development and public policy.* New York: Cambridge University Press.

Korbin, J. E. (1992). Introduction: Child poverty in America. *American Behavioral Scientist, 35,* 213–219.

Krause, N. M., & Jay, G. M. (1994). What do global self-rated health items measure? *Medical Care, 32* (9), 930–942.

Lykken, D. T. (1995). *The antisocial personalities.* Hillsdale, NJ: Lawrence Erlbaum Associates.

Maccoby, E. E. (1999, August). *Parenting effects: Issues and controversies.* Paper presented at the conference, Parenting and the Child's World, sponsored by NICHD and the Robert Wood Johnson Foundation, Washington, DC.

McGroder, S. (2000). Parenting among low-income, African-American single mothers with preschool-age children: Patterns, predictors, and developmental correlates. *Child Development, 71* (3), 752–771.

McGroder, S., Zaslow, M. J., Moore, K. A., & LeMenestrel, S. (2000). *The National Evaluation of Welfare-to-Work Strategies: Impacts on young children and their families two years after enrollment: Findings from the Child Outcomes Study.* Washington, DC: U.S. Department of Health and Human Services and U.S. Department of Education.

McLoyd, V. C. (1990). The impact of economic hardship on black families and children: Psychological distress, parenting, and socioemotional development. *Child Development, 61* (2), 311–346.

Moffitt, R. (1999). Presentation at the congressional briefing, "Is Welfare Reform Working? The Impact of Economic Growth and Policy Changes," sponsored by the Consortium of Social Science Associations.

Moore, K. A., Evans, V. J., Brooks-Gunn, J., & Roth, J. (1998). What are good child outcomes? Washington, DC: Child Trends.

Moore, K. A., Zaslow, M. J., Coiro, M. J., Miller, S. M., & Magenheim, E. B. (1995). *How well are they faring? AFDC families with preschool-aged children in Atlanta at the outset of the JOBS evaluation.* Washington, DC: U.S. Department of Health and Human Services.

NICHD Early Child Care Research Network. (1998). Early child care and self-control, compliance and problem behavior at twenty-four and thirty-six months. *Child Development, 69* (3), 1145–1170.

NICHD Early Child Care Research Network. (2000). The relation of child care to cognitive and language development. *Child Development, 71* (4), 960–980.

Ogawa, J., Weinfield, N., & Egeland, B. (1999, April). All in a day's work: Maternal employment and mother–child relationships in a low-income sample. Presented at the biennial meeting of the Society for Research in Child Development, Albuquerque, NM.

Olds, D. L., Henderson, C. R., Kitzman, H. J., Eckenrode, J. J., Cole, R. E., & Tatelbaum, R. C. (1999). Prenatal and infancy home visitation by nurses: Recent findings. In R. E. Behrman (Ed.), *The future of children: Home visiting: Recent program evaluations* (pp. 44–65). Los Altos, CA: David and Lucile Packard Foundation.

Peterson, J., & Zill, N. (1986). Marital disruption and behavior problems in children. *Journal of Marriage and Family, 48,* 295–307.

Polit, D. F. (1996). *Self administered teacher questionnaire in the New Chance 42-month survey.* New York: Manpower Demonstration Research Corporation.

Quint, J., Bos, H., & Polit, D. (1997). *New Chance: Final report on a comprehensive program for young mothers in poverty and their children.* New York: Manpower Demonstration Research Corporation.

Radloff, L. S. (1977). The CES-D scale: A self-report depression scale for research in the general population. *Applied Psychological Measurement, 1,* 385–401.

Rothbaum, F., & Weisz, J. R. (1994). Parental caregiving and child externalizing behavior in nonclinical samples: A meta-analysis. *Psychological Bulletin, 116,* 55–74.

Rowe, D. C. (1994). *The limits of family influence: Genes, experience, and behavior.* New York: Guilford Press.

Suomi, S. J. (1999). *A biobehavioral perspective on developmental psychopathology: Excessive aggression and serotonergic dysfunction in monkeys.* Manuscript in preparation.

Vandell, D. L., & Ramanan, J. (1992). Effects of early and recent maternal employment on children from low-income families. *Child Development, 63,* 938–949.

Wahlsten, D. (1994). The intelligence of heritability. *Canadian Psychology, 35* (3), 244–258.

Weinfield, N. S., Egeland, B., & Ogawa, J. R. (1998). Affective quality of mother–child interactions. In M. J. Zaslow & C. A. Eldred (Eds.), *Parenting behavior in a sample of young mothers in poverty: Results of the New Chance Observational Study.* New York: Manpower Demonstration Research Corporation.

Wertheimer, R. (1999). *Children in working poor families.* Washington, DC: Child Trends.

Wilson, J. B., & Ellwood, D. T. (1993). *Welfare to work through the eyes of children: The impact on children of parental movement from AFDC to employment.* Cambridge, MA: Malcolm Weiner Center for Public Policy, John F. Kennedy School of Government.

Zaslow, M. J., Dion, M. R., Morrison, D. R., Weinfield, N., Ogawa, J., & Tabors, P. (1999). Protective factors in the development of preschool-age children of young mothers receiving welfare. In E. M.

Hetherington (Ed.), *Coping with divorce, single parenting, and remarriage: A risk and resiliency perspective.* Mahwah, NJ: Lawrence Erlbaum Associates.

Zaslow, M. J., & Eldred, C. A. (Eds.). (1998). *Parenting behavior in a sample of young mothers in poverty: Results of the New Chance Observational Study.* New York: Manpower Demonstration Research Corporation.

Zaslow, M. J., & Emig, C. A. (1997). When low-income mothers go to work: Implications for children. *Future of Children, 7* (1), 110–115.

Zaslow, M. J., McGroder, S., Cave, G., & Mariner, C. (1999). Maternal employment and measures of children's health and development among families with some history of welfare receipt. *Research in the Sociology of Work, 7,* 233–259.

Zaslow, M. J., Moore, K. A., Morrison, D. R., & Coiro, M. J. (1995). The Family Support Act and children: Potential pathways for influence. *Children and Youth Services Review, 17,* 231–249.

Zaslow, M. J., Oldham, E., Magenheim, E., & Moore, K. A. (1998). Welfare families' use of early childhood care and education programs, and implications for their children's development. *Early Childhood Research Quarterly 13* (4), 535–563.

Zill, N. (1985). *Behavior Problems Index.* Washington, DC: Child Trends.

Zill, N. (1999). *Setting an example: The health, medical care, and health-related behavior of American parents.* Washington, DC: Child Trends.

Zill, N., & Coiro, M. J. (1992). Assessing the condition of children [Special issue]. *Children and Youth Services Review, 14,* 119–136.

17

Family Structure and Resources and the Parenting of Children With Disabilities and Functional Limitations

Dennis P. Hogan

Brown University, Providence, RI

Michael E. Msall

Brown Medical School and Child Development Center, Hasbro Children's Hospital and Rhode Island Hospital

INTRODUCTION

Child disability is rarely discussed in studies of parenting. This chapter presents evidence that the disability of a child is salient to many American families. For families with a child with disability, the special needs of the child present added challenges to successful parenting. How the parents deal with these challenges may greatly impact the lives of their children. The effects of child disability pervade the family, influencing husband–wife relationships, reducing the stability and economic security of the family, altering the life course of mothers, and impacting on both the family life of the child with the disability and the siblings. We base this chapter both on prior

Address correspondence to: Dennis P. Hogan, Population Studies and Training Center, Box 1916, Brown University, Providence, RI 02912, Phone: 401-863-1656, Fax: 401-863-3351, e-mail: Dennis_Hogan@brown.edu research findings of other investigators and on our own research on functional limitations in children with disabilities and children with special health care needs.

DATA

The information used to describe the relationship of family structure and resources with the parenting of children with disabilities is drawn from two complementary nationally representative population surveys. The National Health Interview Survey (NHIS) annually provides demographic, socioeconomic, and health information for a nationally representative sample of noninstitutionalized persons and their households. In 1994 and 1995 the National Center for Health Statistics broadened the scope of the NHIS to include Disability and Family Resources Supplements, and Longitudinal Follow-Back one year later of persons who have chronic medical conditions, medication, or physician care, or are functionally limited (NHIS-D). The NHIS-D included an unusually extensive battery of questions to measure functional limitations and disability. In addition, it is unique among the population samples in its collection from parents of extensive information on medically diagnosed problems or conditions, the use of medical facilities, medications, special diets and equipment, along with participation in special programs or activities. The Disability Follow-Back, conducted one year later, is an especially rich source of information about medical services and rehabilitation inputs, including the use of special services, equipment, programs, and environmental modifications. It also asked parents direct questions about the impact of their child's disability on family life (U.S. Department of Health and Human Services, 1996).

Beginning in 1988, the National Center for Health Statistics conducted the National Maternal and Infant Health Survey (NMIHS). This major survey of maternal and infant health was designed to collect information to study factors related to poor pregnancy outcomes, including congenital malformation and infant mortality (Sanderson, Placek, & Keppel, 1991). This study is extremely complex in its sampling of birth certificates (collecting information on fetal deaths as well as live births and infant deaths). The natality component included oversamples of low- and very-low-birth-weight infants. The final sample included 11,000 women who had live births in 1988 and 6,000 women who had infants who died in 1988 between their births and first birthdays. Records were constructed for each birth (whether ending in infant death or infant survival) with data from the birth and death certificates, and additional information was collected from a survey of the mothers and health care providers about 9 months after the birth. Children of the NMIHS who were alive in 1988 and 1991 were included in the baseline and follow-up study through maternal interview. This information can be used to measure and analyze functional limitations and disability among the children, linking such outcomes to congenital anomalies at birth and to family conditions, social support, and medical inputs from birth to ages 32 to 38 months.

HOME-BASED DISABILITY

Even in children with severe and profound developmental disabilities, the major programmatic emphasis has been the development of community and nonnursing home placements. Thus, while many older persons with disabilities leave their homes for institutions, 98% of children with disabilities live at home (Hogan, Msall, Rogers, & Avery, 1997). Their needs are managed and coordinated by the family, and it is the family that defines and structures much of their lives. Until the passage of the Americans with Disabilities Act of 1990 and the 1991 Individuals with Disabilities Education Act (representing a continuation and expansion of the 1975 Education for All Handicapped Children Act), they were not uniformly entitled to specialized government assistance (Bowe, 1995).

Many American families face child disability. Of American families with school-age children, 12.3% have a child who is limited in the ability to perform everyday tasks (Figure 17.1). These limitations can take many forms, such as difficulty communicating basic needs to others, toileting or eating, getting around the house, or learning what others their age can learn.

The impact of a child with disability on families is even greater than these numbers suggest. Twenty percent of school-age children live in families with a child who is disabled (Figure 17.1). Of these, 8.6% of children are functionally limited but have no disabled sibling, 3.7% are limited in functioning and have a sibling who is disabled, and 7.7% have no limitation themselves but live with a

Percent of children functionally limited

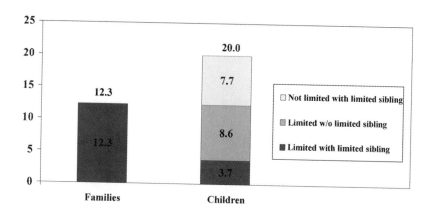

Source: 1994 National Health Interview Survey, Disability Supplement

FIG. 17.1. Disabled children age 5 to 17 in American families.

sibling who has a disability. Overall, 9.9 million children age 5 to 17 years are growing up in a family in which they or a school-age sibling is limited in age-appropriate tasks.

This creates a potentially stressful situation for families. Husbands and wives unexpectedly may face time and resource demands typically not associated with childrearing. They will be confronted with the need to make decisions about specialized medical services and developmental rehabilitation inputs with which they have little if any firsthand knowledge. In the cases of children with severe or life-threatening chronic conditions, parents must face the prospect that their children may not survive or become sufficiently functional to lead independent adult lives. In these cases, the family itself can become organized around the disability, potentially transforming the life course of the parents and altering parental attention and resources across their children.

Six million school-age American children have one or more functional limitations. Of all school-age children, 10.6% are limited in learning, 5.5% in communication, 1.3% in mobility, and 0.9% in self-care. To understand how serious these limitations are, we examined each of these four functional domains (mobility, self-care, communication, and learning) and classified the extent of limitation as relatively mild or severe. (A child in the NHIS-D who has a mild limitation in mobility, for example, is one who has some difficulty getting in and out of a chair; a child with a severe mobility limitation either is unable to get in and out of a chair or needs special equipment and help. In other population studies, mild mobility limitation often is defined as difficulty in climbing a long flight of stairs,

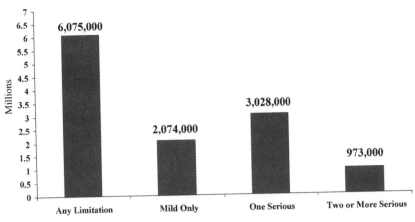

Number of Children with Functional Limitations

Source: 1994 Health Interview Survey, Disability Supplement

FIG.17.2.   The population of disabled children.

walking distances greater than one block, or getting in and out of a bathtub.) Severe limitations would include the inability to climb a flight of stairs or the necessity to use special equipment to get around.

Figure 17.2 describes the six million school-age children who are limited in function and the severity of their limitations. Of these, approximately two million have mild limitations, and three million have one serious limitation (and may have mild limitation in other domains). Nearly one million children have serious limitations in two or more areas of functioning relating to mobility, self-care, communication, or learning limitations. These multiply limited children present special challenges to families. They draw heavily on societal resources for medical care, rehabilitation services and devices, and special education supports.

CHRONIC HEALTH CONDITIONS

Stein and Silver (1999) estimate that 10.3 million children (14.8% of all children) ages 0 to 17 years have a chronic health condition, as indicated by medical service use or need beyond routine care for age, the use of compensatory mechanisms, or a limitation in functioning. This definition includes rehabilitation services (physical therapy, occupation therapy, speech/language therapy) and special education supports. Two thirds of children with chronic health conditions are functionally limited. The other children have a chronic condition that is not disabling, have been protected by medical intervention, or have not yet developed a limitation in function (Newacheck & Taylor, 1992; Newacheck & Halfon, 1998).

CONCEPTUALIZING DISABILITY

Disability is not easily conceptualized or analyzed. Yet the large number of children and families impacted by disability make it imperative that we have a conceptual framework to understand the process. The Institute of Medicine has recommended a conceptual framework for the study of disability. It is based on the application of the recently developed National Center for Medical Rehabilitation Research (NCMRR) disability classification (National Institutes of Health, 1993; Brandt & Pope, 1997). The NCMRR framework focuses on the measurement of limitation in functional tasks and disability in activities, and its associated rehabilitation actions. While designed for all age groups, this framework is appropriate to the study of children from birth to age 17 (see Figure 17.3 for definitions and examples). The advantage of this framework is that it provides a medically grounded and socially informed basis for conceptualizing, identifying, and measuring the various aspects of the disability process. Using this framework, this chapter examines how family factors—family structure, maternal education, and poverty—have played a part in the process of child disability and rehabilitation.

Pathophysiology	The interruption of or interference with normal physiological and developmental processes or structures. (Example: Severe intraventricular hemorrhage in very low birth weight preterm infants secondary to hypoxemic respiratory failure.) Medications to restore functioning are one aspect of rehabilitation (Example: Maternal corticosteroids and postnatal surfactant to enhance pulmonary maturity and decrease hypoxemia).
Impairment	The loss or abnormality of cognitive, emotional, physiological, or anatomical structure or function, including all losses or abnormalities, not just those attributable to the initial pathophysiology. (Example: Motor control of lower extremity, strabismus, learning disabilities.) Rehabilitation includes surgery, specialized therapies, or prosthetic or orthotic interventions.
Functional Limitation	The restriction or lack of ability to perform an action in the manner or with the range consistent with the purpose of an organ or organ system. (Example: Difficulty walking 150 feet.) Rehabilitation strategies include different approaches to completing tasks using remaining physical abilities, substituting actions previously used for performing another function, and replacing lost function through assistive devices (such as crutches, walker or wheelchair).
Disability	The inability or limitation in performing tasks, activities, and roles to levels expected in physical and social contexts. (Example: Can no longer walk to school or participate in after school recreation.) Rehabilitation includes establishing and maintaining support for transportation, counseling to maintain emotional stability, and school program assistance to redefine school tasks and recreational activities.
Societal Limitation	The restriction, attributable to social policy or barriers (structural or attitudinal), which limits fulfillment of roles or denies access to services and opportunities that are associated with full participation in society. (Example: Cannot move freely around school due to stairways and doors that are obstacles to someone in a wheel chair.) Rehabilitation involves the restructuring of physical or social arrangements to permit persons with disability to have physical mobility and attend school.

Source: NIH, NCMMR (1993: 33–38).

FIG. 17.3.   Conceptualizing disability.

GENETIC DISORDERS

One of the key needs for families with children with genetic impairments is to understand the long-term impact of the genetic disorder on the child's development. Msall and Tremont (1999) examined the functional status of children with Down syndrome, spina bifida, congenital limb anomalies, congenital heart disease, urea cycle disorders, DiGeorge Malformation Sequence and severe multiple disabilities, of early childhood onset. In many cases this condition may be genetically linked to one of the parent's genetic history, and associated with uncertainty of outcome, fear of stigma, and guilt. In autosomal chromosomal disorders with multifactorial inheritance, parents do not have the genetic disorder themselves. However, the genetic impact is on reproductive options and risk to child health. Though most childhood genetic disorders are not autosomal dominant (i.e., if one of the parents has the condition 50% of their children at risk for the condition). The childhood conditions with autosomal dominant inheritance include neurofibromatous, tuberous sclerosis, Marfan syndrome achrondroplasia and Crouzon's disease. Each of these genetic conditions can result in varied outcomes for children depending on early diagnosis and medical intervention, functional assessment and monitoring, and family support for the functional development that optimize self-care, mobility, communication, and learning. Especially with a genetically based disability, it is very important to promote functional competencies. Yet the ability of families to participate in medical management of the condition and provide a home environment that supports functional development may be limited by the parent's physical or mental health status or limitation in function, conceptualization of the disorder, struggle with accessing supportive health services, and the tremendous stresses associated with disorders that are progressive.

The cognitive impairment of children with genetic disorders does not necessarily predict the child's prospects to become a functioning member of society. For example, the average IQ of children with Down syndrome at kindergarten entry is 2 to 3 standard deviations below peers, but many of these children are able to learn letters and numbers and apply these concepts to functional academic tasks of reading and mathematics. Nor is the low IQ score predictive of a child's ability to run, dress, maintain continency, communicate basic needs, or play a game with friends.

FAMILY FACTORS IN THE DISABILITY PROCESS

The social conditions of the child's family are central to understanding the process of disability—identification and diagnosis, treatment, and rehabilitation responses (Link & Phelan, 1995; McLloyd, 1998; Newacheck & Stoddard, 1994). It is critical to understand these aspects of the role of family circumstances in disability if the consequences of disability for families are to be better understood. Children who have more highly educated mothers, better socioeconomic situations, and parents who are married when a pregnancy occurs are more likely to receive early prenatal care, have better prenatal health care on average, and experience fewer serious birth-related and neonatal health complications (Hogan & Park, 2000). They also are less likely to be at risk for fetal alcohol syndrome (caused by maternal alcoholism), which is associated with mental retardation and for the effects of other substance abuse (including cocaine), which may also affect prenatal and subsequent postnatal development. After birth, children in disadvantaged environments may be exposed to higher risks that increase injury as well as missed opportunities for developmental stimulation. Yet in so far as the children in these disadvantaged families receive less than optimal medical care, they also are more likely to receive later diagnoses and fragmented interventions to prevent disability and to optimize functioning. Seven to ten percent of very-low-birth-weight survivors have parenchymal brain injury (the major predictor of cerebral palsy), but poverty is the major predictor of low IQ and educational disabilities in very-low-birth-weight children without cerebral palsy (Msall, Bier, & LaGasse, 1998).

FAMILY STRUCTURE, CULTURE, AND RESOURCES

Favorable social conditions may buffer children significantly from potential functional limitations and disability in activities associated with impairment as shown for maternal education in Figure 17.4 (House & Kahn, 1985). The scope and generosity of government programs for such assistance affects access to early medical assistance. The timing and type of health remedies sought differ among cultural groups (Aneshensel, Fielder, & Becerra, 1989; Angel & Guarnaccia, 1989; Angel & Worobey, 1988; Mechanic & Hansell, 1989). Family social conditions also buffer children: More highly educated parents may recognize symptoms of the disabling condition earlier. Such recognition may lead to earlier medical intervention limiting the course of the disabling condition or to earlier therapy, education, and environmental restructuring. Families in poverty or lacking health insurance are likely to have less access to specialized medical care and recommended services; thus formal medical inputs may be reduced (Kogan et al., 1995; Newacheck & Halfon, 1998; Takeuchi, Bui, & Kim, 1993). In addition, the stresses of poverty may limit interventions intended to enhance a child's development and resiliency. These dimensions also are associated with the extent to which health care professionals' recommendations are followed and the learning environment of the home.

There are multiple risks within the biological realm, including prematurity, low birthweight, prenatal teratogens, genetic disorders, and other medical conditions at birth, and these interact with family variables. Maternal education

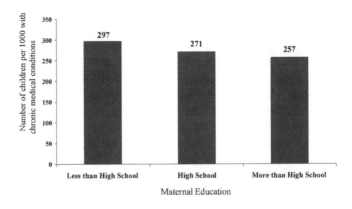

Source: 1988/91 National Maternal and Infant Health Survey

FIG. 17.4. Maternal education in the chronic medical conditions of children age 32 to 36 months with birth weight under 1,500 grams.

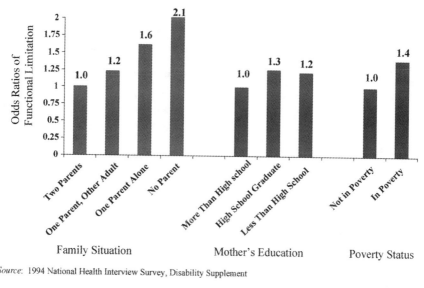

Source: 1994 National Health Interview Survey, Disability Supplement

FIG. 17.5. Family factors in the functional limitation of children age 5 to 17.

and other family characteristics often can modify the severity of disability associated with a genetic condition. In some situations, this relationship can be selective—women of higher education more often give birth to a baby who is very low birthweight and of greater risk of a disability. Among children who are very low birthweight, a more favorable socioeconomic environment can sometimes lessen morbidity. By age 32 to 38 months, for example, the greater the mother's education the less likely children with a very low birth weight have a chronic medical problem. More than one fourth of these high-risk babies have chronic medical conditions at age 32 to 38 months (Figure 17.4). The relationship of maternal education to impairment is evident in these rates, ranging from a rate of 297 per 1,000 for children whose mothers have less than a high school education to 257 per 1,000 for those whose mothers have more than a high school diploma.

We next turn to the relationship of family variables to limitation in function among children (Figure 17.5). We do this by estimating a complex statistical model that predicts the presence, severity, and number of dimensions of limitation. The model provides estimates of the unique effects of family structure, parental education, and poverty. In these models a number of 1.0 indicates the category used as the comparison. Other coefficients in the model indicate the extent to which the likelihood of limitation is greater for persons in that category to persons in the comparison group. (The coefficients are like betting odds—for example, a value of 1.5 indicates odds of 1.5 to 1.0.)

There are strong differences in children's functional status by family structure. Using a two-parent family as the standard, families in which one parent and another adult are present are 23% more likely to have a limitation. For a single parent alone, this increases to 62%. Children living with neither parent are twice as likely as children living with two parents to be limited, in part because such families include foster parent arrangements that may be a consequence of their biological families being unable to meet their special needs.

Children of parents with a high school education or less are about one fourth more likely to be limited compared to parents who are better educated. Children living in poverty are 40% more likely to be functionally limited. However, it is important to recognize that family structure and poverty may partly be a consequence of child disability, such as when divorce is associated with parental conflict about care of a special needs child or when family resources are depleted as a consequence of medical bills. Nonetheless, the family situation is strongly related to child disability status.

Causal relationships are clearer when looking at the effects of these factors on the use of rehabilitation services for children with limitation in function (Figure 17.6). These models indicate the likelihood of children with equivalent functional limitations and medical conditions having implants (e.g., gastrostomy, tracheotomy, middle-ear tubes), devices (e.g., hearing aid, walker, crutches, wheelchair, inhaler), rehabilitation specialists, and mental health services. There

Rehabilitation	Medical Condition					Functional Limitation				Family Situation		
	Life Threatening	Chronic	Episodic, Injury	Genetic/Neurological	Mental, Learning, Drug	Mobility	Selfcare	Communication	Learning Ability	Poverty	Family Type	Education
Devices			•	•		•	•					
Implants	•			•		•	•					
Mental Health/Substance Abuse Services	•				•			•			•	•
Rehabilitation Specialists			•	•		•	•	•				

Note: Analysis restricted to children with functional limitations. Net effects of family situation controlling for severity of functional limitation and medical condition. Asterisks indicate statistically significant Relationships.

Source: 1994/95 National Health Interview Survey, Disability Supplement and Follow-back

FIG. 17.6. Family factors in use of rehabilitation services for children age 5 to 17.

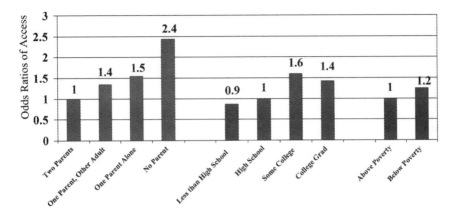

Note: Analysis restricted to children with functional limitations. Net effects of family situation controlling for severity of functional limitation and medical condition.

Source: 1994/95 National Health Interview Survey, Disability Supplement

FIG.17.7. Family factors in access to mental health services for children age 5 to 17.

are no differences in the receipt of implants, devices, or rehabilitation services by family structure, parental education, or poverty. This is heartening in that it suggests that once their medical conditions are diagnosed and their functional limitations assessed, children share equal access to some rehabilitation services. This is due in part to Supplemental Security Income (SSI) and Medicaid support for families with children with disability, and the access to many rehabilitation services at no cost through the schools.

Mental health services are used more often by children whose parents have some college education and by children who do not live with their parents (Figure 17.7). This latter relationship might reflect the serious behavioral challenges regarding mental health supports among children in special foster care arrangements.

EFFECTS OF DISABILITY ON THE FAMILY

We now consider the impact of a child with a disability on the family. The stresses, time and resource requirements, and challenges of a child with special needs (Hall, 1997) are likely to change the family circumstances when a child has a disability.

Mauldon (1992) established that children with a disability and children in frail health destabilize marriages by increasing the risk of divorce once they reach age 6. Less evidence exists to show that children with a disability destabilize marriage before age 6.

Even if the parents remain together, families with a child who has a disability may be less able to fully participate in the labor market, thus significantly reducing family income. Labor force participation may not be possible for mother-headed households in which extreme child disability (for example, with self-care or mobility) requires 24-hour care and supervision. This leaves the family at high risk of poverty and gaps in insurance. The use of financial resources for the care of children with a disability may further reduce families' financial security, leaving them cumulatively less able to respond to financial demands associated with a special needs child.

Families with a child who is limited in function may experience many types of hardship, including labor force transitions of discontinuing work (13.7%), reducing hours worked (13.7%), or working fewer hours (12.1%). These outcomes differ substantially by the type and seriousness of the child's limitation (Rogers, 1999). Two thirds of families with a child with self-care limitations and one half of the families with a mobility limitation have such labor force outcomes. Overall, the experience of a range of hardship—labor force transition, impoverishment, or sleep deprivation—affects 17% of families whose child has mild limitations in functioning, 22% of children who have one serious limitation, and 46% whose child has two or more types of severe limitation (Figure 17.8).

Brady, Meyers, and Luks (1998) find that child disability has a more substantial impact on welfare dynamics, increasing the likelihood of a move to Supplemental Security Income (SSI) and reducing the ability of families to become independent of SSI and welfare. In fact, these investigators note that a

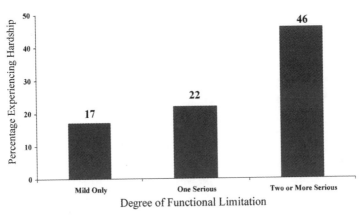

Note: Family hardship due to health of child refers to any change or limitation in employment, recent disruption due to financial stress, or need to change sleep patterns, due to health of child.

Source: 1994/95 National Health Interview Survey, Disability Supplement and Follow-Back (Rogers 1999).

FIG.17.8. Percentage of families with a functionally limited child experiencing hardship.

child with severe disability has an effect that is approximately double that of not having a partner in the household or about a four-year reduction in educational level. Clearly, research on issues of family well-being and welfare dependence need to be informed about child disability and also parental disability.

FAMILY LIFE OF CHILDREN WITH DISABILITY

Because of the dynamic interplay among family conditions, child characteristics, and the disability process, the family's social conditions must be viewed as changing over time. These changes often tend to produce a pattern of cumulative disadvantage for children with a disability. Figure 17.9 shows some of these outcomes for children viewed at only one point in time. Children with a disability less often live in families in which two parents are present (76% for children with no limitation and 59% for those with two or more serious limitations). They also are more likely to have a parent with less than a high school education (12% for children without disability compared to 19% of children with two or more serious limitations), and more often in poverty (18% vs. 29%, respectively).

Many other correlates, and perhaps consequences, of these family and child dynamics are observed as well. For example, exposure to secondhand smoke

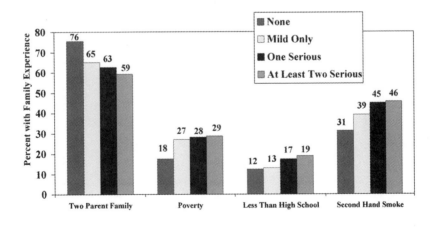

Source: 1994/95 National Health Interview Survey, Disability Supplement and Follow-back

FIG.17.9. Differences in family environment of children by functional limitation.

increases from 31% for children without limitations to 46% for children with the most serious limitations (Hogan, Rogers, & Msall, 2000). This relationship may reflect stress that make it more likely parents will smoke, or perhaps indicate the added impact of smoking as a lifestyle variable associated with other family dynamics, as well as documented increases in respiratory illness in young children.

IMPACT OF CHILD DISABILITY
ON SIBLINGS

The family situations of siblings of children with a disability presumably are also affected by changes in the family and household situations. But the consequences of these common changes will differ for siblings insofar as time and material resource reallocation within the household, reducing their well-being and later life potential unfavorably impact them.

Figure 17.10 provides an indication of this impact. About one fifth of children in households in which no child with disability is present are poor, compared to 32% who have a sibling with limitations. In the extreme case of two or more school-age children with disabilities, 42% are in poverty. An additional indication of the stress created in a family when a child with a disability is present also is seen in data on age-grade delay of two years or more in schooling. Overall, 4% of children who are not disabled and have no disabled sibling show such an

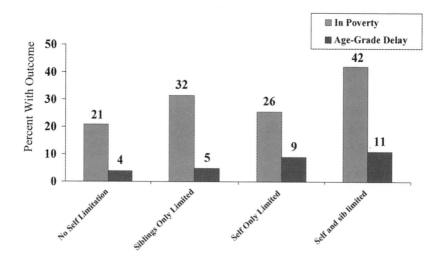

Source: 1994/95 National Health Interview Survey, Disability Supplement and Follow-back

FIG. 17.10.   Effects of siblings with disabilities.

age-grade delay. This increases very slightly to 5% for a child whose sibling has a disability. Nine percent of children who themselves are disabled are age-grade delayed, increasing to 11% for children with a disability who come from families with two or more children with disabilities.

CONCLUSION

This chapter has provided a sample of findings that confirm the multiple relationships between child disability and families. Some children are born with conditions that are potentially disabling. For many others, a serious chronic medical condition or injury after birth alters their acquisition of normal functional skills and participation in age-appropriate activities. For all of these children the critical issue in terms of societal participation involves their ability to achieve adequate skills in self-care, mobility, communication, and learning.

An estimated 12% of American children have a limitation in mobility, self-care, communication, and/or learning. For many of these children the limitations are severe and involve multiple areas of functioning. Those with severe disabilities can provide multiple challenges and difficulties to families. Although as Glidden has discussed in this book, there also can be benefits and perceived rewards.

The stresses of a childhood disability on the parents' relationship can be serious and may increase over time. In a family in which two parents work, full-time care needs of a child with disability often make it necessary for one parent to give up work, creating a substantial income loss. The financial burdens of child disability can be considerable, including modifications to the home, the purchase of special equipment, rehabilitation services, and in-home care. Time pressures on parents can be severe, especially for parents of children whose disability requires round-the-clock care, as well as requirements for special education meetings, after-school supports, and financial paperwork.

Children with disability more often grow up in a single-parent family that is in poverty. The family situations of children in turn affect the course of their treatment, education, and eventual severity or impact of their original risk condition or disability. This includes the diagnosis of potentially disabling conditions; medical treatment; the emergence of limitations in functioning; and the course of intervention or rehabilitation. For affected families, parental resources promote effective parenting for the coordination of medical and rehabilitative services, and work with schools to mobilize resources so that a disabled child is as fully as possible a participant in society. Effective parenting also involves dealing with the special time and resource constraints and other challenges in a way that permits parents and siblings to thrive.

Studies that ignore the 12% of American families with a child who has a disability misrepresent the special conditions for parents associated with children's disabilities. For these children, then, parents are crucial in helping to meet their needs. In the case of children who are severely limited, access to peers will be circumscribed, further emphasizing the key role of parents. Studies that do not recognize child disability also fail to understand the situations of the other children in the family. Their allocation of resources will be reduced if the child with a disability requires a disproportionate amount of parental time and financial resources. The entire family environment may contain different levels of stress. For all of these reasons, it is imperative that we include a consideration of child disability in all of our studies of children and families to improve our understanding of this key population group. Attention to children with disability also is likely to provide insights into the structure and dynamics of family functioning by looking at families under unusual distress.

ACKNOWLEDGMENTS

This research was supported by NICHD/NCMRR Grant No. 1 R03HD35376, "The Demography of Child Disability and Rehabilitation," Dennis P. Hogan, principal investigator and by an NCMRR supplement to the Brown University NICHD P30 Population Center Grant. Dr. Msall's efforts were also supported in part by MCH Grant MCJ-449505-02-0. We thank Meghan Hogan for her insightful comments on this chapter.

REFERENCES

Aneshensel, C. S., Fielder, E. P., & Becerra, R. M. (1989). Fertility and fertility-related behavior among Mexican-Americans and non-Hispanic white female adolescents. *Journal of Health and Social Behavior, 30,* 56–76.

Angel, R., & Guarnaccia, P. J. (1989). Mind, body, and culture: Somatization among Hispanics. *Social Science Medicine, 28,* 1229–1238.

Angel, R., & Worobey, J. L. (1988). Single motherhood and children's health. *Journal of Health and Social Behavior, 29,* 38–52.

Bowe, F. G. (1995). Population estimates: Birth-to-5 children with disabilities. *Journal of Special Education, 28,* 461–471.

Brady H. E., Meyers, M. & Luks, S. (1988). *The Impact of child and adult disabilities on the duration of welfare spells.* San Francisco: Public Policy Institute of California.

Brandt, E. N., Jr., & Pope A. M. (1997). *Enabling America: Assessing the role of rehabilitation science and engineering.* Washington, DC: Institute of Medicine: National Academy of Sciences.

Hall, J. G. (1997). The impact of birth defects and genetic diseases. *Archive of Pediatric Medicine, 151,* 1082–1083.

Hogan, D. P., Msall, M. E, Rogers M. L., & Avery R. C. (1997). Improved disability population estimates of functional limitation among American children aged 5–17. *Maternal and Child Health Journal, 1,* 203–216.

Hogan, D. P., & Park, J. M. (2000). Family factors and social support in the developmental outcomes of children who were very low birth weight at 32 to 38 months of age. *Seminars in Perinatology,* 27: 433–459.

Hogan, D. P., Rogers, M. L., & Msall, M. E. (in 2000). Children with disability: Functional limitations and key indicators of well-being. *Archives of Pediatric and Adolescent Medicine, 154,* 1042–1048.

House, J., & Kahn, R. (1985). Measures and concepts of social support. In S. Cohen, & S. Syme (Eds.), *Social Support and Health* (pp. 83–105). Orlando, FL: Academic Press.

Kogan, M. G., Alexander M., Teitelbaum B., Jack M., Kotelchuck, M., & Papas, G. (1995). The effect of gaps in health insurance on continuity of a regular source of care among preschool-aged children in the United States. *Journal of American Medical Association, 274,* 1429–1435.

Link, B. G., & Phelan J. (1995). Social conditions as fundamental cause of disease [Special issue]. *Journal of Health and Social Behavior,* 80–94.

Mauldon J. (1992). Children's risks of experiencing divorce and remarriage: Do disabled children destablize marriages? *Population Studies, 46,* 349–362.

McLloyd, V. (1998). Socioeconomic disadvantage and child development. *American Psychologist, 53,* 185–204.

Mechanic, D., & Hansell, S. (1989). Divorce, family conflict, and adolescents' well-being. *Journal of Health and Social Behavior, 30,* 105–116.

Msall, M. E, Bier J., LaGasse, L., Tremont, M., and Lester, B. (1998). The vulnerable preschool child: The impact of biomedical and social risks on neurodevelopmental function. *Seminars in Pediatric Neurology, 5,* 52–61.

Msall, M. E., & Tremont, M. R. (1999). Measuring functional status in children with genetic impairments. *American Journal of Medical Genetics (Seminars in Medical Genetics), 89,* 62–74.

National Institute of Health/NICHD. (1993). *Research Plan for the National Center for Medical Rehabilitation Research. NIH Publication* No. 93–3509.

Newacheck P., & Halfon, N. (1998). Prevalence and impact of disabling chronic conditions in childhood. *American Journal of Public Health, 88,* 610–617.

Newacheck, P., & Stoddard, J. (1994) Prevalence and impact of multiple childhood chronic Illnesses. *Journal of Pediatrics, 124,* 40–48.

Newacheck, P., & Taylor, W. (1992). Childhood chronic illness: Prevalence, severity, and impact. *American Journal of Public Health, 82,* 364–371.

Rogers, M. L. (1999). Family consequences of child disability. Paper presented at the annual meeting of the Population Association of America, New York.

Sanderson, M., Placek P. J., & Keppel, J. M. (1991). The 1988 National Maternal and Infant Health Survey: Design, Content and Availability. *Birth, 8,* 26–32.

Stein R. E. K, & Silver, E. J. (1999). Operationalizing a conceptually based moncategorical definition: A first look at U.S. children with chronic conditions. *Archives of Pediatric Medicine, 153,* 68–74.

Takeuchi, D. T., Bui, K. V. T. & Kim, L. (1993). The referral of minority adolescents to community mental health centers. *Journal of Health and Social Behavior, 31,* 43–57.

U.S. Department of Health and Human Services. (1996) *1994 National Health Interview Survey on Disability, Phase 1.* Machine Readable Data. CD-ROM Series 10-8 (SETS Version 1.22a).

18

Parenting Children With Developmental Disabilities: A Ladder of Influence

Laraine Masters Glidden
St. Mary's College of Maryland

In 1968, Richard Q. Bell began his seminal *Psychological Review* article, "A Reinterpretation of the Direction of Effects in Studies of Socialization" with the following statement: "It is not too surprising to find that most research on parent-child interaction has been directed to the question of effects of parents on children" (p. 81). Bell then went on to review various lines of research that provided evidence that the direction also operates in reverse, *viz.,* that children are likely to influence parents in their interactions with them. Interestingly, among the sources of evidence he reviewed were studies of children with various kinds of disabilities—schizophrenia, mental retardation, and hyperactivity—used to demonstrate the importance of child characteristics in determining parental interaction behavior.

In the field of developmental disabilities, this notion of child influencing parent was not a novel one. Indeed, in that era, a version of it dominated the research *Zeitgeist.* By 1968, a substantial number of studies of parents and their children with developmental disabilities had been published, and they all focused on the effect of the child on the parents or family (Farber, 1959, 1960a, 1960b; Olshansky, 1962; Schonell & Watts, 1956; Schonell & Rorke, 1960; Solnit & Stark, 1961). Actually, it is more accurate to describe these studies as ones that focused not on the child's effect on the parents, but on the effect of the child's

Address correspondence to: Laraine M. Glidden, St. Mary's College of Maryland, 18952 E. Fisher Road, St. Mary's City, MD. 20686, Phone: 240-895-4922, Fax: 240-895-4443, e-mail: Lmglidden@smcm.edu disability on the parents. A paper by Holt (1958) is typical. In an interview study of 201 families rearing at least one child with mental retardation, the investigator documented problems of burden of care and emotional distress in detail. The children with retardation were regarded as homogeneous, with their disability being the only important characteristic that influenced how their parents and other family members reacted. This approach of viewing the child with a disability as nothing but a disability was typical of much of the research at this time.

Not surprisingly, then, the conclusions of this research tended to be dominated by this unidimensional conceptualization of the child. Because it seemed obvious that the presence of a disability was negative, it was negative effects that were mostly sought and uncovered. A conclusion by Mitchell (1973) exemplifies this approach: "The impact of a handicapped child on a family is never negligible, usually damaging, and sometimes catastrophic. A few families with great spiritual strength may be bound more firmly together by the experience, but in most, the stresses imposed far outweigh any benefit" (pp. 767–68).

Although investigators writing about the impact of a child with disabilities have become slightly less negative over the ensuing several decades, a literature review as late as 1993 found that most theoretical or empirical writings still posit negative rather than positive hypotheses and assumptions. As a collaborator and I wrote in our summary of the literature, investigators "almost always formulate research designs that include the stressors that families encounter, but rarely involve the rewards that families frequently experience in their everyday interactions with their children who have disabilities" (Helff & Glidden, 1998, p. 461).

THE MACROENVIRONMENT

Despite this early and almost exclusive focus on the child's disability influencing parents, there is certainly evidence that parents and the environment did and do provide influence on the child. This evidence can be seen most clearly when one views the "big picture" or the macroenvironment. The concept of macroenvironment and how it affects the developing and developed organism has been discussed extensively by others (Bronfenbrenner, 1979; Elder, 1995; Goodnow, 1995; Roopnarine & Carter, 1992; Sameroff, 1983). Although different writers may define and characterize the macroenvironment somewhat differently from each other, the most general definition of macrosystems are those "broad ideological, demographic, and institutional patterns of a particular culture or subculture" (Garbarino & Kostelny, 1995, p. 423).

In the field of developmental disabilities, many macrosystemic issues have been and continue to be focal ones. Beliefs about whether people with disabilities have rights identical to those of other citizens; whether people with intellectual disabilities are educable or not; whether the community has the responsibility to embrace persons with disabilities as inclusive members of their society; and

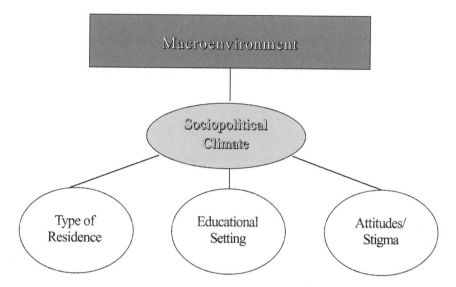

FIG. 18.1.   The macroenvironment and some of its domains.

many others reflect the macrosystem. The individual with a developmental disability does not directly interact in a macroenvironment the way he or she does in a microenvironment, but is influenced enormously by it nonetheless.

Figure 18.1 represents a sampling of macroenvironmental issues that have and do affect the development of persons with developmental disabilities. The sociopolitical climate is a reflection of the beliefs that citizens have about the nature of the human condition, and the relations that the society has to the individual. Is government responsible for the welfare of the individual? In all domains of living or just in some? For all individuals, or just for children, or not even for children? What is the value of a human life? What defines being human? Depending on what answers a society gives to these questions, different laws will be written and enforced, and different policies will be in effect. These answers and the level of agreement of the citizenry on these answers will influence whether we advocate for institutions or home rearing for inclusive, segregated, or no schooling at all. The sociopolitical climate will dictate the attitudes of the members of the society and the degree of stigma associated with being disabled. Moreover, neither the sociopolitical climate nor the specific manifestations of it, are static over time. Indeed, the history of developmental disabilities in the 20th century is a history of change with regard to this climate (Hickson, Blackman, & Reis, 1995, chapter 1).

Not only is the macroenvironment an important element to the understanding of developmental disabilities, it also has been the primary focus in most of the research about parenting until quite recently. In the field of developmental disabilities, we have spent relatively few of our research dollars answering questions about what kinds of parenting are better than others. Rather, we have been almost singularly occupied with convincing ourselves and others that almost any kind of parenting, short of that which is neglectful or abusive, makes a difference. There are good reasons for this emphasis.

Living Environments

During the 20th century, the variability in usual living environments has been much greater for children with disabilities than those without. This variability is apparent in the work of Stephen Richardson and his colleagues, who have written extensively about the mentally retarded members of a cohort born between 1952 and 1954 in Aberdeen, Scotland. In 1996, Richardson and Koller described their 22-year longitudinal study, providing a chilling example of just how variable the family environments of children with mental retardation are. In their sample of 178 children with mental retardation, only 62% lived with one or both biological parents throughout their childhood. Most of the remaining 38% lived in some kind of institution or residential home, frequently moving several times during childhood. For example, one of the children, Molly, had been placed in a residential nursery during infancy either because of parental abandonment or death—the records were unclear as to which. With the exception of one short-term foster placement as a toddler, she lived in a variety of residential homes until she aged out of the system. Although Molly's case may seem extreme, it was not atypical for about a third of the sample. In this sample, and in others, even children who are eventually placed in good adoptive or foster homes frequently experience some degree of "foster care drift"—movement from one short-term setting to another—before their permanent placements.

In my own work studying children with developmental disabilities who are adopted by parents who know that these children have disabilities, I have found many children who have had multiple placements before their home environment stabilizes. For example, in one study, 39% of 56 adopted children had been in more than one previous placement before arriving at their adoptive home, and all but one of these children with two or more previous placements had been in at least one institution (Glidden, 1989). Although we do not have data specifically on how children with developmental disabilities are affected by multiple placements, we can speculate that problems with social-emotional development will be more likely, including especially attachment disorders (Groze, 1994; Gruber, 1978; Pinderhughes & Rosenberg, 1990).

Institutions

Although there were and are strong beliefs about the adverse effects of institutions, and there is an extensive pre-1980 scientific literature about the effects of institutionalization on the development of personality and intelligence, it is not completely edifying with regard to personality. Research conducted primarily in the 1950s and 1960s, when there were large numbers of individuals with mental retardation in institutions, focused on characteristics such as heightened motivation for social reinforcement, overdependency, wariness, and high expectation of failure. It is fair to say that the results of this research were far from definitive. The best that Ed Zigler, undeniably at least one of the heads in this monster body of research, could do by way of summary in 1979 on institutions and personality was as follows:

> Institutions do have an impact on the personality development of their residents. Institutions differ from one another, however, and their effects are not nearly as monolithic as has often been assumed . . . the question of the effects of institutionalization is a very complex one . . . four classes of variables need to be considered: (1) the characteristics of the persons (e.g., age, gender, diagnosis); (2) the nature of the person's preinstitutionalization life experience; (3) the nature of the institution both in demographic and social/psychological terms; and (4) the particular characteristic indexed as a dependent variable." (Balla & Zigler, 1979, p. 163)

All these issues are also critical for explicating the effect of institutions on the development of intelligence, a research domain that was quite active in the 1960's and 1970's. A variety of studies during these decades did find, for the most part, that children who were institutionalized at an early age suffered decrements in cognitive abilities in comparison to children who were home reared, especially those who were being reared in relatively stimulating environments. (Centerwall & Centerwall, 1960; Donoghue, Kirman, Bullmore, Laban, & Abbas, 1970; Elliott & MacKay, 1971). A British study published in 1979 by Ludlow and Allen is illustrative. They studied a cohort of children with Down syndrome born in one county between 1960 and 1969. The 143 children were divided into three groups based on living arrangements and the intensity of services provided. Group 1 consisted of children who were home reared with extensive services for children and parents; Group 2 children were those who were home reared with minimal services for children and parents; and Group 3 contained children who were placed in residential care before age 2, many at birth. The children were followed until age 10, with significant differences emerging in developmental functioning early on, and increasing over time. By age 10, the home-reared children who had received extensive services had developmental quotients that were 24 points higher than the children who were in residential care, and 6 points higher than the home-reared children who had received minimal services.

Because of these kinds of data and also more humanitarian concerns, institutions were viewed rather monolithically as bad places for persons to be, and both psychological research and parent advocacy were influential in the massive deinstitutionalization movement that began in the late 1960s. In 1967, 98.58 residents per 100,000 of the general population lived in MR/DD institutions (194,650 persons) in comparison to 56,161 or 20.72 per 100,000 in 1997 (Anderson, Lakin,

Mangan, & Prouty, 1998). In 1997, fewer than 3,000 children aged 0 to 21 lived in institutions in the United States (Lakin, Prouty, Braddock, & Anderson, 1997). In 1967, the comparable number was approximately 91,000. Thus, there has been a sea of change in the type of environment in which children with developmental disabilities are reared. At last, vindication came to parents who had been ignoring the advice of their pediatricians and other health care professionals to "institutionalize the child, or ruin your life and your family." Today, very few children with mental retardation and other developmental disabilities are cared for outside a home environment, and almost none in institutions.

Adoptive Homes

A manifestation of this massive macroenvironmental change is in the adoption of children with developmental disabilities. Earlier in this century, children with disabilities other than those that were mild and correctable were considered unadoptable (Isaac, 1965; Kornitzer, 1952; Wolkomir, 1947). In contrast, now, at the beginning of the 21st century, a variety of agencies and workers specialize in the adoption of children with disabilities. Moreover, the federal government via the Children's Bureau has announced a national strategic plan that includes as its first goal an increase in the number of children with disabilities that are adopted (Spaulding for Children, 1996).

The adoption of children with disabilities is taking place on a large-enough scale that investigators are able to study it scientifically rather than anecdotally. The results of this research have indicated generally positive outcomes for the families (Groze, 1996; Lightburn & Pine, 1996; Marx, 1990; Todis & Singer, 1991). I have reached similar conclusions in my own work. For example, in one follow-up study, we recontacted families 12 years after their adoptions and found good adjustment outcomes on several variables (Glidden & Johnson, 1999). None of the adoptions had disrupted, and when children moved out of their adoptive homes it was as young adults to age-appropriate settings. Mothers reported more benefits than problems, describing the importance of giving and receiving love, the positive characteristics of their children, and pride in their child's achievements. Importantly, 50% of the sample had adopted at least one additional child in the intervening years since the original interview, and 82% of these subsequently adopted children had developmental disabilities.

In ongoing work with a sample of 123 adoptive families, we are replicating these findings of excellent adjustment. Data collected approximately 5 and 11 years after the children were placed in their adoptive homes indicated that both mothers and fathers experienced low depression and high subjective well-being (Flaherty & Glidden, 2000). Their scores on marital adjustment and family strength were comparable or better than those of families rearing children without disabilities. When asked whether they would do the adoption again, 96% of the mothers responded that they were certain that they would.

Moreover, good adjustment approximately five years after the child's placement predicted good adjustment 11 years after the placement (Flaherty & Evans, 1998). A cluster analysis of scores on outcome variables measured approximately five years after placement grouped only 8% of the adoptive mothers into a "poor" functioning category. The remainder were classified as average (32%) or high (60%) functioning. When these mothers were reexamined six years later, the mothers in the high-functioning group were still functioning substantially better than the mothers in the other two groups combined. They had lower depression and sense of personal burden, higher subjective well-being, and lower perception of parenting hassles. It is noteworthy, however, that even the "lower" functioning group was low only in comparison to their extremely high-functioning peers. The former were still doing quite well when compared to samples normed on families rearing children without disabilities.

Parental Advocacy

The change in residential living patterns for children with developmental disabilities—out of institutions and into adoptive homes or remaining with their parents of origin—has not been an isolated phenomenon in the history of mental retardation. As important as parents were in this change, they were even more important as advocates for educational services. As early as the 1950s, parents of children with mental retardation organized as the National Association for Retarded Children, most recently the Arc, an organization that has lobbied effectively at the local, state, and national levels. At times, parents have encountered seemingly overwhelming barriers. Nonetheless, both the important litigation and legislation of the 1960s and thereafter that extended a variety of rights to individuals with developmental disabilities was, at least in part, the result of parent advocacy efforts. And these advocacy efforts continue. Once federal law mandated access to public education, issues relating to the quality of that education became paramount. Inclusion and entitlement to a variety of services now dominate the contemporary educational landscape.

Furthermore, parental efforts do not typically end when the son or daughter reaches adulthood. Most adults with developmental disabilities remain in contact with their families of origin, frequently living with their parents or another family member (Heller, 1997; Seltzer & Krauss, 1994). Thus, the active parenting role often continues until one or both parents becomes too health-impaired to prolong it. For example, in Seltzer's and Krauss' groundbreaking longitudinal research of several hundred families caring for a son or daughter with mental retardation, the average age of the mother at the beginning of the study was 66 years, and they were caring for their adult children with mental retardation, ranging in age from 19 to 51 years (Seltzer & Krauss, 1989).

Even more importantly, these parents reported that they viewed this caregiving in primarily positive terms, describing the gratifications they have received from it (Seltzer, 1992). Moreover, these gratifications were accompanied by: physical health that was actually better than that of their age peers who were not caring for a dependent family member; and greater life satisfaction than age peers who were caring for an elderly relative. These parents had accepted their role, had given it positive meaning in their lives, and had effectively managed it as part of their life experience (Krauss & Seltzer, 1993).

In sum, when viewed from the perspective of the macroenvironment and in the context of the history of the 20th century, there can be little doubt that parents have influenced the intellectual and social-emotional development of their children with developmental disabilities because of what they have done on behalf of their children. They have accepted the personal responsibility of rearing children where the burden of care is sometimes extraordinary. They have influenced their children's development by working singly or with other parents and groups to advocate for improvements in the educational, medical, residential, and other support services that a responsible society must provide to normalize the lives of individuals with developmental disabilities. And, as I describe in the next section on microenvironment, they frequently have expectations that help to elevate the functioning of their children with disabilities in a positive version of a self-fulfilling prophecy. They think that their children can learn, so they create favorable environments in which to teach them, and thus they do learn more than they would in less favorable environments. Because of parental efforts, the kinds of scenes depicting loneliness and debilitation that Burton Blatt and colleagues published in their 1966 and 1979 books, *Christmas in Purgatory* and *The Family Papers: A Return to Purgatory*, are less frequent than they were. They have been mostly replaced by family interaction, school and community integration, and employment opportunity.

Community Integration

A case study, described in both written (Andrews, 1995) and cinematic form (Andrews, 1987), is an apt segue from the macro- to the microenvironment. John Mcgough is a man with Down syndrome who was born in 1957. His parents were advised to institutionalize him but did not. Instead, they raised John in a loving home environment. When he was a young adult, John and his mother moved to Mendocino, California. It was here that John's story became one of fulfillment and renewal because of a community whose members were accepting in both ideology (macroenvironment) and daily interactions (microenvironment). Town members were both his teachers and his students. They welcomed him into work and recreational activities, including art and music, which were important modes of individual expression. They described how John taught them to listen, to reexamine their most basic values. An artist who was one of John's mentors explained, "What John illustrates is that there is only one truly fine dimension to art—that the highest point of art that we can reach is the art of human relationships—that transcends the making of physical stuff. And John is a supreme artist in that sense. The relationships he builds are a model for all of us" (Andrews, 1995, p. 114).

THE MICROENVIRONMENT

It seems to be a clear conclusion that parents of children with developmental disabilities have influenced their children by creating a macroenvironment that is more salutary than the macroenvironment of a presumably bygone era. But as scientists we are also interested in microenvironments and in experimental designs that allow us to make statements about how parents with certain characteristics create particular family environments that lead to particular outcomes in children. On this issue of microenvironments for children with disabilities we are much less knowledgeable. The research on early intervention as well as other teaching–learning environments tells us that microenvironments do make a difference (e.g., Burchinal, Campbell, Bryant, Wasik, & Ramey, 1997; Guralnick, 1998; Hemmester & Kaiser, 1994; Kaiser, Hemmester, Ostrosky, & Alpert, 1995; Kaiser & Hester, 1996; Lowry & Whitman, 1989; Ramey & Blair, 1996; Ramey, Mulvihill, & Ramey, 1996; Ramey & Ramey, 1998). Moreover, the entire parent-training movement is predicated on the value of educating parents to what they can do to make a difference in the behavior of their children with developmental disabilities (Baker, 1996; Lutzker & Steed, 1998). Indeed, it has long been assumed that much of the mental retardation in this country is a function of both genetic and environmental causality, with the latter consisting of specific environmental causes such as toxins and injuries, as well as generalized environmental deprivation or disadvantage frequently associated with poverty (Drew, Hardman, & Logan, 1996; Ellis, 1979). Therefore, it follows that an enriched environment can prevent or reverse the retardation that is caused by the impoverished environment.

Despite this preponderance of premise, the research on specific parenting attributes is not conclusive as to whether and what parental attributes and behavior influence the intellectual/cognitive and social/emotional development of children with disabilities. An essential component to understanding how parents might influence their children with developmental disabilities is the analysis of parent–child interactions and how those interactions are affected by variability and individual differences across families. Of course, this is no easy task. The microenvironment, along with the variables that influence it, is complex and multidimensional (Belsky, 1984; Borkowski et al., 1992). It includes structural variables such as one- or two-parent families and number and age of siblings, as well as individual parental characteristics such as personality variables like mental stability, and parental experience in childrearing and related endeavors. Nonetheless, examples from two research programs are illustrative of the progress that we are beginning to make.

The work of Frank Floyd and his colleagues is noteworthy (Floyd & Saitzyk, 1992; Floyd & Phillippe, 1993; Floyd, Costigan, & Phillippe, 1997; Floyd & Gallagher, 1997; Floyd, Gilliom, & Costigan, 1998; Floyd & Zmich, 1991). In an interactive setting, family members are videotaped for 50 minutes while they engage in an activity of their choosing. Extensive coding provides details of activities, actors, and actions as well as a variety of behavioral domains such as positive and negative exchanges and various behavior management techniques such as coercion and directiveness. Although parents of children with mental retardation demonstrate some differences in comparison to parents of typically developing children, patterns are frequently quite similar. For example, Floyd and Phillippe (1993) found that parents of children with mental retardation engaged in relatively more behavior management attempts and were less likely to be playful and positive with the child. However, this behavior seemed to be a compensation for the larger number of behavior problems of the children with mental retardation. Despite these problems, the children with mental retardation exhibited the same degree of compliance as did the typically developing children. Thus, this relation may be an example of the child influencing the parent, who, in turn, influences the child.

Another example from Floyd's work demonstrates a longitudinal effect over a 5-year period (Gallagher & Floyd, 1997). For mothers, fewer commands that were vague and nagging, and less negative behavior including reciprocal mother–child behavior at Time 1, was associated with greater community self-sufficiency five years later even after controlling for adaptive skills at Time 1. These data, then, substantiate the claim that parenting does matter.

The research program of Ron Gallimore and colleagues at UCLA also uses longitudinal methodology to assess the role of parental influence on child development (Gallimore, Weisner, Kaufman, & Bernheimer, 1989; Gallimore, Coots, Weisner, Garnier, & Guthrie, 1996; Gallimore, Keough, & Bernheimer, 1999). Project CHILD began with 103 children who exhibited developmental delays when they were 3 years old. Various child, parent, and family measures were collected when the children were 3, 7, and 11 years old. Among these measures were parent expectations with regard to the future functioning of the child: Would he or she catch up, have a marginal handicap, or a permanent disability? IQ data were among those collected for the children. Not surprisingly, parental expectations were related to concurrent child functioning, with correlations varying between .36 and .56. Obviously, no one—and certainly not the investigators—would argue that these were causal.

Somewhat more interesting, however, and quite relevant to the issue of parent influence on child functioning, was the relation between parental expectations when the child was 3 with the child's functioning at age 11. There was no significant influence on IQ scores, suggesting that parental expectation at an earlier time period does not influence intellectual development, but there was an influence on daily living competence. A path analysis of the data revealed that this influence was transactional, with parent expectations influencing daily living competence at each age and daily living competence predicting parent expectations at the next age. Behaviorally, it is reasonable that parents who expect more of their children influence their children to achieve more. Such parents may spend more time themselves teaching their children what they believe these children can learn, or they may work to ensure that the children receive a panoply of services that they think will be beneficial for them.

It may not be accidental that in both the Floyd and Gallimore examples, the impact of parental behaviors was not on a global measure such as intelligence, but rather on more limited, albeit important, skills such as daily living competence, compliance, and community self-sufficiency. These child behaviors are less broad-based, more easily operationalized, and, perhaps, more mutable and more subject to environmental influence than are generalized intellectual abilities. On both macro and micro levels, this environmental influence, is substantially different than what it once was. As we begin a new century and a new millennium, persons with IQs in the severely retarded range live very differently than they did 100 years ago. No longer are they spending most of their lives in institutions with little to occupy them and nothing to contribute. Rather, they may be living semi-independently in houses or apartments, using public transportation, and doing useful work in the community.

SUMMARY AND CONCLUSIONS

In sum, parenting children with developmental disabilities can be conceptualized as a ladder of influence. The bottom rung of the ladder is the microenvironment, and the top rung is the macroenvironment. As I have described in this chapter, parents as a group stand on both rungs, frequently straddling them as they operate on two levels simultaneously. They help to change the macroenvironment (top rung), an effect that can be seen most clearly over longer periods of time and in the context of research that belongs most obviously in the historical domain. They also do this in the microenvironment (bottom rung) by the kinds of interactions they have with their children and the accommodations they make because of their children, which in turn cause changes in the children.

About these latter effects, we still know little. For the most part, our models and hypotheses are extrapolated from those developed for and from work with typically developing children. For example, Belsky (1984) introduced a model of parenting that included parental personality, work, and social network, as well as marital relations. He recognized that child characteristics also were a likely influence on how parents parent. Of course, all of these factors are probably important for children with disabilities as well as those without disabilities. However, we must ask some fundamental questions as we think about extending and modifying this model or other similar ones: Will factors need to be weighted differently, or will the process by which a factor operates differ when one of the child characteristics is a disability? Perhaps the social network is more (or less) important in successfully rearing children with disabilities than it is for children without disabilities. Or perhaps the difference for social networks is not one of degree, but kind. If so, differentially weighting factors may not be a sufficient solution. The actual process by which a parental factor operates to influence parenting may be different depending on the child's disability—whether the child has one or not and what kind of disability it is (Hodapp, 1995). The social network, for instance, may be important to provide information and solve problems when the child has a disability, but not important as an emotional support group.

Similarly, it is possible that some parental personalities are "better" for rearing children with disabilities, whereas others are "better" for children without disabilities. A certain characteristic, such as a high level of directiveness, might result in poor outcomes for typically developing children, but good outcomes for children with developmental disabilities. As illustration, Roach, Barratt, Miller and Leavitt (1998) interpreted the parent–child interaction differences they found between parents of Down syndrome and typically developing children as appropriate adaptations to the behavioral differences of the children, in contrast to earlier conclusions of insensitive parenting. Moreover, it could be that a characteristic that is important in creating the best environment for typically developing children is irrelevant for children with certain types of disabilities. For example, some parents may be very good at providing an intellectual and aesthetic environment for their children, an environment that might be very valuable for a gifted child but which could be irrelevant for one with profound mental retardation.

Existing models are a good place for us to start, but we have barely begun the task of assessing to what degree the models and hypotheses are appropriate or need to be modified for parenting children with developmental disabilities. Nonetheless, it is essential that research on parents and children with developmental disabilities be an integral part of research on all parents and children. We do not yet know to what degree it is even useful to categorize children as disabled or not in our research endeavors. It is possible that other traits or behaviors are far more important than whether or not a child has a disability.

Finally, we must recognize that these models should be multidimensional and contextually sensitive as an adequate representation of parenting itself. As I and others have written (Glidden, Rogers-Dulan, & Hill, 1999; Rogers-Dulan & Blacher, 1995) the role of ethnicity and culture is crucial to understanding parenting. In the first part of this chapter, I described the ways in which parents of children with developmental disabilities have influenced the macroenvironment. Of course, we should not forget that models of parenting must recognize the degree to which the macroenvironment also influences parenting, and ultimately, therefore, child development.

ACKNOWLEDGMENTS

Prepared, in part, with the support of Grant No. HD21993 from the NICHD and from faculty development grants from St. Mary's College of Maryland.

REFERENCES

Anderson, L. L., Lakin, K. C., Mangan, T. W., & Prouty, R. W. (1998). State institutions: Thirty years of depopulation and closure. *Mental Retardation, 36,* 431–443.

Andrews, S. (Camera and editor). (1987). *And then came John: The story of John Mcgough* [Videotape]. (Available from Filmmakers Library, Inc., 124 East 40th Street, New York, NY 10016)

Andrews, S. S. (1995). Life in Mendocino: A young man with Down syndrome in a small town in northern California. In S. J. Taylor, R. Bogdan, & Z. M. Lutfiyya (Eds.), *The variety of community experience: Qualitative studies of family and community life* (pp. 101–116). Baltimore: Paul H. Brookes.

Baker, B. L. (1996). Parent training. In J. W. Jacobson, & J. A. Mulick (Eds.), *Manual of diagnosis and professional practice in mental retardation* (pp. 289–299). Washington, DC: American Psychological Association.

Balla, D., & Zigler, E. (1979). Personality development in retarded persons. In N. R. Ellis (Ed.), *Handbook of mental deficiency, psychological theory and research* (2nd ed., pp. 143–168). Hillsdale, NJ: Lawrence Erlbaum Associates.

Bell, R. Q. (1968). A reinterpretation of the direction of effects in studies of socialization. *Psychological Review, 75,* 81–95.

Belsky, J. (1984). The determinants of parenting: A process model. *Child Development, 55,* 83–96.

Blatt, B., & Kaplan, F. (1966). *Christmas in purgatory.* Boston: Allyn and Bacon.

Blatt, B., Ozolins, A., & McNally, J. (1979). *The family papers: A return to purgatory.* New York: Longman.

Borkowski, J. G., Whitman, T. L., Passino, A. W., Rellinger, E. A., Sommer, K., Keogh, D., & Weed, K. (1992). Unraveling the "new morbidity": Adolescent parenting and developmental delays. In N. W. Bray (Ed.), *International review of research in mental retardation* (pp. 159–196). San Diego, CA: Academic Press.

Bronfenbrenner, U. (1979). *The ecology of human development: Experiments by nature and design.* Cambridge, MA: Harvard University Press.

Burchinal, M. R., Campbell, F. A., Bryant, D. M., Wasik, B. H., & Ramey, C. T. (1997). Early intervention and mediating processes in cognitive performance of children of low-income African American families. *Child Development, 68,* 935–954.

Centerwall, S. A., & Centerwall, W. R. (1960). A study of children with mongolism reared in the home compared with those reared away from home. *Journal of Pediatrics, 25,* 678–685.

Donoghue, E. C., Kirman, B. H., Bullmore, G. H. L., Laban, D., & Abbas, K. A. (1970). Some factors affecting age of walking in a mentally retarded population. *Developmental Medicine and Child Neurology, 12,* 781–792.

Drew, C. J., Hardman, M. L., & Logan, D. R. (1996). *Mental retardation: A life cycle approach* (6th ed.). Edgewood Cliffs, NJ: Prentice-Hall.

Elder, G. H., Jr. (1995). The life course paradigm: Social change and individual development. In P. Moen, G. H. Elder, Jr., & K. Lüscher (Eds.), *Examining lives in context: Perspectives on the ecology of human development* (pp. 101–139). Washington, DC: American Psychological Association.

Elliott, R., & MacKay, D. N. (1971). Social competence of subnormal and normal children living under different types of residential care. *British Journal of Mental Subnormality, 17,* 48–53.

Ellis, N. R. (1979). Introduction. In N. R. Ellis (Ed.), *Handbook of mental deficiency, psychological theory and research* (2nd ed., pp. xxv–xxix). Hillsdale, NJ: Lawrence Erlbaum Associates.

Farber, B. (1959). Effects of a severely mentally retarded child on family integration. *Monographs of the Society for Research in Child Development, 24* (2, Whole No. 71).

Farber, B. (1960a). Family organization and crises: Maintenance of integration in families with a severely mentally retarded child. *Monographs of the Society for Research in Child Development, 25* (1, Whole No. 75).

Farber, B. (1960b). Perceptions of crisis and related variables in the impact of a retarded child on the mother. *Journal of Health and Human Behavior, 1,* 108–118.

Flaherty, E. M., & Evans, J. N. (1998, March). Stability or instability? Predicting long-term personal and family well-being of adoptive and birth parents raising children with developmental disabilities. In L. M. Glidden (Chair), *"Ho-hum? Or Aha!?" The expected and unexpected in families rearing children with developmental disabilities.* Symposium conducted at the Gatlinburg Conference on Research and Theory in Mental Retardation and Developmental Disabilities, Charleston, SC.

Flaherty, E. M., & Glidden, L. M. (2000). Positive adjustment in parents rearing children with Down syndrome. *Early Education and Development, 11,* 407–422.

Floyd, F. J., Costigan, C. L., & Phillippe, K. A. (1997). Developmental change and consistency in parental interactions with school-age children who have mental retardation. *American Journal on Mental Retardation, 101,* 579–594.

Floyd, F. J., & Gallagher, E. M. (1997). Parental stress, care demands, and use of support services for school-age children with disabilities and behavior problems. *Family Relations, 46,* 359–371.

Floyd, F. J., Gilliom, L. A., & Costigan, C. L. (1998). Marriage and the parenting alliance: Longitudinal prediction of change in parenting perceptions and behaviors. *Child Development, 69,* 1461–1479.

Floyd, F. J., & Phillippe, K. A. (1993). Parental interactions with children with and without mental retardation: Behavior management, coerciveness, and positive exchange. *American Journal on Mental Retardation, 97,* 673–684.

Floyd, F. J., & Saitzyk, A. R. (1992). Social class and parenting children with mild and moderate mental retardation. *Journal of Pediatric Psychology, 17,* 607–631.

Floyd, F. J., & Zmich, D. E. (1991). Marriage and the parenting partnership: Perceptions and interactions of parents with mentally retarded and typically developing children. *Child Development, 62,* 1434–1448.

Gallagher, E. M., & Floyd, F. J. (1997, March). *Child behavior problems and parent–child interactions in families of children with and without disabilities.* Paper presented at the Gatlinburg Conference on Theory and Research in MR/DD, Riverside, CA.

Gallimore, R., Coots, J. J., Weisner, T. S., Garnier, H. E., & Guthrie, D. (1996). Family responses to children with early developmental delays II: Accommodation intensity and activity in early and middle childhood. *American Journal on Mental Retardation, 101,* 215–232.

Gallimore, R., Keough, B. K., & Bernheimer, L. P. (1999). The nature and long-term implications of early developmental delays: A summary of evidence from two longitudinal studies. In L. M. Glidden (Ed.), *International review of research in mental retardation* (Vol. 22, pp. 105–135). San Diego, CA: Academic Press.

Gallimore, R., Weisner, T. S., Kaufman, S. Z., & Bernheimer, L. P. (1989). The social construction of ecocultural niches: Family accommodation of developmentally delayed children. *American Journal of Mental Retardation, 94,* 216–230.

Garbarino, J., & Kostelny, K. (1995). Parenting and public policy. In M. H. Bornstein (Ed.), *Handbook of parenting: Vol. 3. Status and social conditions of parenting* (pp. 419–436). Mahwah, NJ: Lawrence Erlbaum Associates.

Glidden, L. M. (1989). Parents for children, children for parents: The adoption alternative. *AAMR Monograph #11.* Washington, DC: American Association on Mental Retardation.

Glidden, L. M., & Johnson, V. E. (1999). Twelve years later: Adjustment in families who adopted children with developmental disabilities. *Mental Retardation, 37,* 16–24.

Glidden, L. M., Rogers-Dulan, J., & Hill, A. E. (1999). "That child was meant?" or "Punishment for sin?" Religion, ethnicity, and families with children with disabilities. *International Review of Research in Mental Retardation, 22,* 267–288.

Goodnow, J. J. (1995). Differentiating among social contexts: By spatial features, forms of participation, and social contracts. In P. Moen, G. H. Elder, Jr., & K. Lüscher (Eds.), *Examining lives in context: Perspectives on the ecology of human development* (pp. 269–301). Washington, DC: American Psychological Association.

Groze, V. (1994). Clinical and nonclinical adoptive families of special-needs children. *Families in Society: The Journal of Contemporary Human Services, 75,* 90–104.

Groze, V. (1996). A 1 and 2 year follow-up study of adoptive families and special needs children. *Children and Youth Services Review, 18,* 57–82.

Gruber, A. R. (1978). *Children in foster care.* New York: Human Services Press.

Guralnick, M. J. (1998). Effectiveness of early intervention for vulnerable children: A developmental perspective. *American Journal on Mental Retardation, 102,* 319–345.

Heller, T. (1997). Older adults with mental retardation and their families. In N. W. Bray (Ed.), *International review of research in mental retardation* (Vol. 20, pp. 99–136). San Diego, CA: Academic Press.

Helff, C. M., & Glidden, L. M. (1998). More positive or less negative? An empirical examination of twenty years of research on adjustment in families of children with developmental disabilities. *Mental Retardation, 36,* 457–464.

Hemmester, M. L., & Kaiser, A. P. (1994). Enhanced milieu teaching: Effects of parent-implemented language intervention. *Journal of Early Intervention, 18,* 269–289.

Hickson, L., Blackman, L. S., & Reis, E. M. (1995). *Mental retardation: Foundations of educational programming.* Boston: Allyn and Bacon.

Hodapp, R. M. (1995). Parenting children with Down syndrome and other types of mental retardation. In M. H. Bornstein (Ed.), *Handbook of parenting: Vol. 1. Children and parenting* (pp. 233–253). Mahwah, NJ: Lawrence Erlbaum Associates.

Holt, K. S. (1958). The home care of severely retarded children. *Pediatrics, 22,* 744–755.

Isaac, R. J. (1965). *Adopting a child today.* New York: Harper & Row.

Kaiser, A. P., Hemmester, M. L., Ostrosky, M. M., & Alpert, C. L. (1995). The effects of group training and individual feedback on parent use of milieu teaching. *Journal of Child Communication Disorders, 16,* 39–48.

Kaiser, A. P., & Hester, P. P. (1996). How everyday environments support children's communication. In L. K. Koegel, R. L. Koegel, & G. Dunlap (Eds.), *Positive behavioral support: Including people with difficult behavior in the community* (pp. 145–162). Baltimore: Paul H. Brookes.

Kornitzer, M. (1952). *Child adoption in the modern world.* London: Putnam.

Krauss, M. W., & Seltzer, M. M. (1993). Coping strategies among older mothers of adults with retardation: A life-span developmental perspective. In A. P. Turnbull, J. M. Patterson, S. K. Behr, D. L. Murphy, J. G. Marquis, & M. J. Blue-Banning (Eds.), *Cognitive coping, families, and disability* (pp. 173–182). Baltimore: Paul H. Brookes.

Lakin, C., Prouty, B., Braddock, D., & Anderson, L. (1997). State institution populations: Smaller, older, more impaired. *Mental Retardation, 35,* 231–232.

Lightburn, A., & Pine, B. A. (1996). Supporting and enhancing the adoption of children with developmental disabilities. *Children and Youth Services Review, 18,* 139–162.

Lowry, M. A., & Whitman, T. L. (1989). Generalization of parenting skills: An early intervention program. *Child and Family Behavior Therapy, 11,* 45–65.

Ludlow, J. R., & Allen, L. M. (1979). The effect of early intervention and pre-school stimulus on the development of the Down's syndrome child. *Journal of Mental Deficiency Research, 23,* 29–44.

Lutzker, J. R., & Steed, S. E. (1998). Parent training for families of children with developmental disabilities. In J. M. Briesmeister, & C. E. Schaefer (Eds.), *Handbook of parent training: Parents as co-therapists for children's behavior problems* (2nd ed., pp. 281–307). New York: John Wiley and Sons.

Marx, J. (1990). Better me than somebody else: Families reflect on their adoption of children with developmental disabilities. *Children and Youth Services Review, 18,* 139–162.

Mitchell, R. G. (1973). Chronic handicap in childhood: Its implications for family and community. *Practitioner, 211,* 763–768.

Olshansky, S. (1962). Chronic sorrow: A response to having a mentally defective child. *Social Casework, 43,* 191–194.

Pinderhughes, E. E., & Rosenberg, K. F. (1990). Family-bonding with high risk placements: A therapy model that promotes the process of becoming a family. In L. M. Glidden (Ed.), *Formed families: Adoption of children with handicaps* (pp. 209–230). New York: Haworth Press.

Ramey, C. T., & Blair, C. (1996). Intellectual development and the role of early experience. In D. K. Detterman (Ed.), *The environment: Current topics in human intelligence.* (Vol. 5, pp. 59–67). Norwood, NJ: Ablex.

Ramey, C. T., Mulvihill, B. A., & Ramey, S. L. (1996). In J. W. Jacobson & J. A. Mulick (Eds.), *Manual of diagnosis and professional practice in mental retardation* (pp. 215–227). Washington, DC: American Psychological Association.

Ramey, C. T., & Ramey, S. L. (1998). Early intervention and early experience. *American Psychologist, 53,* 109–120.

Richardson, S. A., & Koller, H. (1996). *Twenty-two years: Causes and consequences of mental retardation.* Cambridge, MA: Harvard University Press.

Roach, M. A., Barratt, M. S., Miller, J. F., & Leavitt, L.A. (1998). The structure of mother–child play: Young children with Down syndrome and typically developing children. *Developmental Psychology, 34,* 77–87.

Rogers-Dulan, J., & Blacher, J. (1995). African American families, religion, and disability: A conceptual framework. *Mental Retardation, 33,* 226–238.

Roopnarine, J. L., & Carter, D. B. (Eds.). (1992). Parent–child socialization in diverse cultures: In I. E. Sigel (Series Ed.), *Annual advances in applied developmental psychology: Vol. 5.* Norwood, NJ: Ablex Publishing.

Sameroff, A. J. (1983). Developmental systems: Contexts and evolution. In P. H. Mussen (Series Ed.) & W. H. Kessen (Vol. Ed.), *Handbook of child psychology: Vol. 1. History, theory, and methods* (4th ed., pp. 237–294). New York: John Wiley and Sons.

Schonell, F. J., & Rorke, M. (1960). A second survey of the effects of a subnormal child on the family unit. *American Journal of Mental Deficiency, 64,* 862–868.

Schonell, F. J., & Watts, B. H. (1956). A first survey of the effects of a subnormal child on the family unit. *American Journal of Mental Deficiency, 61,* 210–219.

Seltzer, M. M. (1992). Family caregiving across the full lifespan. In R. L. Taylor & L. Sternberg (Series Eds.) & L. Rowitz (Ed.), *Disorders of human learning, behavior, and communication: Mental retardation in the year 2000* (pp. 85–100). New York: Springer-Verlag.

Seltzer, M. M., & Krauss, M. W. (1989). Aging parents with adult mentally retarded children: Family risk factors and sources of support. *American Journal on Mental Retardation, 94,* 303–312.

Seltzer, M. M., & Krauss, M. W. (1994). Aging parents with co-resident adult children: The impact of lifelong adult caregiving. In M. M. Seltzer, M. W. Krauss, & M. P. Janicki (Eds.), *Life course perspectives on adulthood and old age* (pp. 3–18). Washington, DC: American Association on Mental Retardation Monograph Series.

Solnit, A. J., & Stark, M. H. (1961). Mourning and the birth of a defective child. *Psychoanalytic Study of the Child, 16,* 523–537.

Spaulding for Children. (1996). A national adoption strategic plan. *The Roundtable: Journal of the National Resource Center for Special Needs Adoption, 10,* 1–5.

Todis, B., & Singer, G. (1991). Stress and stress management in families with adopted children who have severe disabilities. *The Journal of the Association for People with Severe Handicaps, 16,* 3–13.

Wolkomir, B. (1947). The unadoptable baby achieves adoption. *Child Welfare League of America Bulletin, 26,* 1–7.

V

Future Research Directions and Translations to Parenting Practices

19

The National Institute of Child Health and Human Development Research on Parenting: Past, Present, and Future Directions

Margaret M. Feerick, Marie Bristol-Power, and Dana Bynum

National Institute of Child Health and Human Development

During the past 20 years, research on parenting has expanded greatly in breadth and scope. Studies have ranged from microanalytic examinations of early infant-caregiver interactions, to demographic studies on the dramatic shifts in timing of pregnancy and incidence of teenage parenthood, to ethological studies of the evolutionary basis of parenting behaviors. Through all of these studies, with their diverse research methodologies and populations, the goal has been an understanding of positive parenting behaviors and their causes and consequences for children, as well as negative or high-risk parenting behaviors and the conditions that surround them. Consistent with its primary mission, the National Institute of Child Health and Human Development (NICHD) has played a leadership role in funding investigations of parenting.

The mission of the NICHD is to ensure that every individual is born healthy and wanted, and has the opportunity to fulfill his or her potential for a healthy and productive life. In pursuit of this mission, the NICHD conducts and supports

Address correspondence to: Margaret M. Feerick, Ph.D., Child Development and Behavior Branch, NICHD, 6100 Executive Blvd., Room 4B05, MSC 7510, Bethesda, MD 20892-7510 Phone: 301-435-6882, Fax: 301-480-7773, e-mail: Feerickm@mail.nih.gov laboratory, clinical, and epidemiological research on the reproductive, neurobiologic, developmental, and behavioral processes that determine and maintain the health of children, adults, families, and populations.

The NICHD administers a multidisciplinary program of research, research training, and public information, nationally and within its own facilities, on reproductive biology and population issues; on prenatal development as well as maternal, child, and family health; and on medical rehabilitation. NICHD programs are based on the concepts that adult health and well-being are determined in large part by episodes early in life, that human development is continuous throughout life, and that the reproductive processes and the management of fertility are of major concern, not only to the individual but to society. NICHD research is also directed toward restoring or maximizing individual potential and functional capacity when disease, injury, or a chronic disorder intervenes in the developmental process.

Since its inception, the NICHD has supported a range of extramural and intramural research and research-training programs related to parenting and the myriad influences of parents on child development. These programs have been supported by the Center for Research for Mothers and Children; the Center for Population Research; the National Center for Medical Rehabilitation Research; the Division of Epidemiology, Statistics, and Prevention Research; and the Division of Intramural Research. Within these functional components, nine different branches or laboratories support a wide range of programs related to children and families, and represent a diversity of disciplines and areas, including child development, anthropology, psychology, pediatrics, sociology, demography, perinatology, pediatrics, developmental biology, and epidemiology. They also represent both basic and applied research examining multiple levels of influence of parents on child development and vice versa, as well as research on processes and mechanisms of development throughout the life span.

TRENDS IN NICHD PARENTING RESEARCH FUNDING DURING THE PAST 20 YEARS

During the past 20 years the NICHD has spent a total of $471,776,606 on parenting research and has supported a total of 983 different research and training projects that examine aspects of parenting and the role of parents in child development. These projects have included a range of different funding mechanisms: research project grants, research training mechanisms (e.g., fellowships and institutional training grants), cooperative agreements, research centers, intramural research projects, and research and development–related contracts and intra- and interagency agreements. More than half of the projects supported have been research project grants, more than a quarter research centers,

TABLE 19.1

NUMBER AND TOTAL DOLLAR AMOUNT FOR PARENTING PROJECTS,
FISCAL YEAR 1982–1999 BY TYPE OF FUNDING MECHANISM

Type of Funding Mechanism	1982–1989			1990–1999		
	Number	Total amount	% of total	Number	Total amount	% of total
Research projects (e.g., R01, R03)	212	$80,713,267	70.8	322	$217,102,156	60.7
Research centers (e.g., P20, P30)	107	$19,013,803	16.7	194	$32,998,444	9.2
Other research grants (e.g., K04, R43)	17	$2,038,234	1.8	26	$56,945,581	15.9
Training (F and T series)	13	$1,704,825	1.5	15	$3,091,247	0.9
Contracts and intra interagency agreements	14	$2,291,038	2.0	21	$22,274,195	6.2
Intramural	23	$8,253,622	7.2	19	$25,350,194	7.1
All types of projects	386	$114,014,789	100	597	$357,761,817	100

Note. Subprojects of program projects and center grants are counted individually.

and more than 4% other research awards. Fewer than 3% of the projects have been research training mechanisms, and fewer than 4% have been research and development-related contracts and intra- or interagency agreements (see Table 19.1).

In terms of the scientific areas represented by the projects, of the total number of parenting research projects supported between 1982 and 1999, approximately 24% have focused on processes of atypical development (e.g., mental retardation and other developmental disabilities), 27% on family and other childcare contexts and their influences on child development, 39% on demographic studies related to families and children, and 10% on biological processes, animal studies, or biobehavioral development (see Figure 19.1). Very few of the projects can be classified as intervention research (e.g., experimental or quasi-experimental studies of the effectiveness of specific intervention or prevention programs, about 4%), applied or translational research (e.g., program evaluation studies, tests of specific instructional tools, or studies of assessment or consent processes, about 3%), or policy-oriented research (e.g., research examining the impact of specific policies such as child support or welfare reform legislation, about 3%). Fewer than 1% of the awards have focused primarily on measurement development or the development of new methodologies.

Figure 19.2 presents the total funds spent on parenting research during the 1980s and 1990s by year. Of the total funds spent by the NICHD on parenting research during the past 20 years, more than 40% has been spent in the area of family and other childcare contexts and their influences on development, and 32% has been spent on demographic studies of families and children. Approximately

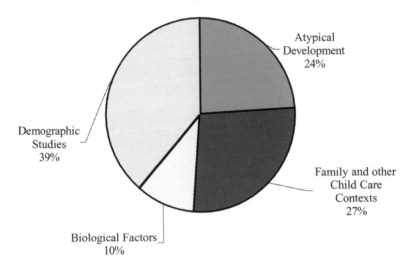

FIG. 19.1. Scientific areas represented by all awards for parenting research.

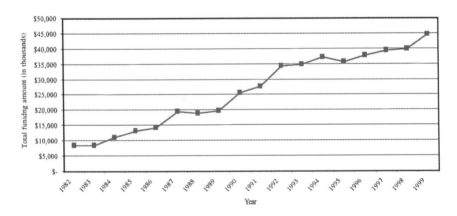

FIG. 19.2. Total funding amount for parenting research, 1982–1999.

19% has been spent on atypical development, and an additional 10% has been spent on biological, biobehavioral, or animal studies. During the 1980s, the total funds spent on parenting research was $114,014,789. During the 1990s, this amount more than tripled, with a total of $357,761,817 spent on parenting research.

The greatest increase in funding during the 1990s occurred in the area of family and other childcare contexts and their influences on development. This area

TABLE 19.2
TOTAL FUNDING OF PARENTING RESEARCH BY RESEARCH AREA,
FISCAL YEAR 1982–1999

Area of Study	Total funding		Change in funding	
	1982–1989	1990–1999	Funding	% Increase
Atypical development	$27,520,377	$60,459,050	+$32,938,673	+120%
Family Context	$33,081,582	$156,124,587	+$123,043,005	+372%
Demographic studies	$36,921,246	$112,577,480	+$75,656,234	+205%
Biological factors	$16,491,584	$28,600,700	+$12,109,116	+73%
Total	$114,014,789	$357,761,817	+$243,747,028	+214%

increased by more than four times, from $33,081,582 during the 1980s to $156,124,587 during the 1990s. Funding for demographic studies of families and children more than tripled, from $36,921,246 in this area during the 1980s to $112,577,480 during the 1990s. Studies of atypical development also increased in funding, from $27,520,377 spent during the 1980s to $60,459,050 during the 1990s. Funding for biological studies, animal studies, and studies of biobehavioral development, increased from $16,491,584 to $28,600,700 (see Table 19.2).

Funds spent on intervention research during the past 20 years were in about the same proportion as numbers of projects, representing slightly less than 7% of the total expenditures on parenting research. The total of funds spent on intervention studies during the 1980s and 1990s was $31,765,295. An additional $10,932,839 was spent on applied or translational research projects and $17,947,279 on policy-oriented research projects. A total of $2,703,904 was spent on projects primarily focused on measurement development or the development of new methodologies.

ATYPICAL DEVELOPMENT

The pattern of funding for studies of atypical development has been similar to that for all parenting research during the past 20 years, with the majority of both projects and dollars supporting research project grants or research centers. Nearly half of the projects supported in this area have been research centers, and more than 45% have been research project grants. Fewer than 2% have been research training mechanisms, and fewer than 3% have been other research grants, research and development-related contracts or intra- and interagency agreements, or intramural research.

Across all mechanisms, the number of projects that can be classified as intervention or applied research is slightly higher than that for all parenting studies supported. Approximately 9% of the projects in the area of atypical development can be classified as intervention research and 5% as applied or translational research, including projects focused on developing tools or techniques to enhance family processes or child development. An additional 1% of projects can be considered policy-oriented research (e.g., projects focused on ethics and social policy issues related to atypical development).

In terms of the scientific content of the awards in this area, approximately 40% focused on family processes or parent-child interactions in families with members having mental retardation or other developmental disabilities. An additional 30% of projects focused primarily on child developmental processes in atypical families, primarily language development, social processes, or social and behavioral adjustment. About 15% of projects focused on parent or family responses and behaviors in relation to children or family members having mental retardation or developmental disabilities, and an additional 6% focused primarily on parental risk factors or maladaptive parenting. Approximately 9% of awards focused on living settings and environments, treatment regimens, or societal variables influencing families with members having mental retardation or developmental disabilities.

A total of $9,814,075 was spent on intervention research in this area. The majority of these funds was spent on projects focusing either on family processes, parent-child relationships, or parent and family responses and behaviors, with a small proportion spent on intervention research in which the primary focus of intervention was the mentally retarded or developmentally delayed child or adult. An additional $2,605,906 was spent on applied or translational research. The majority of these funds was spent on projects focused primarily on parent or family responses and behaviors, although a small proportion was spent on applied or translational projects in which the focus was on child developmental outcomes, family processes, or parent-child relationships in atypical families. A total of $1,036,945 was spent on policy-oriented research, primarily studies of ethical and social policy issues related to families with children or adults having developmental disabilities.

FAMILY AND OTHER CHILDCARE CONTEXTS

The majority of projects addressing family and other childcare contexts and their influences on child development have focused on processes of normal parenting behaviors and child developmental outcomes. Similar to the overall trends in parenting research, the majority of projects in this area (more than 60%) have been research project grants. An additional 13% have been other research mechanisms including career development awards, cooperative agreements, and research conferences, and 7% have been research training mechanisms. Fewer than 1% have been research and development–related contracts or intra-and interagency agreements, and approximately 14% have been intramural research projects. Approximately 5% of the projects in this area can be classified as intervention research. An additional 5% of projects can be classified as applied or translational research, including projects involving parenting and parent skills training programs, education tools, and child development materials. About 1% of projects have focused on the development of new measurement tools or methodologies for parenting and/or child development research.

In terms of the scientific content of the projects in this area, approximately 30% focused on family processes or parent-child interaction, primarily in typical families. An additional 26% focused on childcare or school settings or societal/cultural variables influencing processes of parenting and child development. Twenty-four percent of projects focused primarily on child developmental outcomes in typical and high-risk families including physical, social, emotional, and cognitive development and the development of specific academic abilities. An additional 13% focused on specific parenting behaviors or parent qualities related to normal child development, and approximately 7% focused on processes of maladaptive parenting or parental risk factors for poor developmental outcomes.

Similar to the total expenditures for intervention research for atypical development studies, a total of $11,512,628 was spent on intervention research related to family and other childcare contexts and their influences on development. Of this amount, approximately one third was spent on interventions focused on parenting and parent behaviors. An additional third was for projects focused primarily on child developmental outcomes, and about 20% for projects focused on family processes or parent-child interaction. Less than a quarter of the funds spent on intervention research was for projects focused primarily on childcare or school settings or societal/cultural variables influencing child development. An additional $7,405,429 was spent on applied or translational research. The majority of these funds was spent on projects focused primarily on maladaptive parenting or parental risk factors and child development outcomes. A smaller proportion of funds was spent on applied or translational projects in which the focus was on family processes, parent-child interaction, or parent qualities or behaviors.

A total of $1,536,122 was spent on the development of new research methodologies. The majority of these funds was spent on projects examining family processes, parent-child interaction, or parenting behaviors. A small proportion of additional funds was spent on measurement/methodology projects in which the focus was on maladaptive parenting or parental risk factors.

DEMOGRAPHIC STUDIES

Demographic studies of children and families have followed trends similar to studies of atypical development, with more than 90% of projects in this area being research project grants or research centers. An additional 8% of projects have been research and development contracts or intra- and interagency agreements. Fewer than 2% of awards have been research training mechanisms or other research mechanisms. None of the awards in this area can be classified as intervention research, although slightly fewer than 1% have been applied or translational research projects. Seven percent of awards have been policy-oriented research, and an additional 1% have focused on measurement or methodology development.

In terms of the scientific content of projects in this area, approximately half of the projects have been studies of family or household dynamics, including studies of family structure, family formation, and changes in household composition. An additional quarter of the projects have focused on economic and employment influences on children and families, approximately 10% have focused on population dynamics or migration and immigration processes, 10% have focused on fertility and sexual behavior, and fewer than 1% have focused on factors affecting morbidity or mortality. Approximately 5% of the projects in this area have focused on childcare and its influence on families and children.

A total of $921,494 has been spent on applied or translational research projects in this area. The majority of these funds was spent on studies of population dynamics or migration and immigration processes, with a total of $847,896 spent on projects of this kind. An additional $73,598 was spent on applied or translational projects focused on family or household dynamics. A total of $16,910,334 was spent on policy-oriented research, including projects focused on welfare reform, economic policies, and child support. The majority of these funds was spent on studies of economic and employment influences on children and families, with a smaller proportion spent on studies of family or household dynamics, studies of childcare, and population dynamics or migration and immigration processes. A total of $1,167,782 was spent on research focused on measurement or methodology development. All of these projects focused on population dynamics or migration and immigration processes.

BIOLOGICAL AND BIOBEHAVIORAL DEVELOPMENT AND ANIMAL STUDIES

Of the total number of parenting research projects that can be classified as studies of biological or biobehavioral development or animal studies, 57% have been research project grants. An additional 35% have been research centers and 5% research training mechanisms or other research awards. Approximately 6% of projects have been research and development-related contracts, intra- and interagency agreements, or intramural research. Approximately 5% of the projects in this area can be classified as intervention research.

Approximately 30% of projects in this area focused on biological processes related to developmental disorders. These include studies of eating disorders, mental retardation and other developmental disabilities, and studies of preterm or low birth weight infants. An additional 22% of projects focused on biological and biobehavioral processes related to pregnancy, prenatal development, and perinatology. Twenty-one percent of projects focused on biological influences on maternal behavior, 9% on processes related to infant development, 6% on biobehavioral development, and about 12% of projects were animal studies.

A total of $10,438,592 was spent on intervention research related to the area of biological and biobehavioral development and animal studies. Of this amount, the majority of funds was spent on studies related to developmental disorders, studies focused on pregnancy, prenatal development, or perinatology, and studies of biobehavioral development.

SUMMARY

During the past 20 years, parenting research has received a substantial amount of funding by the NICHD. Funds spent on parenting research continued to grow throughout the 1980s and 1990s, and more than tripled between 1982 and 1999. The majority of awards made during this period were for research project grants or centers, with research and development-related contracts or intra- and interagency agreements, research training mechanisms, and other research projects representing less than 15% of all parenting research projects supported. Approximately 24% of all parenting projects focused on processes of atypical development, 27% on family and other childcare contexts and their influences on development, 39% on demographic studies of families and children, and 10% on studies of biological or biobehavioral development or animal studies. Only about 10% of all projects supported can be considered intervention research, applied or translational research, or policy-oriented research, and fewer than 1% can be classified as focused on measurement or methodology development.

The majority of research projects within each scientific area have been research project grants or research centers. A smaller proportion of projects have been intramural research, research training awards, research and development– related contracts, intra- and interagency agreements, or other research. Within each scientific area, spending on intervention or applied research and policy-oriented research has represented a small proportion of total expenditures, with very few funds spent on projects focused on measurement or methodology development. Despite the continual increase in funds allocated to study parenting and the involvement of so many programs of the NICHD, there have been several areas of importance that have received little attention over the years. These gaps need to be addressed in coming years both by the NICHD and the scientific community.

Research Gaps in NICHD Funding

Although the NICHD and the other National Institutes of Health (NIH) institutes have supported much important research on parenting and families over the past two decades, there are a number of gaps remaining in our knowledge. Although some of these gaps are being explicitly addressed by the NICHD and other NIH institutes through current program initiatives (described below), in all cases more investigator-initiated research is also needed to address these and other notable gaps in current parenting/family research. As indicated in the discussion of funding trends in the previous section, there are some research questions that have already been receiving attention from NICHD-funded researchers, and some questions are only beginning to draw the attention they warrant. In this section we outline some of the more prominent areas of research on parenting that are of growing interest to the NICHD.

KEY RESEARCH NEEDS

In general, in parenting/family research, more studies are needed that assess the dramatic changes in the demographics and contexts of American families in terms of family structure, immigration, ethnicity, employment, and the changing context of childcare. In addition, more cross-cultural and cross-disciplinary research and multilevel studies of parenting and child development in social and cultural contexts are needed, especially those examining multiple layers of the child's ecology and processes and mechanisms of change over time and in different social, cultural, and ethnic contexts. Although some research is being conducted that examines parenting and child development in different social and cultural contexts, there is a clear need for more research of this kind, as well as research which examines the complex interplay among the different contexts in a child's life. While a few current studies examine multiple systems in the child's life, most focus on only one or two, and few examine the processes by which these systems and contexts interact to influence and shape development.

Similarly, there is a need for more research specifically focused on the multiple influences on health in the lives of children and families. Although some studies have addressed stressors in families, there are few data relating parenting to actual health outcomes for either children or parents. Additionally, there are almost no data that adequately address disparities in health care availability and access by persons of different ethnic groups, socioeconomic status, or race, and the impact of such disparities on both morbidity and mortality for children or parents. Especially important is the role of parents in the development of those health habits in childhood that lead to adult disease, such as obesity in children and behaviors that put young people at risk for early pregnancy, drug use, violence, or other problems of adolescence (see chapter by Dishion and Bullock). At the same time, we are just beginning to understand the dynamics of resilience in children and the factors that lead to adaptation in children growing up in less than optimal circumstances. Longitudinal studies of early predictors of psychopathology or atypical socioemotional or behavioral development are thus especially needed.

Although there are a number of studies of parent–child relationships in infancy and the preschool years, the field's interest in these relationships during middle childhood and adolescence has been limited. In particular, little is known about successful transitions into and out of adolescence, and those factors that promote healthy adjustment, particularly during periods of transition. Additionally, little research to date has explored mediators of developmental change and the nature of developmental processes from preschool through the elementary school years. Similarly, with increasing attention being paid to educational outcomes for children, more research is needed to address parental roles in school achievement, both in school readiness and in academic success throughout the school years (see chapters by Morrison and Cooney and by the Cowans). Moreover, the role of schools themselves as powerful influences on child development, and the ways in which parental and school practices shape conditions such as violence in the schools (see chapter by Dodge) needs further study. Of particular importance in this regard are detailed studies of classroom interactions, studies of change in interpersonal contexts, and research that addresses how schooling is affected by family and culture. Similarly, there is a need for more research on the role of neighborhoods and communities in shaping the contexts in which children live (e.g., neighborhood violence) and processes of risk and resilience.

There is also a need for greater use of biological indicators (see chapters by Embry and Dawson, and by Rowe) that can capture the influence of biology on both child and family development. Especially important would be studies utilizing innovative designs allowing scientists to disentangle the complex relationships between genes and environment in determining parenting behaviors. As more sophisticated measurements become possible, the biological underpinnings of areas such as affective and social development and the development of self-regulation also take on increased importance. Finally, researchers working with animal models are able to study more directly biological and evolutionary processes underlying optimal and negative parenting behaviors and their relations to child outcomes (see chapter by Suomi).

As a number of chapters in this volume point out, there is also a need to expand the context in which parenting is viewed to extend beyond mothers. We need more study of the roles of fathers, siblings, grandparents, peers, communities, and electronic media in shaping the development of children. Recently, some researchers have begun to examine parenting in homosexual families, while others are beginning to focus on the roles of fathers and other secondary caregivers. In all cases, *parent* has become to mean more than "mother," and more accurately reflects the diversity in family arrangements in our society. Still, with a few notable exceptions (some of which are described in this volume, see chapter by Masters-Glidden), there are few data on adoptive parenting. This is especially true for the area of "special needs" adoptions, or those adoptions involving older children or children with special needs such as emotional or developmental disabilities.

Finally, there are only limited data that assess over time the differential impact of parenting factors and practices on child outcomes and studies that focus specifically on parental risk factors and maladaptive parenting (see chapter by Borkowski and colleagues). This is true for both typical families and for families of children with diagnosed disabilities (see chapter by Hogan and Msall). While particular parenting practices may be appropriate and adaptive at one age, at another stage in the child's development they may be potentially harmful or abusive. How parenting practices change and develop over time and in different social, ethnic, and cultural settings, and how abusive or neglectful parenting impacts on child developmental processes needs to be empirically examined. Recent studies examining the impact of the marital relationship on child outcomes suggest the need to develop even more complex models of parenting practices, examining the parent-child relationship within a system that includes parent relationships and other social and cultural relationships as well.

Although the role of the media in violence has begun to be addressed, there is only limited information regarding both positive and negative influences of children's interactions with electronic media, especially computers and video games, that take up an increasing portion of children's days. How such media impact on children's social, cognitive, and affective development and the role of such media in fostering healthy or unhealthy behaviors is yet to be determined.

RESEARCH DESIGN AND MEASUREMENT

As the field evolves, so too must the research designs and measurement strategies utilized by scientists. As noted in the previous section, very few research funds in recent years have been spent specifically on measurement and methodology research, despite the tremendous need for development and refinement in this area. As fields advance, researchers must start to explore methodological refinements, such as blinded ratings and new measurement tools that are particularly essential in correlational research. With more advanced and complex methodologies come more complex statistical analyses that must be carefully considered and tested for appropriateness. Recent efforts to develop and evaluate interventions for at-risk parents are only beginning to suggest effective, proactive strategies researchers may develop to enhance the possibilities for optimal child outcomes. Such efforts strongly indicate the need for more sophisticated research designs and methodologies that can capture the multiple levels of influence of social and cultural factors and variables on child development processes. They also indicate the need for more research integrating quantitative and qualitative research methods, and for the development of measurement techniques for the assessment of change and contexts, and the role of contexts as mediators of change.

Although scientists have become increasingly sensitive to the need for studies of cultural and cohort differences, more sophisticated sampling strategies and research designs directly comparing groups are somewhat limited in number. In addition, more research is needed taking advantage of efforts across sites and in analyzing data already available. Although secondary data are widely used in sociological and economic research, there has been little availability of funding to make extensive, extant psychological databases widely available. There is a need for greater availability and use of extant data banks, often collected at considerable government expense.

Finally, for all areas of parenting and family research, there is a need to have parenting and family measures included in very large, prospective, longitudinal studies that evaluate the mutual impact of behavior and biology on child development. Only in this context can the reciprocal nature of these influences be identified and a research base for needed parenting and family intervention be established.

RESEARCH TRAINING

Although parenting and family research has expanded in breadth and scope in recent years, paralleling similar changes in the behavioral sciences, research training in this area to date, has been largely neglected. However, with the expansion of research areas and new methodologies, there is a clear need for greater training opportunities at pre- and postdoctoral as well as mid-career levels. Especially needed are programs that can prepare individuals for research careers that integrate different disciplines (e.g., cognitive psychology, developmental neuroscience, behavioral and molecular genetics, and computational modeling) and methodologies (e.g., experimental and imaging techniques) to address emerging issues in parenting and family research, cognitive science, and child social and emotional development. Also needed are research training opportunities in cross-cultural research and research with ethnic and minority populations, including research training in techniques to measure change in different social contexts and change over time.

Finally, there is a need for research training in advanced research methods as well as translational and applied research. Training opportunities are needed in advanced research design and measurement, including experimental, observational, and longitudinal research, as well as both quantitative and qualitative measurement strategies. Also needed are training opportunities that enhance training in one's chosen field and include a formal emphasis on the translation of research to practice. This should include training at the predoctoral level to prepare students to translate research applications to policy, to communicate research findings to the public, and to influence those who work with at-risk children.

SUMMARY

Although the NICHD and NIH have supported much research on parenting and families in recent years, a number of research gaps remain in our knowledge, and several key research needs can be identified. These include the need for more research examining changes in the demographics and contexts of American families; for cross-cultural, cross-disciplinary, and multilevel studies of parenting and child development; for research on health outcomes and the dynamics of risk and resilience in the lives of children who are at risk or who have disabilities; for research on middle childhood and adolescence and mediators and mechanisms of developmental change over time; for research on the role of schools and other social contexts in shaping child development; for greater use of biological indicators of development; for research on the different contexts of parenting; and for research on the role of the media in affecting child developmental processes.

Also needed is more research focused specifically on research design and measurement and the development of new methodologies, particularly multimethod and longitudinal designs and techniques that can capture the complex contexts in which children live, and more sophisticated sampling strategies and research designs to address child development in different social and cultural settings. Similarly, there is a tremendous need for research training in parenting and family research, especially in interdisciplinary research, advanced research methods, and translational and applied research.

NICHD and NIH Current Initiatives in Parenting Research

While many research gaps can be identified, in recent years the NICHD and other NIH institutes have initiated a number of programs designed to further our understanding of parenting and the role of parents in child development. Specific efforts in recent years have focused on a number of the gaps above, especially in the areas of health disparities and maladaptive or abusive parenting. However, a number of gaps still remain, particularly in terms of research design and measurement as well as research training.

In the past year, the NIH has developed a 5-year *NIH Strategic Research Plan to Reduce and Ultimately Eliminate Health Disparities.* This trans-NIH initiative focuses on eliminating the disparities in health and death experienced by many minority groups in the United States. Part of the NICHD's goal in participating in this initiative is to study the biological, social, and behavioral processes of development and how they are mediated by family structure. Of particular interest is how parents guide the child's social and cognitive development, respond to health needs and disabilities, and how parenting interventions can influence or mitigate injury and violent behavior. The NICHD is also interested in the impact of poverty on parenting and child development, with a particular interest in the impact of poverty on early childhood development.

The NICHD has also had a specific interest in research on the role of parents in child development during the preschool years. In the early 1990s, the NICHD issued an initial request for applications (RFA) on the "Effects of Nonparental Infant Daycare on Child Development." The overall goal of this RFA was to study the long-term development of children placed in childcare during infancy. This project is an ongoing longitudinal study of more than 1,000 children from a variety of ethnic, economic, and geographical backgrounds whose parents are diverse in their levels of education and childrearing practices. The study examines the impact of the family, childcare, school, and poverty on child development, and the effects of culture, neighborhood, peers, and electronic technology on children in middle childhood (see Chapter, this volume).

The process of reading and writing begins before children enter elementary school. Parents guide their child's developing literacy by exposing them to print and spoken language in the home. In 1999, the NICHD, in partnership with the Department of Education, issued an RFA on the "Development of English Literacy in Spanish-Speaking Children" to help understand the cognitive, sociocultural, and instructional factors that affect the acquisition of English reading and writing skills in children whose native language is Spanish. This initiative was designed to encourage research on both the school and home contexts of Spanish-speaking children as they develop English literacy skills.

Parents play an important role in their children's physical and emotional development, and it is important to understand the special challenges that are faced by parents of children who have developmental or physiological disorders or require special care. The NICHD is specifically interested in research on the pathophysiology of autism and autism spectrum disorders (ASDs). Autistic disorder is the most notable of the pervasive developmental disorders (PSDs), and is a significant public health issue since it is typically of lifelong duration. The NICHD joined other institutes in issuing a program announcement in 1998 on "Research on Autism and Autism Spectrum Disorders." The goal of this initiative was to encourage research to understand the epidemiology of autism by examining the brain mechanisms and genetics involved, as well as clinical research that will lead to the diagnosis and treatment of this developmental disorder. Many of the treatments for autism are behavioral interventions that often focus on parent-child interactions in the home. In addition to the study of family histories in understanding the biological basis of the disorder, research is needed on the contextual factors in the parent-child relationship that will lead to effective interventions and the specific impact of family involvement in treatment planning.

Parents play an important role in helping their children develop good health habits that will remain with them through adolescence and into adulthood. The NICHD has joined other institutes of the NIH in promoting research that looks at how children develop health habits from childhood through adolescence. For example, obesity is a serious public health issue that leads to serious health problems associated with being overweight. The prevalence of adults and children who are obese has been increasing over the past 10 years. In 1999, the NICHD participated in a multi-institute RFA on "Innovative Approaches to the Prevention of Obesity," to solicit research to address the genetic, behavioral, and environmental factors that contribute to obesity as well as prevention and intervention strategies. It is important to identify factors that influence obesity in childhood, since obese children are more likely to become obese adults. It is especially important to understand the influence of the family environment on obesity and how interventions in the home can prevent childhood obesity.

Parents of children in middle childhood also play important roles in preventing the risk behaviors that lead to unwanted pregnancy, sexually transmitted diseases, and transmission of HIV. In 1999, the NICHD issued an RFA on the "Prevention of Health Risk Behaviors in Middle Childhood," which encouraged research to investigate the role that the family, school, peers, and community play in influencing health-risk behaviors that lead to risky sexual behavior. The quality of the parent's relationship with the child impacts the child's resilience, or ability to make appropriate behavioral decisions, especially in situations of risk. Research is needed to examine what factors are most effective in contributing to resilience, particularly as it pertains to health risk behaviors.

Parents also contribute to their child's emotional development. Recently, the NICHD joined other NIH institutes in re-issuing a program announcement (PA) on "Basic and Translational Research in Emotion" to expand research on the processes and mechanisms involved in the expression of emotion. The quality of the parent-child relationship in infancy influences the child's emotional development and may impact the child's interpersonal relationships throughout the life span. Research is also needed to examine how different parenting styles impact the child's affective development. One goal of this initiative is to expand the sophistication of research on basic processes of emotion while also encouraging research focused on translating basic research findings to practice.

Youth violence has become an increasing problem in our society, with the homicide rate for young males in our country being the highest of any industrialized nation. The NICHD recently joined with other institutes of the NIH in issuing an RFA on "Research on the Development of Interventions for Youth Violence," to solicit research projects on behavioral interventions for youth violence. The goal of this research initiative is to study and develop interventions focused on changing the behaviors in children, at an early age, which would later lead to violence. One specific focus of the RFA was for studies to examine the relationship between the parent, or adult caretaker, and the child, and how the aggressive or violent behavior of the parent influences aggressive behavior in the child.

Another public health problem that has received attention in recent years is the problem of child abuse and neglect. Child abuse and neglect have many negative health consequences such as physical injuries, disabilities, and behavior problems. Abused and neglected children are also at an increased risk for health problems due to lack of medical and dental care, malnutrition, and poor hygiene. Children who are maltreated also fall behind academically when parents permit truancy and fail to enforce and nurture their child's education. The NICHD has been an active member of the NIH Child Abuse and Neglect Working Group, and as part of this group participated in two recent initiatives to enhance our understanding of the etiology and impact of child abuse and neglect on development: an RFA on "Research on Child Neglect" and a PA on "Career Development Awards: Child Abuse and Neglect Research." Both of these initiatives were designed to encourage research on the relationship between the child and other family members, and interventions within the family to reduce abuse and neglect.

Finally, the NICHD is also involved in two initiatives that look at how various family factors impact child well-being. In 1998, the "Family and Child Well-Being Research Network" PA was released with the purpose of encouraging researchers to use secondary data analyses to examine the impact of the family on child development. In June 2000, the NICHD and the National Institute of Mental Health (NIMH) issued a PA inviting researchers to apply to be a part of "The Science and Ecology of Early Development" program. The purpose of this initiative is to encourage research examining the impact of families, schools, communities, and cultures on the development of children in poverty. Children in poverty are at a higher risk for health problems and academic failure. Many children come from single-parent households where the primary caregiver works outside of the home and the children are in nonparental daycare. Research is needed to focus on how this affects child development. This initiative also seeks to encourage research that addresses the roles that fathers play in the child's development, especially in situations where fathers are not living in the home, not contributing to the family income, and may not have a strong relationship with mothers. Of particular interest is how the father's relationship with the child is influenced by the child's age, the family's economic resources, and the family's culture.

CONCLUSIONS

Although in recent years the NICHD and other NIH institutes have instituted a number of initiatives and programs to increase the scope and breadth of research on parenting and the role of parents and other social influences in child developmental processes, many gaps in our knowledge remain. To bridge these gaps research needs to address the increasing complexity and diversity of environments in which children develop, while expanding boundaries between disciplines to allow for greater collaboration and integration among different disciplines related to the role of parents and families in child development, and encouraging new methodologies, measurement tools, and training mechanisms that can advance research in these areas. In the future, addressing these gaps will require the joint efforts of agencies that fund research on parenting and families and individual investigators in order to develop specific initiatives and to encourage investigator-initiated research.

20

Parenting Research: Translations to Parenting Practices

John G. Borkowski
University of Notre Dame

Sharon L. Ramey
University of Alabama at Birmingham

Christina Stile
National Institute of Child Health and Human Development

PARENTING RESEARCH: TRANSLATION TO PARENTING PRACTICES

Since the late 1960s—the end of the "Ozzie and Harriet period" of American family life—rapid social changes in the fabric of the American family have made it more difficult to parent children with confidence and competence. The increased birth rate to single mothers, the high divorce rate, changes in the safety and quality of neighborhoods, the staggering amount of television and other electronic media devoted to violence and violent sexuality, and a reduction in the size and availability of parents' social support systems—brought on by our highly mobile society and very busy lifestyles—combine to complicate the task of parenting America's children. Today's parents need specific information about how to combat the negative forces that undermine their rightful influence on children's development. In addition, many parents, such as single

Address correspondence to: John G. Borkowski, Notre Dame, IN, 46556, Phone: 219-631-6549, Fax: 219-631-8883, e-mail: souders.1@nd.edu

mothers, are in need of consistent and effective support from established institutions, including community agencies, schools, churches and temples, and
clinics.

This chapter draws upon the research presented both in this book and from
the broader literature to provide parents with useful information about "best"
parenting practices. First, we present a sketch of *what parents need to
know*, compiled from a research-based model of effective parenting principles.
Then we translate this model into a format mothers and fathers can use to
reflect on their parenting approaches and styles, to solve immediate problems,
and to develop proactive attitudes and behaviors that can guide their childrearing practices. Our message to parents is called *RPM3: Responding,
Preventing, Monitoring, Mentoring, and Modeling Your Way to Being a Successful Parent.*

WHAT PARENTS NEED TO KNOW

While some parents feel overwhelmed by the enormous challenges that face them
as they rear their children from birth to adulthood, almost all care deeply about
improving their parenting practices so that they can positively influence their
children's development. The principles described in this chapter will, hopefully,
assist parents in carrying out their responsibilities more effectively and efficient-
ly. Indeed, all parents can take steps that will enhance their children's intellectual,
emotional, and social development. If parents systematically and consistently use
the information we provide in this chapter, their children will likely experience
the following benefits:

- Positive progress in school
- Improved social and emotional adjustment
- Decreased risky behaviors

In general, becoming a better parent involves two steps: first, acquiring knowledge about the best parenting practices; and second, translating this knowledge
into actual practice. This second step works best when parents are willing to be
open, flexible, and honest in their self-appraisal of what is working and what is
not. Parents can be more successful if they enlist help from others—their extended families, other parents, school personnel, competent community-based professionals, and others concerned about safety, decent living environments, and good
schools and jobs.

The information and advice we offer here is not meant to cover the gambit of
research on good parenting practices. Rather, this information addresses specific
aspects of parenting that research has shown really matter—producing better

outcomes for children and improving the quality of family life on a day-to-day basis.

Most of the information has a solid foundation in research; that is, it has been observed in practice or substantiated in laboratory research. Additionally, successful families have much wisdom to pass down from one generation to the next; additionally, many parents developed their own creative and effective approaches to parenting. When integrated into a model of effective parenting, the combination of research-based knowledge and culturally rooted, historically based approaches acquired from personal experience offer a powerful guide to improving parenting practices.

Creating a Mental Map or Model of Parenting Practices

We believe that all parents can benefit from having a clear mental map or "model" of how they want to parent and help their children grow and prosper. These mental models give parents several distinct advantages:

- Models help parents to develop a program for action that is appropriate for today as well as tomorrow. These models are not limited by a child's current stage of development, but also charts where the child is going next. This allows parents to figure out how they can support positive growth and development appropriate for each successive age level.
- Models enable parents to not just respond to problem behaviors or crises, but also to prevent them from occurring in the first place and to enhance the positive aspects of human development.
- Models provide a starting point for discussion and a talking point for parents, both in the home and with other parents.
- Most importantly, models of parenting can be adjusted, through experience and new knowledge, to guide parenting behavior in many different domains. Because models are built on a family's value system, personal experiences, and scientific knowledge that is generated from analyses of children and families in today's world, they are owned by individual parents. Hence, models are both personal and flexible.

Once equipped with a dynamic model of parenting knowledge, parents can adjust or change their current practices and prepare for the future, thereby fostering their children's development, especially in the areas of academic achievement, language development, social development, emotional well-being, and health-promoting behaviors. A detailed mental map of parenting practices also allows parents to anticipate risks and potential harmful influences and to identify ways to minimize these risks long before they become imminent threats.

What Should a Mental Map of Parenting Contain?

To be truly useful, a mental map should incorporate as much information as possible *about the parenting behaviors that can make a meaningful difference in children's development.* When it comes to summarizing what we really know about effective parenting—the facts, not the opinions—the 1999 conference on parenting convened by the National Institute of Child Health and Human Development and the Robert Wood Johnson Foundation revealed several major conclusions that are contained in this book:

- Parents who are highly responsive to their children in terms of warmth, affection, and sensitivity have the most positive parent–child relationships and raise children who are usually successful in their social, emotional, and intellectual development.
- Parents who actively encourage and direct their child's development, provide consistent and authoritative guidance, and set reasonable and appropriate behavioral limits have greater success than those who are too lax or overly restrictive, punitive, and critical.
- Parents who directly monitor their children's behavior are more likely to prevent harmful influences that are often associated with the following: violence portrayed on television, videos, electronic games, or computer-based activities; poor-quality child-care or after-school programs; negative or marginal peer groups; and poor teaching and/or disciplines in schools. When parents take action to minimize or stop these harmful influences, children almost always benefit.
- Seeking outside help or treatment for suspected problems, whether for children or parents, can benefit the whole family. When children or parents have health concerns, learning problems, difficulty with anger management, depression, substance abuse, or conditions associated with disabilities, early detection and vigorous treatment usually make a significant difference.

In the following sections, we elaborate on four important themes—*responsive parenting, modeling, mentoring, and seeking help*—that we believe are the major components of a model of effective parenting practices.

Warm, Sensitive, and Responsive Parenting

From birth onward, parents need to convey a sense of love and commitment to their children. Infants need secure attachment to an adult, usually a parent or caregiver, to develop good social competence. The bond between a parent and a baby that develops during the formation of secure infant attachment across the first 12 months of life will serve the growing child well into his or her later years, likely resulting in a young adult capable of true intimacy and real concerns for others. The same kind of positive bond can be formed when older children are adopted, though at times more difficult to establish.

Behaviors to focus on during infancy are *warmth, sensitivity to the baby's needs, and a consistent concern for the infant's welfare and optimal development through active and responsive parenting.* Parents need to maintain this same sensitivity to individual needs and loving, warm concern throughout childhood and adolescence. Responsiveness does not create a spoiled child; to the contrary, responsive parents have children who are socially connected and caring. The following behaviors are related to warm and responsive parenting:

- Picking up a crying infant quickly to determine why he or she is upset
- Providing positive family routines and a somewhat orderly (but not rigid) daily schedule and home life for infants, youth, and school-age children
- Showing pleasure and joy when interacting with the child, especially in response to the infant's emerging skills and efforts to try new things
- Speaking with the child, from birth on, in ways that are interactive, enjoyable, interesting, and educational; singing, repeating nursery rhymes, and teaching new sounds and words facilitate language development
- Responding with interest to the child's questions and requests for help as an opportunity to encourage curiosity and teach about things of interest to the child
- Showing care and concern for the child's feelings and talking about your own and your child's emotions, especially sadness and anger; as the child gets older, expressing empathy about other people's problems and offering encouragement "to imagine" what other people are feeling and why

Guiding and Modeling

All parents have a unique opportunity to help mold their child into a happy and constructive member of society. Parents do this best by setting behavioral rules and establishing clear limits of acceptable behavior for their child—those that are appropriate for his or her age—and then enforcing these rules consistently and fairly. Parents should avoid styles of parenting that are either too permissive or too restrictive and harsh. Children prosper in an atmosphere of loving direction, guidance, and reasonable expectations.

Parents can also be a key source of help to their children's achieving more in school, as most children are capable of doing. Three of the best tactics for school readiness that parents can use with preschool children are: *talking with them often, reading to them, and encouraging them to read books on their own.* Parents of school-age children can help improve their child's performance by having conversations about what the child is studying in school and its relationship to broader issues or to more general world events, by helping the child acquire self-discipline and high standards, and by "coaching" the child through times of failure and self-doubt. Further, parents can help schools by being supportive and by communicating any special individual needs or family concerns directly to the child's teacher, using a positive, constructive approach.

Equally important in childrearing is a parent's own behavior—or what precisely a parent models to the child. What a parent says and does provides an important message and template for the child's own growth and development. If a parent models or demonstrates hard work in obtaining goals; kindness, respect, and courteousness to others; a sense of self-control and discipline; and a willingness to try new strategies when old ones are not working, the child will be more likely to emulate these qualities and behaviors. Parents also can point out others who demonstrate or live out the characteristics that parents desire for their children by telling stories about family members and friends, reading biographies about men and women who have made the world a better place, and discussing values and the behaviors that can translate a person's values into concrete actions.

Finally, when parents have disputes and conflicts, which are inevitable in any family, they should resolve these situations in positive ways. This process teaches children that "fights," disagreements, and other interpersonal conflicts can be settled through effective communication and social problem solving. This approach is especially important in both married and divorced families, where unresolved parental conflicts can cause serious problems for children's development. The following behaviors are related to successful guiding and modeling activities:

- Setting limits for the child's behavior and having consequences associated with not following these limits; parents should always explain, at the child's level of understanding, the importance of these limits and the value of positive behaviors
- Spending time helping a child with homework (but not doing it for the child)
- Teaching the child about some of the parent's favorite activities; helping the child acquire new skills (in music, art, sports, and academic subjects) or exploring a new interest (collecting, reading about a new topic, or visiting a museum)
- Doing volunteer work or community service with the child in order to put values into action
- Talking about conflicts or problems the parent has experienced and how they were resolved in the past, including letting the child hear an apology, compromising to settle differences of opinion, or admitting a mistake

Monitoring the Child's World

At all stages of development, parents need to be vigilant in monitoring their child's activities. In the early years, concerns about health and safety are paramount, so childproofing a house and being active in monitoring the care the child receives from others (child-care providers, other relatives, and babysitters) are vital. During the school years, parents need to be attentive to the quality of the child's school experience to make sure the child is actively engaged in the learning process and provided with good teaching.

The most important aspect of successful monitoring, however, is knowing where children are and what they are doing. Without this information, a child can fall into destructive patterns of behavior or under the influence of negative peers. Adolescents especially need parental direction and monitoring in order to help them find and maintain close, constructive friendships and to engage in healthy, positive extracurricular activities.

A very important behavior to monitor concerns television viewing, as well as the nature of interactions with other electronic media. Parents may want to limit how much time their children spend watching television or playing video or computer games. Just as important, parents should know the content of programs and games their children experience; examples of violent or disrespectful behavior should be minimized.

Seeking Outside Help for Problems

What starts off as a small family problem can quickly become much larger. All too often, this occurs because the family is reluctant to admit that there is trouble, viewing "problems" as a sign of personal weakness or as something that will just disappear with time. Because family members depend upon one another, when one person is experiencing difficulty, the entire family feels the repercussions. Many new and effective treatments and interventions are available for a wide variety of personal problems. For instance, mothers with depression who seek help early can prevent the harmful effects often seen in young children whose mothers are unable to be responsive and warm because of their own emotional problems. Similarly, children with early signs of excessive aggression and inappropriate social behaviors can learn new ways to play with others and control their anger, especially when parents and teachers work together to help redirect the child's behavior. However, if families wait until things become intolerable, they may find the problem is far more serious; the uphill battle they may be forced to deal with can result in a family that is less functional and happy because of the long-term stress it has already endured.

In addition, parents can also be important "agents of change" in their communities. Parents of children with physical and learning disabilities have long advocated on their children's behalf and have, in a sense, created a world where there are more opportunities for their children than ever before. Parents of all children can reach out to other parents, talk about their common concerns or problems, and share solutions that may be helpful and inspirational to others. Sometimes parents need to find a new neighborhood or a new school to solve serious problems; at other times parents need to discontinue relationships with friends or family members who may be a negative influence on (or directly harmful to) their children. Regardless of the situation, the underlying message is clear: Parents need to take constructive actions to minimize problems or dangers in their children's lives. In many cases, parents cannot solve these problems entirely on their own and need the help of others.

Many parents fear that their children will become the victims of violence, have learning or attention problems, or become incapacitated by personal problems such as depression or excessive shyness. To combat these fears, parents need to be proactive in preventing behavior problems. If parents, teachers, or peers recognize early signs of childhood problems such as depression, inattention and lack of self-control, or antisocial tendencies, parents should seek out professional advice to establish a thoughtful, competently run plan of action, incorporating both parents and professionals.

One of the worst feelings in the world is the loneliness and abandonment a parent experiences when he or she believes no one is available to help and support them in rearing a child who is having trouble. Society needs to increase the number of competent counselors, clinicians, and pediatricians to help parents successfully overcome some of these burdens. Parents also need active support groups so that they can function well in the other parts of their lives—especially in maintaining close family, spouse, or partner relationships.

Summing Up: Making Good Choices

Parenthood is filled with tough choices: Can I find a high-quality daycare arrangement for my child? Can I identify the best school, and within that school, a teacher with my child's best interests in mind? Do I have the time and energy to prepare my child for school and, once there, to navigate safely and successfully through it? Can I help my son or daughter find a good friend, positive outside-the-home activities, and a constructive peer group with whom to associate? Can I make time in my life to monitor my child's daily activities over a span of 18 years or more? Am I willing to talk with my son or daughter frankly, yet compassionately, during his or her preadolescent years about sensitive topics such as sexuality and sexual behavior, personal choices related to health and safety, right and wrong personal decisions regarding drinking and drugs, and how to solve difficult social problems?

Answers to these questions and the choices that we, as parents, must make about childrearing practices are difficult; yet it is essential to face these issues from an informed perspective. Reasonable, thoughtful, and practical decisions about parenting and the corresponding parental actions that flow from these choices will help ensure that warm, loving, and responsive parents will successfully steer their children into adulthood with a sense of pride and accomplishment.

Communicating the Message to Parents

Researchers face an additional difficulty in trying to find the best messages, right format, and most appropriate language or medium to translate this model of effective parenting—with its multiple interacting principles—to parents in such a way as to produce positive changes in parenting practices. The following text represents one such attempt to communicate with parents about improving their parenting practices as they raise their children from infancy to adolescence.

RPM3: RESPONDING, PREVENTING, MONITORING, MENTORING, AND MODELING YOUR WAY TO BEING A SUCCESSFUL PARENT

Have you heard the latest advice about parenting? Of course you have. From experts to other parents, people are always ready to give you parenting advice. Parenting tips, parents' survival guides, dos, don'ts, shoulds, and shouldn'ts— new ones come out every day. But with so much information available, how can anyone figure out what *really* works? How do you know whose advice to follow? Isn't parenting just common sense anyway? How can the experts know what it's like to be a parent in a *real* house?

What's a Parent to Do?

Try RPM3—a no-frills approach to parenting from the National Institute of Child Health and Human Development (NICHD). For over 30 years, the NICHD has conducted and supported research in parenting and child development. We've talked to experts. We've talked to parents. We've talked to children. We've collected the statistics, identified the myths, and tested the suggestions. The result is RPM3.

The RPM3 guidelines aren't meant to be just another parenting "how to" telling you what to do. Instead, RPM3 separates the useful information from the not-so-useful so that you can make your own decisions about parenting. RPM3 does more than tell stories about what people *think* about parenting; it incorporates 30 years of NICHD research to tell you what really works. RPM3 confirms something that you already know: parents *do* matter. *You* matter. Read on to find out just how much.

> **RPM3 stands for:**
>
> **R**esponding to your child in an appropriate manner
>
> **P**reventing risky behavior or problems before they arise
>
> **M**onitoring your child's contact with his or her surroundings
>
> **M**entoring your child to support and encourage desired behaviors
>
> **M**odeling your own behavior to provide a consistent, positive example for your child
>
> FIG. 20.1.

So Where Do We Start?

The first thing you need to know is that there are no perfect parents. The words "good" and "bad" don't apply to parenting the same way they apply to other parts of life. Parenting isn't an all-or-nothing situation. Successes *and* mistakes are part of being a parent. So, for the rest of this chapter, take the words *good* and *bad* out of your head. Instead, think in terms of the type of parent you want to be. RPM3 offers research-based guidelines for being:

- An *effective* parent—your words and actions influence your child the way you want them to.
- A *consistent* parent—you follow similar principles or practices in your words and actions.
- An *active* parent—you participate in your child's life.
- An *attentive* parent—you pay attention to your child's life and observe what goes on.

By including responding, preventing, monitoring, mentoring, and modeling in your day-to-day parenting activities, you can become a more effective, consistent, active, and attentive parent. Once you have learned about each RPM3 guideline, go to the section that describes your child's age to see how you might use RPM3 in your everyday parenting. The type of parent you want to be is up to you.

Keep in Mind . . .

As you learn about the RPM3 guidelines and read the examples, remember that responding, preventing, monitoring, mentoring, and modeling have their place in parenting every child—including those children with special or different needs. All children—be they mentally challenged, mentally gifted, physically challenged, physically gifted, or some combination of these—can benefit from the guidelines in RPM3. The children described in the booklet's examples might be in wheelchairs; they could have leukemia or asthma; they may take college-level courses; or they might be in special classes for kids with attention deficit disorder. The stories don't specifically mention these traits because even kids in special situations need day-to-day parents. The guidelines presented in RPM3 focus on how to handle day-to-day parenting choices, in which a child's abilities or disabilities are not the most important factors. The booklet's examples also apply to families of any culture, religion, living arrangement, economic status, and size. They address situations that all families experience, even if the specific details are slightly different.

Let's begin by learning the lessons that RPM3 has to teach, starting with *R*—responding to your child in an appropriate manner.

Responding to Your Child in an Appropriate Manner

Here we go. It's only the first guideline and already the words don't say anything, right? *Wrong*! The words are actually saying two different things: make sure you're *responding* to your child, not reacting; and make sure your response is *appropriate*, not overblown, or out-of-proportion.

Are You Reacting or Responding to Your Child?

Many parents *react* to their children. That is, they answer with the first word, feeling, or action that comes to mind. It's a normal thing to do, especially with all the other things people do every day.

When you react, you aren't making a decision about what outcome you want from an event or action. Even more than that, if you react, you can't *choose* the best way to reach the outcome you want.

Responding to your child means that you take a moment to think about what is really going on before you speak, feel, or act. Responding is much harder than reacting because it takes more time and effort. The time that you take between looking at the event and acting, speaking, or feeling is vital to your relationship with your child. That time, whether it be 30 seconds, 5 minutes, or a week, allows you to see things more clearly in terms of what is happening right now and what you want to happen in the long-run.

Did you know . . . ?

How you feel affects your child.
Your child tunes into your thoughts, feelings, and attitudes. He or she can sense how you feel about something, even if your words say that you are feeling something different. So a negative reaction or outburst from your child may not be without reason. It could be your child's way of telling you how *you* feel.

FIG. 20.2.

What is an Appropriate Response?

An appropriate response is one that fits the situation. Both your child's age and the specific facts of the occasion are important in deciding what a fitting response is. For example, a fitting response for a baby who is crying differs from a fitting response for a 10-year-old who is crying. A fitting response for an instance in which a child is running depends on whether that child is running into a busy street or running to the swing set on the playground. Your child's physical or emotional needs may also alter your decision about a fitting response. Responding to your child in an appropriate manner allows you to:

- **Think about all the options before you make a decision.** This will help you choose the best way to get from the current situation to the outcome that you want. By taking time to see both sides of a problem, for instance, you can select the most fitting response.

- **Answer some basic questions.** Do your words get across what you are trying to say? Do your actions match your words? Are your emotions getting in the way of your decision making?

- **Consider previous, similar events and recall how you handled them.** You can remind your child of these other times and their outcomes to show that you are really thinking about your decision. You can use your past experiences to judge the current situation, decide the outcome you want, and figure out how to reach that outcome.

> **Did you know . . . ?**
>
> **Parents *do* matter!**
> Of all the things that influence your child's growth and development, one of the most important is the reliable, responsive, and sensitive care your child gets from you. You play a key role in your child's development, along with your child's intelligence, temperament, outside stresses, and social environment.
>
> FIG. 20.3.

- **Be a more consistent parent.** Your child will know that you are not making decisions based on whim, especially if you explain how you made your choice. Your child will be more likely to come to you with questions or problems if he or she has some idea of what to expect from you. Warm, concerned, and sensitive responses will also increase the likelihood of your child coming to you with questions or problems.

- **Offer a stable example of how to make thoughtful decisions.** As your child gets older, he or she will know your decision-making process and will appreciate the time you take. Your child might even pattern him or herself after you.

- **Build a solid but flexible bond of trust between you and your child.** A solid bond holds up to tough situations; a flexible bond survives the changes in your child and in your relationship with your child that are certain to occur.

Now consider the *P* in RPM3.

Preventing Risky Behaviors or Problems Before They Arise

Seems easy enough. You "childproof" your house to make sure your toddler can't get into the cleaning products or electrical outlets. You catch your 8-year-old jumping on the bed and make her stop. You make your 12-year old wear his helmet when he rides his bike, no matter how "dumb" he thinks it makes him look. But prevention goes beyond just saying "No" or "Stop." There are two parts to prevention: spotting possible problems; and knowing how to work through the problem. Let's look at each one a little closer.

Spotting Possible Problems

Some problems are obvious, like drugs, alcohol, smoking, and violence. But what about those not-so-obvious ones? Consider these methods for spotting problems before they turn into full-blown crises:

Did you know . . . ?

Parents have a profound influence on children from the beginning of their children's lives.
As a parent, you can have close contact with your child from the time he or she is small. That type of contact builds trust; with trust comes commitment. Parents who are committed to their child's well-being can have a very positive effect on their child.

FIG. 20.4

- **Be actively involved in your child's life.** This is important for all parents, no matter what the living arrangements. Knowing how your child usually thinks, feels, and acts will help you to notice when things begin to change. Some changes are part of your child's growing up, but others could be signs of trouble.
- **Set realistic limits and enforce them consistently.** Be selective with your limits by putting boundaries on the most important behaviors your child is engaged in. Make sure you and your child can "see" a limit clearly. If your child goes beyond the limit, deal with him or her in similar ways for similar situations. If you decide to punish your child, use mostly nonphysical methods, like restriction or time-outs; make sure the harshness of the punishment fits your child's "crime." As your child learns how limits work and what happens when he or she goes past those limits, he or she will trust you to be fair.
- **Create healthy ways for your child to express emotions.** Much "acting out" stems from children not knowing how to handle their emotions. Feelings can be so intense that usual methods of expressing them don't work. Or, because feelings like anger or sadness are viewed as "bad," your child may not want to express them openly. Encourage your child to express emotions by crying, yelling into a pillow, or drawing dark scribbles on a piece of paper; let your child see you doing things to deal with your own emotions. Once these feelings are less powerful, talk to your child about how he or she feels and why. Make sure your child knows that *all* emotions are part of the person that he or she is, not just the "good" or happy ones. Once your child knows his or her range of emotions, he or she can start to learn how to handle them.

Knowing how to Work Through the Problem

Because problems are quite different, how you solve them also differs. To solve "bigger" problems, you may need more complex methods. Keep these things in mind when trying to solve a problem:

• **Know that you are not alone.** Talk to other parents, trusted friends, or relatives. Some of them might be dealing with or have dealt with similar things. They may have ideas on how to solve a problem in a way you haven't thought of. Or, they might share your feelings, which can also be a comfort.

• **Admit when a problem is bigger than you can handle alone or requires special expertise.** No one expects you to solve every problem your family has by yourself. Some problems are just too big to handle alone, not because you're a "bad" parent, but simply because of the nature of the problem. Be realistic about what you can and can't do on your own.

• **Get outside help, if needed.** There will be times when you just won't know how to help your child; at other times, you won't be able to help your child. That's okay; someone else may know how to help. Use all the resources you have to solve a problem, including getting outside help when you need it. Remember that it's not important how a problem is solved, just that it is.

Where can I go for parenting help?

◆ Other parents
◆ Family members and relatives
◆ Friends
◆ Pediatricians
◆ School nurses and counselors
◆ Social workers and agencies
◆ Psychologists and psychiatrists
◆ Pastors, priests, rabbis, ministers, and reverends
◆ Community groups

FIG. 20.5.

The *M3* in RPM3 describes three complex but central principles of parenting: monitoring, mentoring, and modeling. Many people are confused by these words because they seem similar, but they are really very different. It might be easier to understand these ideas if you think of them this way:

Did you know . . . ?

All parents should maintain positive relationships with their children.

One parent, two parents, grandparents, foster parents, weekend parents, step parents. Regardless of whether or not you live with your child, it's important that you maintain a positive relationship with him or her. A positive relationship gives your child a stable environment in which to grow, so that you are one of the people your child learns to depend on.

FIG. 20.6.

• Being a monitor means that you pay careful attention to your child and his or her surroundings, especially his or her groups of friends and peers.
• Being a mentor means that you support your child's development and changes in that development as he or she learns more about him- or herself, how the world works, and his or her role in that world.

- Being a model means that you examine your own words and actions to decide what kind of example you want to be for your child and showing your beliefs, values, and attitudes in action on a daily basis.

Now let's look at each one more closely. Monitoring your child seems pretty straightforward, so let's start there.

Monitoring Your Child's Contact with His or Her Surrounding World

Do you need to be a superhero with X-ray vision and eyes in the back of your head to be a careful monitor? Of course not. You don't need to be with your child every minute of every day, either. Being a careful monitor combines asking questions and paying attention, with making decisions and setting limits.

When your child is young, monitoring seems easy because you are the one making most of the decisions. You decide who cares for your child; you decide what your child watches or listens to; you decide who your child plays with. If something or someone comes in contact with your child, you're one of the first to know.

Things may change as your child gets older, especially in the preteen and teen years. Many parents and kids have a tough time getting through some of these years. As kids begin to learn about their own personalities, they may clash with their parents' personalities. A parent's ability to actively monitor is often one of the first things to suffer from this clash.

Parents need to monitor their children's comings and goings through every age and stage of growth. Being an active monitor can be as simple as answering some basic questions:

- **Who** is your child with?
- **Where** is your child?
- **What** is your child doing?
- **When** will your child be home/leaving?
- **How** is your child getting there/home?
- **What** do you know about the person(s) your child is with?

You won't always know detailed answers to these questions, but it's important to know most of the answers, most of the time. You may also want to keep these things in mind when being an active monitor:

- **Open the lines of communication when your child is young and keep those lines open.** It sounds like a line, but honest communication is crucial. When your child is young, talk openly about things you do when you aren't with your child; then ask your child what he or she does during those times. As your child gets older, keep up this type of communication. Both you and your child have to take part in open, two-way communication.

• **Tell your child what thoughts and ideals you value and why.** For instance, if being respectful to adults is an ideal you want your child to have, tell him or her; even more importantly, tell him or her *why* you think it's important. Don't assume that your child knows your reasons for valuing one practice or way of behaving over another.

• **Know what your child is watching, reading, playing, or listening to.** Because TV, movies, video games, the Internet, and music are such a large part of many of our lives, they can have a huge influence on kids. Be sure you know what your child's influences are. You can't help your child make positive choices if you don't know what Web sites he or she visits or what he or she reads, listens to, watches, or plays.

• **Know the people your child spends time with.** Because you can't be with your child all the time, you should know who is with your child when you're not. Friends have a big influence on your child, from preschool well into adulthood. Much of the time, this influence is positive, but not always. With a little effort from you, your child might surround him- or herself with friends whose values, interests, and behaviors will be "pluses" in your child's life. Your child also spends a lot of time with his or her teachers. Teachers play a vital role in your child's development and well-being, so get to know your child's teachers, too.

• **Give direction without being rigid.** In some cases, *not* being allowed to do something only makes your child want to do it more. Is the answer just plain "no," or does it depend on the circumstances? "Yes, but only if . . . " is a useful option when making decisions.

A special note to those of you with pre-teens or teenagers

Keep in mind that even if you're the most careful monitor, your child may have friends and interests that you don't understand or don't approve of. You may not like the music she listens to, or the clothes he wears, or the group she "hangs out" with. Some of these feelings are a regular part of the relationship between children and adults. Before you take away the music or forbid your child to see that friend, ask yourself this question: **Is this (person, music, TV show) a *destructive* influence?** In other words, is your child hurting anyone or being hurt by what he or she is doing, listening to, wearing, or who he or she is spending time with? If the answer is "no," you may want to think before you act, perhaps giving your child some leeway. It's likely that taking music away, not letting your child watch a certain show, or forbidding your child from spending time with that friend will create a conflict between you and your child. Make sure that the issue is important enough to insist upon. Think about whether your actions will help or hurt your relationship with your child, or whether your actions are necessary for your child to develop healthy attitudes and behaviors. You may decide that setting a volume limit for the radio is better than having a fight about your child's choice of music.

FIG. 20.7.

Monitoring is an important way to protect your child from harm. Being your child's *mentor* can also keep your child from being hurt by encouraging him or her to act in reasonable ways. Let's think about mentoring.

Mentoring Your Child to Support and Encourage Desired Behaviors

Have you watched TV lately? If so, you may have seen various TV stars and sports celebrities talking about becoming a *mentor.* Since the early 1980s, the number of mentoring programs has grown into the thousands, with many programs enjoying a great deal of success. These programs share a common goal: guiding children in need to a healthy, happy adulthood. These programs some-times forget, however, that *all children need mentors*; even more importantly, the message that **parents make great mentors** often gets little or no mention.

What Does it Mean to be a Mentor?

A mentor is someone who provides support, guidance, friendship, and respect to a child. Sounds great. But what does *that* mean?

Being a mentor is like being a coach of a sports team. A caring coach sees the strengths and weaknesses of each player and tries to build strengths and lessen weaknesses. In practice, coaches stand back and watch the action, giv-ing advice on what the players should do next, but knowing that the players make their own game-time decisions. Coaches honestly point out things that can be done better and praise things that are done well. Coaches listen to their players and earn players' trust. They give their players a place to turn when things get tough.

Mentors do the same things: develop a child's strengths; share a child's interests; offer advice and support; give praise; listen; be a friend. Mentors help kids to reach their full potential, which includes mistakes and tears, as well as successes and smiles. Mentors know that small failures often precede major successes; that in mind, they encourage kids to keep trying because those successes are right around the corner.

Did you know . . . ?

Kids who have mentors are less likely to take part in risky behaviors.

Children who have mentors are 46% less likely to use illegal drugs, 27% less likely to use alcohol, and 52% less likely to skip school than kids who don't have mentors. Kids with men-tors also report that they are more confident of their school performance, more likely to get along with others, and less likely to hit someone.

—*Big Brothers Big Sisters Impact Study, 1995*

FIG. 20.8.

What can I do to be a Mentor?

There is no magic wand that turns people into caring mentors. Just spending time with your child helps you to become a mentor. You can do ordinary things with your child, like going grocery shopping together; you can do special things with your child, like going to a museum or a concert together. The important part is that you do things *together,* which includes communicating with one another. You may want to keep these things in mind as you think about being a mentor:

• **Be honest about your own strengths and weaknesses.** If you know the answer to a question, say so; if you don't, say so. To build a trusting, but real relationship with your child, you only have to be human. All humans make mistakes; you have and your child will, too. Your child can benefit from hearing about your mistakes, including what you thought before you made them, how your thoughts changed after you made them, and how you changed your thoughts or behaviors to avoid them. A child who thinks his or her parent is perfect builds expectations that parents can't possibly live up to.

> **Did you know . . . ?**
>
> **Your approval or disapproval teaches your child about desirable behavior.**
> Parents need to be careful with how they you express approval or disapproval. Parents who are harsh in their disapproval may hurt their children's self-esteem; parents who never express disapproval may raise children who can't deal with any criticism. Try to find a balance between expressions of approval and disapproval. Be consistent in your rewards and punishments.
>
> FIG. 20.9.

• **Respect your child's thoughts and opinions without judging them.** Even if you don't agree with your child, make it clear that you want to know what his or her thoughts are, without the threat of punishment. If your child is afraid of being punished, he or she may stop sharing things entirely. Let different points of view co-exist for a while; they will allow your child to think more about an issue. Remember that there is an important difference between "I disagree with you," and "You're wrong."

> **Did you know . . . ?**
>
> **The feedback and advice that parents give can guide children to make more positive decisions.**
> By supporting desired behaviors, parents help their children build self-esteem and self-confidence. These traits give children the inner strength they need to make better decisions when faced with a challenge. It's important for parents to keep the lines of communication open, so that vital advice and feedback gets to their children.
>
> FIG. 20.10.

• **Support your child's interests and strengths, but don't force things.** Kids spend their childhood trying to figure out who they are, how the world works, and how they fit into that world. Make sure your child has enough room to explore. If your child has no interest in an activity or topic, don't push. Your child will soon begin to dread the "forced activity" and will find ways to get out of doing it.

• **Introduce your child to things that you like to do.** This is a useful way for your child to learn more about you. It's sometimes hard for kids to picture their parents doing things that other people do, like playing an instrument, volunteering at a nursing home, watching movies, playing a sport, or knowing about art. If your child *sees* you doing these things, you become more of a "regular person" rather than "just a parent."

Mentoring gives kids the support they need to become they people they are meant to be. But what about you? Are you the person you want to be? Take some time to think about becoming a better *model* for your child.

Modeling Your Own Behavior to Provide a Positive Example for Your Child

"When I grow up, I want to be just like you."

Has your child ever said this to you? It's a bittersweet statement for a parent to hear. On the one hand, it's touching to have your child look up to you in this way; on the other, being a role model comes with great responsibility.

Role models come in all shapes and sizes; they do all kinds of jobs; they come from any country or city. Some children view athletes as their role models; other children look up to authors or scientists. And, believe it or not, many children see their parents as role models.

> **Did you know . . . ?**
>
> **Children are great copycats.**
> Have you ever said a curse word in front of your child, only to hear him or her repeating that word later (usually at the worst possible time)? Kids are highly imitative, with both words and actions. If you are aggressive, your child will copy you to be aggressive, too. If you are very social, your child will probably be very social, too. Make sure you are a strong, consistent, and positive role model, to foster better behaviors in your child.
>
> FIG. 20.11.

All too often, parenting behavior is guided by adults reacting to their own childhoods; that is, many parents think: I don't *ever* want to be like my parents; or it was good enough for me, so it's good enough for my kids. Remember that reacting prevents you from making decisions that can change the outcome of a situation. To be a more effective, consistent, active, and attentive parent, it's best to focus on your children and their lives.

Does this mean that you have to be perfect so your child will grow up to be perfect, too? Of course not. No one is perfect. But you do need to figure out what kind of example you are setting for your child. You may want to be the kind of role model who does the following:

• **Do as you say *and* say as you do.** Children want to *act* like their role models, not just talk like them. Children learn as much, if not more, from your actions as they do from your words. Don't just tell your child to call home if he or she is going to be late; make sure that *you* call home when you know you're going to be late. Don't just tell your child not to shout at you; don't shout at your child or at others. This kind of consistency helps your child form reliable patterns of the relationship between attitudes and actions.

• **Show respect for other people, including your child.** For many children, the word *respect* is hard to understand. It's not something they can touch or feel, but it's still a very important concept. To help your child learn about respect, you may want to point out when you are being respectful. For instance, when your child starts to pick out his or her own clothes, you can show respect for those choices. Tell your child, "That wouldn't have been my choice, but I respect your decision to wear that plaid shirt with those striped pants."

• **Be honest with your child about how you are feeling.** Adults get confused about emotions all the time, so it's no surprise that children might get confused, too. For instance, you might have a short temper after a really stressful day at work, but your child might think you are angry with him or her. If you find yourself acting differently than you usually do, explain to your child that he or she isn't

---

Did you know . . . ?

How parents act in their relationships with one another has a significant impact on child development.

Regardless of the living arrangements, parents should consider their children when dealing with each other. Your child sees how you work through everyday issues and uses your interactions as the basis for his or her own behavior in relationships. The next time you interact with your spouse, significant other, or partner, ask yourself whether or not you are providing a positive example for your child. Do you want your child to act the same way you are acting with that person or another person? If not, you may want to reconsider your behavior.

FIG. 20.12.

---

to blame for your change in "typical" behavior; your child can even help you by lightening your mood or altering your attitude. You can prevent a lot of hurt feelings and confusion by being honest with your child about your own emotions.

• **Make sure your child knows that being angry does not mean "not loving."** Disagreements and arguments are a normal part of most relationships. But many children can't separate love from anger; they assume that if you yell at them, then you don't love them anymore. Even if you think your child has a solid grasp of emotions, you may want to be specific about this point. Otherwise you run the risk of having your child think he or she is not loved every time you raise your voice.

• **Pinpoint things that you wouldn't want your child's role model to do, and make sure you aren't doing them.** For instance, suppose your child sees a sports player as his or her role model. If you found out that player used illegal drugs or was verbally or physically abusive to others, would you still want your child to look up to that person? Probably not. Now apply that same standard to your own actions. If you don't want your child to smoke, then you should stop smoking. If you want your child to be on time for school, make sure you are on time for work and other meetings. If you don't want your child to use curse words, then stop using those words in front of your child. Reviewing your own conduct means being honest with yourself about yourself. You may need to make some changes in how you act, but both you and your child will benefit in the end.

Now What Should I Do?

Now that you know about RPM3, it's time to put these ideas into action. Take some time to think about the examples and make decisions about how RPM3 can fit into your style of parenting. You might consider forming a discussion group in which you share this model, talk about common problems, and propose various solutions in light of the principles that are at the heart of RPM3. For a complete copy of this text, including age-specific stories that show these parenting guidelines in practice, call the NICHD clearinghouse at 1-800-370-2943.

THE NEED FOR TRANSLATIONAL RESEARCH

Translational research is needed to assess the specific impact of text-based (such as RPM3) and video-based messages on parenting practices. Do attitudes and behaviors change as a result of reading, viewing, and discussing these messages? Are long-term changes produced by short-term interventions? Are booster sessions or discussion groups necessary for generalized changes in parenting practices? Are different messages required for various racial and ethnic groups? What unique parenting practices need to be emphasized for mothers and fathers who raise children with special needs, such as autism, mental retardation, depression, or learning disabilities? These and other issues need to become the focus of the next generation of translational research that aims to bridge the gap between basic research findings and actual parenting practices. Parenting research has much information to offer the public at large. However, multiple approaches to the dissemination of that knowledge—and their systematic evaluation—represent an important new agenda and challenge for social science research.

ACKNOWLEDGMENTS

The writing of this chapter was supported in part by grants from the National Institutes of Health (HD-26456) and the Robert Wood Johnson Foundation.

Subject Index